PASSION AND VIRTUE:
ESSAYS ON THE NOVELS OF
SAMUEL RICHARDSON

Portrait by Sir Joshua Reynolds (1723–92) of his niece, Miss Theophila Palmer, reading *Clarissa* by Samuel Richardson. Reproduced by kind permission of the Trustees of the Fourth Lord Hillington's 1962 Heirlooms Settlement.

Passion and Virtue

Essays on the Novels of Samuel Richardson

Edited by
DAVID BLEWETT

UNIVERSITY OF TORONTO PRESS
Toronto Buffalo London

Printed on acid-free paper

National Library of Canada Cataloguing in Publication Data

Main entry under title:

Passion and virtue : essays on the novels of Samuel Richardson

Includes index.
ISBN 0-8020-3503-5

1. Richardson, Samuel, 1689–1761 – Criticism and interpretation.   2. Virtue
in literature.   I. Blewett, David, 1940–   .
PR3667.P37 2001   823′.6   C2001-930196-0

University of Toronto Press acknowledges the financial assistance to its
publishing program of the Canada Council for the Arts and the Ontario Arts
Council.

University of Toronto Press acknowledges the financial support for its publishing activities of the Government of Canada through the Book Publishing
Industry Development Program (BPIDP).

fuo

Contents

Contributors

RACHEL K. CARNELL, Assistant Professor of English at Cleveland State University, has published articles in *Eighteenth-Century Studies, Nineteenth-Century Literature*, and *Studies in the Novel*. She is completing a book on the connections between eighteenth-century political debate and the rise of the novel.

LOIS A. CHABER teaches at the American Intercontinental University in London and has published several essays on the eighteenth-century novel, particularly Defoe and Richardson. She is working on a book dealing with an aspect of family history.

MARGARET ANNE DOODY is John and Barbara Glynn Family Professor of Literature, University of Notre Dame. Her most recent full-length book is *The True Story of the Novel* (1996). She is writing a book on Apuleius.

JOHN A. DUSSINGER, Professor of English at the University of Illinois (Urbana-Champaign), is the author of *The Discourse of the Mind in Eighteenth-Century Fiction* (1974), *In the Pride of the Moment: Encounters in Jane Austen's World* (1990). He is at work with other Richardson scholars on a projected scholarly edition of the printer-novelist's correspondence.

ROBERT A. ERICKSON is Professor of English at the University of California, Santa Barbara. He is the author of *The Language of the Heart, 1600–1750* (1997) and *Mother Midnight: Birth, Sex, and Fate in Eighteenth-Century Fiction* (1986). He was Fulbright Professor in Comparative Religion at the University of Helsinki, 1999–2000, teaching and writing on Milton, epic, shamanism, and the Finnish national epic, the *Kalevala*.

DANIEL P. GUNN is Professor of English and Chair of the Department of Humanities at the University of Maine at Farmington. His essays on the English novel and the theory of the novel have appeared in the *Georgia Review, Twentieth-Century Literature, Studies in the Novel, Nineteenth-Century Literature*, and elsewhere.

GEORGE E. HAGGERTY, Professor of English at the University of California, Riverside, has published *Unnatural Affections: Women and Fiction in the Later Eighteenth Century* and *Men in Love: Masculinity and Sexuality in the Eighteenth Century*. He has also edited *Professions of Desire: Lesbian and Gay Studies in Literature* and *Gay Histories and Cultures: An Encyclopedia*. He is at work on a study of the life and work of Horace Walpole.

JOCELYN HARRIS holds a personal chair at the University of Otago, New Zealand. She edited Richardson's *Sir Charles Grandison* and is the author of *Samuel Richardson* and *Jane Austen's Art of Memory*.

WENDY JONES is the author of articles on the English novel and popular culture. She is currently completing a manuscript about the ideology of love in the English novel.

JULIET MCMASTER is University Professor at the University of Alberta, and a Fellow of the Royal Society of Canada. She has published books on Thackeray, Trollope, Dickens, and Jane Austen, as well as many articles on other British novelists, and she is completing a study on reading the body in the eighteenth-century novel.

JOHN B. PIERCE is Associate Professor of English at Queen's University, Kingston, where he teaches courses in eighteenth-Century and romantic literature and in literary theory. He is the author of *Flexible Design: Revisionary Poetics in William Blae's Vala or the Four Zoas* and of articles on Blake and Shelley. He is also co-editor, with Shelley King, of Amelia Opie's *Adeline Mowbray*.

ALBERT J. RIVERO is Professor of English and Director of the Honors Program at Marquette University. A member of the Editorial Board of The Works of Tobias Smollett, he is collaborating on a critical edition of Samuel Richardson's complete correspondence. He is the recipient of a National Endowment for the Humanities Fellowship for 2000–2001 and is also editing a critical edition of *Gulliver's Travels*.

BETTY A. SCHELLENBERG is Associate Professor of English at Simon Fraser University. She has published *The Conversational Circle: Rereading the English Novel, 1740–1775* (1996) and co-edited *Part Two: Reflections on the Sequel* (1998). Her current book projects are on the professional careers of several mid-eighteenth-century women writers and on the eighteenth-century sequel.

PEGGY THOMPSON is Professor of English at Agnes Scott College. She has published widely on Restoration and eighteenth-century literature and on relationships between literature and religion.

Acknowledgments

There are debts that are a pleasure to acknowledge. *Eighteenth-Century Fiction* is sponsored by McMaster University and receives a grant from the Program of Aid to Learned Journals of the Social Sciences and Humanities Research Council of Canada. Their support sustains the journal, and our debt to both institutions is considerable. I would like to thank the readers of the manuscript for the University of Toronto Press, who made helpful suggestions for improving the book, and to the editors at the Press, Kristen Pederson, Barbara Porter, and Suzanne Rancourt, for their diligence and expertise. The Arts Research Board of McMaster University provided a grant for the index, which Ruth Pincoe prepared, and I am grateful to both. I am also very much in debt to John Robinson, who furnished me with a computer and a fax machine when they were unexpectedly needed in the midst of a holiday visit to Jamaica. I am, as always, indebted to Judy Williams, the copy editor of *ECF* and of this volume, and to Richard Morton, the Associate Editor of *ECF*, for his invaluable editorial advice. My last and greatest obligation is to Elaine Riehm, the Managing Editor of *ECF*, whose meticulous care and exemplary patience in putting together this book, and the many volumes of the journal itself, have made my task easier.

A Note on Texts

Richardson's Editions of His Novels

The publication history of Samuel Richardson's novels is complex for two reasons. In the first place he was the publisher of his own works and in the second an inveterate reviser. As a result all his novels appeared in several editions, each with a competing claim on our attention as the representation of a stage in the evolution of the author's intentions.

Pamela

The first edition of *Pamela* (vols 1 and 2, in duodecimo) appeared anonymously in November 1740 (dated 1741 on the title-page).[1] Four revised editions were published in 1741 and a continuation of *Pamela* (vols 3 and 4, in duodecimo, now often referred to as *Pamela* 2) in December of that year. In May the following year, 1742, a sumptuous edition (in octavo and illustrated) was published, containing the sixth edition of vols 1 and 2 (the original *Pamela*) and the third edition of vols 3 and 4 (*Pamela* 2). The Shakespeare Head *Pamela* (1929) is based upon this edition. The first part of *Pamela* was reprinted in

---

1 The publication history of Richardson's first novel is provided by Peter Sabor in a helpful "Note on the Text" to the Penguin edition of *Pamela* (1980), pp. 21–22. There is a more detailed "Chronological Table of *Pamela* and the *Pamela* Vogue in England" in the Riverside edition of *Pamela*, ed. T.C. Duncan Eaves and Ben D. Kimpel (1971), pp. xvii–xxii. See also T.C. Duncan Eaves and Ben D. Kimpel, "Richardson's Revisions of *Pamela*," *Studies in Bibliography* 20 (1967), 61–88.

1746 and 1754, and in 1761, following Richardson's death, all four volumes were reprinted (dated 1762). The final version of both parts of *Pamela* was published in 1801, from a copy preserved by Richardson's daughters of his elaborate revision of the octavo edition of 1742, prepared by Richardson but not published before his death. In 1810 this edition was reprinted with corrections made probably by Richardson's daughter Anne. Richardson's final version of *Pamela* (1801) was published in facsimile by Garland Publishing in 1974.

Clarissa

Clarissa was first published over fourteen months in groups of duodecimo volumes: vols 1 and 2 in November 1747 (dated 1748), vols 3 and 4 in April 1748, and vols 5 to 7 in December 1748.[2] The type size was reduced at letter 19, vol. 6 in order to bring eight volumes into seven. The second edition appeared in 1749, seven volumes in duodecimo, of which the first four volumes had been extensively revised. This edition included a fifty-page table of contents, which was also published separately. In 1751 Richardson published a carefully and extensively revised third edition (eight volumes in duodecimo) and a fourth edition (seven volumes in octavo). These editions incorporated (and added to) the many changes of the first four volumes of the second edition and provided extensive changes to the final volumes. In the two editions of 1751 Richardson adopted the unusual expedient of indicating the changes by marking each line of added material with a bullet in the margin. In 1751 he also published the *Letters and Passages Restored from the Original Manuscripts of the History of Clarissa*, which made the additional passages printed in the third edition (and the more important additional passages in the second edition) available to purchasers of the earlier editions. The final edition of *Clarissa* in Richardson's lifetime was published in 1759, confusingly described as the fourth edition, that is, the fourth duodecimo edition. This edition reprinted the third duodecimo edition

2 The publication history of Richardson's masterpiece is provided by Florian Stuber in the Introduction to the Clarissa Project edition (AMS Press, 1990). See also T.C. Duncan Eaves and Ben D. Kimpel, "The Composition of *Clarissa* and Its Revision before Publication," *PMLA* 83 (1968), 416–28; Shirley Van Marter, "Richardson's Revisions of *Clarissa* in the Second Edition," *Studies in Bibliography* 28 (1975), 107–32; and her "Richardson's Revisions of *Clarissa* in the Third and Fourth Editions," *Studies in Bibliography* 28 (1975), 119–52.

but omitted the bullets indicating added material as well as the "Collection of Sentiments" compiled from the novel and presented to Richardson by an "ingenious Gentleman." The Shakespeare Head edition (1929) is based on the third edition (with a few readings adopted from the first edition in doubtful cases), but, like the 1759 edition, with the omission of the bullets and of the "Collection of Sentiments." The AMS Press edition is a facsimile reprint of the third edition.

Sir Charles Grandison

The first edition (seven volumes in duodecimo) of *Grandison* was published in instalments: vols 1–4 in November 1753; vols 5–6 in December 1753; and vol. 7 in March 1754.[3] The second edition in octavo was published at the same time but in six volumes. It was extensively revised, as was the third edition (in duodecimo) of 1754. In 1762, the year after Richardson's death, the fourth edition was published. Finally, in 1810 a "new edition, with the last corrections by the author" was published by Anna Laetitia Barbauld.

Modern Editions

There is no uniform modern scholarly edition of Richardson's novels. The texts listed below and cited in this volume are considered the best available modern editions. No attempt has been made to restrict references to a single edition of a novel, since the choice of edition may be crucial to the discussion. Contributors have agreed, however, to cite the editions listed here and, when an edition is not readily available, to provide a parallel reference to another edition. For example, neither the Shakespeare Head nor the AMS Press edition of *Clarissa* is widely available. When references are to one of these editions a parallel reference is given, whenever possible, to the Penguin edition. Of course, that is not possible when the citation is

3 The publication history of Richardson's last novel is provided by Jocelyn Harris in a "Note on the Text" to the Oxford University Press edition of *Sir Charles Grandison* (1972). See also R.C. Pierson, "The Revisions of Richardson's *Sir Charles Grandison*," *Studies in Bibliography* 21 (1968), 163–89.

from a passage added in the third edition, as the Penguin edition is based on the first edition.

Pamela 1

Pamela or, Virtue Rewarded, ed. T.C. Duncan Eaves and Ben D. Kimpel, Riverside edition (Boston: Houghton Mifflin, 1971), based on the first edition, 1740. A new and more accurate edition of *Pamela,* ed. Thomas Keymer and Alice Wakely, Oxford World's Classics (Oxford: Oxford University Press), based on the first edition (with the second edition introductory material included in an Appendix), is scheduled for publication in 2001.

Pamela; or, Virtue Rewarded, ed. Peter Sabor (Harmondsworth: Penguin Books, 1980), a reprint of the posthumous 1801 edition of the first two volumes of the novel.

Pamela 1 and 2

Pamela; or, Virtue Rewarded, Shakespeare Head edition, 4 vols (Oxford: Basil Blackwell, 1929), based on "the Sixth Edition, corrected, of Vols I & II" and "the Third Edition, corrected, of Vols III & IV," 1742. The *Recommendatory Letters* and *Introductory Preface,* which were omitted in the edition, have in the Shakespeare Head reprint "been re-placed from the third edition of the first two volumes published in 1741."

Pamela; or, Virtue Rewarded, the revised text of 1801, 4 vols (New York and London: Garland Publishing, 1974). A facsimile reprint.

Clarissa

Clarissa or The History of a Young Lady, ed. Angus Ross (Harmondsworth: Penguin Books, 1985), based on the first edition, 1747–48 (modernized in accidentals).

Clarissa or, The History of a Young Lady, Shakespeare Head edition, 8 vols (Oxford: Basil Blackwell, 1930), based on the third edition, 1751.

Clarissa. Or, The History of A Young Lady, ed. Florian Stuber, The Clarissa Project, 8 vols (New York: AMS Press, 1990), a facsimile reprint of the third edition, 1751.

Sir Charles Grandison

The History of Sir Charles Grandison, ed. Jocelyn Harris, 3 vols (London: Oxford University Press, 1972), based on the first edition, 1753–54.

The History of Sir Charles Grandison, Shakespeare Head edition, 6 vols (Oxford: Basil Blackwell, 1931), based on the second edition (in octavo), 1753–54.

Letters

Selected Letters of Samuel Richardson, ed. John Carroll (Oxford: Clarendon Press, 1964).

The Correspondence of Samuel Richardson, ed. Anna Laetitia Barbauld, 6 vols (London: R. Phillips, 1804). A new complete correspondence is projected, which, when published, will replace Mrs Barbauld's inaccurate edition.

Richardson's novels are available in an electronic edition, *Eighteenth-Century Fiction on CD-ROM* (Cambridge: Chadwyck-Healey, 1996):

Pamela, 4 vols (the first edition of both *Pamela* 1 and the continuation, *Pamela* 2)
Pamela, 4 vols (the sixth edition, as described on the title-page, 1742. Actually the sixth edition in octavo of *Pamela* 1 and the third edition in octavo of *Pamela* 2)
Clarissa, 7 vols (the first edition, 1747–48)
Clarissa, 8 vols (the third edition, 1751)
Sir Charles Grandison, 7 vols (the first edition, 1753–54)

These novels are also available to subscribing libraries on line at http://lion.chadwyck.co.uk or http://lion.chadwyck.com.

PASSION AND VIRTUE

Joseph Highmore (1692–1780), *Samuel Richardson* (1750). By courtesy of the National Portrait Gallery, London.

Introduction   David Blewett

The essays in this volume have been collected from among the thirty essays on Samuel Richardson that have appeared in *Eighteenth-Century Fiction* in the first dozen years of publication. As the largest and strongest group of essays on a single author, they are testimony, if one were needed, to the vitality of Richardson studies today. The critical excitement that his novels continue to generate constitutes a powerful response to one of the most passionate of novelists. Richardson's great theme is human passion, both in its ennobling and its destructive aspects, that is, as love and as lust, but also in the Christian sense of suffering. We have selected fourteen essays on *Pamela*, parts 1 and 2, *Clarissa*, and *Sir Charles Grandison*, vigorous responses to Richardson's deeply felt and compelling analyses of the conflict of human emotions and the formidable struggle to safeguard virtue.

Both John Pierce and John Dussinger, though in very different ways, read the fable-like *Pamela* as a product of print culture. Pierce draws our attention to the degree in which the maturing consciousness of the surprisingly literate heroine is expressed through her use of texts. In sacred and secular analogies, with the Bible and with Aesop's *Fables*, she creates, like a novelist, an account of her plight that enables her to resist "the potentially paralysing force of the abduction, captivity, and threat of rape" (p. 15). Dussinger, also emphasizing the resemblance between Pamela's tale and the "tendentious fables of Aesop" (p. 1), sees a connection with Richardson's own experience, caught up in the "ferocious print wars" (p. 1) of the period. Virtue for Pamela, as for Richardson, is "moral strength in resisting temptation" (p. 16). The central action of the novel—passion and resistance—is resolved in the triumph of Pamela, "the power of the written word over the presumptive aristocratic social hierarchy" (p. 21), an apt description, as it happens, of the riposte to Lord Chesterfield of Richardson's friend Samuel Johnson, in his famous letter written in February 1755.

Albert J. Rivero offers a subversive reading of the Sally Godfrey episode, "the unpleasant secret" (p. 2) concealed from Pamela and the reader alike throughout most of the novel. Sally Godfrey is a type of Pamela, a grim reminder of an earlier sexual passion that, standing in stark and exemplary contrast to Pamela's virtuous conduct, ends in exile and separation. But the providential "happy" resolution to Sally Godfrey's story, as Rivero points out, is rooted in hypocrisy, "predicated on secrecy, on deceit, on a providential rewriting that allows the seducer the pleasant exercise of pitying his victim" (p. 17). In a rare essay on *Pamela* 2, Betty Schellenberg makes the case for the often derided sequel, seen not as a falling off from the narrative vigour of the first part, but as a conservative portrayal of a social alternative. (Her argument, *mutatis mutandis*, applies to the second part of *Pilgrim's Progress*, to *Sir Charles Grandison*, and to *Amelia*.) Passion gives way to a virtuous and disciplined authority, though the extended London masquerade section harks back to the old excitement of part 1.

Several of the essays on *Clarissa* examine the major political, economic, philosophical, moral, and religious ideas at work in the novel, the turbulent undercurrents stirring beneath the surface of the vast expanse of Richardson's great work, creating its apparent—and real—inconsistencies. Three essay turn outward to the major intellectual disputes of the seventeenth and eighteenth centuries. Jocelyn Harris links the struggle between passion and virtue to its philosophical correlatives in the "two vigorously competing worldviews of his time" (p. 2), Hobbes's materialist philosophy and Christian Platonism, embodied in Lovelace and Clarissa. Rachel K. Carnell links the story of Clarissa's terrible struggles with her family

and then with Lovelace to the debate over tyranny, brilliantly articulated by Robert Filmer in *Patriarcha* (1680) and by John Locke in
Two Treatises on Government (1689). Clarissa, by making her story public, raises a tale of domestic violence to the level of tragedy, making
it "as worthy of public scrutiny as is state tyranny" (p. 16). Daniel P.
Gunn challenges Christopher Hill's notion that Clarissa "is an expression of militant bourgeois ideology" (p.1), that of the thrusting
Harlowes, who stand against the "feudal-cavalier" and aristocratic values of Lovelace and his family. Instead he argues that the clash is
between "two visions of morality and passion" (p.12), one backward-
looking, since it has its roots in a medieval tradition of self-denial
and the annihilation of the passions of this world, the other forward-
looking, a progressive ideology which responds to the moral emphasis upon freedom and openness. In other words, Clarissa, like
a medieval ascetic, renounces passions and the world. But her benevolent heart—her susceptibility to passion—makes her superior to
the cold-hearted Lovelace.

The second three essays on *Clarissa* turn inward to the religious,
moral, and emotional sources of Richardson's creative imagination.
In "Abuse and Atonement: The Passion of Clarissa Harlowe," Peggy
Thompson sets the novel in the context of the theological considerations of Christian atonement, outlining three theories of atonement
then current. This procedure allows her to examine the suffering of
Clarissa as a type of Christ's passion. Like Robert Erickson, she makes
the important point that Clarissa through her passion becomes an
exemplar herself. Erickson, demonstrating the rich allusiveness of
Richardson's literary experience, shows the depths of meaning in
passion and virtue. Richardson provided "a new representation of inner experience, most notably the 'Passions,' centring on love" (p. 2).
He sees that "the central dynamic" of the novel "is a parable of the redemption of the heart," "a regenerative process of unexampled trust
and suffering for the new Christian hero, a woman and a writer" (p.
5). Margaret Anne Doody, in a wide-ranging investigation of Gnosticism, detects the presence within *Clarissa* of the Gnostic story of "the
Fall and Rise of the Virgin Sophia" (p. 53), Christ's sister and counterpart. Like others, though from a very different perspective, she
sees Clarissa's passion as a counterpart of Christ's. Clarissa's virtue

is, of course, Sophia, or Divine Wisdom, that is, she descends from a higher sphere, again like Christ, and longs to return to it, a goal she attains.

Four writers consider *Sir Charles Grandison*, a novel that was a favourite of both Jane Austen and George Eliot, and in the nineteenth century, as Juliet McMaster points out, "undoubtedly *the* Richardson novel." Its loss of popularity in the twentieth century has often been attributed to the lower emotional pitch of a novel in which female vulnerability is no longer paramount, as if Richardson's imagination required stimulation of a rather prurient kind. But the question arises as to whether we are reading *Sir Charles Grandison* in the wrong way—in effect blaming Richardson for not writing another *Clarissa*—and failing to read the novel on its own terms. The final four essays, by probing beneath the surface "in order to expose and explore disquieting views which both complicate and enrich the text," in Lois Chaber's words, invite an overdue reassessment of the significance of Richardson's most neglected work.

One of the chief problems for modern readers is that the hero is entirely virtuous. The result, as Juliet McMaster points out, is that the women are considerably more interesting. In this novel, in which the situations are less extreme than those in *Pamela* or *Clarissa*, the major theme is "the issue of the proper relation of mind to body" (p. 6), not so much in Grandison, who is perfect already, but in the women, especially the admirable Harriet Byron. Harriet, who falls in love with Sir Charles—"almost a virtue in itself" (p. 9)—achieves the desirable "consonance of mind and body" (p. 10). She is contrasted with Clementina, who fails the test, and with Charlotte, who succeeds, though not with the aplomb of Harriet. Lois Chaber detects beneath the surface of the novel a profound anxiety born out of the uncertainty of human destiny. She traces Richardson's sense of the "precariousness of human fate" (p. 10) to Anglican homiletic writings with which Richardson was familiar. Richardson generates anxiety through "two key strategies" (p.9)—his frequent use of the subjunctive mood and of the *alter ego* or double (a device first used in the Sally Godfrey episode in *Pamela*). As a result, "tragedy hovers over the seemingly comic world of *Grandison*" (p. 14).

In her analysis of Richardson's typology of love, Wendy Jones argues that *Grandison* is Richardson's clearest and most complete anatomy of "the different sorts of love" (p. 8). Companionate love, by the eighteenth century the basis for marriage, at least in the middle classes, was based upon "esteem," or respect for the "intellectual and moral qualities" of the other person, that is, upon virtue (p. 9). But the love of Harriet and Grandison is raised to a higher plane because he is "so much more virtuous than other men" (p. 14). Theirs is a "perfect kind of love," "a fully mutual, erotic response to moral excellence" (p. 19). George Haggerty also addresses the expression of love in the novel, pointing out the degree to which passion must be articulated if it is to lead, as it ought, to "self-knowledge" (p. 12) and "self-realization" (p. 13). As in all Richardson's novels, "Deception and dishonesty of any kind are deplored" (p. 12).

Passion and virtue are the twin themes of this volume. Both are important words in Richardson's moral vocabulary, as Samuel Johnson observed when he said of Richardson that he "enlarged the knowledge of human nature, and taught the passions to move at the command of virtue" (*Rambler* 97). Virtue can withstand passion, as in *Pamela* or *Clarissa*, or may be the appropriate reward of passion, as, in different senses, it is in all three novels.

Pamela's Textual Authority

John B. Pierce

Removed from her parents, harassed and imprisoned by her employer, nearly driven to suicide, Richardson's Pamela attempts to forge a personal identity that balances conflicting claims of authority.[1] As the novel proceeds, Pamela tries to embody her parents' injunctions and to correct the abuses of aristocratic privilege by Mr B.[2] Her maturing process culminates in a struggle between Mr B.'s will to power over Pamela and her will to profess and practise virtue. Unfortunately, the authority of Pamela's appeals to truth and virtue is threatened by her subordinated roles as adolescent, woman, and servant, roles which pose contradicting claims against a mature male aristocrat.[3] Thus even though her moral stance may be justified by her belief in the correspondence between inward virtue and outward honesty, it is supported by little that is tangible in

1 John A. Dussinger, "What Pamela Knew: An Interpretation," *Journal of English and Germanic Philology* 69 (1970), 379. "Pamela's Textual Authority" was first published in *Eighteenth-Century Fiction* 7:2 (1995), 131–46.

2 Dussinger, p. 381, and Nancy K. Miller, *The Heroine's Text: Readings in the French and English Novel* (New York: Columbia University Press, 1980), pp. 39–40, discuss the parents' role in shaping Pamela. See also Christopher Flint, "The Anxiety of Affluence: Family and Class (Dis)order in *Pamela: or, Virtue Rewarded*," *SEL* 29 (1989), 497.

3 Patricia Meyer Spacks, *The Adolescent Idea: Myths of Youth and the Adult Imagination* (New York: Basic Books, 1981), discusses Pamela's identity as part of the three subordinated groups of the adolescent, woman, and servant (p. 26).

terms of age, sex, or social status. The only identity, the only authority, and the greatest degree of power she has are manifest in her
writing, a textuality giving voice to an identity Mr B. would willingly
debase and silence. A closer examination of the manner in which
Pamela invokes different texts—in particular, her own and those of
scripture and fable—to strengthen her claims to truth and authority reveals the complexity of the character's and novel's textuality.
Mr B.'s charges that she is fabricating a "romance"[4] would take on
some merit if she did not write truth, and she would become a temp-
tress, a Lucretia, or a Shamela, manipulating a frustrated lover out of
self-interest and caprice.[5] Essentially, Pamela's text as a discourse of
authority, as a virtually sacred record of events, manifests personal
identity supplemented by sacred and secular texts, and reinforces
her personalized claims to textual authority.

Pamela's "Text"

In an off-hand remark addressed to Mrs Jewkes during her imprisonment at Lincolnshire, Pamela talks in a "prattling Vein," offering
what she calls "a little History of myself" (p. 173). Pamela's claim
that she creates a history follows in the tradition of eighteenth-
century writers who seek to obtain a greater degree of credibility
for their narratives by invoking an empirical bias to set against the
idealizing impulse of romance. As Michael McKeon has pointed out,
the generic and epistemological claims of the term "history" are in-
tertwined with, and set in opposition to, those of "romance." Romance emerges in the period "as not only a distinct generic, but
also as a broadly epistemological, category whose meaning is over-
whelmingly trivialized or pejorative." History, on the other hand,
becomes increasingly connected to empirical truth, "exploiting especially the techniques of authentication by first-hand and documentary witness." In McKeon's terms, Pamela is a "naïve empiri-
cist," a character refuting the fabrications of romance compiled by

4 Samuel Richardson, *Pamela or, Virtue Rewarded*, ed. T.C. Duncan Eaves and Ben D. Kimpel,
  Riverside edition (Boston: Houghton Mifflin, 1971), p. 201. References are to this edition.

5 For discussions of Mr B. as romance writer, see Michael McKeon, *The Origins of the English
  Novel 1600–1740* (Baltimore: Johns Hopkins University Press, 1987), pp. 357–64, and Sheila
  C. Conboy, "Fabric and Fabrication in Richardson's *Pamela*," *ELH* 54 (1987), 85–86.

Mr B. in favour of "an empirical epistemology that derives from many sources." Pamela's sources include her first-hand observations, which are fixed, verified, and verifiable when she records them in written form. Borrowing from Elizabeth Eisenstein, McKeon outlines the argument that writing, but more particularly print, is connected to the development of the idea of objective history.[6]

Pamela's assertion that her story is a "history" gives authority to her account. What might seem personal and subjective becomes more general and objective when set against the structures of history. The possibility that her reports are distorted by emotionalism or unreliability is somewhat circumscribed, and the reader's sympathy and judgment are simultaneously engaged. More important, the move to historicity, by fixing experience in written form, creates a text which is the arbiter of truth in the dispute between Mr B. and Pamela. It can be reviewed and revisited for confirmation or refutation of the "facts" of Pamela's imprisonment and her treatment. Indeed, when Mr B. disputes Pamela's assertion that she has no serious intention of marrying Parson Williams, she refers him to "the Text" of her journal:

Why, said he, you discourage his [Parson Williams's] Address in Appearance; but no otherwise than all your cunning Sex do to ours, to make us more eager in pursuing you.
    Well, Sir, said I, that is your Comment; but it does not appear so in the Text. (p. 200)

The force of this argument is direct and far reaching. Mr B. argues for a form of authority that reads codes of "Appearance" and that is invariably tied to false seemings hiding manipulative interests. Pamela's appeal to authority resides in the mediated form of the "Text." She bypasses questions of subjectivity perhaps because it is her own subjectivity that is at stake. The "Text" acts as an objectified form for Pamela, having a reflective security and stability produced from but outside the constant threats to her virtue. She tells Mr B. that her sincerity and honesty are clearly evident in her letter, thereby raising it to the status of a work having a self-evident truth.

6 See McKeon, pp. 27, 46–47, 21, and 43.

Samuel Richardson, *Pamela, or, Virtue Rewarded,* 4 vols (London, 1742), vol. 3, opposite p. 161. Engraved by Hubert François Gravelot (1699–1773) after a drawing by Francis Hayman (1708–1776). Reproduced by permission of McMaster University Library.

By confining the flow and swirl of experience to letters, Pamela gives
reported experience a truth that is tangible, fixed, examinable, and
therefore confirmed as truth. Ultimately, reference to "the Text" reinforces her own sense of empirical truth and encourages a certain
degree of sympathy in the reader for such views. Moreover, Pamela's
absolute reference to "the Text" suggests she believes it is a full and
authentic report of her actions and a reflection of her intentions.
She thereby grants a certainty to language that a modern writer is
not likely to give and that a contemporary such as Sterne would easily ridicule. She sees words as directly connected to truth, arguing
quite flatly, "I have only writ Truth" (p. 206). The schisms between
signifier and signified, intention and meaning, are denied or glossed
over; the expressive and referential values of language also have
equal value in this empirically based textuality. The text as arbiter,
authority, and object thus delivers power to Pamela that transcends
the limitations of sex, class, and circumstance.

Difficulties arise, however, in as much as Pamela's truth is rather
malleable, a truth that one critic has called "iffy."[7] Pamela's notion of
truth may be more sharply defined in light of Patricia Meyer Spacks's
distinction between truths of representation and those of doctrine.[8]
Truth of representation is the claim of the practitioner of realism or
verisimilitude, and in literature it purports to record faithfully actual
events and people in written form with a verifiable referential accur-
acy. Truth of doctrine is a "moral or ethical" one constituted from
the framework of social thought.[9] Pamela's claim to an authoritative
truth, like that of many authors, is problematic, since she does not
differentiate between the truths of representation and doctrine, the
facts of the referential and the estimates of the ethical. Moreover,
such claims to truth and authority are complicated by the strong
emotive or expressive dimension of her observations and writing.

The resulting truth may seem "iffy," but it is inclusive. Her central concern is "to establish her sincerity: her letters faithfully express

7 Patricia McKee, "Corresponding Freedoms: Language and the Self in *Pamela*," *ELH* 52
(1985), 632.

8 Patricia Meyer Spacks, *Desire and Truth: Functions of Plot in Eighteenth-Century English Novels*
(Chicago: University of Chicago Press, 1990), pp. 1–2.

9 Spacks, *Desire and Truth*, p. 2.

her feelings at the time of her suffering."[10] With disarming honesty she argues, "tho' I don't remember all I wrote, yet I know I wrote my Heart; and that is not deceitful" (p. 200). The sincere heart as a measure of truth opens the way to the novel and heroine of sentiment[11] and, additionally, sets referential and expressive modes of discourse on an equal footing. The bull Pamela thinks she sees outside the gates in Lincolnshire, for instance, may later be understood to have been only a cow (p. 137), but her early view of it as a bull accurately expresses her sexual fear of Mr B. and reflects a more personal truth than a verifiable description of the actual object would.[12] While Pamela tends to subsume representational and doctrinal truths within the framework of personal observation and felt experience, what seems crucial to the heartfelt truth of her text is that this mix supports rather than diminishes her authority. This form of truth and authority is bolstered by the adaptation of other textual forms, specifically those of scripture and fable.

Sacred Texts: The Bible

Pamela's status as a Christian heroine has been suggested by Roger Sharrock,[13] but her use of the Bible has not adequately been commented on. Pamela's use of the Bible places her in a Judeo-Christian heritage strongly modified by the Puritan tradition of the spiritual

---

10 Lars Harveit, *The Art of Persuasion: A Study of Six Novels* (Bergen: Universitetsforlaget, 1977), p. 18.

11 For more on Pamela's journal as embodying her "heart," see Roy Roussel, "Reflections on the Letter: The Reconciliation of Distance and Presence in *Pamela*," *ELH* 41 (1974), 387–88.

12 Conboy comments on the way in which Pamela's "imagination subsumes the 'facts,' and she projects them onto the world in new ways" during her imprisonment (p. 87). Her sight of the bull illustrates how "her fear of phallic attack has impaired her vision, rendering her unable to effect the escape she desires" (p. 88). Yet this "impaired ... vision" offers the most accurate view of Pamela's experience of the moment. See also Stuart Wilson, "Richardson's *Pamela*: An Interpretation," *PMLA* 88 (1973), 85–86, for a commentary on the bull as an incarnation of Pamela's sexual fears.

13 Roger Sharrock, "Richardson's *Pamela*: The Gospel and the Novel," *Durham University Journal* 58 (1966), 67–74. Margaret Anne Doody, *A Natural Passion: A Study of the Novels of Samuel Richardson* (Oxford: Clarendon Press, 1974), also describes *Pamela* as "a Christian fable" (p. 34).

biography. As J. Paul Hunter points out, spiritual autobiographies "could formulate causes and effects to exhibit the purposeful nature of God's plan for an individual, and they could portray 'examples' for the imitation or evitation of the reader, so that, like providence books, their function was not only polemical but moral." For Pamela, the effect of participating in this tradition is to validate her experience and align "even ... seemingly trivial happenings" with profound events containing a divine shape.[14] Thus her actions and, more particularly, the records of them take on an even greater significance as her text inscribes the empirical concerns of history within the spiritual contexts of divinity. References to scripture go beyond acts of simple piety, complementing the empirical truths of secular history with the spiritual truth of sacred revelation, and her mandate as recording angel for her own book of fate shifts from passive recording to active interpretation. As part of a Puritan tradition she reinterprets her subjective experience as part of a larger struggle of spiritual endurance elevating both her role and her record.

Her direct references to the Bible during her imprisonment in Lincolnshire identify her state with that of the dispossessed and enslaved Israelites. Despondent over her imprisonment and prohibition from going to church on Sunday (p. 127), Pamela constructs her own updated version of Psalm 137. The importance of this psalm is revealed just before her wedding when Pamela's version is compared, stanza by stanza, with a traditional version contained in Mr Williams's "little Pocket Common-prayer Book."[15] In this case, the reader is given conscious clues about how the text is to be read and the kind of agreed-upon authority it has within the fictional world of the novel. Close discussion of Pamela's version of the psalm seems purposely delayed so that its public appearance coincides with her entrance into the social sphere of aristocratic privilege. Although Mr B. controls the text at this point—it comes from his pocket—in the course of the scene it moves into the public domain and passes from

14 J. Paul Hunter, *The Reluctant Pilgrim: Defoe's Emblematic Method and Quest for Form in "Robinson Crusoe"* (Baltimore: Johns Hopkins University Press, 1966), pp. 76–77.

15 In the following discussion, I will quote from the version in Williams's "Common-prayer Book" (pp. 267–71).

a private text of personal suffering to a public account of heroic action. Comments by the ladies suggesting that it is "very pretty" and by Lady Jones declaring the psalm "a new Instance of [Pamela's] ... Genius and Accomplishments" (pp. 268, 269) bolster Pamela's confidence at this precarious juncture and reinforce the sense that the products of her personal sufferings are congruent with norms of larger aristocratic society. The censure of the ladies directed against Mr B. and his own admission that he "should get no Credit by shewing" the psalm are a recognition and an admission of guilt on Mr B.'s part and recommend the great forbearance and fortitude on Pamela's. The general approval of Pamela's rendering of the psalm in such a public forum and in conjunction with the public ritual of the wedding reinforces the authority of her account as filtered through the psalm. This social acknowledgment reconstructs the earlier, isolated act of creation in personal suffering, removing any lingering sense of self-pity, solipsism, or manipulative purpose.

Psalm 137 records the constancy in sorrow of a dispossessed Israelite community and their curse against their imprisoners. Pamela describes it as "a little touching" (p. 127), meaning, of course, that it touches or reflects her current emotional state; the tactile image, however, is fitting in a perspective based on sensibility. She writes that she "turn'd to it, and took the Liberty to alter it to my Case more; I hope I did not sin in it: But thus I turn'd it" (p. 127). The key word here is "Liberty"; textual revisionism seems the only certain evidence of freedom she has. The empowerment experienced in turning to the psalm and turning it to her case shows a consciousness self-determined within Christian ideology. The self determined is limited by the fear of sin—"I hope I did not sin in it"—but at least the attempted freedom is possible. Pamela's turning of the psalm to reflect her "Case more" shows the expressive potentiality of this Puritan tradition. In adapting and transforming biblical events to her own life, she makes herself, as a figure of virtue, part of a pattern of faith in an oppressive landscape and portrays herself as one of the chosen people.

In revising the psalm, Pamela also echoes the authorial function of Richardson and other eighteenth-century novelists. The transformation of "Babylon" to "B——n-hall" and "Harp" to "Spinnet" involves

Pamela in a process of literary displacement in which mythic and archetypal images are translated into the objects of formal realism.[16]
This hermeneutic action, reflecting the process and claims made by
the novel itself, reinforces Pamela's claims to authoritative representation. In addition, the temporal displacement involved in fusing
Pamela's contemporary experience with that of the ancient Hebrews
extends a certain degree of novelistic authority over the modulation
of time. At the very least, the manipulation of place, objects, and
time offers a surrogate liberty, a mental freedom, that counterbal-
ances her physical imprisonment. Like the novel writer, she may be
constrained by the room she writes from, but seeks her liberty in
the transformation of the literary sources within it. The eradication
of temporal difference emphasizes the similarity of human experience, making Pamela's individual drama more universal, lifting her
out of the prison of self-enclosure.

Pamela's revision of the psalm thus has a self-reflexive quality that
mingles realistic sentimental vision with the ability to adapt ancient
tradition to modern experience. Beyond the simple displacement of
"Babylon" to "B——n" and "Harp" to "Spinnet," Pamela replaces the
theme of faith in Jerusalem and Jehovah of the original psalm with a
concern for "innocence" and "chastity," and introduces the implied
metaphor that chastity itself is the walled city of Jerusalem.

Mrs Jewkes, not Mr B., is depicted as the central assailant of this
jewelled city:

> Remember, Lord, this Mrs. Jewkes,
>   When with a mighty Sound,
> She cries, Down with her Chastity,
>   Down to the very Ground!
>
> Ev'n so shalt thou, O wicked One,
>   At length to Shame be brought;
> And happy shall all those be call'd
>   That my Deliv'rance wrought.

The Old Testament version contains imprecations against the Edom-
ites, heirs of Esau and therefore exiled from the immediate grace of

---

16 See Northrop Frye, "Myth, Fiction and Displacement," *Fables of Identity: Studies in Poetic
Mythology* (New York: Harcourt, Brace, Jovanovich, 1963), p. 36.

God. But in the curse against Mrs Jewkes, Pamela, not surprisingly, moderates the tone of vindictiveness against the oppressor, replacing the famous image of dashing out babies' brains with "Even so shalt thou, O wicked One, / At length to Shame be brought." The outlines of Pamela's mythic universe become clearer even as she engages in an act of literary displacement. Equal to the destruction of infants is the bringing of shame on the persecutors. Shame involves a destruction of the outward fortifications of the self, of honour, honesty, and truth, to reveal outward appearances as false, the self as a negation of value. Pamela, obsessed with building a self of larger significance, obviously feels that this loss of self is as abhorrent as infanticide. Her emphasis on Mrs Jewkes perhaps suggests the deep fear of a female anti-Pamela, one whose false chastity can lead only to shame. Yet, in addition, the localizing of blame in Mrs Jewkes serves as a method of psychological damage control; by limiting Mr B.'s involvement, she possibly reveals the degree of her attachment to him. Indeed her final stanza suggests the desire for a male deliverer:

> Yea, blessed shall the Man be call'd
> That shames thee of thy Evil,
> And saves me from thy vile Attempts,
> And thee, too, from the D—l.

At this point in the novel Pamela may consciously believe Williams the deliverer, but she subconsciously hopes it is Mr B. himself. Later in the novel Pamela's restraint in this regard will strike Mr B., if not the reader, as another sign of the generosity of her soul and the appropriateness of her social elevation. The moment is well prepared for by the dialogue between Pamela, Mr B., Williams, and a silent Mrs Jewkes:

Now, good Sir, said I, oblige me; don't read any further: Pray don't! O pray, Madam, said Mr. *Williams*, let me beg to have the rest read; for I long to know who you make the Sons of *Edom*, and how you turn the Psalmist's Execrations against the insulting *Babylonians*.

  Well, Mr. *Williams*, reply'd I, you should not have said so. O, said my Master, that is one of the best things of all. Poor Mrs. *Jewkes* stands for *Edom*'s Sons; and we must not lose this, because I think it one of my *Pamela*'s Excellencies, that tho' thus oppress'd, she prays for no Harm upon the Oppressor. (pp. 269–70)

Interestingly, Williams's sycophancy is set off against Mr B.'s authoritarianism here, and only Pamela's virtue seems to emerge unscathed.

Pamela's other references to the Bible emphasize servitude. In the degree of certainty Pamela arrogates to her writing as history, she comes close to usurping divine omniscience. As we have seen, the errors of emotionalism humanize the scope of her observations for the reader but are overlooked by her and are not seen in conflict with the authority of her version of truth. McKeon notes that while she nears the "sin of sufficiency," "she is consistently on her guard against the temptation to arrogate to her own ingenuity the praise for 'Contrivances' that are truly due only to 'the Author of all my Happiness.'"[17] The concern that she not "sin" in transforming biblical texts offers a check against the presumptuous and hubristic. While struggling against the "Kindness" (p. 180) of Mr B., she speaks in a biblical cadence derived directly from David as he is about to face Goliath:

But I trust, that that God, who has deliver'd me from the Paw of the Lion and the Bear; that is, his and Mrs. *Jewkes*'s Violences; will also deliver me from this *Philistine*, myself, and my own Infirmities, that I may not defy the Commands of the Living God!

The heroic stature gained is moderated by the limitation of the self before a divine source of power and authority. And much later, in a debate over the text for her wedding, Pamela chooses one that reinforces her role as servant: "I am sure ... if any body ever had Reason, I have, to say, with the blessed Virgin, *My Soul doth magnify the Lord; for he hath regarded the low Estate of his Handmaiden,—and exalted one of low Degree*" (p. 263). The social victory is replaced by subjection to the divine.[18]

Spiritual servitude supplants the physical servitude she faces under Mr B. and within the structures of social and gender-based identity. She plays out the paradoxical ideal of liberation in the idea that she is never entirely free until enslaved to God.[19]

17 McKeon, p. 362.

18 McKeon, pp. 378–80.

19 Compare John Donne's Sonnet XIV, *The Divine Poems*, ed. Helen Gardner (Oxford: Clarendon Press 1952), p. 11.

Secular Texts: The Fable

In his Preface to *Pamela*, Richardson indicates his indebtedness to the tradition of the fable when he notes that the work is designed "*to* Divert *and* Entertain, *and at the same time to* Instruct, *and* Improve *the Minds of the* YOUTH *of both Sexes ... as well as ... Persons of* maturer *Years and Understandings*" (p. 3). Such indebtedness is not surprising considering the moral import of the work and the fable's importance in the eighteenth century. In addition, the fact that he published a revised version of Sir Roger L'Estrange's *Aesop* barely a year before *Pamela* and referred to this edition in the novel (p. 77) indicates more than a casual influence.[20]

Particularly appropriate for use in the novel, the fable frames instruction and delight within a form that bridges barriers of age and social class. Locke, for instance, argues that Aesop's *Fables* are unique in their suitability for all ages; the *Fables*, while "apt to delight and entertain a Child, may yet afford useful Reflections to a grown Man."[21] In his own preface to L'Estrange's *Fables*, Richardson writes that the fables are "fit for the instruction of the youth of both sexes, at the same time that we hope it [the book] will not be found unworthy of the perusal of persons of riper years and understandings."[22] As the fable is also a didactic form that functions outside the divisions of social class,[23] it is a credible form for Pamela, a young girl of low social status, to learn from and to adapt to her own personal station, that of her parents, and Richardson's audience, a broad mixture of social classes. The wide appeal of the fable does not necessarily make it apolitical, however. Margaret Anne Doody, one of the few critics to

20 For a discussion of the importance of the fable in this period see Thomas Noel, *Theories of the Fable in the Eighteenth Century* (New York: Columbia University Press, 1975), pp. 1–13. On the background of Richardson's publication of *Aesop's Fables* see T.C. Duncan Eaves and Ben D. Kimpel, *Samuel Richardson: A Biography* (Oxford: Clarendon, 1971), pp. 76–80; Katherine Hornbeak, "Richardson's Aesop," *Smith College Studies in Modern Languages* 19 (1939), 30–50; and Doody, pp. 25–28.

21 John Locke, *Some Thoughts Concerning Education, The Educational Writings of John Locke: A Critical Edition with Introduction and Notes*, ed. James L. Axtell (Cambridge: Cambridge University Press, 1968), p. 259.

22 *Aesop's Fables*, ed. Samuel Richardson (1940; New York: Garland, 1975), p. xii.

23 Noel, p. 10.

comment directly on Richardson's use of the fable, has noted that "Like a fable, the story [of *Pamela*] has an indirect bearing on a broader political and social situation." She goes on to offer a concise summary of the story in terms of fable morality: "The holder of rank and power over-extends his authority treacherously, until taught a lesson, and those in the pay of the powerful are haughty-minded and foolish counsellors."[24] The fable as adopted in *Pamela* offers a moral truth and common-sense wisdom compatible with the sacred truth of scripture and the empirical truth of history.

In invoking the fable of the "Grasshopper and the Ants," for instance, Pamela presents herself and her reader with an object lesson that admonishes any tendency to sloth through the enjoyments of luxury and illustrates the rather precarious nature of her social and economic status. She sees herself as the grasshopper, making a "fine Figure with my Singing and Dancing" when she returns to her parents, drawing attention to the fact that Lady B. has educated her far beyond the social station of her birth. She hopes, upon her return, to become like one of the ants and "get a little Plain-work, or any thing to do" (p. 77), yet this regressive social move is conveyed as a form of self-mortification and clearly runs counter to Pamela's desires and the direction of the fiction towards self-definition and self-fulfilment. She follows the fable with the story "of a good Bishop that was to be burnt for his Religion; and he try'd how he could bear it, by putting his Fingers into the lighted Candle" (p. 77). Her equation of this mortification of the self to the scouring of "Pewter Plate" (p. 78) and the getting of "Needle-work" (p. 78) borders on excessive self-pity, luckily interrupted by the appearance of "our *Hannah* with a Message from Mrs. *Jervis*" (p. 78). Pamela's self-indulgence emerges not just as a sign of her egotistic immaturity but also as an indicator that she already participates in the expectations of a higher social class.

The use of the fable dramatizes Pamela's circumspection when facing an impending change in which her singing and dancing at Brandon Hall will be exchanged for scrubbing and sewing in the house of her parents. In the choice of such an apt fable, Pamela

24 Doody, p. 33.

demonstrates a sharpness of mind capable of accurately evaluating present circumstances, yet the choice of a fable—rather than, say, a biblical text, philosophical axiom, or learned allusion—illustrates the common sense of a simple country girl. Pamela's statement that she has of her own accord read this fable "in my Lady's Books" (p. 77) is designed to impress the reader by showing that her mind is capable of educating itself, and evaluating her personal situation through the application of learned generalizations. The fable, when applied to human experience, demonstrates learning as an applied part of human life; the emphasis on Pamela's mental acuity prepares the reader for an acceptance of her individual merit that justifies her social elevation at the end of the novel. Moreover, the speculation that her singing and dancing at Brandon Hall shall make her "unfit for a May-day Holiday-time; for these Minuets, Rigadoons, and *French* Dances, that I have been practising, will make me but ill Company for my rural Milkmaid Companions that are to be" (p. 77) explicitly suggests that Pamela, knowingly or not, is constitutionally suited to a genteel life. Her innate intelligence coupled and her constitution adapted to the life of a gentlewoman perhaps compensate for her low birth. Yet the cautionary impact of the tale is not lost on Pamela; she demonstrates "an humble, and a teachable Mind" in her willingness to forego the personal inclination to retain the attributes of her genteel lifestyle in favour of that which is "honest."

Immediately following these speculations, Pamela has further opportunity to illustrate her acuity through another fable. After abruptly breaking off from speculation about what she will do when she returns home, she characterizes her nervousness in terms of the fable of the city mouse and the country mouse: "'Twas only our *Hannah* with a Message from Mrs. *Jervis!*—But, good Sirs, there is some body else!—Well, it is only *Rachel.* I am as much frighted as were the City Mouse and the Country Mouse in the same Book of Fables, at every thing that stirs" (p. 78). In the fable, a country mouse visits her sister in the city. Despite the plenty of the city, the country mouse comes to see that she would "much rather lie knobbing of crusts, without fear or hazard, in my own hole, than be mistress of all the delicacies in the world, and subject to such terrifying alarms and dangers."[25] The use of the fable to comment on the immediate interruption of her writing shows her spontaneous response controlled by an automatic intellectual and moral framework. The fable gives articulate form to innate character, a character refined through education.

A later fable illustrates Pamela's ability to rework and revise the basic elements of the fable narrative. As Mr B. supports Mrs Jewkes in a series of accusations against her, Pamela blurts out, "I have a strange Tribunal to plead before. The poor Sheep, in the Fable, had such an one; when it was try'd before the Vultur, on the Accusation of the Wolf" (p. 162). The allusion is to fable 29 in Richardson's *Aesop's Fables* in which a dog, not a wolf, brings legal action for some hay long overdue. A kite, wolf, and vulture stand as biased witnesses against the sheep and no judge is mentioned. Pamela's revision of the fable seems intentional here, bringing it closer to her situation and highlighting her isolation in a community of three. The reactions to Pamela of Mr B. and Mrs Jewkes also illustrate the "Moral" Richardson attaches to this fable in his *Aesop*: "It is not a straw matter, whether the main cause be right or wrong, or the charge be true or false, where the bench, jury and witnesses are in a conspiracy against the prisoner." The "Reflection" upon the fable also fits Mr B. and Mrs Jewkes with a surprising allegorical suggestiveness: "No innocence can be safe where power and malice are in confederacy against it."[26]

Pamela's transformation of the basic components of a pre-existing narrative into a more expressive form illustrates her creative autonomy; she rewrites Aesop within the didactic boundaries of conventional morality but at the same time adapts the literary dimensions of the fable to express more accurately her own experience. The constancy of her didactic truth, evident in the appropriateness of Richardson's Moral and Reflection to Pamela's revised narrative, stabilizes the protean shifts of literary embellishment. The literary components chosen are not random but derive from a confluence of Aesop's *Fables* and the literal and figurative aspects of her own

25 *Aesop's Fables*, p. 9.

26 *Aesop's Fables*, p. 23.

experience. The literal conflict between Pamela, on one side, and
Mr B. and Mrs Jewkes, on the other, works clearly as a moral tale
of innocence in conflict with corrupt authority, and the figurative
equation of Pamela with the sheep, Mrs Jewkes with the wolf, has a
source within the imagery created by the characters in the novel. The
raw materials for such figuralism are provided in an earlier dialogue
between Pamela and Mrs Jewkes:

And now I have not five Shillings left to support me, if I *can* get away!— Was
ever such a Fool as I! I must be priding myself in my Contrivances indeed!
Said I, was this in your Instructions, *Wolfkin?* for she called me *Lambkin.*
Jezebel, you mean, Child, said she!—Well, I now forgive you heartily; let's
buss and be Friends!—Out upon you, said I! I cannot bear you. But I durst
not call her Names again; for I dread her huge Paw most sadly. (p. 121)

The initial comparison of Pamela to a "*Lambkin*" and Mrs Jewkes
to a "*Wolfkin*" offers a static representation of the ongoing conflict
between them, but it becomes dynamic when adapted to fable form
in her argument with Mr B. and Mrs Jewkes. Pamela expands the
conflict of simple opposition between the lamb and wolf into a more
wide-ranging scenario of a sheep outnumbered and outranked by
two representative antagonists. The background of Aesop's fable
hints at the fate of innocence when social and political structures
are abused, especially when to the advantage of a wanton aristocracy.
The conflict of predator and victim is enlarged into a commentary
on an exploitive social hierarchy and an abusive political structure.
Richardson's Reflection for this Aesop's fable—"There is no living ...
without law" (p. 23)—underlines the urgency of proper governance
in the social and political body.

The responses of the other two characters are revealing. Mr B.
comments:

So, Mrs *Jewkes,* said he, you are the Wolf, I the Vultur, and this the poor
innocent Lamb, on her Trial before us.—Oh! you don't know how well this
Innocent is read in Reflection. She has Wit at Will, when she has a mind
to display her own romantick Innocence, at the Price of other People's
Characters.

Well, said the aggravating Creature, this is nothing to what she has called
me; I have been a *Jezebel,* a *London* Prostitute, and what not?—But I am
contented with her ill Names, now I see it is her Fashion, and she can call
your Honour a Vultur. (p. 162)

These responses demonstrate the presence of an interpretive community within which there is common understanding of the basic outline of morality, even if it is not adhered to or applied to everyday existence out of rampant self-interest (as with Mr B.). One of the central struggles in the novel is for control over the nature of the hermeneutic for this community. Pamela has the natural advantage, since she is the source of information about this world, but Mr B. and Mrs Jewkes constantly attempt to discredit her claims to honest and authoritative representation. Despite the social and political superiority of Mr B., Pamela derives additional authority by fabricating or transforming a literary form—the fable—to reflect her expressive response and the descriptively based facts of the moral battle that rages around and within her. Mr B. attempts a similar process by citing romance tales such as those of Lucrece, but his transformations are more properly distortions born out of immorality and self-interest. The obvious corruption in Mr B. and Mrs Jewkes in the first half of the novel also undermines their claims to authority, literary or personal, and shifts possession of an authoritative fiction to Pamela. Indeed, Pamela's implicit claims to authority seem validated by the recognition brought to Mr B. (and others) when he reads and is transformed by Pamela's journal as a whole. Distance from his own anger allows calmer recognition of his own failures. While the fable may be reductive in its portrait of human manners, it seems an appropriate educational tool, illuminating the most obvious abuses in a complex network of personal, social, and political relationships.

Pamela shows additional felicity with the fable form by creating one of her own. While fishing with Mrs Jewkes, she stumbles upon an object lesson for herself. At this moment she has no external writings to draw on but develops her own text of life. The transformation of experience into fable comes in a moment of self-discovery:

She baited the Hook, and I held it, and soon hooked a lovely Carp. Play it, play it, said she; I did, and brought it to the Bank. A sad Thought just then came into my Head; and I took it, and threw it in again; and O the Pleasure it seem'd to have, to flounce in, when at Liberty!—Why this? says she. O Mrs. *Jewkes!* said I, I was thinking this poor Carp was the unhappy *Pamela*. I was likening you and myself to my naughty Master. As we hooked and deceived the poor Carp, so was I betrayed by false Baits; and when you said, Play it, play it, it went to my Heart, to think I should sport with the

Destruction of the poor Fish I had betray'd; and I could not but fling it in again: And did you not see the Joy with which the happy Carp flounced from us! O! said I, may some good merciful Body procure me my Liberty in the same manner; for, to be sure, I think my Danger equal! (p. 120)

The "sad Thought" demonstrates a literary self-consciousness born out of self-recognition. Such understanding portrays her relationship as one of betrayal and the destruction of "Liberty"; her recognition of this and refusal to be manipulated by Mrs Jewkes into participating in the same kind of "play," even with a fish, demonstrate her refusal to be an accomplice in her own moral or physical "destruction." In the following paragraph, Pamela creates an alternate fable, telling Mrs Jewkes, "I will plant Life then, if I can, while you are destroying it. I have some Horse-beans here, and I'll go and stick them into one of the Borders, to see how long they will be coming up; and I will call them my Garden" (p. 120). As an alternate activity, the planting of life stands in opposition to the carp-playing of Mr B. and Mrs Jewkes, setting seeds and letters side by side under the earth to foster a new existence Pamela hopes will be outside the gates of Lincolnshire. By creating her own fables, Pamela demonstrates her total assimilation of a moral universe ready for application to everyday experience. Outside the sphere of her parents' influence, she begins to replicate an authoritative text in accord with their beliefs but modified and personalized in terms of her own individual experience.

The ability to recognize and frame such a fable suggests a degree of detachment necessary to Pamela if she is to surmount the potentially paralysing force of the abduction, captivity, and threat of rape. Detachment and analysis are a necessary adjunct to the developing identity of Pamela and signal a maturing consciousness. The self-created fable registers the consciousness of her victimized status and illustrates the potential hopelessness and hopefulness of her situation. It also reflexively illustrates Pamela's spontaneous creativity. Through her reworking of the materials of human experience into a form blending the literary and didactic, she illustrates definitively her role as artist. As A.M. Kearney points out, "Pamela's role ... is that of the novelist himself: by bringing literary ability and sufficient reflection to bear upon the crude stuff of personal experience, he shapes it as didactic art."[27] As in her use of biblical texts, the relative truths of her everyday experience are united to long-standing traditions of interpreting and viewing the world. The fable is used as a nodal point that alerts the reader and the character to larger thematic concerns set forth in the whole of the novel or experience. By crystallizing the main themes of hundreds of pages of text in one paragraph, the fable gives the truths of a single utterance greater validation.

Conclusion: The Composite Text

The composite text wrought of empirical discourse modified by emotive value, biblical allusiveness, and moral didacticism combines to form the autonomous creative personality at the heart of Richardson's novel. As ingredients in what Richardson called "a new species of writing,"[28] the combination of texts enhances the character of Pamela's complexity, reinforcing her solid grounding in the Bible and Aesop's *Fables* while linking her to an intellectual acuity that suits her rise to a privileged social position. These textual structures create a difficult balance between the radical relativism of individual perception and the oppressive authoritarianism of imposed texts, received commandments, and repressive moralities. Pamela's free manipulation of a variety of textual forms is at the centre of her liberty, as it is of the privileged status accorded her character. Ultimately, the balancing of conflicting claims to authority is achieved by the assimilation of all received influences and by their realignment in terms of individual human experience. Pamela's letters and journals demonstrate that an authoritative account containing a truthful representation of human experience is not reducible either to the exactness of referential truth or to the subjectivism of entirely personal truth. The former is the truth of a tyrant; the latter, that of an egoist. Pamela's authority, instead, derives from the assimilation of universal forms to the honesty of human sentiment.

27 A.M. Kearney, "Richardson's *Pamela*: The Aesthetic Case," *Review of English Literature* 7:3 (1966), 89.

28 Letter to Aaron Hill (1741), *Selected Letters of Samuel Richardson*, ed. John Carroll (Oxford: Clarendon Press, 1964), p. 41.

"*Ciceronian* Eloquence": The Politics of Virtue in Richardson's *Pamela*

John A. Dussinger

It has usually been taken for granted that the author of *Pamela* was wholly sympathetic with the titular heroine in her struggle against her master to maintain her chastity and that her triumph in reforming this upper-class rake was the reward of virtue. I argue here, however, that the novel has a much larger significance in the history of the printing press as a paradoxical and dialogical rendering of the conflict between private expression and public authority. More concretely, Richardson's long experience as a London printer before producing his first novel at just past the age of fifty, especially his role during the tumultuous years of Robert Walpole's ministry, helps to account for the central action in *Pamela* about desire and resistance. In the context of the ferocious print wars between opposition writers and government defenders, the novel's erotic focus on a fifteen-year-old servant-girl trying to withstand seduction by the power of her pen resembles the tendentious fables of Aesop, which Richardson had edited shortly before composing his novel.

While her young master indulges her love of scribbling and is her most avid reader, he is nevertheless worried about the damage done to his reputation by some of the news she is spreading outside his household. At times when the narrative draws our attention to the heroine's secreting away her supplies of pens, ink, paper, wax, and wafers, she becomes at one with the whole scribal technology that subverts all efforts of authority either to silence it or at least to control its news-making capacity. Throughout the story, Mr B. tries to exert his authority as the censor of Pamela's writing, intercepting her mail before it goes out of the house and sometimes withholding seditious information. Yet, ironically, despite times when her known writing utensils are confiscated at Lincolnshire, as the most assiduous reader of her letters, Mr B. does not really want to eradicate her activity and rob himself of his voyeuristic pleasures. Although this seesaw between freedom of expression and censorship also exists in Richardson's later novels, especially in *Clarissa*, the fable-like quality of *Pamela* helped to make it instantly a popular success while casting the seemingly innocent protests of moral virtue in a generally unstable discourse.[1]

As critics have emphasized, the many imitations of the Pamela story also exerted an enormous influence on its immediate reception, notably Henry Fielding's brilliant parody, *An Apology for the Life of Mrs. Shamela Andrews* (1741), which ridicules the "*Ciceronian* Eloquence" of this epistolary narrative. Since at first Richardson was so secretive about his authorship of this work that not even his closest friends knew the truth, when writing this satire Fielding apparently either suspected that Conyers Middleton was the author of *Pamela* or at least wanted to compare the novel to the latter's highly acclaimed biography of Cicero, which had appeared only two months before the publication of *Shamela* in April. Thus, Parson Oliver writes to Parson Tickletext:

1 See Tom Keymer, "*Pamela*'s Fables: Aesopian Writing and Political Implication in Samuel Richardson and Sir Roger L'Estrange," *XVII-XVIII: Bulletin de la société d'études anglo-américaines des XVIIe et XVIIIe siècles* 41 (1995), 81–101; and Jayne Elizabeth Lewis, *The English Fable: Aesop and Literary Culture, 1651–1740* (Cambridge: Cambridge University Press, 1996), pp. 29–30. For the vogue of *Pamela*, see Bernard Kreissman, *Pamela-Shamela: A Study of the Criticisms, Burlesques, Parodies, and Adaptations of Richardson's "Pamela"* (Lincoln: University of Nebraska Press, 1960); and James Grantham Turner, "Novel Panic: Picture and Performance in the Reception of Richardson's *Pamela*," *Representations* 48 (1994), 70–96. "'*Ciceronian* Eloquence': The Politics of Virtue in Richardson's *Pamela*" was first published in *Eighteenth-Century Fiction* 12:1 (1999), 39–60.

Indeed I was in hopes that young Woman would have contented herself
with the Good-fortune she hath attained; and rather suffered her little Arts
to have been forgotten than have revived their Remembrance, and endeavoured by perverting and misrepresenting Facts to be thought to deserve
what she now enjoys: for though we do not imagine her the Author of the
Narrative itself, yet we must suppose the Instructions were given by her, as
well as the Reward, to the Composer. Who that is, though you so earnestly
require of me, I shall leave you to guess from that *Ciceronian* Eloquence,
with which the Work abounds; and that excellent Knack of making every
Character amiable, which he lays his hands on.[2]

To judge by this passage, "*Ciceronian* Eloquence" appears to mean
"perverting and misrepresenting Facts" to inflate one's moral character. Since elsewhere he usually speaks approvingly of Cicero, Fielding's attack on Middleton as well as on Colley Cibber, the poet laureate, is politically motivated and has little or nothing to do with the
great Roman orator. Middleton had obsequiously dedicated his biography to his patron Lord Hervey, Pope's "Miss Fanny" and "Sporus,"
and major Court Whig and ally of Walpole.[3] Although a work of substantial scholarship, Middleton's *Life of Cicero* was essentially a monument to the Hanoverian establishment in answering the opposition
writers' tendency to extol the virtues of Cato of Utica, that other
Republican martyr in resisting Caesar's seizure of power. Against
critics who questioned Cicero's often vacilliating behaviour towards
the Triumvirate despite his orations on civic virtue, Middleton implicitly compared Walpole's flexible, pacific course as statesman to
this great Roman consul.[4] The main point here is that Fielding de-
tected in Richardson's novel a bond with other manipulative texts
from the Court Whig writers.

2 Henry Fielding, *Joseph Andrews* and *Shamela*, ed. Sheridan Baker (New York: Crowell, 1972),
    p. 13. References to *Shamela* are to this edition.

3 See Robert Halsband, *Lord Hervey: Eighteenth-Century Courtier* (New York and Oxford: Ox-
    ford University Press, 1973), pp. 175–78.

4 Conyers Middleton, *The History of the Life of Marcus Tullius Cicero*, 3 vols (London, 1741).
    See Reed Browning, *Political and Constitutional Ideas of the Court Whigs* (Baton Rouge and
    London: Louisiana State University Press, 1982), pp. 210–56. J.G.A. Pocock has analysed
    incisively the civic humanism surrounding the term "virtue" as "devotion to the public
    good" in this era. See "Virtues, Rights, and Manners," *Virtue, Commerce, and History* (Cam-
    bridge: Cambridge University Press, 1985), pp. 37–50. Given the social transformation that
    Pamela brings about by remaining steadfast and converting her master, it may be only a
    slight exaggeration to say that her virtue is also a "devotion to the public good."

Except in the broader sense of ideology, *Pamela* is not overtly a political novel. Like Middleton in setting forth his quasi-Walpolean portrait of the Roman statesman, Richardson is at pains to avoid any partisan allusions and in the guise of letters allows the "facts to speak for themselves"[5] or rather the character to speak for herself. Not even the printer's social identity as a London businessman is immediately evident in his rendering of this peasant-heroine's upward mobility. Some of Richardson's last revisions to *Pamela*, which appear in the 1801 edition, reveal his interest in Mr B.'s dilemma as a young master temporarily unstable about his house, if not also his mind. The very first letter of this novel shows the heroine in her late mistress's dressing-room being interrupted by her master. What is most significant is her guilty behaviour upon being found writing this letter:

I have been scared out of my Senses. ... Good Sirs! how I was frightned! I went to hide the Letter in my Bosom, and he seeing me frighted, said smiling, Who have you been writing to, *Pamela?*—I said, in my Fright, Pray your Honour, forgive me!—Only to my Father and Mother. He said, Well then, Let me see how you are come on in your Writing![6]

5 "*I have taken care always to leave the facts to speak for themselves, and to affirm nothing of any moment without an authentic testimony to support it,*" Middleton, *Life of Cicero*, 1:xvi. Although there is no evidence that Middleton read *Pamela*, this reliance on Cicero's letters to tell the story bears a striking resemblance to the novelist's epistolary strategies. Richardson cautiously praised Middleton's *Cicero*: "It is a fine piece; but the Doctor, I humbly think, has played the panegyrist, in some places in it, rather than the historian. The present laureate's [Colly Cibber's] performance on the same subject, of which Dr. Middleton's is the foundation, is a spirited and pretty piece." *Selected Letters of Samuel Richardson*, ed. John Carroll (Oxford: Clarendon Press, 1964), pp. 211–12.

6 Unless otherwise indicated, references to *Pamela* are from the first edition of 1740. For the original novel in two volumes, I use the reprint of this edition, ed. T.C. Duncan Eaves and Ben D. Kimpel, Riverside edition (Boston: Houghton Mifflin Company, 1971). For the sequel that apeared in 1741, *Pamela 2*, as vols 3 and 4, I use the database *Eighteenth-Century Fiction on CD-ROM* (Cambridge: Chadwyck-Healey, 1996). Since the Shakespeare Head edition of *Pamela* is rare and since there is no scholarly edition of the sequel, I also refer to the facsimile reprint of the sequel: *Pamela; or, Virtue Rewarded*, the revised text of 1801, 4 vols (New York and London: Garland Publishing, 1974), vols 3–4. For the sake of comparison to the first edition, I refer to *Pamela; or, Virtue Rewarded*, ed. Peter Sabor (Harmondsworth: Penguin Books, 1980), which is a reprint of the 1801 edition of the first two volumes of the novel. The quotation here is from the Riverside edition, p. 26. Cf. Penguin, p. 44.

Pamela repeatedly begs forgiveness as if she had committed a crime. After reading her letter, however, Mr B. returns it and remarks what a good girl she is to be so kind to her old father and mother: "I am not angry with you. Be faithful, and diligent; and do as you should do, and I like you the better for this." But in italics Richardson added the following ominous clause in the 1801 edition: "*though you ought to be wary what tales you send out of a family.*" In light of the cautionary advice in the *Collection of Moral and Instructive Sentiments*, to be examined below, we may assume that here Richardson sympathizes with Mr B.'s predicament of losing his reputation through this servant-girl's reports.[7]

Despite their differences in class, Richardson could probably see himself in Mr B.'s predicament in losing authority over his domestic affairs and consequently over his public life as well. Richardson's own admirable tact in regulating both his printing trade and his private household is well documented; and it reflects indirectly his professional caution about regulating information for the sake of keeping the peace.[8] Taking into account his businesslike dealings both at home and at the office, we can see that Richardson's moral sentiments extracted from his three novels are no less than his own practical wisdom from years of successful personnel management.

7 Fielding playfully mimics this predicament in a letter that Joseph Andrews writes to his sister: "you know, *Pamela*, I never loved to tell the Secrets of my Master's Family. ... Don't tell any body what I write, because I should not care to have Folks say I discover what passes in our Family," *Joseph Andrews*, ed. Martin C. Battestin (Middletown, Conn.: Wesleyan University Press, 1967), book 1, chap. vi, p. 31.

8 In contrast to the hostile anecdotes about this novelist in Boswell's *Life of Johnson*, Catherine Talbot gives an eloquent description of her visit to the Richardson family newly removed to Parson's Green: "Walking around all the Offices with him I could see every domestic Countenance brightening up as he came near them with Unaffected Joy, while he asked every one en passant some kind question." Catherine Talbot to Mrs George Berkeley, 9 August [1756], B.M. Add. Ms. 39,311, ff. 83–85. Richardson's prominence as a London printer inspired the Oxford law professor William Blackstone to request advice from him about how to reform Oxford University Press to make it more economically competitive with the commercial presses. In his long letter to Blackstone, on 10 February 1756, Richardson stressed the need for developing good relations "between the Masters and Workmen (who will be always for encroaching)." *Letter from Samuel Richardson to William Blackstone 10 February 1756*, reproduced in "William Blackstone and the Reform of the Oxford University Press in the Eighteenth Century," *Oxford Bibliographical Society Publications*, n.s., vol. 6 (1953), 39. See also Dussinger, "Masters and Servants: Political Discourse in Richardson's *A Collection of Moral Sentiments*," *Eighteenth-Century Fiction* 5 (1993), 239–52.

In *A Collection of the Moral and Instructive Sentiments*, Richardson repeatedly stresses the need for maintaining a proper distance from servants. Because of the danger of gossip to the reputation of the master, secrecy as well as discretion in general is usually crucial to good governance. Despite Pamela's precocious insight that "Women in their education ... are generally forced to struggle for knowlege like the poor feeble infant who is pinioned, legs, arms, and head, on the nurse's lap," Richardson nevertheless seems reluctant to allow her too much leash and has her disapproving of novels and romances because of their raising false expectations and disturbing family authority.[9] Even more so than the ephemeral entertainers, really "good Writers" need to be wary "of propagating lewdness and immorality; since the works of such are likely to live after them."[10] Pamela anticipates here the Rambler's warning that "it is necessary to distinguish those parts of nature, which are most proper for imitation: greater care is still required in representing life, which is so often discoloured by passion, or deformed by wickedness."[11] Yet, notwithstanding the ventilation of sentiments favouring the woman's independence elsewhere in this novel, Richardson has Pamela wanting to burn her letters rather than risk having them misinterpreted after her death. The maxim in the *Collection* deriving from *Pamela* implies that the woman has more to fear than the man from readers of posthumous letters:

A prudent woman will not preserve such letters and papers, however innocent, as she cares not her husband should see, lest any doubts, in case of his survivorship, should arise from them of her conduct, when she is *no more*, and which the papers themselves do not fully explain, iii. 475 [376].[12]

9 *Samuel Richardson's Published Commentary on "Clarissa," 1745–65*, vol. 3, *A Collection of the Moral and Instructive Sentiments, Maxims, Cautions, and Reflections, Contained in the Histories of Pamela, Clarissa, and Sir Charles Grandison* (1755), introduction by John A. Dussinger and afterword by Ann Jessie Van Sant (London: Pickering and Chatto, 1998), pp. 28, 70–71. Cf. *Pamela*, 1st ed., 4:335–36, 440–41; Garland, 4:277, 373–74.

10 *Collection*, p. 82. Cf. *Pamela*, 1st ed., 3:238; Garland, 3:200.

11 Samuel Johnson, *The Rambler*, ed. W.J. Bate and Albrecht B. Strauss, 3 vols, The Yale Edition of the Works of Samuel Johnson (1969; New Haven and London: Yale University Press, 1979), 1:22.

12 *Collection*, p. 33. Cf. *Pamela*, 1st ed., 3:408; Garland, 3:334–35.

When we try to understand Richardson's position on censorship in the public sphere, a moment like this in his fiction is far more subtle than the dualistic polemic about freedom and restraint in the journalism of his time.[13] As an innovator himself in creating "private space," Richardson doubtless knew the necessity of at least self-imposed censorship, while still regretting that the evils of invasive state power usually outweigh the benefits accrued. Not surprisingly, Richardson's maxims derived from *Clarissa* reflect a much more sinister and dangerous world than those from *Pamela*, where news leakage can destroy a family rather than just embarrass it:

A Master's communicativeness to his Servants, is a means for an enemy to come at his secrets, ii.226 [309].[14]

For an enemy to come at his secrets. Since workers are by nature the enemy, the master, whether Mr B. or Samuel Richardson, must finesse the strategies of governance needed to contain this enemy; and distance and secrecy are crucial to maintain authority.

Perhaps reflecting this relatively more tolerant atmosphere for the liberty of the press, even when it undermines his reputation disarmingly, Mr B. does not really want to quash Pamela's writing activity. At first, he does complain, "That Girl is always scribbling; methinks she might find something else to do, or to that purpose"; and he asks Mrs Jervis to bid Pamela "not spend so much time in writing."[15] But we hear nothing about whether the orders were carried out. We do know, however, that Mr B. has stolen Pamela's letter in this scene and is apparently off reading it somewhere. Later, in the sequel, in his long review of his struggle to overcome his love for Pamela, Mr B. confesses: "I used to watch for her Letters, tho' mere Prittle-prattle and Chit-chat; receiv'd them with burning Impatience, and read them with Delight, tho' myself was accused in them, and stigmatiz'd

13 See, for example, Fredrick Seaton Siebert, *Freedom of the Press in England, 1476–1776: The Rise and Decline of Government Control* (Urbana: University of Illinois Press, 1965), pp. 364–92; Simon Varey, *Henry St. John, Viscount Bolingbroke* (Boston: Twayne Publishers, 1984), pp. 34–77; and Michael Harris, *London Newspapers in the Age of Walpole: A Study of the Origins of the Modern English Press* (Rutherford, Madison, Teaneck: Fairleigh Dickinson University Press, 1987), pp. 134–54.

14 *Collection*, pp. 159–60.

15 Riverside, p. 37. Cf. Penguin, p. 58.

as I deserv'd."[16] Hence, by merely invading the writer's privacy, he finds in even commonplace communication an erotic allure.

Despite the considerable evidence of Richardson's belief in the necessity of rigorous control over what is represented, whether on stage or in print, because of a focus on the central action in *Pamela* and *Clarissa* as the woman's struggle for the freedom to inscribe herself in her narrative, some readers have erroneously inferred that this skilful businessman was himself militant against press censorship. What needs to be stressed, on the contrary, is Richardson's sympathy with Mr B.'s predicament as master struggling to gain control over himself as well as over his house. It is doubtless the relatively weaker fictional rendering of the master's dilemma that has resulted in critical disagreement about Richardson's intentions in the protagonists' conflict. Thus, over the past forty years or so commentators have taken diametrically opposed stances towards Richardson's views of censorship. T.C. Duncan Eaves and Ben D. Kimpel, authors of the standard biography, state flatly that Richardson "was certainly no proponent of the freedom of the press"; and in a footnote to a contrary view, they declare: "One of the strangest readings of *Pamela* and *Clarissa* interprets them as allegorical attacks on the Licensing Act of 1737." As Eaves and Kimpel point out, moreover, in a letter written on 14 January 1757, Richardson "regretted to Young that no legal authority stood sentinel over it [the press], to prevent 'Infidelity, indecency, libel, faction, nonsense.'"[17] If the first three terms indicate a concern with religion and morality, the last two surely imply political threats to the public peace. Thus, in the *Daily Gazetteer* (2 October 1735), Francis Walsingham (William Arnall) rebuts an article from the *London Evening Post* that boasted of the strong opposition to the government from the Country party: "Here they [the Whigs] are plainly told, that the *Country Interest* is a Faction formed in

16 *Pamela*, 1st ed., 3:208. Cf. Garland, 3:173.

17 T.C. Duncan Eaves and Ben D. Kimpel, *Samuel Richardson: A Biography* (Oxford: Clarendon Press, 1971), p. 549. Their footnote is to R. Baird Shuman's "Censorship as a Controlling Theme in *Pamela* and *Clarissa*," *Notes and Queries* n.s. 3 (1956), 30–32. Commenting on this article, Terry Eagleton remarks mysteriously that Richardson's actual approval of censorship was "a fact not available to Shuman at the time of writing." *The Rape of Clarissa* (Minneapolis: University of Minnesota Press, 1982), p. 49. The evidence that Eaves and Kimpel educed in their biography was already available in Richardson's known letters and pamphlets about the need of censorship and reform of the stage and press.

opposition to them, their *Principles,* and their *Interests* ... that so long as these *Country Patriots* unite with their Collegues, whom we must understand to be *Jacobites* or *Tories,* the Endeavours of the *Whigs* are to be defeated."

Like Arnall, by "Faction" Richardson means any partisan opposition to the government. Yet, despite his explicit fear of anarchy caused by an unrestricted press, two prominent Richardsonians have recently seen his novels as political allegories of Tory resistance to corrupt power. Jocelyn Harris comments on the comic "trial" scene in *Pamela*: "In this mock court-room Mr B. jests about seizing the 'treasonable Papers' of a 'great Plotter,' but Pamela very sullenly and gravely defends the privacy of her thoughts." Similarly, while trying to connect the printer's early experiences to his novels, Margaret Anne Doody argues: "What Richardson learned in his earlier years of running an independent business was the power of censorship—and the brutal ugliness with which censorship appears to those on the receiving end. If one thinks of it, all his works reflect this sense of the horror of censorship, the injustice of taking someone's words away."[18] How do we resolve this discrepancy between literary historians over Richardson's attitudes towards censorship and freedom of the press?

One approach might be to separate for the sake of argument the Court Whig printer from the perhaps psychologically more complex fictional "editor" of this erotic epistolary novel as if the author had a Jekyll-and-Hyde personality. Here again, however, we would be back to the dubious notion of the "unconscious artist" in creating probably the first model of dramatic form for the English novel. A less speculative approach might focus on Richardson's career as printer to provide a context for his first novel. The stark fact is that in the formative years before, during, and after the composition of *Pamela,* Richardson was printing the chief organ of propaganda for the Walpole government—the *Daily Gazetteer;* and it has hardly received the attention it deserves. Despite William Sale's pioneering bibliographical work, not even Eaves and Kimpel, who discounted the import-

18 Jocelyn Harris, *Samuel Richardson* (Cambridge: Cambridge University Press, 1987), p. 22; Margaret Anne Doody, "Richardson's Politics," *Eighteenth-Century Fiction* 2 (1990), 119.

ance of politics in Richardson's career, pursued this thread in their otherwise invaluable biography.[19]

But Richardson's part ownership of the *Gazetteer* as well as his apparent role in editing as well as printing it since its inception in 1735 down to 1744 cannot be ignored if we are to understand the complex reception of his first novel. Like many of his fellow London tradesmen, having witnessed the economic improvements despite its controversial policies, Richardson seems at last to have made his peace with the Walpole administration after the excise tax crisis in 1733. Notwithstanding his votes for some Tory candidates during the 1720s, Richardson was nevertheless a close friend of Arthur Onslow, the Whig Speaker of the House of Commons from 1728 to 1760, and doubtless on good terms with the government while printing the *Journal of the House of Commons*. Uppermost in Richardson's mind was the City's interests, whatever the party involved; and his long support of Sir John Barnard, an Independent Whig, was in principle not inconsistent with his later accommodation with Walpole's ministry.[20]

19 William M. Sale, Jr, *Samuel Richardson: Master Printer* (Ithaca: Cornell University Press, 1950), pp. 34–76. Although Sale long ago provided an excellent overview of Richardson's political affiliations as a London printer and traced his shift from opposition Whig to supporter of Walpole by the middle 1730s, when he was printing the government's official paper, more recent scholars have tended to avoid the matter. Eaves and Kimpel summed up their view: "Richardson's political views do not seem to have played a large part in his life" (p. 545). While pressing her interpretation of Richardson as a Tory ideologue, Doody fails to mention Richardson's association with the *Gazetteer*. See "Richardson's Politics." On the other hand, in his careful analysis of subversive oppositional encoding in L'Estrange's *Æsop*, which remains in Richardson's self-declared expurgated edition, Keymer does not follow up his insights by reference to the printer's apparent loyalty to Walpole at the time these fables and *Pamela* were in the press. Michael Harris, however, believes that among the various printers getting involved in the commercial newspaper business Richardson was the most important and points out that by 1736 his interests included two weekly papers, the *Weekly Miscellany* and the *London Journal*, and two dailies, the *Daily Journal* and *Daily Gazetteer*. See *London Newspapers in the Age of Walpole*, p. 84. Thus, Fielding's satiric reference to the *Daily Gazetteer* may target Richardson as well as Walpole: "'It is a dirty News-Paper,' replied the Host, 'which hath been given away all over the Nation for these many Years to abuse Trade and honest Men, which I would not suffer to lie on my Table, tho' it hath been offered me for nothing.'" *Joseph Andrews*, book 2, chap. xvii, p. 183.

20 William Sale is the only modern scholar to identify Richardson's probable motives in doing business with his old enemy: "During Walpole's administration the printer and the publisher of newspapers could not escape the political implications of their contracts. Consequently a survey of Richardson's relations with newspapers is an index to his political thinking. Such a survey reveals nothing original in his political thought, but it shows the extent to which he identified himself with the citizenry of London, the extent to which he felt

It was Barnard's unsuccessful bill in 1735 to restrict the number of theatres in the City that anticipated Walpole's Licensing Act two years later. Besides voting for Barnard in 1735, Richardson also wrote *A Seasonable Examination of the Pleas and Pretensions of the Proprietors of, and Subscribers to, Play-Houses, Erected in Defiance of the Royal Licence,* a polemic on behalf of Barnard's bill concerning the theatres. Perhaps most revealing, although Barnard was mainly interested in restricting the number of theatres, Richardson, by contrast, added a new ingredient to the bill—censorship of plays deemed immoral or subversive. The gist of this pamphlet was the need to protect the working classes of the City from the contamination of the upper-class theatres in the West End. Richardson was especially concerned with the fact that many plays at this time ridiculed tradesmen and made heroes out of criminal types. One of the most subtle complaints concerns the dangerous consequences of over-stimulating the working class on the grounds that besides the time lost in attending the theatre, images of the stage spectacles would distract their minds afterwards while on the job.[21]

Against opposition writers who hotly condemned Walpole's Licensing Act, letters and articles in the *Daily Gazetteer* defended this legal restraint on the liberty of speech and writing by condemning

that London was a citadel within the kingdom. Like many of his fellow-citizens he at first opposed Robert Walpole; like many of these same citizens he grew to see that accommodation with Walpole was preferable to alliance with his somewhat irresponsible opponents" (pp. 34–35).

21 "Because of the Danger of the Mind's being too much diverted from Business by those Representations. If a Person has a Taste for 'em, as is justly observed, the Musick will always play upon his Ears, the Dancers will constantly swim before his Eyes." *A Seasonable Examination,* p. 18. This pamphlet was first identified by Alan Dugald McKillop in "Richardson's Early Writings—Another Pamphlet," *Journal of English and German Philology* 53 (1954), 72–75. Part of McKillop's attribution of this pamphlet to Richardson derives from quoted material from Richardson's earlier pamphlet *Apprentice's Vade Mecum,* which this scholar also discovered. See "Samuel Richardson's Advice to an Apprentice," *Journal of English and German Philology* 42 (1943), 40–54. The second pamphlet more specifically addresses Barnard's bill. For further confirmation of these pamphlets as Richardson's see also Eaves and Kimpel, p. 54. Both pamphlets concern the need of censorship to protect the work force in the City from the upper-class diversions in the theatres. For interpretation of Richardson's attitudes towards the working class as a special constituency of the City, see Tom Keymer, *Richardson's "Clarissa" and the Eighteenth-Century Reader* (Cambridge: Cambridge University Press, 1992), pp. 145–49. See also Dussinger, "'The Working Class of People': An Early Eighteenth-Century Source," *Notes and Queries* (1996), 299–302.

the licentiousness of the age.[22] Even if we have no proof that Richardson himself wrote any of these essays, nothing published here on behalf of censorship runs counter to his known views; and a cluster of ideas from the Court Whig strategy of defending Walpole's policy bears on the style and action in *Pamela*. Against the opposition writers of the *Craftsman*, the *Gazetteer* argues generally that no era of British history has ever been as free as the present one. On 2 May 1737, nearly the whole front page is devoted to "*A General* VIEW *of* CIVIL LIBERTY, *its* Extent, *and* Restraints," signed "Solon." Its main argument distinguishes between a tyranny that gratuitously puts "a severe and criminal Construction upon Words, which can bear another and harmless Sense," on the one hand, and the "malicious, busy and deliberate inveighing against the Government; a loading it with false Aspersions, and exposing it to the Contempt and Hate of the Governed," on the other. According to this view, writing that carries a double meaning, innuendo, is acceptable now in contrast to the Restoration period when Roger L'Estrange had attempted to clamp down on seditious writing that insinuated disaffection or treason towards the monarchy.[23] Direct attacks on government figures, however, are still held liable. Solon observes: "No Country, therefore, not even this Country, the freest of all others, can permit an universal Latitude of Speaking and Writing; and the *Liberty of the Press*, so highly and so justly valued amongst us, is and must be subject to certain Bounds." More specifically, in a subsequent issue (7 May 1737) a letter signed by "An ADVENTURER in POLITICKS," while upholding more lattitude for printed satire than for stage productions, points out that, even though it introduced contemporary politics in

---

22 For Richardson's anticipation of this bill, see Vincent J. Liesenfeld, *The Licensing Act of 1737* (Madison: University of Wisconsin Press, 1984), esp. pp. 42–44.

23 As evidence of the general recognition that Walpolean political discourse had introduced ways of insinuating opinions, see the anonymous *The Doctrine of Innuendo's Discuss'd; or The Liberty of the Press Maintain'd* (London, 1731). In *Considerations and Proposals in Order to the Regulation of the Press: Together With Diverse Instances of Treasonous, and Seditious Pamphlets, Proving the Necessity thereof* (London, 1663), L'Estrange drew up an ambitious plan to make everyone involved in the production of books liable to prosecution. The persons responsible would be not only the author, bookseller, and printer, but also the compiler, proof-reader, letter-founder, metal smith, and carpenter at the press. Moreover, even all the agents employed in news distribution would be held accountable: the stitchers, binders, stationers, hawkers, mercury-women, pedlars, ballad-singers, posts, carriers, hackney-coachmen, boatmen, and mariners.

plays, Fielding's *Pasquin* could be tolerated because it mentioned no names, whereas *The Historical Register* was intended "to make a *Minister appear ridiculous to a People*." Fielding's crime was in using the stage medium to undermine the government, a medium that did not allow a riposte from the government as easily as the journalistic essay. Just as Richardson seemed to fear the licentiousness of the theatre as more dangerous than printed matter, so the Licensing Act of 1737 did not interfere with the publication of plays prohibited from being acted on stage. On the contrary, the fact that a play was banned by the government was usually mentioned in advertisements for the printed versions, obviously with the insight that forbidden fruit must be all the more savoury.[24] Again, on 8 June 1737, an anonymous article claims to uphold nearly unlimited freedom of the press but fears the result if the same freedom should be allowed the stage: "If, because Licentiousness in *Writing* ought to be suffered, therefore Licentiousness in *all* other instances has an equal Right to be tolerated, no government can support itself. There must be a Power in the Legislature to determine in *what* Instances Licentiousness shall be suffered; or the certain Consequence will be Anarchy and Confusion." To judge by the *Daily Gazetteer's* emphasis, it is probably already in his capacity as this newspaper's printer and part-owner that Richardson had developed his antipathy towards Fielding.[25] What matters most is to preserve government itself, and by now the decades of partisan debate in the press no longer seemed to threaten that authority, partly, no doubt, because Walpole had learned the power of bribery, in particular, as well as of persuasion, in general, in converting his Grub Street opponents. If his administration learned to tolerate a "cool" medium like the essay, it was still not modern enough to tolerate the devastating parodies performed on stage, which must have excited audiences in ways similar to today's interactive media coverage of political events.

24 In 1738, Henry Brooke's *Gustavus Vasa* was the first play to be banned by the Lord Chamberlain, followed soon by James Thomson's *Edward and Elenora*, and William Paterson's *Arminius*, for their satirical parallels between their historical heroes and the Walpole ministry. The publicity caused by the government prohibition, however, helped to promote the publishing of these plays subsequently. See James Sambrook, *James Thomson, 1700–48: A Life* (Oxford: Clarendon Press, 1991), pp. 191–201, *passim*.

25 Sale, p. 64.

With an obvious pointing of the finger at Jacobites among the opposition forces, the *Gazetteers* repeatedly contrasted British liberty under Walpole to the tyranny suffered in France, where one sees *"disguised Informers*, in almost every publick Place, with blank *Lettres de Cachet* ready to fill up with the Names of such, as dare barely inquire, in a Manner different from the Sense of the Court, into the State of Affairs, and a *Bastille* always open to receive them. Go a little further, and cross either Ridge of Mountains: A *Holy Inquisition*, and the *Gallies*, offer their Service to the *State*, as well as to *Religion*." A similar condition, they argued, was also commonplace in Britain before the Revolutionary Settlement of 1688–89. When Mr B. mockingly threatens force to get at Pamela's letters, he alludes to the Spanish Inquisition:

O my Girl! said he, many an innocent Person has been put to the Torture, I'll assure you. But let me know where they [the letters] are, and you shall escape the *Question*, as it is called abroad.

Sir, said I, the Torture is not used in *England*, and I hope you won't bring it up. Admirably said! replied the naughty Gentleman.—But I can tell you of as great a Punishment. If a Criminal won't plead with us here in *England*, we *press* him to Death, or till he does plead. And so now, *Pamela*, that is a Punishment shall certainly be yours, if you won't tell without.[26]

In the context of the journalistic debate over freedom of the press, this comic dialogue subverts the chauvinistic contrast between British liberty and Roman Catholic tyranny of the day: after conceding that Pamela is safe from the methods of torture employed by the Spanish, he then jokingly reminds her of the comparable savagery still permitted in the English courts—pressing the victim, a scarcely concealed sexual threat in her case. Since one of the *Craftsman*'s most penetrating attacks on the government singled out the increase of crimes punishable by death as part of the social evils brought about by Walpole's leadership, Richardson the novelist seems to be having it both ways—playfully undermining the Court Whig pro-

26 Riverside, p. 203. Cf. Penguin, p. 270.

paganda by invoking opposition criticism that, partisanship aside, carried moral weight.[27]

One of the more effective counterattacks by ministry writers concerned the hypocrisy of Viscount Bolingbroke's posing as a patriot champion of liberty. In the *Gazetteer* (13 June 1737), while reviewing the history of the British stage, an anonymous letter points out what was an untenable opposition stance: "In the Tory Part of Queen *Anne's* Reign, 'tis well known that *Bolingbroke*, the Craftsman's Patron, survey'd all the Plays before they were acted; and, for Example, struck out, as I remember particularly two Verses in *Rowe's Jane Shore*, because of something in them, tho remote, that displeas'd them." By contrast to the Stuart era, despite the opposition's complaints about government suppression in general, and about such violent measures against printers like Franklin and Haines in particular, "from the late 1720s a more coherent policy of rebuttal began to emerge, aimed at discrediting or at least answering opposition newspaper attacks."[28]

While exposing Bolingbroke's bogus libertarian posture, the *Gazetteer* emphasized the relative lack of freedom of the press during the Elizabethan and Stuart reigns; yet, it also insisted on the need for regulation. Hence, an anonymous article in the *Gazetteer* (7 July

27 In the *Daily Gazetteer* (27 November 1735), Francis Walsingham (William Arnall) vigorously answered an attack in *Fog's Journal* (13 November 1735) on the government's abuse of capital punishment: "But if the GREAT OBJECTION to the present System of Law, be as FOG hath so pathetically urged it ... that so innocent a Crime as Smuggling is liable to severe Penalties; if it be the *lamented* Reproach of our Constitution, that such Depredations on the fair Trader are obnoxious to publick Justice ... then must I rejoice that I live in such a Country, under such Laws, and such a Government." By way of justifying the twenty or thirty executions per year in London, Walsingham calculates that in a population of a million, only one in fifty thousand suffered the death penalty. In contrast to the arbitrary methods used during the Elizabethan period, he also points out that the present government is overly lenient.

28 Harris, *Newspapers in the Age of Walpole*, p. 116. See also Laurence Hanson, *Government and the Press, 1695–1763* (London: Oxford University Press, 1936); Siebert, pp. 323–45; and Alan Downie, "The Growth of Government Tolerance of the Press to 1790," *Development of the English Book Trade 1700–1899*, ed. Robin Myers and Michael Harris (Headington: Oxford Polytechnic Press, 1981), pp. 36–65. As I hope my use of the lower case "o" in "opposition" here indicates, I am indebted throughout this essay to Alexander Pettit's *Illusory Consensus: Bolingbroke and the Polemical Response to Walpole, 1730–1737* (Newark: University of Delaware Press; London: Associated University Presses, 1997) for demonstrating the real disunity among the many journalists attacking the Walpole government.

1737) serves warning that a less tolerant ministry might in the future resort to repression to end the abuses of freedom:

> Happy would it be for this Nation, if a Method could be found out for restraining the Licentiousness of the Press, with as little Inconvenience and as few ill Consequences attending it; for it is very much to be feared, that if ever Power should get into less moderate and less indulgent Hands than at present, the People, by things that are daily published, would furnish out Arguments enow, to those that were otherwise well disposed to it, to deprive us intirely of that great and valuable Privilege.

Again, the ideal of regulating the press that Richardson conveyed to Young in 1757, of a "legal authority" to guard against "Infidelity, indecency, libel, faction, nonsense," finds expression here; and the cautionary phrases "with as little Inconvenience but as few ill Consequences" imply that at least some price has to be paid for *any* government intervention. In the early twenty-first century, when the term "rights" is bandied about for almost any cause, the *Gazetteer*'s understanding of the liberty of the press as a *privilege* only, no matter how precious, must seem tepid, indeed. In the *Gazetteer* (9 July 1737) the "ADVENTURER in POLITICKS" defends censorship of the drama by a curious comparison: "It is no more than what is practised by the College of Physicians, who have a Right to depute some of their Body to inspect into the Drugs of the Retailers." By this analogy the Licensing Act is supposedly no less than a means of protecting mental hygiene, the same objective, we have seen, that was proposed in Richardson's pamphlet in support of Barnard's bill to control the playhouses.

Just as the Licensing Act was intended to prevent libellous attacks on individuals in power, so an article of the *Gazetteer* (31 March 1738), signed "R. Freeman" (Ralph Courteville), advises against *ad hominem* attacks in the journals and recommends instead fair discussion of the issues at stake: "Under such a Regulation as I have proposed, it might very probably come to pass, that *Polemical Writings* might become not only *harmless* but *useful*. It is very certain, that most Subjects are capable of being considered in various *Lights*, and that the more *Lights* they are considered in, the better they are sifted and discussed." In the long run, of course, this plea for disinterestedness might transcend political journalism altogether and result in the genre of the moral essay, the category of writing that best suited both Richardson and his friend Samuel Johnson. Despite this high-minded plea for non-partisan discussion, however, because of his vicious personal attacks on Fielding, Courteville won the sobriquet "Court-evil" from his enemy. In any case, apparently upon Richardson's urging, Courteville did tone down the paper's political bickering and varied the content with moral essays, including two that coincide remarkably with important themes in *Pamela*—the one on despair and suicide (17 November 1738) and the other on the reward of virtue (29 November 1738). Even though Sale and succeeding scholars have never mentioned the possibility, I see no reason why Richardson may not have at least collaborated with Courteville in writing these essays.[29] Given the proximity of all three of these essays to the time of composing his first novel, Richardson might very well have written them in their entirety.

In the essay on suicide, Freeman emphasizes that it is a failure of circumspection, an act of madness: "DESPAIR, is throwing away of *Reason* and *Hope*, that is, the Means of *bearing* Misfortunes, and the Prospect of being *delivered* from them. A Man, who falls into *Despair*, falls into a *Belief*, that the *Misery* he feels, is greater than can or ought to be borne, and that it is such a one as he can never be freed from." The basic logic in this essay reappears in the pond scene in *Pamela*. When momentarily tempted to drown herself after suffering an injury while trying to escape the house at Lincolnshire, Pamela reasons her way out of it: "This Act of Despondency, thought I, is a Sin, that, if I pursue it, admits of no Repentance, and can therefore claim no Forgiveness.—And wilt thou, for shortening thy transitory Griefs, *heavy* as they are, and *weak* as thou fanciest thyself, plunge both Body and Soul into everlasting Misery?" As usual, Pamela also worries about appearances and perhaps fears most the consequence of being denied a "decent Funeral" and of having to submit to the "dreadful Stake, and the Highway Interrment." Still another dread is of being vulgarized by the media when made the "Subject of their

---

29 Martin C. Battestin, with Ruthe R. Battestin, *Henry Fielding: A Life* (London and New York: Routledge, 1989), p. 287. For Richardson's influence on the contents of this newspaper, see Robert L. Haig, *The Gazetteer 1735–1797: A Study in the Eighteenth-Century Newspaper* (Carbondale: Southern Illinois University Press, 1960), pp. 13–14. Only two letters between Courteville and Richardson are on record. One urges Richardson to produce the sequel to *Pamela* by way of stemming the profits made by imitations of this popular novel. See Eaves and Kimpel, p. 68.

[young people's] Ballads and Elegies."[30] Although avoiding reference to the orthodox Christian view against suicide, Freeman's essay urges the therapy of a "Chearfulness of Mind" against all odds and compares unfavourably various ancient Romans who died by their own hand. But perhaps the major difference between Courteville's moral essay on suicide and the fictional rendering of despair and death wish is not its argumentative strategy but rather the mimetic effect of Richardson's internalizing the issue as the mental soliloquy of a young female hostage.

Freeman's essay on virtue rewarded is based on "the Reason of Things, that the Practice of Virtue is profitable," the very heart of Fielding's virulent parody. Richardson's novel, of course, never explicitly admits that Pamela's chastity has a market value, but her subsequent joy after earning her way into the marriage contract and to a place as mistress of Mr B.'s properties surely implies as much. Freeman unabashedly takes a businesslike approach and argues that honesty is the best policy: "The Practice of moral Virtue, is a Part of Natural Religion; and, it is so; because the Light of our Reason shews us, that the greatest Profit, the greatest Pleasure we are capable of attaining in this World, can only this Way be obtained." While repeating these truisms from Latitudinarian thought, Freeman is quite frank in acknowledging that his belief here "differs very little, if at all, from what *Epicurus* recommended under the Name of *Pleasure*; yet this does not hinder the Thing from being *true*, or take off at all from its *Value*." With such tinkling cymbals, it is understandable how Fielding suspected *Pamela* to be the work of the "*Ciceronian* Eloquence" fostered by the government propaganda machine. Taken together, Freeman's two essays teach a lesson: no matter what misfortunes befall one, suicide is never a reasonable response because the world is governed by laws that always reward virtue with eventual happiness.

But what is virtue in Freeman's and Richardson's texts? Mimicking Pamela's own words, Shamela leaves little doubt that it is no more than technical chastity: "I thought once of making a little Fortune by my Person. I now intend to make a great one by my Vartue."[31]

30 Riverside, pp. 152–53. Cf. Penguin, pp. 212–13.

31 *Shamela*, letter 10, p. 36.

Pamela's mother herself implies as much when fearing that her daughter will be too grateful to Mr B. "and reward him with that Jewel, your Virtue, which no Riches, nor Favour, nor any thing in this Life, can make up to you."[32] But a more comprehensive meaning of virtue recurs throughout this story: the idea of moral strength in resisting temptation. As normative readers of her letters, for instance, her parents supposedly gain greater self-esteem despite their poverty in her exemplary steadfastness against bribery: "O my dear Child, your Virtue has made me, I think, stronger and better than I was before. What blessed Things are Trials and Temptations to us, when they be overcome!"[33] Virtue, of course, is also presumably important for the man as well as for the woman. Sir Simon Darnford, we hear, "is not a Man of extraordinary Character for Virtue."[34] As an oily compliment to Mr Williams during the scheme to have his servant-girl married while doubling as his mistress, even Mr B. has the foresight to pretend to hope that Pamela will find as a husband "a Man of Virtue and Probity."[35]

When Pamela quotes freely a line from George Stepney's translation of Juvenal, "Virtue *is the only nobility*,"[36] the ideological implication is that hereditary power has no moral foundation. The original line is as follows: "Virtue alone is true Nobility." Again, the contemporary import of this apothegm would not be lost on Fielding and other politically hostile readers. In the dedication to Lord Hervey for his *Life of Cicero*, Middleton observes that the Roman Republic was a meritocracy: "In old Rome there were no hereditary honors; but when the virtue of a family was extinct, its honor was extinguished too; so that no man, how nobly soever born, could arrive at any dignity, who did not win it by his personal merit." By contrast, Britain has a family system that perpetuates an aristocracy by inheritance. Nevertheless, Middleton praises Lord Hervey for having "emulated that ancient spirit": "though born to the first honors of Your country,

32 Riverside, p. 27. Cf. Penguin, p. 46.

33 Riverside, p. 46. Cf. Penguin, p. 69.

34 Riverside, p. 122. Cf. Penguin, p. 172.

35 Riverside, p. 131. Cf. Penguin, p. 185.

36 Not in 1st ed., but in 6th ed.,1:73. Cf. Penguin, pp. 83, 521n.

yet disclaming, as it were Your birthright, and putting Yourself upon the foot of a Roman, You were not content with inheriting, but resolved to import new dignities into Your family."[37] In this model of "*Ciceronian* Eloquence" eulogizing his patron at Court, Middleton implicitly defends a government continually under attack by opposition writers for supposedly destroying civil liberty through a system of coercion and bribery. The key element in his praise of Hervey is the comparison to Cicero's example of civic virtue: neither the Roman nor the British statesman could ever "think any private interest an equivalent, for consenting to the ruin of the public."[38]

If virtue comes to mean a devotion to the public good and corruption a pursuit of private gratifications, the conflict between Pamela and her master entails not only a sentimental resolution but also, throughout the narrative, a sexual interest in the various consumer goods surrounding them as well as in each other. In general, material objects, especially clothing, in this story have such a peculiar power to contend with virtue that it takes considerable effort by both Pamela and Mr B. to resist them. What D.H. Lawrence aptly described in Richardson as the combination of "calico purity and under-clothing excitements" surely applies to the female as well as male gazer.[39] The scene where Mr B. models his "Birth-day Suit" privately before Pamela and asks for her opinion of its fit is another "teazing" to be surmounted. When hearing that not only is her master about to attend Court for the king's birthday but, so it is rumoured, is "to be made a lord," Pamela reacts predictably: "I wish they may make him an honest Man, as he was always thought; but I have not found it so."[40] Yet, in almost the same breath she cannot help but remark: "His Waistcoat stood an End with Gold Lace, and

37 *Life of Cicero*, p. xi.

38 *Life of Cicero*, p. xii.

39 Quoted in Ian Watt, *The Rise of the Novel: Studies in Defoe, Richardson and Fielding* (London: Chatto and Windus, 1960), p. 203. Despite the many attempts to replace Watt's classic study of the early English novel, no one can match the wit and verve of his remarkable insight into *Pamela*: "a work that could be praised from the pulpit and yet attacked as pornography, a work that gratified the reading public with the combined attractions of a sermon and a strip-tease" (p. 173). No one has summed up better the "*Ciceronian* Eloquence" of this novel since Fielding!

40 Riverside, p. 70. Cf. Penguin, p. 100.

Samuel Richardson, *Pamela, or, Virtue Rewarded*, 4 vols (London, 1742), vol. 3, opposite p. 451. Engraved by Hubert François Gravelot (1699–1773). Reproduced by permission of McMaster University Library.

he look'd very grand."[41] At this moment in the story, Mr B. wears the uniform of his public role as hereditary aristocrat who has yet to demonstrate his virtue as protector of the public good, which includes all of his dependants on his country estates. In other words, he is still a long way from the exalted position that Middleton attributed to Lord Hervey as Whig statesman. To make matters worse, at the end of this scene Mr B. makes a lewd joke about having Mrs Jervis and Pamela keep a house together in London for the entertainment of members of Parliament happy to pay a good price in return.

Despite early impressions of his wrongdoing as manager of his estate, Mr B. is finally not intended to be politically very different from Sir Charles Grandison as Whig squire. After the altercation with Lady Davers made Pamela late in arriving at the Darnfords', Sir Simon greets her with a dark jest:

Adad! Madam, said he, I'm glad to see you here. What, it seems you have been a Prisoner! 'Tis well you was, or your Spouse and I should have sat in Judgment upon you, and condemned you to a fearful Punishment for your first Crime of *Læsæ Majestatis* (I had this explained to me afterwards, as a sort of Treason against my Liege Lord and Husband).[42]

His vague hint about turning "over a new Leaf with our Wives" and having Mr B. "shew us the Way" seems to imply that an imagined period of permissiveness is about to come to an end. Probably intended to represent a "Tory" country squire, much like Squire Western in *Tom Jones*, Sir Simon in alluding to the Latin name for the crime of treason may evoke the much more repressive authority exerted against the press in Roger L'Estrange's era. If she had read the *Daily Gazetteer* (26 April 1736), Pamela would have seen a lead article about a rebellion in Hungary that resulted in the sentencing of the culprits for the crime of *Læsæ Majestatis* to horrendous punishment by being broken on a wheel alive, quartered, and beheaded, with the body parts tied to gibbets throughout the country. One motive for emphasizing such front-page news about a remote

41 Riverside, p. 71. Cf. Penguin, p. 100.

42 Riverside, p. 334. Cf. Penguin, p. 426.

place might have been to serve notice to opposition writers who allegedly attacked the king as well as prime minister in ways that could be construed as treasonable. The mere fact that partisan journalism had gone so far evidenced the unusual liberty of speech enjoyed by the British in contrast to other European nations. As Sir Simon's remark suggests, transgressions against domestic authority should be taken as seriously as those against the state. Later in her marriage, Pamela complains, "Could you ever have thought ... that Husbands have a Dispensing Power over their Wives, which Kings are not allowed over the Laws?"; and she debates with Mr B. his contention that "if a Wife thinks a Thing her Duty to do, and her Husband does not approve of her doing it, he can dispense with her performing it, and no Sin shall lie at her Door?"[43] Whether Richardson believed this himself is moot; rather, it may be simply his experience as newspaper editor to welcome differing points of views in a controversey without demanding closure.

Despite the appearance of Toryism in endorsing a husband's power over his wife in the above passage, in matters of state Mr B. reaffirms the Court Whig view that the king's authority is subordinate to the law. In the symbolic action of the game of whist at the Darnfords', for instance, when Pamela wins, Mr B. emerges as a quiet defender of the Walpole ministry by the encoded allusions in the four trump cards of whist—the king, queen, ace, and knave. Although Mr Perry regards whist as a "court game" and identifies the knave as "the prime Minister," Mr B. sees a deeper historical significance in this card game:

[I] have consider'd Whist as an *English* Game in its Original; which has made me fonder of it than of any other. For, by the Ace, I have always thought the Laws of the Land denoted; and, as the Ace is above the King or Queen, and wins them; I think the Law should be thought so too; tho', may-be, I shall be deem'd a *Whig* for my Opinion.[44]

By *English*, Mr B. appears to discountenance the Stuart ties with France and absolute government and to uphold the Whiggish principle that the law is above the monarchy, and by implication declares

43 *Pamela*, 1st ed., 3:389–90. Cf. 6th ed., 3:467–68; not in Garland.

44 Riverside, pp. 335–36. Cf. Penguin, pp. 427–28.

himself a defender of the Revolutionary Settlement of 1688–89, which according to zealots had introduced a "new England" based on constitutional reform. Thus, in the *Gazetteer* (16 August 1735), Francis Osborne (James Pitt) wrote: "The King has *now* no Prerogative, but *Legal Rights*; so that the People have nothing to fear but when they violate the Laws; nor is it possible they should *lose their own Rights*, till they break in upon and invade the *Rights of others*." A "mixed government" implies a limited monarchy and an independent House of Commons.

More cryptic, however, are the innuendoes about the role of the knave as the prime minister in this game. In a passage finally omitted in the 1801 edition, both Mr Perry and Mr B. "think the Distinctions of *Whig* and *Tory* odious" and have only given their vote for the "publick Good."[45] By 1740, any claim to serving the "publick Good" would again invoke images of the Ciceronian vision of the selfless statesman as opposed to the corrupt place-seeker. In Richardson's later years, however, his last revisions to *Pamela* reveal an effort to distance his novel yet further from the political discourse of the Walpole period. Subsequently, Mr B. hints darkly that in practice politics necessarily involves a certain give-and-take that belies moral rigour— something less, in other words, than Pamela's monistic insistence on virtue:

But you see, said he, by my *Pamela's* Hand, when all the Court-cards get together, and are acted by *one Mind*, the Game is usually turn'd accordingly. Tho' now-and-then, too, it may be so circumstanced, that *Honours* will do them no Good; and they are forced to depend altogether upon *Tricks*.[46]

As if to personify her as the "*one Mind*," the "public Good," and most significantly as his own rapprochement with his former enemy Walpole, Richardson has her comment ingenuously on this lesson from her master:

I thought this way of Talking prettier than the Game itself. But I said, Tho' I have won the Game, I hope, Sirs, I am no *Trickster*. No, said my Master, God forbid but *Court-cards* should *sometimes* win with *Honour*! But you see,

45 Riverside, p. 336. Not in Penguin.

46 Riverside, p. 336. Not in Penguin.

for all that, your Game is as much owing to the *Knave*, as the *King*, and you, my Fair one, lost no Advantage, when it was put into your Power.[47]

When we recall that Pamela had as her partner Mr Perry (Country Whig?) against Mr B. and Miss Boroughs (urban constituency?), her winning the game illustrates all the more the disinterestedness of her power play by having "done Justice to my Partner" even if it means beating her husband. And as a stalwart constitutional Whig, Mr B. heartily approves of this justice. Again, as if future readers might no longer be aware of, or care about, the lessons learned during the Walpole years, Richardson deleted this passage in the 1801 text.

Notwithstanding Richardson's usual discretion about insinuating contemporary partisan views, this symbolic play of cards seems to leave little doubt about the need of a prime minister to broker the various interests in Parliament and in the country at large. In the sequel or *Pamela* 2 as well as in the *Collection of Moral and Instructive Sentiments*, Richardson again refers sparingly—and vaguely—to the necessary balance of power in electoral politics. But the general point seems transparent: sometimes opposition is called for, on the one hand; sometimes the government may be right, on the other. No matter how apparently non-committal, such sentiments probably represent an *Apologia pro Vita sua* for Richardson the London printer and City Whig whose constituency had finally given their support for Walpole in his last years in office. In sum, not only Pamela but also Mr B. seems to have grown wiser politically towards the end of the novel; but even from the first nervous moments of the story, he demonstrates little real power as a tyrant over the wily letter-writer. On the contrary, in the spirit of the Walpole era, when newspapers and periodicals were gaining an increasingly wider circulation, government censorship remained a threat, but for the most part there seemed to be a prevailing sense that persuasion was the safer means of effecting political change and hence that a free press was at best an evil necessity. Pamela's triumphant virtue was no less than the power of the written word over the presumptive aristocratic social hierarchy, but without Mr B.'s complicity as sympathetic reader it could not have prevailed.

47 Riverside, p. 336. Not in Penguin.

The Place of Sally Godfrey in Richardson's *Pamela*

Albert J. Rivero

Near the end of her journal to her parents, while relating the events of her sixth day of happiness, Pamela describes her not-so-happy quarrels with Lady Davers. Angered by her brother's foolish act of exogamy, Lady Davers fulminates against the docile Pamela with all the aristocratic hauteur she can muster. The scenes, anticipating and answering many of the criticisms raised by the novel's program of social levelling, display the nastiness and vulgarity of the high-born. Indeed, Lady Davers's desperate strategies of subjection recall Mr B.'s treatment of Pamela before his conversion, suggesting that her behaviour is typical of her class. Showering epithets like "creature" and "wench" on her victim, threatening to "confine" her if she fails to obey her commands, Lady Davers stands as the last obstacle to be removed before the heroine's assumption into Mr B.'s social sphere can be considered successful.[1]

Another obstacle is raised by Lady Davers when she reveals the existence of "poor Sally Godfrey": "Poor *Sally Godfrey*," she tells Pamela,

1 On Lady Davers—and the "rights" of gender and class—see Michael McKeon, *The Origins of the English Novel 1600–1740* (Baltimore and London: Johns Hopkins University Press, 1987), pp. 378–81. "The Place of Sally Godfrey in Richardson's *Pamela*" was first published in *Eighteenth-Century Fiction* 6:1 (1993), 29–46.

"never had half the Interest in him, I'll assure you!"[2] From this point on, "poor Sally Godfrey"—she is rarely mentioned without the adjective—becomes a narrative obsession, both for Pamela and, I suggest, for Richardson. It seems as though the novel cannot end until Sally Godfrey has been disposed of. I say "disposed of" because Sally Godfrey is the unpleasant secret this narrative has concealed from both its heroine and its readers until near the end, only to be blurted out by a character who has been instrumental in keeping "poor Sally Godfrey" in her proper place, out of everyone's sight and knowledge. Now that the secret is out, Pamela must discover the secret within the secret and what she discovers is what Richardson wants her and his readers to discover. That, however, is not the whole story.

Given its prominent place in Richardson's narrative, the Sally Godfrey story has elicited surprisingly little critical attention, perhaps because, as several readers have noted, it appears in that part of the novel where, after concluding the energetic narration of Pamela's struggles with herself and Mr B., Richardson turns his attention to demonstrating why Pamela belongs in high life. As Nancy Armstrong has brilliantly shown, one context in which to read eighteenth-century novels in general—and *Pamela* in particular—is that of contemporary conduct books; after Pamela and Mr B. agree to marry, the novel begins to sound more and more like a conduct book and less and less like a romantic tale.[3] As the narrative energy flags, our interest is likely to do so too. Thus Sheldon Sacks remarked that

2 Samuel Richardson, *Pamela or, Virtue Rewarded*, Riverside edition, ed. T.C. Duncan Eaves and Ben D. Kimpel (Boston: Houghton Mifflin, 1971), p. 356. References are to this edition. Since Richardson continued to revise *Pamela* throughout his life, adding a second part in late 1741, and leaving at his death a corrected copy eventually published in 1801, several editions of the work exist. The Eaves and Kimpel edition reprints the first edition of 1740 (though 1741 appears on the title-page). I have used it as my text because my reading here hinges, among other things, on the placement of the Sally Godfrey story at the end of the novel as it first appeared. When Richardson added a second part, he revised portions of the Sally Godfrey story to anticipate future developments in his narrative (for instance, Miss Goodwin's becoming part of the B.s' household). Since the 1801 edition of the first part of *Pamela* is now available from Penguin (ed. Peter Sabor), I shall record in these notes, whenever a change in phrasing might alter my argument, significant variants between it and the 1740 edition.

3 Nancy Armstrong, *Desire and Domestic Fiction: A Political History of the Novel* (New York: Oxford University Press, 1987).

"though the final section—especially the auspicious solution of the problem of Sally Godfrey—deftly resolves the action, it is anticlimactic and detracts from the novel's effectiveness."[4]

Margaret Anne Doody, one of Richardson's most astute and sympathetic readers, while acknowledging the change in narrative strategy, does not see it as detracting, since she, like Armstrong, agrees that this part of the narrative is crucial to establishing Pamela in her new station. Doody, however, concedes that something is wrong with the "Sally Godfrey sequence": "The Sally Godfrey section is but clumsily done, resembling the inset story so common in novels of the time."[5] Yet Doody shares Sacks's view that the problem is given an "auspicious solution," since it shows that "in this first major trial within her marriage she [Pamela] comes up trumps, not by complaisant yielding through prudence as the conduct books suggest, nor by calculation, but by spontaneous emotional reaction."[6] This auspicious solution of the Sally Godfrey problem strengthens Doody's reading of *Pamela* as "pastoral comedy."

An equally auspicious reading of Sally Godfrey is offered by Mark Kinkead-Weekes, who sees in the episode a "decisive break with orthodox morality," though his reading indicates that his own assumptions about what women do and what they deserve are at least as objectionable as the supposedly "orthodox morality" Pamela breaks with: "Sally Godfrey not only failed to resist seduction but to a great extent took the initiative in her own disaster. Only, she was so affected by the warning of her 'childbed terrors' that she rushed into exile to avoid falling again, though she was still in love with her seducer. We might expect Pamela to rail against her for her fall; instead she voices a judgment that excludes the fall altogether."[7]

Given these representative examples, I wish to offer the preliminary hypothesis that any "auspicious" reading of Sally Godfrey must

4 Sheldon Sacks, *Fiction and the Shape of Belief* (Berkeley: University of California Press, 1964), p. 64.

5 Margaret Anne Doody, *A Natural Passion: A Study of the Novels of Samuel Richardson* (Oxford: Oxford University Press, 1974), p. 66.

6 Doody, p. 67.

7 Mark Kinkead-Weekes, *Samuel Richardson: Dramatic Novelist* (Ithaca: Cornell University Press, 1973), p. 68.

be predicated on the suppression of Sally Godfrey herself. Sally Godfrey must be sacrificed to save Pamela, to show Pamela's goodness, to emphasize her forgiveness, to cement her love for Mr B., to complete the narrative. But what if we resist the pressure of the text and refuse to participate in this auspicious reading? A suspicious reading of the Sally Godfrey incident, one that questions its ideological assumptions, leads to some troubling conclusions.[8] It also raises the question of our ethical responsibility as readers of Richardson at the beginning of the twenty-first century.

The question of ethical responsibility is raised by Richardson himself. The Sally Godfrey story is an exemplum, to be read ethically. The reader is asked to pass judgment on the characters' actions and to adjudicate praise or blame. That act of judgment is both facilitated and complicated by the way in which Richardson transmits the story to his readers. The story is reluctantly told by Mr B. to Pamela, who, in turn, relates it to her parents in the journal which makes up over one half of the novel we are reading, a journal which will be read—or has already been read—by Pamela's parents, Mr B., and Lady Davers, as well as, of course, all of Richardson's readers since

---

8 Several critics of *Pamela* have questioned and resisted Richardson's ideology in the latter part of the novel, as Pamela, in Patricia Meyer Spacks's Congrevian borrowing, "dwindles into a wife." *The Adolescent Idea: Myths of Youth and the Adult Imagination* (New York: Basic Books, 1981), p. 29. For example, see Terry J. Castle, "P/B: *Pamela* as Sexual Fiction," *Studies in English Literature* 22 (1982), 469–89; Terry Eagleton, *The Rape of Clarissa: Writing, Sexuality and Class Struggle in Samuel Richardson* (Minneapolis: University of Minnesota Press, 1982), pp. 29–39; Patricia Meyer Spacks, *Imagining a Self: Autobiography and Novel in Eighteenth-Century England* (Cambridge and London: Harvard University Press, 1976), pp. 193–226; and Janet Todd, "*Pamela*: or the Bliss of Servitude," *British Journal for Eighteenth-Century Studies* 6 (1983), 135–48. None of these critics has pondered the crucial place of Sally Godfrey in Richardson's narrative of Pamela's dwindling. One critic, however, has dealt with the political implications of this incident. While reviewing the largely auspicious readings of *Pamela* found in Nancy Armstrong's *Desire and Domestic Fiction* and Michael McKeon's *The Origins of the English Novel*, Charlotte Sussman argues that, even though these critics approach Richardson's novel from different perspectives (Armstrong adopts a Foucauldian model; McKeon, a Marxist), they elide the nasty ideological implications in the Sally Godfrey story. See Charlotte Sussman, "'I Wonder Whether Poor Miss Sally Godfrey Be Living or Dead': The Married Woman and the Rise of the Novel," *diacritics* 20 (1990), 88–102. In spite of her title, however, Sussman devotes less that two pages (pp. 97–98) to the Sally Godfrey story.

1740. Every act of reading entails an act of judgment. Prompted by
Pamela, Mr B. offers moral observations on the actions he relates.
His reading is modified by these promptings and our reading is modified or guided by his reading and Pamela's. Pamela's reading is, of
course, modified by the "facts" Mr B. presents to her, facts already interpreted in his telling. For Richardson, the act of reading is seldom
solitary. It is done in community, by readers whose ethical responses
are both to be sought and to be directed. We know that Richardson solicited and supervised the reading of his (mostly female) first
readers while composing his novels. And, as the conversion of Mr B.
from rake to husband testifies, Richardson believed that reading, in
its appeal to the reader's conscience, can modify behaviour. As we
read *Pamela*, our (usually) solitary reading is shaped by those other
readings—Mr B.'s, Pamela's, Richardson's—embedded in the text,
readings we can accept or resist. We can be converted by this text's
ideology—or we can resist it.

How does Richardson, then, want us to read the story of Sally
Godfrey? Auspiciously, of course—and the clues to that reading
have been dutifully picked up by readers such as Sacks, Doody, and
Kinkead-Weekes.[9] Richardson explicitly points up the "moral" at the
end of the first part of his novel, "in a few brief Observations, which
naturally result from [this little History]; and which will serve as so
many Applications, of its most material Incidents, to the Minds of
the Youth of both Sexes" (p. 409).[10] What is interesting to note here

9 In fairness to Doody, I must emphasize that her reading of the Sally Godfrey story is a
relatively minor part of her immense contribution to Richardson studies, and that her
reading is two decades old. I doubt that the author of the definitive biography of Frances
Burney—as well as of numerous feminist studies of eighteenth-century literature—would
read the Sally Godfrey story quite so auspiciously now.

10 This section, deleted after the addition of the second part of the novel, does not appear in
the Penguin edition. Although my reading is confined to the first part of *Pamela*, it should
be noted that the Sally Godfrey story has a sequel in the second part, as Miss Goodwin (as
indicated above) comes to live with the B.s and, as we learn in the novel's conclusion, "at
the Age of Eighteen, was married to a young Gentleman of fine Parts, and great Sobriety
and Virtue: And that both she and her Spouse ... emulated the great and good Examples
set them by Mr and Mrs *B.*" (4:454). References to Sally Godfrey and Miss Goodwin in the
second part include 3:33–34, 39, 48, 62–64, 99, 119, 424–29; 4:54, 243 (Pamela to Lady
Davers: "I am to be favoured with the Care of Miss *Goodwin*"), 270–82, 287–88, 361–62,
371–73, 380–84, 391, 436–38, 442– 52. References are to the Shakespeare Head Edition of
Pamela, 4 vols (Oxford: Basil Blackwell, 1929).

is that Richardson feels that there is a "natural" connection between story and moral. That he must point out that "natural" connection indicates that the connection may not be so natural, that readers can always wander off from the prescribed path and arrive at their own readings, a situation Richardson experienced most acutely with the first readers of *Clarissa* and which he tried to remedy in future editions by adding prefaces, footnotes, and other helpful interpretive devices to ensure a "natural" reading.[11] Here, then, is the moral Richardson "naturally" derives from the Sally Godfrey story:

The poor deluded Female, who, like the once unhappy Miss Godfrey, has given up her Honour, and yielded to the Allurements of her designing Lover, may learn from her Story, to stop at the *first Fault*; and, by resolving to repent and amend, see the Pardon and Blessing which await her Penitence, and a kind Providence ready to extend the Arms of its Mercy to receive and reward her returning Duty. While the abandon'd Prostitute, pursuing the wicked Courses, into which, perhaps, she was at first *inadvertently* drawn, hurries herself into filthy Diseases, and an untimely Death; and, too probably, into everlasting Perdition afterwards. (p. 410)

Here the story is read as another version of the Fall, which always presupposes a "poor deluded female" as well as a "designing" male (it is no accident that Pamela has often called Mr B. a "devil"), but since the story of the Fall is not complete in itself—in typological terms, as we learn in Romans 5:14, the story of the first Adam makes complete sense only if understood in the context of the story of Christ,

---

11 See William Beatty Warner's controversial treatment of this topic in his *Reading Clarissa: The Struggles of Interpretation* (New Haven: Yale University Press, 1979). For a more temperate account of Richardson's editorial improvements, see Florian Stuber's introduction to the AMS Press reprint of the third edition (1751; New York, 1990), pp. 1–53. On Richardson's footnotes, the subject of much heated debate, Stuber writes: "Editorial footnotes had appeared in the First Edition of *Clarissa*, providing cross-references between letters and in some cases providing narration of facts letter-writers could not or would not mention. The Second Edition contained several new editorial footnotes, all of which are retained in the Third. ... [Richardson's] footnotes draw the readers' '*Attention* ... to what lies before them,' and what lay before them in the Third Edition was essentially the same as in the First and the Second" (p. 31). While Stuber suggests that Richardson is simply pointing out what is already there, he grants, albeit reluctantly, that "the editorial footnote offers an editorial reading" (p. 32). Whether one agrees with Warner or Stuber, the point is that Richardson wanted to "guide" his readers to the "correct" reading of Lovelace's character and of the novel's tragic ending.

the second Adam—a "kind Providence" has reclaimed Sally Godfrey from perdition and the consequent bodily and spiritual ravages
which will "too probably" be inflicted by that "kind Providence" on
those who fail to repent. Sally Godfrey as prodigal daughter is a type
of Pamela, who, but by the "Grace" (p. 393) of that same Providence, would have been, in Mr B.'s words, "*Sally Godfrey* the Second"
(p. 399).

Yet we immediately recognize that this connection between Sally
Godfrey and Pamela is neither natural nor warranted. If nothing
else, Pamela's story of her own life demonstrates that she is *sui gen-
eris*, like nobody but herself. It is Mr B. who believes that there is a
connection between Pamela and Sally Godfrey and it is because of
this assumption that he has attempted to seduce Pamela. But Pamela
does not resemble Sally Godfrey either in social class or in behaviour. Indeed, Richardson himself, in his elucidation of the moral
cited above, indicates that the reader of the Sally Godfrey story is
"the poor deluded Female" likely already to have fallen. Pamela, in
short, does not need to hear the story of Sally Godfrey, since it has
no application to herself except in the terms prescribed by Mr B.
That Pamela accepts those terms indicates that she has begun to read
her own story as Mr B. wishes her to read it, that she has become a
"poor deluded Female" in a sense other than Richardson perhaps
intends, that her voice has begun to acquire the inflections of the
patriarchal voice she had so vigorously fought at the beginning of
her story. That patriarchal voice urges "poor deluded females" to
yield to their "designing" lovers and suffer the consequences, in loss
of reputation, in the pain of childbirth.

What is particularly disturbing, then, about the prescribed reading of the Sally Godfrey story, prominently placed at the end of
Pamela, is that that patriarchal voice, which Pamela, and Richardson, attempt to silence (or at least question) through the narrative
of her struggles with Mr B., returns at this point as the voice of
Providence, not to be questioned but to be obeyed as the final arbiter of any reading that is to be regarded as ethical, as "natural." Mr
B., the once diabolical rake, now becomes the agent of Providence,
whose "Goodness," as Pamela earlier suggests, may "be said to be
God-like" (p. 233). If the story of Sally Godfrey establishes Pamela's

nobility of character, it does so only because, in her world, nobility of character is best exemplified by submission to the patriarchal order, now redefined as providential. Like Pamela, Sally Godfrey refuses, at one point, to submit to Mr B.'s script, yet the sequel—her convenient transportation to Jamaica and marriage to a suitably deceived husband—writes a satisfactorily providential, *male* ending to her story. What is silenced is the voice of the female, Sally Godfrey's own voice, a voice which my reading will attempt to recuperate.

The suppression of Sally Godfrey begins with her name, a name that both captures and denies her identity. "Sally," with its connotations of breaking of restraints, of going beyond the boundaries of passion, of desire—as in Steele's sentence, with its tellingly female subject, "she [is] apt to fall into little Sallies of Passion" (*Tatler* no. 172, 16 May 1710)—is joined to the patronymic "Godfrey," suggestive of both conflict with ("fray") and denial of ("free") the godhead. "Sally," for Richardson, seems to have been a generic name for godless, fallen women, such as Sally Martin in *Clarissa*, the prostitute who, by failing to repent, meets the horrible fate reserved for her kind. This act of naming traps Sally Godfrey in the figure of prosopopeia, an abstraction without a voice. Yet this is an abstraction which has left several traces or *vestigia*, in the "hint" Lady Davers gives Pamela, in the daughter whom Pamela meets, and in the story eventually told by Mr B. In the first instance, however, Sally Godfrey is hinted at in such a way that Pamela wonders "*whether poor Miss Sally Godfrey be living or dead!*" (p. 370). And when Pamela meets Sally's daughter, she cannot tell who she is because she goes under the name "Miss Goodwin." This (pseudo)-name, Mr B. tells Pamela, "her Mother chose ... for her ... because she should not be called by her own" (p. 392). Little Miss Goodwin, the living testimony of transgression, is denied her own identity, in an act of maternal abnegation which Mr B. seems to approve of because it allows him to keep her guilty origins secret. Pamela and (I suggest) Richardson approve of it because such an act testifies to Sally's repentance of her wickedness. Sally Godfrey must deny her daughter in order to survive in a patriarchal society that frowns on her behaviour, giving her daughter a name—"good win"—that plots the trajectory of Sally's spiritual reclamation by "a kind Providence," an ironic reminder that, to attain the kingdom of heaven, one must sever earthly ties, break away from one's kind, deny one's identity, restrain (or at least rename) one's desires or passions. Sally's "choice" is not her own, as Mr B. would like us to believe, but determined by social and religious imperatives.

Yet under all these acts of renaming, of suppression, the faint voice of Sally Godfrey may be heard, but only because other women conspire to exhume her from the narrative death she seems to have wished for herself.[12] Like other women in Richardson (Mrs Jewkes, Mrs Sinclair) who help a man exercise his natural male prerogative of seducing and disposing of "poor deluded females," Lady Davers plays a prominent part in the Sally Godfrey affair. She arranges for a private lying-in and takes "upon herself the Care of the Little-one" (p. 395). It is significant that she fails to elaborate on her "hint," that Pamela will not hear the full story from her: "I had once a good mind to have asked her Ladyship about Miss *Sally Godfrey*; but I thought it was better let alone, as she did not mention it herself." Pamela then reveals, in turn, her curiosity, her dread of finding out, her darkest suspicion (already voiced a few pages earlier): "May-be, I shall hear it too soon. But I hope not!—I wonder, tho', whether she be living or dead!" (p. 376).[13] The full revelation of the secret, which occurs in three stages, each stage disclosing more and more detail in a sort of narrative striptease, is reserved for Mr B. The final disclosures take place after his theatrical presentation of Miss Goodwin to Pamela.

The revelation of Sally Godfrey's story might be prompted by Lady Davers's "hint" and helped along by Pamela's curiosity—though Pamela wishes she could unspeak what Lady Davers has "spoken": "For it has given me a Curiosity that is not quite so pretty in me" (p. 372)—but the pace and terms of that revelation are controlled

12 In the second part, Sally Godfrey undergoes another renaming: her first name is restored to the more formal "Sarah" and her new married surname is the highly evocative Mrs Wrightson (4:274).

13 In the Penguin version (p. 476), "May-be, I shall hear it too soon. But I hope not!" is deleted; so is the exclamation point after "dead," thus muting Pamela's emotional dread of making a discovery.

by Mr B. Sally Godfrey survives in fragments of compromised speech, in a morally charged name and surname, in Lady Davers's ill-natured outburst, in a female child who, though born of her, does not bear her name, in a narrative controlled by her seducer. Unlike Pamela, who, though once able to voice her own oppositional discourse, now seems to welcome the appropriation of her voice by Mr B.'s— becoming, in Terry Castle's words, "a mouthpiece for those patri-archal values which have everywhere ordered her experience"[14]— Sally Godfrey never gets a chance to tell her own story, except through the agency, the projections, the obfuscations of others. Her voice can be heard only within the discourse of the "master," a dis-course transmitted to us by a sympathetic "female" who, having mar-ried the "master," becomes virtually indistinguishable from him, as Richardson himself, his task of impersonating Pamela nearly fin-ished, labours to provide a satisfactorily male ending to the story of his heroine. In this sense, Pamela may be read as "Sally Godfrey the second," though she prefers to sign herself—or have Mr B. complete the signature for her—"Pamela——" (pp. 302–3), a name hinted at but never spelled out. Although Pamela might know the surname, the reader must fill in the inviting blank. At crucial points in the Sally Godfrey story, the figure of aposiopesis, silent in itself, calls for our imaginative speech.

It is precisely in those hints before they are fully spelled out, be-fore the fragments of "female" speech are shaped into a providen-tial narrative, before the heroine writes herself or is written into the "master" plot, that our reading must begin. We must, in other words, arrest the narrative death of Sally Godfrey, catch her before she is entombed in the "master" plot, and imagine her as living, as really suffering the ills she is reported to have suffered. Our sympathy for her plight must not be allowed to become—like Pamela's—the pat-ronizing pity of the morally superior. Reading her from above, from a providential perspective, we transform her experience into a dead moral metaphor, killing her with textual kindness. Instead, we must read the signs of her suffering without the comfort of "a kind provid-ence," through the eyes of all those "poor deluded females" whose

---

14 Terry Castle, *Clarissa's Ciphers* (Ithaca: Cornell University Press 1982), p. 169.

bodies have been mutilated and punished to prove an ideological point. We must resist the providential closure offered by Richardson and read, as Pamela does before her identification with Mr B., in a spirit of contradiction.

Pamela's last act of contradiction, of saying something against the discourse of the master, occurs in the form of her often pert comments on the "Rules" she extracts from the "awful Lecture" (p. 369) she hears from Mr B. after their reconciliation with Lady Davers. Unlike her extensive answers to Mr B.'s earlier articles of cohabitation (pp. 164–68), where her writing and Mr B.'s march side by side down the page—her writing often overwhelming his—her comments on these "rules" are brief and intermittent, vestiges of the old Pamela, now nearly extinct. The sixth rule—"That I must bear with him, even when I find him in the wrong"—elicits a spirited rejoinder: "*This is a little hard, as the Case may be!*"[15] And, immediately, as if by an associational reflex, she exclaims, "*I wonder whether poor Miss Sally Godfrey be living or dead!*" (p. 390). Sally Godfrey's intrusion into Pamela's thoughts in this context is suggestive. By introducing her name, Lady Davers has momentarily disrupted the progress of the narrative harmony towards which Pamela and Mr B. seemed to be headed. This discordant note will continue to be sounded in Pamela's head, much like her suspicions of a "Sham-marriage" (p. 223), until silenced by Mr B. By cropping up at this point, after a "rule" that appears to call for an act of moral compromise on a case yet to be named, Pamela's wonderings about Sally Godfrey prepare the reader for the presentation of that ethically hard case. Pamela is enjoined to "bear with" or suffer Mr B. even when she finds him in the wrong. This "bearing with" calls for Pamela's complicity in bearing or giving birth to a "story" that would allow them to keep up appearances. As Mr B., with consummate casuistical skill, remarks of the many narratives concocted to keep secret the Sally Godfrey affair, "in the whole Story on both sides, the Truth is as much preserv'd as possible" (p. 396). If

15 In the Penguin version (p. 467), this sentence is rendered "*This may be a little hard, as the case may be circumstanced.*" Again, with the removal of the exclamation point, the sentence becomes less emotional. While Richardson may have changed "is" to "may be" to make the sentence grammatically correct, he may also be anticipating, with the addition of "circumstanced," Mr B.'s "affair" at the masquerade in the second part.

Pamela's reading of "poor Miss Sally Godfrey" progresses from "Uneasiness" to "Compassion" (p. 385), from questioning to accepting Mr B.'s version of "truth," ours need not follow that providential trajectory but may retain her initial posture of uneasiness. Although Richardson might have intended the Sally Godfrey story to have a providential ending, his text, with its strategies of disruption and deferral, encourages its readers to adopt those strategies and thus enables them to bear witness to their own versions of the truth.

We have noted that Mr B.'s version of the Sally Godfrey story is imparted to Pamela gradually, in three instalments. The first of these occurs immediately after Lady Davers drops her hint; the other two occur side by side nearly forty pages later, after Pamela meets Miss Goodwin. In the interval, the story is kept alive in Pamela's obsessive recollections: "Foolish thing that I am, this poor Miss *Sally Godfrey* runs in my Head!" (p. 361). The first instalment is self-contained and, in its apparent closure—with Mr B.'s peremptory valediction to Pamela, "And now, my Dear, you may withdraw" (p. 357)—does not seem to look forward to future elaborations. Yet Pamela does not withdraw; Lady Davers "beseeches" her to stay, prolonging the scene until Mr B. bursts "out of the Parlour" (pp. 357–58). Mr B.'s absence does not end the echoings in Pamela's head, nor is his later effort to prevent Lady Davers from uttering "the Name" successful in suppressing her memory: "Well, said [Lady Davers], you will quite forget my fault about Miss—— He stopt her before she could speak the Name, and said, For ever forget it!" (p. 360). It is not only because Sally Godfrey remains alive in Pamela's own internal narrative, or in Lady Davers's not so subtle reminders, that she eventually returns. She returns because there is yet another secret to be revealed and explained, namely the existence of Miss Goodwin. Living or dead, Sally Godfrey has left behind a memorial of herself, a living document that cannot be so easily suppressed.

But let us return to the first version Pamela hears, for in it Mr B. suppresses not only the existence of Miss Goodwin but also his own culpability. As we read his account, we are asked to believe that Mr B. was not so much the seducer of Sally Godfrey as the "prey" of her "artful" mother:

When I was at College, I was well received by a Widow Lady, who had several Daughters, and but small Fortunes to give them; and the old Lady set one of them; a deserving good Girl she was; to draw me in to a Marriage with her, for the sake of the Fortune I was Heir to; and contriv'd many Opportunities to bring us and leave us together. I was not then of Age; and the young Lady, not half so artful as her Mother, yielded to my Addresses, before the Mother's Plot could be ripened, and so utterly disappointed it. This, my *Pamela*, is the *Sally Godfrey* this malicious Woman, with the worst Intentions, has inform'd you of. (p. 357)[16]

As always with Mr B., any flaws in his character, like his fortune, can be traced to the female line. Earlier in the narrative, for example, Pamela finds a maternal origin for his dislike of contradiction: "His poor dear Mother spoil'd him at first" (p. 210). Pamela extends this paradigm when, in distributing the blame for her own travails, she attributes the larger share to Mrs Jewkes: "O what a black Heart has this poor Wretch! So I need not rail against Men so much; for my Master, bad as I have thought him, is not half so bad as this Woman!— To be sure she must be an Atheist!" (p. 212). Pamela's tendency to blame the female indicates that she has internalized the master plot of patriarchal society—in Mr B.'s terse formulation, "Your Sex is the D——l!" (p. 360)—the originary account of the Fall in Genesis, which blames the female, reserves for her the most exquisite torture as atonement, the pain of childbirth, and reiterates her subjugation to her husband: "And unto the woman he [the Lord God] said, I will greatly multiply thy sorrow and thy conception, in sorrow thou shalt bring forth children; and thy desire *shall be* to thy husband, and he shall rule over thee" (3:16, King James version).

Following centuries of misogyny, of placing the blame for mankind's ills on "wikked wyves"—to use the Wife of Bath's wonderfully evocative phrase—Mr B. casts himself as the victim of the "Mother's Plot." What is concealed in his self-serving reading is the economic necessity that has driven Mrs Godfrey to this expedient: she has several daughters and small fortunes to give them. Mr B. rereads her desperate act in allegorical terms, drawing his language from the

16 In addition to several changes in specific words (for example, "Addresses" becomes "importunities," to play off "Opportunities" and to reveal that there was nothing honourable about Mr B.'s intentions, something Sally Godfrey's mother chose to overlook), the Penguin version (p. 452) omits the explicit reference to Mr B.'s fortune.

aristocratic lexicon of the hunt, thus anticipating Lovelace's use of like images in *Clarissa*, though Lovelace seldom forgets that he is the predator. Like a ruthless hunter, Mrs Godfrey chooses from among her kennel of daughters and sets "one of them" loose on Mr B. to trap him in marriage. What had first appeared rather harmless— "I was well received"—now turns out to be a hunter's ruse, to lull the nearly infantilized Mr B. ("I was not then of Age") into a false sense of security. Fortunately, because of the relative lack of art of the daughter, Mr B. "disappoints" the mother's plot by resorting to that most masculine of procedures, the seduction of the "deserving good Girl," an ironic epithet since, by the end of Mr B.'s relation, it is clear that Sally Godfrey "deserves" what she gets, as she is made to suffer both for her sin and her mother's. Her sin, ripening in her womb, will eventually become a sign—to borrow Milton's pun from *Paradise Lost* (2:760)—that must first be concealed, then revealed, and eventually incorporated into Pamela's own narrative body. As Mr B.'s initial account of the Sally Godfrey affair draws to a close, he withholds the name of his victim until near the end, momentarily smears her with what first appears to be a phrase in apposition to her name, "this malicious Woman," and then elides effortlessly, as his sentence winds its way to its final syntactical alignment, into the attribution of that wandering phrase to his sister.[17] With all these women thus bearing the blame for his actions, Mr B. is justified in expecting that Pamela will perform her own exculpatory part and, like "kind Providence," "clasp" Miss Goodwin "in [her] Arms" (p. 392).

Although the scene in which Pamela meets Miss Goodwin is stage-managed by Mr B., it is presented, by Pamela, as a series of discoveries she seems to make on her own. Pamela and Mr B. arrive "at this truly neat House," where Pamela, upon meeting its inhabitants, is "much pleased with the Neatness of the good Woman, and Daughter, and Maid." Whether Pamela noted this "Neatness" while on her visit or later as she reflects upon the completed scene in her writing closet is perhaps impossible to ascertain, though it seems as the narrative progresses that she is discovering what she already knows. In any case, the favourable description of the "Farm-house, noted

17 This syntactical ambiguity is removed in the Penguin version: "This, my Pamela, is the Sally Godfrey that Lady Davers, with the worst intentions, has informed you of" (p. 452).

for a fine Dairy" serves to condition the reader's response. We enter a female household, similar to the household in which Sally Godfrey grew up, though this one is presided over by a "good Woman" who, unlike Sally Godfrey's mother, earns an honest living, by serving breakfast, not her daughters, to "the neighbouring Gentry" (p. 391). While Pamela and Mr B. are breakfasting in one apartment, "four Misses, all pretty much of a Size" arrive and are "shewn another little neat Apartment, that went thro' ours." Pamela steps into this inner room and begins to ask questions of the little girls, eventually singling out Miss Goodwin as "the genteelest shap'd Child," though she does not discover the child's real identity until Mr B. explains the double mystery of Miss Goodwin's calling him "Uncle" and Sally Godfrey's choice of another name for her.

Pamela's discovery of Mr B.'s secret thus occurs in a public place, a place marked by "neatness" and "goodness," yet a place that allows for secrecy, in inner apartments. The "Farmhouse" is a double place, poised on the boundary between public and private, between its "neat" appearance and the secrets, sordid or otherwise, that may be revealed or concealed within its walls. Mr B.'s secret literally walks by Pamela into one of those inner apartments, disguised as one of four nearly indistinguishable little girls. Pamela's quest for knowledge is spatially rendered, as she enters the inner apartment and interrogates the "little ladies." Yet Mr B.'s secret is not spatially confined, though spatial confinements, as we shall see, are crucial to the narrative he tells. Miss Goodwin is also concealed under a false familial relation and an assumed name. Words, in short, conceal her identity. It is significant, then, that Pamela recognizes that there is a connection between Mr B. and Miss Goodwin by reading the little girl's *body* language: "Miss *Goodwin* made a particular fine Curchee to my Master." The ensuing verbal revelation, that Mr B. is her uncle, is another narrative tease, one that holds in suspension the true relation for a moment, to allow Pamela to "embrace" first the little girl and then, after the revelation is completed, the smiling Mr B., who now redefines, ironically though not entirely so, his sister's "Hint" as "good-natur'd" (p. 392). As Pamela "embraces" Miss Goodwin and Mr B., she incorporates his secret into her own body, a move reminiscent of her earlier strategy of concealing her writing about her person to protect her body from sexual penetration. In this instance, however, Pamela uses her body and her writing to protect Mr B. from the full consequences of his sexual penetration of Sally Godfrey, thus becoming, in this respect at least, Lady Davers the second. Unlike Sally Godfrey, now exiled and separated from her child, Mr B. can continue, with his doting wife's co-operation, to keep up the charade of his avuncular connection to his own daughter. When he hears of Pamela's project to have "sweet Employment and Companionship" with Miss Goodwin, he urges her, "in Prudence," to "put some Bounds to [her] amiable Generosity" (p. 393). Pamela is free to "love" Miss Goodwin, so long as the little girl continues to call Mr B. "uncle" and does not live in his house. Pamela's desire for physical proximity must be accommodated to her husband's need for space, for distance, for secrecy. Her maternal instincts now redefined as "amiable Generosity," Pamela is enjoined to curb her bodily discourse with "Prudence," to confine her exuberant "female" narrative, punctuated by excited questions and exclamations, within the reasonable boundaries prescribed by her "Master."

As we have already seen, transgressions of prescribed boundaries punctuate Mr B.'s own version of the Sally Godfrey story. In his second instalment, although he offers "Particulars of this Affair, additional to what he had before mention'd," he continues to cast women in the villains' roles. Though "of a good Family, and the Flower of it," Sally Godfrey is prostituted by her own mother, the word "mother" neatly capturing Mrs Godfrey's twofold character as unnatural parent and scheming bawd. Throughout this account Mr B., while attributing his own flaws to the "natural" instincts of a youth of his class, blames the mother not only for her betrayal of her maternal duties but also for her active co-operation: "When she had Reason to find him unsettled and wild, and her Daughter in more Danger from him, than he was from her; yet she encouraged their Privacies."[18] Even after discovering her daughter and her seducer "in a way not so creditable to the Lady," she persists in her scheme, arranging for a "surprise" meeting, in which her former footman and "a Half-pay Officer, her Relation" attempt "to frighten [Mr B.] into

18 At this point, the Penguin version (p. 498) restores Mrs Godfrey's financial motive—"as she knew that he was heir to a great estate"—omitted on p. 452.

a Marriage with the Lady." Borrowed from Restoration comedy and a variant on the statute allowing husbands to collect money for the criminal conversations of their wives (dramatized, for instance, in Fielding's *The Modern Husband*, 1732), this farcical plot fails to work. Suspecting "from some strong Circumstances, that Miss was in the Plot," Mr B. vows "to break off all Correspondence with the whole Family" (p. 394). "In order to clear herself," Sally Godfrey sets up a meeting with him and "she there was obliged, naughty Creature as he was! to make herself quite guilty of a worse Fault ... to clear herself of a lighter."[19] Their "guilty Lessons" continue "till, at last, the Effect of their frequent Interviews grew too obvious to be concealed," at which point "the young Lady ... when she was not fit to be seen, for the Credit of the Family, was confined, and all manner of Means were used, to induce him to marry her." With Lady Davers's assistance, however, Mr B. manages to frustrate Mrs Godfrey's final scheme. He then settles some money "upon the dear little Miss ... fit for a Gentlewoman." Having paid his way out of this unpleasantry, Mr B. concludes with a lukewarm acceptance of responsibility not exactly supported by his actions: "I am far from making a Boast of, or taking a Pride in, this Affair: But since it has happen'd, I can't say, but I wish the poor Child to live, and be happy; and I must endeavour to make her so" (p. 395).[20]

Mr B.'s second account, then, places the blame squarely on the shoulders of Mrs Godfrey for her malicious scheming and on Sally Godfrey for her foolish pursuit of him after he had chosen to break with her. While Mr B. can easily slide out of any threatened confinement—in rooms, in marriage—Sally Godfrey is trapped in the inevitable facts of female physiology. Following the script outlined in Genesis, she is trapped by her desire for her "husband," while he, with no particular attachment to her except the urgings of

19 The phrasing in the Penguin version is more explicit about the nature of Sally Godfrey's "fault": "But there, poor lady! she found herself betrayed (wicked man!) into the grossest fault a young woman can be guilty of, in order to convince him of her innocence in a less" (p. 499).

20 In the 1740 text, this exchange is followed by Pamela's request to "have [Miss Goodwin] home," a request Mr B. ignores. In the Penguin version, as Richardson looks forward to that homecoming, Pamela writes, "He made no answer in words; but tenderly grasped my hand, and looked pleased" (p. 500).

hyperactive animal spirits, can keep his wits about him and defeat the mother's plot. When Sally Godfrey's belly grows beyond pre-scribed boundaries, she must be confined, a prisoner of her body as well as of the ideological assumptions of her society. Mr B.'s second account, filtered through Pamela's clumsy indirect discourse,[21] is characterized by a hurried and weary tone, indicating that what is being described is precisely what is to be expected under the circum-stances. Pamela's ventriloquizing of this account is troubling, since it becomes nearly impossible to ascertain whether the expressions of pity for Sally Godfrey ("poor Lady!") and blame for Mr B. ("Naughty Creature as he was!") are hers or her husband's (though exclama-tion points usually denote Pamela's speech and "poor Lady" is one of her oft-repeated expressions), and whether the misogyny evident throughout is his or hers. In any case, Pamela renders her mas-ter's speech while silencing and voicing her own curiosity about Sally Godfrey: "I wanted him to say if the poor Lady was living or dead" (p. 395). Picking up Pamela's hints about wanting to hear more— "I see you want to know what's become of the poor Mother!"—Mr B. offers his final account, as a reward for earlier narrative teasings: "I was willing to see how the little Suspence would operate upon you. ... I think you have had a great deal of Patience, and are come at this Question so fairly, that you deserve to be answer'd" (pp. 395–96). In this final account, Sally Godfrey seems, at last, to be allowed to present her own case. But that presentation, granted and sanc-tioned by Mr B., is problematic, an act of narrative kindness masking the brutal facts of political repression.

The first thing Mr B. reveals about Sally Godfrey is that she is alive and well and living in Jamaica, "and very happily too." Mr B.'s as-sertion that Sally Godfrey is "happy" and "happily married" evokes a double response from Pamela: "Poor Lady! said I; how her Story moves me!—I am glad she is so happy at last!" To Mr B.'s insinu-ation that Pamela is "glad" because "she [Sally Godfrey] is so far off," Pamela replies, "I cannot be sorry, to be sure, as she is so happy; which she could not have been here." Pamela then launches into a series of moral reflections, in which she castigates Mr B.—"I doubt

21 Virtually every sentence begins with a formulaic "that," dropped in the 1801 text.

you would have proceeded with your Temptations, if she had not gone"—while praising Sally Godfrey for the enormous sacrifices she has made "to preserve herself from further Guiltiness": "That she could leave her native Country, leave all her Relations, leave you that she so well lov'd, leave her dear Baby, and try a new Fortune, in a new World, among quite Strangers, and hazard the Seas."

Pamela's sympathy is genuine and felt along the heart: "I bleed for what her Distresses must be ... I am grieved for her poor Mind's Remorse, thro' her Childbed Terrors, which could have so great and so worthy an Effect upon her." Pamela then attributes Sally Godfrey's renunciations to "God Almighty's Mercies" and asserts "that her present Happiness is the Result of his gracious Providence, blessing her Penitence and Reformation" (p. 396).[22] What is disturbing in Pamela's "happy" reading is that, while recognizing Sally Godfrey's pain, she sees it as a necessary component of her "Reformation." Sally Godfrey is happy because she has suffered, thus anticipating the movement of Pamela's own narrative. Mr B., the real villain in both cases, gets off relatively easily, with a few rhetorical slaps for his "naughty Purposes" (p. 397). In Richardson's rewritings of the story of Job—*Clarissa* provides a particularly terrifying instance, in which the heroine, after being physically and psychologically tortured and eventually raped, is rewarded with transportation to the next world—"kind Providence" reclaims women through "Childbed Terrors" or, if unregenerate, smites them with "filthy Diseases" before hurrying them off "into everlasting Perdition" (p. 410). Like some kind of Kafkaesque agent, Richardson's Providence inscribes its trials and its judgments on women's bodies, blessing and damning them with nearly indistinguishable gestures.

The rest of Mr B.'s narrative details Sally Godfrey's strategies to frustrate Mr B.'s designs, for, as Mr B. confesses, "I did not believe her so much in Earnest" (p. 396). Sally Godfrey demonstrates her resolve by arranging for her exile to the New World, relating her reasons in a letter (p. 397) whose contents, though unremarkable in themselves, recapitulate almost point by point Pamela's own sympathetic projections concerning the physical and mental distresses

22 In the Penguin version, Pamela's reaction becomes less visceral, as "bleed" is changed to "grieve" (p. 501).

of the "poor Lady." It seems as though Mr B. tailors the contents of Sally Godfrey's letter—the letter exists only in his paraphrases—to fit the moral reflections he has just heard from his wife. One suspects that Mr B. rewrites the letter to follow the providential script adduced by Pamela, in yet another case of narrative collusion that silences Sally Godfrey's voice while appearing to give it utterance.[23] Moreover, as Mr B. narrates the events surrounding his pursuit of Sally Godfrey down to Gravesend—a happily evocative place name, as it launches the narrative "death" of the barely "living" Sally Godfrey—to prevent her sailing, he manages to wring sympathy not only for her plight but also for his. Their parting "affected every one present, Men, as well as Ladies," and, as Mr B. leaves Sally Godfrey confined in the ship, we witness the forlorn and abandoned lover gazing "at the Ship, *till* and *after* I had landed, as long as I could discern the least Appearance of it" (p. 398). After this affecting parting and a restless night, Mr B. sets out for the country, eventually gets over his disappointment, and, "five or six Years afterwards," attempts to "make" Pamela into "*Sally Godfrey* the Second" (p. 399).

The "happy" sequel to these events we already know. Pamela blesses God for Mr B.'s reformation and Mr B., in turn, chimes in with a blessing of his own, adding that "I can truly abhor my past Liberties, and pity poor *Sally Godfrey*, from the same Motives that I admire my *Pamela*'s Virtues; and resolve, by the Grace of God, to make myself as worthy of them as possible." Pamela then rounds out Mr B.'s narrative with a picture of their domestic felicity: "These agreeable Reflections, on this melancholy, but instructive, Story, brought

---

23 A letter from Sally Godfrey to Pamela does appear in the second part (4:270–74). In it we learn that, unlike the "*Happy, deservedly happy, dear Lady*" to whom she is writing, "*Mrs.* Wrightson (*formerly Miss* Sally Godfrey)" is still "unhappy." Though married to a "rich," "tender," and "generous" spouse, she is still troubled by "reflection" on her "past Conduct," which, "like a Winter-Frost, nips in the Bud every rising Satisfaction!" (p. 273). Moreover, Sally Godfrey's letter is once again presented to us in somebody else's discourse. The letter we are reading is a "copy" included by Pamela in a letter she writes to Lady Davers; Pamela's letter also includes her reply to Sally Godfrey as well as a short missive from Miss Goodwin to her "dearest, dear Mamma," with a brief note "subjoined" by Mr B., "the affectionate Admirer of your Piety" (p. 277).

us in View of his own House; and we alighted, and took a Walk in the Garden till Dinner was ready" (p. 399). Unlike Sally Godfrey, Mr B. remains safely in "his own House"—*his* house, not Pamela's— to indulge in "agreeable Reflections" on his past conduct, with such squirely comforts as amiable walks in his garden and well-prepared meals. There is nothing agreeable about Sally Godfrey's fate. The presumably "happy" "poor Lady"—in Pamela's own oxymoron—sails away to inhabit a narrative limbo, dead to her child, living with a husband happily unaware of her shameful secret. Happiness in *Pamela* seems to be predicated on secrecy, on deceit, on a providential rewriting that allows the seducer the pleasant exercise of pitying his victim, in a fatuous display of his "generous Mind" (p. 399).[24] Readers troubled by the ethical and political implications of accepting Richardson's "auspicious" solution of the Sally Godfrey story cannot share that happiness.

24 As William Blake notes in "The Human Abstract" (lines 1–4), such acts of generosity are often screens for oppression: "Pity would be no more / If we did not make somebody Poor; / And Mercy no more could be / If all were as happy as we." *Complete Writings*, ed. Geoffrey Keynes (Oxford: Oxford University Press, 1974), p. 217.

Enclosing the Immovable: Structuring Social Authority in *Pamela* 2

Betty A. Schellenberg

I n *The Sense of an Ending* Frank Kermode dismisses as "simple fictions" those which do not speak of "dissonance, the word set
against the word"; opposite these he sets narratives which "continue
to interest us" because they "move through time to an end," because
"they live in change, until, which is never, *as* and *is* are one." Realistic
fictions, in other words, portray the aspiring individual in inevitable
and sustained tension with his or her social environment. Where the
eighteenth century is concerned, *Pamela, Clarissa,* and even *Tom Jones*
should "continue to interest us," while the *Pamela* sequel, *Sir Charles
Grandison,* and *Amelia* can simply "go on to the dump with the other
empty bottles" after the opium of their harmonious social circle has
been consumed.[1] Richardson's sequel to *Pamela* has provided an easy

---

1 Frank Kermode, *The Sense of an Ending: Studies in the Theory of Fiction* (London: Oxford University Press, 1966), p. 179. Ian Watt's *The Rise of the Novel: Studies in Defoe, Richardson and
Fielding* (London: Chatto and Windus, 1957) has of course been very influential in associating the origins of the novel with individualistic and teleological concepts of the self in
eighteenth-century England. While I believe that the resulting genealogy has limited our
critical understanding of early fictions that resist the forces of change by portraying alternative social models, these conservative fictions ultimately confirm Watt's study in its
identification of the individual-in-society issue as central to the eighteenth-century novel.

target for neat summaries such as that of T.C. Duncan Eaves and Ben D. Kimpel: "the great fault of the continuation of *Pamela* is that there was nothing which could happen in it, and the best excuse that can be offered for it is that Richardson was evidently forced to write it, without any urge from inside."[2]

In her examination of the sequel, Terry Castle discusses the novel's masquerade sequence as a "capsule of narrative delight in a narrative of few delights," a happy accident resulting from the coincidence of Richardson's and his reader's repressed desires for a repetition of part 1's subversive, disorderly plot. Reading part 1 as a narrative of carnivalesque desire fulfilled and part 2 as imaginatively successful only inasmuch as it repeats part 1's "sheer transgressive energy," Castle applies to the novel a Bakhtinian version of the assumption that the essence of the genre is found in the individual radically subverting socially acceptable codes and discourses. She focuses upon the masquerade as "an indispensable plot-catalyst"; by its means "the novel, above all other genres, registered most symptomatically the paradoxical carnivalization of eighteenth-century society."[3]

Early British prose fiction, however, includes a significant number of texts which deliberately attempt to create a sociable, consensual, static structure for the "new species of writing."[4] In *Political Constructions: Defoe, Richardson, and Sterne in Relation to Hobbes, Hume, and Burke*, Carol Kay argues that to view the early eighteenth century as post-revolutionary is to perceive "social stability not as a given, but as a goal, ardently pursued and arduously maintained, by authors

---

In Samuel Richardson's *Pamela* 2 and *Sir Charles Grandison* and in Henry Fielding's *Amelia* the dynamics of successful author, established audience, and preceding text combine to reinscribe the protagonist within a stable social circle modelled on the intimate conversational group. I have discussed such socially conservative fictions at greater length in *The Conversational Circle: Rereading the English Novel, 1740–1775* (Lexington: University Press of Kentucky, 1996). "Enclosing the Immovable: Structuring Social Authority in *Pamela* 2" was first published in *Eighteenth-Century Fiction* 4:1 (1991), 27–42.

2 T.C. Duncan Eaves and Ben D. Kimpel, *Samuel Richardson: A Biography* (Oxford: Clarendon Press, 1971), p. 149.

3 Terry Castle, *Masquerade and Civilization: The Carnivalesque in Eighteenth-Century English Culture and Fiction* (Stanford: Stanford University Press, 1986), pp. 132, 134, viii–ix.

4 Richardson to Aaron Hill, *Selected Letters of Samuel Richardson*, ed. John Carroll (Oxford: Clarendon Press, 1964), p. 41.

as well as by other authorities." She sees the status and authority conferred upon an author through literary recognition represented in "the rise in status and authority of central characters from first novel to second novel." Richardson's work in general, she suggests, reflects his hope of "social reconciliation and unification ... invested in the authority of moral discourse."[5] While Kay focuses on Clarissa as Richardson's response to Pamela's popular success, I contend that part 2 of Pamela more expressly formalizes an exemplary model of social authority as an alternative to the fictional structure patterned upon opposition between the individual and the group.

The ostensible failures of Pamela 2 can be reread in terms of the sequel's own claim to bring words into congruence, to make as and is one, through strategies that deflect conflict and draw the unidirectional line of individualistic desire into a static social circle. As a result, the ultimately conservative project of its precursor is made formally explicit.[6] Richardson's at least partial success in stabilizing Pamela's comic plot is precisely what intrigues me in the sequel. As Terry Eagleton reminds us, the fact that we may not be sympathetic to the ideological values served by Richardson's forms does not in itself justify dismissing these forms on aesthetic grounds.[7] I will show that the text attempts formally to resolve tensions its author has most often been seen to avoid or mismanage. This purportedly plotless, directionless work carefully centralizes authority in the figure of Pamela and controls the forces of individualistic desire by drawing the other characters into an admiring and imitative orbit around

5 Carol Kay, Political Constructions: Defoe, Richardson, and Sterne in Relation to Hobbes, Hume, and Burke (Ithaca: Cornell University Press, 1988), pp. 23, 8, 127.

6 See Robert Allan Donovan, The Shaping Vision: Imagination in the English Novel from Defoe to Dickens (Ithaca: Cornell University Press, 1966), pp. 54–55. See also Margaret Anne Doody, A Natural Passion: A Study of the Novels of Samuel Richardson (Oxford: Clarendon Press, 1974), pp. 67–81; Robert Folkenflik, "A Room of Pamela's Own," ELH 39 (1972), 595; and Morris Golden, Richardson's Characters (Ann Arbor: University of Michigan Press, 1963), p. 144.

7 Terry Eagleton, The Rape of Clarissa: Writing, Sexuality and Class Struggle in Samuel Richardson (Oxford: Basil Blackwell, 1982), p. 36.

her. Potentially disruptive social energies and their stylistic manifestations are either concentred according to the terms of Pamela's discourse or deflected and excluded from her circle.

Richardson's retrospective comment that *Pamela* includes the portrayal of a "Libertine ... perfectly reclaimed" by his wife[8] indicates that, in his mind, the two parts of the work comprise a coherent movement, a movement of return to personal integrity achieved through correct alignment with fundamental social and moral values. Pamela's rather glib opening affirmation in part 1 that "God will not let me want"[9] is severely tried by Mr B.'s initial reluctance to recognize and acquiesce in his role in the scheme. The heroine's initial statements of faith in an economy of the individual life divinely ordered within a defined social structure are ultimately confirmed by experience, but only after this pattern—a conflict with only one possible victor—has been radically reformulated according to an ideal of moral and social, female and male, personal and communal consensus. Pamela's oft-repeated hymn to "the wonderful ways of Providence" underlines the mysterious and superior nature of this revised pattern, visible only when the prospect of her marriage elevates her above the usually limited perspective of "us poor short-sighted Mortals" (p. 261). Pamela's exemplary response to her marriage, the hope that she has thereby been made "an humble Instrument in the Hand of Providence to communicate great Good to others" (3:110), determines the sequel within the same divinely ordered economy.

Writing within the bounds of an idealized marriage calls for a structuring of narrative upon a model other than one of conflict, aspiration, and self-exploration. Whereas in part 1 Pamela, defending female honour and the value of the low-born soul as equal to that of a high-born man, inevitably appears radically to oppose a social structure which does not reflect that equality, the heroine of part 2, as a wife, becomes the centre of moral authority and interpretation within the social structure. In the sequel social realities must be

---

8 Samuel Richardson, *The History of Sir Charles Grandison*, ed. Jocelyn Harris (Oxford: Oxford University Press, 1986), preface, p. 3.

9 Samuel Richardson, *Pamela or, Virtue Rewarded*, ed. T.C. Duncan Eaves and Ben D. Kimpel (Boston: Houghton Mifflin, 1971), p. 26. References are to this edition. References to *Pamela* 2 are to the Shakespeare Head edition (Oxford: Basil Blackwell, 1929), vols 3 and 4.

acknowledged and the great conflict between the encroaching and the defending sexes must be deflected or channelled if the direst consequences to personal happiness are to be avoided. Similarly, the moral and aesthetic authority of the virtuous female writer must be both empowered and contained by the domestic sphere. Thus the focus, in part 1, upon the defence of besieged virtue in precarious social limbo becomes, in the sequel, a careful placing of female behaviour within the boundaries describing its acceptable manifestations. The original's correspondingly reactive, breathless structure of counter-intrigue and breach-stopping gives way to a text radiating outwards in methodical alignment from a centre of disciplined self-regulation. "To perfect the Design" of *Pamela* is Richardson's goal, and as a result, "there cannot, *naturally*, be the room for Plots, Stratagem and Intrigue in the present Volumes as in the first."[10]

The first portion of the sequel maps out the domestic circle within which Pamela's wifely role will be played out, while using the members of that circle as an audience within the text to reflect and record the success of her performance. In one such sequence Pamela makes explicit the mirror-like nature of this dynamic, beginning with praise of herself for "an Understanding which comprehended every thing, and an Eye that penetrated into the very Bottom of Matters in a Moment," and continuing:

Judge how pleasing this was to my best Beloved, who found, in their kind Approbation, such a Justification of his own Conduct, as could not fail of being pleasing to him, especially as Lady *Davers* was one of the kind Praisers.

Lord *Davers* was so highly delighted, that he rose once, begging his Brother's Excuse, to salute me, and remained standing over my Chair, with a pleasure in his Looks that cannot be expressed, now-and-then lifting up his Hands, and his good-natured Eye glistening with Joy, which a Pier-glass gave me the Opportunity of seeing, as sometimes I stole a bashful Glance towards it, not knowing how or which way to look. (3:244–45)

Within this tightly reflexive circle Pamela gradually loses all her lower-class uncertainties and youthful idiosyncrasies to become, finally, "Virtue itself" (4:196).[11] The story of Pamela, star of the divine

10 Richardson to Ralph Allen and Stephen Duck, *Selected Letters*, pp. 51, 53.

11 Elizabeth Deeds Ermarth, *Realism and Consensus in the English Novel* (Princeton: Princeton University Press, 1983), pp. 140–42.

social comedy, concludes in a fixed present tense with her thinly disguised autobiography of the allegorical Prudentia, who "shines, to her last Hour, in all the Duties of domestic Life, as an excellent Wife, Mother, Mistress, Friend, and Christian; and so confirms all the Expectations of which her Maiden Life had given such strong, and such edifying Presages" (4:452). In other words, Pamela's destiny as wife is figured not in terms of progress towards a defined if unattainable happiness, but in terms of an ever-increasing atemporality and typology as the centre of a stabilized circle, the still point gradually aligning a spinning social world around its morally fixed self.

Pamela's master acts as her primary reader in part 1; a growing, while resolutely domestic, circle of admirers focuses all attention on her in part 2. Pamela becomes, according to Lady Davers, "a Means of saving half a hundred Souls" (4:386); when her fame reaches overseas, the former Sally Godfrey credits her with ensuring "the Good of Thousands" (4:274). This audience, however, not only responds to her, but also, mediating for Providence, assigns the roles which Pamela will perform, thus absolving her of the charge of self-aggrandizement. In elaborate and ceremonial exchanges Mr B. and others plead with Pamela to speak to such issues as the awarding of titles and church livings, overruling her demure disclaimers and then responding to her words with grateful tears or ecstatic praise later reinforced by the accolades of correspondents. This increasingly broad social authority is carefully channelled through her husband, who proclaims, "Whenever I put Power into your Hands for the future, act but as you have now done, and it will be impossible, that I should have any Choice or Will but Yours" (3:299). Kay has described this "Humean realization of mutual satisfaction in limiting the full play of power" as "the necessary precondition" of the B.s' "marriage bargain."[12]

Pamela's willing acceptance of limitations to her power is most fully illustrated by the explicit use of a feminist subtext as an adaptive rather than a subversive strategy. Her running commentary on

12 Kay, p. 152.

Mr B.'s curtain-lecture in part 1 is expanded into a conversational exchange between women, of whom the principals are the heroine, Lady Davers, and Polly Darnford. This exchange claims for itself such privileges as the discussion of strategies for circumventing Mr B.'s "haughty way of speaking of our Sex" (3:71) and the sharing of specifically female experiences as matters "upon which our Sex may write to one another; but ... Gentlemen should not desire to see" (3:420). Because the contexts of these statements uphold humility and extreme delicacy as the only appropriate strategies for maintaining a circumscribed form of female power, however, the function of this dialogue is to encourage mutual acquiescence in the realities of patriarchy. Indeed, Pamela's educational counsels include the maxim, "In your *Maiden State*, think yourself *above* the Gentlemen, and they'll think you so too, and address you with Reverence and Respect. ... In your *marry'd State*, which is a kind of State of Humiliation for a Lady, you must think yourself subordinate to your Husband; for so it has pleased GOD to make the Wife" (4:447). Since Pamela's roles are assigned by the dual authorities of Providence and her husband, her role-playing is not theatrical in a deceptive and therefore transgressive sense, as Castle would have it; rather it proves her essential fitness for her destined part.[13] Desireless, prescribed, and yet perfectly consistent with her essential self, Pamela's role-playing provides an exemplary contrast to the masquerade, where "many Ladies ... are so very free, that the Censorious will be apt to blame the whole Sex for *their* Conduct, and to say, their Hearts are as faulty as those of the most culpable Men, since they scruple not to shew as much, when they think they cannot be known by their Faces" (4:99).

As Pamela's roles change with her marriage, it is not surprising that her attributes—humility, honour, duty, and pride—alter their manifestation. In part 1 the harassed servant-girl can describe her master's behaviour as "poor and mean" (p. 36), yet in part 2, as his proper bride, she carefully attributes her "only Glory and Merit"

---

13 Castle, pp. 143–44. See also Cynthia Griffin Wolff, *Samuel Richardson and the Eighteenth-Century Puritan Character* (Hamden, Conn.: Shoe String Press, 1972), pp. 47–48; and Patricia Meyer Spacks, *Imagining a Self: Autobiography and Novel in Eighteenth-Century England* (Cambridge: Harvard University Press, 1976), pp. 209, 218.

to having "had the Grace to withstand the greatest of Trials and Temptations, from a Gentleman more worthy to be beloved both for Person and Mind, than any Man in *England*" (3:232). Similarly, she cannot directly prefer her low-born relations, although she herself has been raised socially by her marriage, because "in the World's Eye ... I must, if I have ever so much Reluctance to [refuse such preferment], appear in a Light that may not give Discredit to his Choice" (3:22). Still later, as an upper-class matron describing the ideal marriage choice for gentlemen, Pamela censures marriage alliances like her own: "I don't mean, that they should all take raw, uncouth, unbred, lowly Girls, as I was, from the Cottage, and, destroying all Distinction, make such their Wives" (4:363). Far from intending that his reader forget the apparent contradiction, Richardson emphasizes it with the phrase "as I was." Together with frequent reviews of her "poor Papers" (3:32), the heroine's memory is thus used to link the sequel with its precursor and to insist upon the continuity of past and present.[14] When Pamela deliberately chooses "to make the best of those natural Defects I cannot master" (4:39), her self-consciousness is more than coyness or canny social instinct. Rather, it is a stylistic embodiment of the unique moral uniformity extending through Pamela's lowly past to her exalted present, a uniformity which contributes to the authority of Pamela and her pronouncements and which by contrast is sadly lacking in the case of the fallen Sally Godfrey who must now live in disguise as Mrs Wrightson.

Within the fixed social structure of part 2, movement is supplied by Mr B.'s spiritual progress, which contrasts with Pamela's unchanging moral status as an instrument of Providence. Pamela retrospectively sums this up in the hope "that one Day, my dear Mr *B*. who from a licentious Gentleman, became a Moralist, would be so touched by the Divine Grace, as to become in time, more than a moral, a *Religious* Gentleman." It is Providence that has again "turn'd that Affair, which once made [her] so uneasy" (4:374), directing a passive Pamela into her position of power as the upholder of social structures based on moral authority. Like the wedding of part 1, as the

---

14 My argument diverges here not only from Castle's reading but also from Ermarth's view of Pamela's memory as merely repetitive without any sense of continuity, and therefore without any capacity for change and growth (pp. 100–104).

day upon which Pamela begins a new calendar counting the "days of her happiness," Mr B.'s spiritual arrival effectively resolves all tension in Pamela's marriage and in Richardson's narrative. It is Pamela's moral "Uniformity" (4:202) in the face of her threatened marriage which is finally and permanently rewarded by Mr B.'s conversion from confidence in his own gentlemanly honour to "RELIGIOUS CONSIDERATIONS," in which Pamela as his guide mingles "the rising Flame" of his devotion "with [her] own" (4:378). Pamela's rhetoric underlines this moment in which "as" and "is" promise to become one: "this *heavenly* Prospect ... added to all my *earthly* Blessings! ... that my dear Mr *B*. is, and will be mine, and I his ... to all Eternity" (4:379).

In *Pamela* 1's "world devoid of neutrality,"[15] final congruence is preceded by a long series of confrontations between Pamela and a sequence of antagonists, increasing her moral and social isolation until the narrative is resolved in favour of the heroine and the values she embodies. In part 2, the unremitting tension of this binary structure is diffused through a homogeneous and expanded social sphere. Pamela is buttressed, in the party of the good, by a large group of like-minded admirers, who reinforce and universalize her values. This social amoeba continually absorbs its opposition, as Mrs Jewkes joins Mrs Jervis, Sir Jacob Swynford follows Lady Davers, and the bold Nun echoes the Countess of C. in praising the "uniform and immovable" domestic virtues (3:207). Indeed, even the masquerade, with its "gaudy prospects" of unregulated desire (4:195), is invaded and interpreted by the emblem of ideal domesticity in the form of Pamela as pregnant Quaker.[16]

Part 2 is constructed according to the predominant clockwork image of a family, in which Pamela is "the Master-wheel, in some beautiful Piece of Mechanism, whose dignify'd grave Motion is to set a-going all the Under-wheels, with a Velocity suitable to their respective Parts" (3:41). Her acts of charity have been regularized into

15 Spacks, p. 210.

16 Castle, on the other hand, interprets this emblem as "the visual embodiment of carnival confusion" (p. 131).

a "*Benevolent Weekly Round*" (3:355), while spiritual and social impulses are perfectly co-ordinated in her "Heaven of a House," so that
"wound up thus constantly once a Week [by Sunday prayers], like a
good Eight-day Clock, no Piece of Machinery that ever was made,
is so regular and uniform, as this Family is" (4:53).[17] Part 1 established the paradox of married time as "a rapturous Circle," both a
timeless repetition of events unfolding "in the same agreeable manner" and an ascending spiral in which "every Hour bring[s] with it
something more delightful than the past!" (p. 306).[18] Restating the
paradox as an equation, Mr B. assures Pamela at the beginning of
the sequel, "How greatly do the innocent Pleasures I now hourly
taste, exceed the guilty Tumults that used formerly to agitate my
unequal mind!— ... One such Hour as I now enjoy, is an ample Reward for all the Benefits I can confer on you and yours in my whole
Life!" (3:2–3). As the chaotic motions of desire are stilled, time—as
a succession of uncontrollable and discontinuous fragments—is defeated by the purposeful subject; one hour of married uniformity is
therefore worth a fortune.

As Richardson's centre of virtue and his standard of reference
in this harmonious domestic construct, Pamela can allow no compromise of established moral principles, and so Mr B. must take on
fully the values of his beloved. When in part 1 he admits that his attempted seduction has failed, he maintains a façade of control by
demanding her papers so as to be "better directed in what manner to wind up the Catastrophe of the pretty Novel" (p. 201). In
part 2, Pamela more bluntly describes his complete resignation of
the prerogative of plot: "when he could not have me upon his own
Terms, God turn'd his evil Purposes to good ones, and he resolved
to submit to mine" (3:84). Such acts of dominance and submission, however, are frequently represented as a discovery of common
terms, as a realignment that undermines the very structure of conflict. Thus when Mr B. tells his version of the story, Pamela's definition of honour turns out to have been his all along: "Yet my Love was

---

17 See Terry Castle, "The Female Thermometer," *Representations* 17 (1987), 20, and Ian Donaldson, "The Clockwork Novel: Three Notes on an Eighteenth-Century Analogy," *Review of
English Studies* n.s. 21 (1970), 14–15.

18 See Ermarth, pp. 96–97.

a Traitor to me: That was more faithful to *her* than to *me*; it had more Honour in it at Bottom, than I had designed" (3:207).

Other textual strategies in the sequel operate to deflect and minimize conflict. Much of the first portion of the sequel reduces long-term tension while introducing mock disagreements to provide immediate momentum. Mr B. pretends to be angry with Pamela only to endorse and enlarge upon her course of action. Her response to his anger reveals that she is one of those "infatuating Creatures" who, "instead of *scornful* Looks darted in Return for *angry* ones, Words of *Defiance* for Words of *Peevishness*, persisting to defend *one* Error by *another*, and returning *vehement Wrath* for *slight Indignation*, and all the hostile Provocations of the Marriage Warfare; ... can thus hide their dear Faces in our Bosoms, and wish but to *know* their Faults, to *amend* them!" (3:133). In fact, the logic of the B.s' marriage allows him to claim that even their disagreements contribute to the mutual good: "Whatever redounds to the credit of my *Pamela*, redounds in Part to my own; and so I have the less Regret to accuse myself, since it exalts her" (3:211).

These contrived tensions, then, develop the only mode of conflict which Richardson can safely allow into the ideal marriage plot: the conflict of misunderstanding, heightened by the sensible female imagination.[19] The insertion into this idyll of the visit to London, with its masquerade episode, provides an opportunity not only to test the sequel's conjugal ideal, but also to illustrate how discord plays itself out in this new context, where the old patterns of opposition are both inappropriate and potentially fatal to the future happiness of both Pamela and Mr B. Richardson thus transforms his original plot by placing it within a new frame, and in so doing demonstrates that its moral logic—virtue that holds steady under trial will be rewarded by the production of good from apparent evil, and by a felicity figured as a rapturous stasis—holds true even within the restricted confines of a wife's experience. Pamela's sense of a moral crisis brought on by Mr B.'s alienated affections and his affair with the Dowager Countess is genuinely felt, and is to be shared by the

19 Mark Kinkead-Weekes, *Samuel Richardson, Dramatic Novelist* (London: Methuen, 1973), reads the role of Pamela's imagination here as a "reinforcement of the original pattern of her fallibility" (p. 82).

reader. But even before she confronts her husband in a mock version of that most conflictual of social encounters, a trial, the reader has been signalled, through the tone and content of Mr B.'s bewildered "What *means* the dear Creature! What *means* my *Pamela!*—Surely your Head, Child, is a little affected!" (4:172), that Pamela's interpretations have been heightened by her post-partum sensibilities. This defusing of oppositional tension continues through to the trial itself, where the debate is as much one of Pamela's and Mr B.'s each insisting that she or he play accused to the other's judge, as it is one of proving Pamela's innocence and Mr B.'s culpability.

Well before this point, however, the reader has been prepared for the fact that the London sojourn will bring a test of this marriage. The orderly regulation of Pamela's rural domestic circle is implicitly contrasted to the disorderly, "over-grown Capital" with its "vast Circumference" and "public Diversions" (4:4). Pamela's repeatedly stated fears invite a view of this test as a case of Mr B.'s straying out of Pamela's orbit; in one instance, she confides: "if I can but find him not deviate, when we go to *London*, I shall have great Hopes, that nothing will affect his Morals again" (3:212).[20] When Mr B. raises "the sleeping Dragon ... *Prerogative* by Name" (3:416) in the argument over the pregnant Pamela's wish to breastfeed her baby, Richardson also indicates that the individualistic masculine will as it opposes itself even to divine authority will be the arena of conflict. While Pamela acquiesces in this matter, her account of the debate establishes clearly the principle that divinely instituted moral imperatives must supersede the authority of a husband.

When Pamela believes that her husband is embarking upon an extramarital relationship amounting to polygamy, she sees herself under just such an imperative to refuse any part in the arrangement. Her authoritative management of the mock-trial scene is therefore allowable, despite the normal limitations of wifely behaviour and despite her heightened female imagination, according to the logic of Pamela's authority in this text: it is explicitly founded both

20 Castle's description of London as a place of "confusion" and "multiformity" is helpful (*Masquerade and Civilization*, p. 154); her discussion of the move to the city as abrupt and without any narrative logic (p. 153) is puzzling, however, in light of the text's repeated hints associating Mr B.'s potential for relapse with his forthcoming exposure to the temptations of London.

upon her social responsibility—"the Character I ought to assume as his Wife"—and upon her moral duty—"to be an humble Means of saving the Man I love and honour, from Errors that might be fatal to his Soul" (4:182–83). As a social role-player whose fitness and prudence have been demonstrated, Pamela's admittedly dramatic behaviour (Lady Davers worries that her "Intellect" has been threatened [4:206], and Pamela feels the need to reassure Mr B. that the "future Conduct" of his "dutiful *Pamela*" "shall [not] be different from what it used to be") is nevertheless evaluated by Mr B. as having had "an Uniformity in it, that is surprisingly just" (4:202).

Castle notes that the affair again raises the suggestion that a high-born wife would have been more suitable for Mr B., and that it is this suggestion which Pamela emphasizes as the primary charge against herself in the trial scene.[21] The real significance of this recurrence, however, is revealed in Pamela's mode of defence. She skilfully turns an acknowledgment of her inferior social origins into an argument that she is superior to the Countess in her moral qualifications, because her love for Mr B. extends beyond his physical attractions to the good of his soul. These are the qualifications which Mr B. himself has equated repeatedly with his social ones, and when Pamela is soon after threatened with the loss of her own physical beauty through smallpox, her husband makes explicit the heightened moral attraction he feels after the London episode: "The last Uneasiness between us, I now begin to think, was necessary, because it has turned all my Delight in you, more than ever, to the Perfections of your Mind" (4:238). The double sense of "last" here is telling; because "the word set against the word," in Kermode's formulation, leaves open the possibility of future change, of renewed conflict, not only Mr B. but also the apparently free-living Countess must be seen to affirm Pamela's values, if not her self-discipline. Thus Pamela formulates the definitive resolution of the affair as an effect of congruence: "I have no Doubt in [Mr B.'s] Honour, and kind Assurances, and hope my next will be a joyful Letter; and that I shall inform you in it, that the Affair which went so near my Heart, is absolutely concluded to my Satisfaction, to Mr *B.*'s, and to the *Countess*'s; for if it be so to all

21 Castle, *Masquerade and Civilization*, pp. 167–68.

Three, my Happiness, I doubt not, will be founded on a permanent Basis" (4:234).

As conflict becomes consensus, part 1's sequential presentation of intensely personal experiences gives way to a static, concentric structure fundamental to socializing the narrative of individual success. Richardson's ideal social and literary structure is modelled on the moral perfection and stasis of heaven. As part of a process events thus become transforming moments which ultimately render death almost superfluous. Most spectacularly, in the mock-trial scene Mr B. undergoes his judgment on earth. Pamela responds to the outcome of this scene as if transposed into a higher, spiritual realm, writing to Lady Davers of "a Thankfulness so exalted, that it left me all light and pleasant, as if I had shook off Body, and trod in Air," and of a husband "in all Probability, mine upon better and surer Terms than ever" (4:198). Mr B.'s ultimate conversion not only seals the moral and social terms of the marriage, but also brings the flavour of eternity into the present, so that Pamela feels herself "already ... ceasing to be mortal" (4:379).

Although the affair's outcome is satisfactory to all three parties, it also fully meets Pamela's terms, reminding us that the heroine remains the centre to which orthodoxy or deviation is referred. The text's repeated movement from divergent perspectives to concurrence with Pamela's vision underlines Richardson's insistence that all lives are essentially and ideally based upon the same plot, and that apparent variations arise only from differing degrees of submission to the providential pattern. Unlike the protracted struggle in part 1 between supporters of Pamela and those of her master, correct moral and social alignments in the sequel are effected at will and almost invariably; Pamela assures her children that "good Masters seldom fail to make good Gentlemen; and good Misses, good Ladies; and GOD blesses them with as good Children as they were to *their* Parents; and so the Blessing goes round!" (4:440). Those aligned with Pamela's ideal figure find themselves, like Lord and Lady Davers, greatly improved in "Conversation" and "Temper" (4:386).

By making Pamela's nature normative rather than normal, however, the author not only shields her social mobility from would-be imitators, but also effectively distances her from all other characters. With all attention focused upon her raised figure, and all desires channelled into emulation, an inward and upward impetus creates a balanced concentric structure which allows almost no escape from its centripetal pull. Significantly, the fallen Sally Godfrey, whose story is a reverse image of Pamela's, writes from "an awful Distance" (4:271) that geographically illustrates her exclusion from the exemplary inner circle, though not from the penitential outer one. The "naughty" characters, whose lot is "*of course*, unhappy" (4:450), remain almost out of sight in this narrative; at best they are glimpsed as their egocentric courses carry them momentarily through Pamela's stable system. Among such characters are the country rakes and the town lawyers, Mr B.'s friends from before his marriage; the only rake who is represented as repeatedly resisting Pamela's influence is Jackey, one of those "Coxcombs" whose "Delights are centred in himself," and who "will not wish to get out of that narrow, that exceedingly narrow Circle" (4:263). Jackey actively excludes himself from the B. circle, choosing rather the disorder of London, where he is made predictably miserable. Other acts of exclusion are suggested through stylistic negations and narrative dismissal.[22] Good children, for example, are "never rude, nor noisy, nor mischievous, nor quarrelsome" (4:439). For the "naughty" (that is, undutiful) sons and daughter of Pamela's nursery tale, divine punishment and their definitive expulsions from the social structure come when seafaring leads to drowning, thieving to hanging, unemployment to exile, and sloth to fatal illness.

After Pamela's London triumph and the family's retirement to the country, imagery of stasis and circularity reinforces the stability of Pamela's clockwork domesticity. The family machinery becomes, if possible, ever more "uniform and methodical," so that Pamela finally has nothing to report but "the same things ... with little Variation, occurring this Year, ... that fell out the last" (4:372). Narrative is frozen into the tableau of the heroine "seated, surrounded with the Joy and

---

22 Peter Sabor, "Richardson and His Readers," *Humanities Association Review* 30 (1979), 162–63.

the Hope of my future Prospects, as well as my present Comforts"
(4:438); present and future are conflated as Pamela's world becomes
perfectly congruent with her values and desires.

As her present becomes a heaven on earth, Pamela's past is treated as
a finished text, detachable from its context as common currency, and
circulated as a mnemonic device to remind others of the heroine's
social and moral fitness. For the onlookers at church, her "Story"
and Mr B.'s "Tenderness to me" are the source of her attraction as
a unique social phenomenon (3:229). For young ladies, her "Story
and ... Example" are the basis for her authority to advise them about
courtship (4:402). Indeed, as Prudentia, Pamela herself becomes an
attribute, fixed in an eternal present tense and passed as a completed plot from one beneficiary to another.

To illustrate the exemplary and universal nature of this life-as-
attribute, Richardson employs a topical and associative narrative logic, rather than the experiential and causal one of part 1. His stated
purpose, in the sequel's preface, of bringing "a multitude of important subjects ... within the compass which he was determined not to
exceed"[23] suggests a strategy of comprehensiveness within enclosure.
Although the text continues to be presented in letter form, these letters are addressed to an audience as varied as Lady Davers's circle,
Pamela's parents, and the Darnford family, and are consequently
rather more generalized than intimate in their mode of expression.
They frequently take the form either of a journal recording weekly
routine or of what Pamela calls "conversation-pieces."[24] In these, the
conversational exchange and gestures of a group of characters in
a domestic setting, in effect replacing the monologic voice of the
isolated letter-writer with a more sociable, leisurely, and digressive
vehicle, give Pamela access to such topics as preferment, correct
behaviour for spinsters and young town gentlemen, and relations

23 Samuel Richardson, *Pamela; or, Virtue Rewarded* (London, 1801; reprinted New York: Garland, 1974), 3:iv.

24 First introduced in the sequel, this term is even used enumeratively by Pamela (see 3:176,
213), suggesting Richardson's deliberate selection of the form as a structuring device.

between the sexes. The result is not heteroglossia, however, but an example of what Mikhail Bakhtin has called "a forensic and polemical discourse,"[25] positing the existence of an absolute and definable standard of social action applicable to all experience and available to certain knowledge.

Pamela's achievement of moral stasis for herself and her world is matched by her establishment of stylistic norms for those genres to which the domestic woman can extend her literary practice. As an alternative to public forms such as the theatre and the opera, she develops her conversation pieces into character sketches of "Persons ... whose Conduct may serve for Imitation or Warning" to young ladies and children (4:437). Despite the increasing formality of her language, which includes elaborately detailed images of Mr B.'s "sunny Sphere" and her own "paler and fainter Beaminess" (4:367), Pamela is frequently commended in the novel for the "Truth and Nature" of her writing, for the "artless Ease" through which "your Gratitude, your Prudence, your Integrity of Heart, your Humility shine so much in all your letters and thoughts" (3:52–53). Proper style, while it may be formal and conventional, must, by inference, be transparently congruent with an individual's identity and values. Transgressions against this principle of transparency are abundantly illustrated at the fateful masquerade, where the mismatch of conversation and appearance shocks and bewilders Pamela, who "had imagined," according to her ideal of role-playing, "that all that was tolerable in a Masquerade, was the acting up to the Character each Person assum'd" (4:94). Characters who recognize Pamela's moral standard must therefore adopt her linguistic one as well. The most remarkable instance of this equation is the transformation of Lady Davers's terms for Pamela from part 1's "Beggar-born" (p. 328) to "unexampled Prudence" (3:53), then to "My charming *Pamela*, my *more than Sister*" (3:238), and finally, in a prayer for Pamela's safety, to "an Example so necessary to us all" (4:105).

In addition to transparency and standardization, simplicity is a necessary component of virtuous language, achieved by the privileging of repetition over variation, whether in diction or imagery.

25 Mikhail Bakhtin, "Discourse in the Novel," *The Dialogic Imagination: Four Essays*, ed. Michael Holquist and trans. Caryl Emerson and Michael Holquist (Austin: University of Texas Press, 1981), p. 335.

The good-naughty system of inclusion and exclusion into which the narrative is repeatedly distilled justifies Aaron Hill's description of Richardson's style as one in which "redundance but conveys resemblance."[26] A stylistically redundant reflection of the perfect social circle is created by mirror-like passages such as the raptures of Pamela's parents, in which, according to her father, they

join Hand in Hand together, and I say to her, Blessed be God, and blessed be you, my Dear. And she, in the same Breath, Blessed be God, and you, my Love—For such a Daughter, says the one—For such a daughter, says the other.—And she has your own sweet Temper, cry I—And she has your own honest Heart, cries she. And so we go on, blessing God, and blessing you, and blessing your Spouse, and blessing ourselves! (3:149–50)

Similarly, Pamela is an "Angel" three times in almost as many lines of her parents' first letter, while images of raised spirits, shining stars, and high-tuned instruments prepare the reader for her apotheosis as Mr B.'s "tutelary Angel" (4:196). Repetition and reflexivity thus strengthen the centripetal impulse of the text.

The sequel would seem to end at the moment in which form overwhelms narrative, in which the individual Pamela has become perfectly transparent as the typological Prudentia and her story has fragmented itself into an anthology of exemplary narratives with lives of their own. In a sense, such a view supports the critical claim that a narrative without a unified plot and without a protagonist embodying individualistic desire is neither viable nor readable. Richardson's text, however, has gone literally to great lengths to arrive at unreadability in the complete frustration of the desire for subversive repetition. His sequel exhibits not repressed desire, but rather anxiety about the social and moral dangers of the new prose fiction. *Pamela* 2 draws itself into a structural, social, and linguistic circle as the most tightly controlled and least penetrable means of portraying an idealized social experience. The reader who is willing to be drawn, at least temporarily, into Pamela's circle will find a text that reveals

---

26 See *The Correspondence of Samuel Richardson*, ed. Anna Laetitia Barbauld, 6 vols (1804; New York: AMS Press, 1966), 1:100.

a great deal about mid-eighteenth-century strategies for modelling social authority through narrative.[27]

27 Among critics who have seen in *Clarissa* an explicit realization of anxiety about the legitimate ability of either social or narrative structures to contain individual desire, John Dussinger draws attention to a link between *Clarissa* and the earlier novel. He sees the marriage portion of *Pamela* as, for Mr B. and Pamela, an attempt at "imposing a static order upon their time-ridden nervousness" which can nevertheless not overcome social and epistemological anxieties. *The Discourse of the Mind in Eighteenth-Century Fiction* (The Hague: Mouton, 1974), p. 68. Dussinger's suspicion of this attempt is in part a result of his view of Pamela's power in marriage as "a miraculous abnegation of male, patriarchal, aristocratic authority" (p. 74), a view which underestimates the careful realignment of moral and social authority achieved in the sequel. I agree with Dussinger, however, that Richardson ultimately moves in *Grandison* towards a fraternal model of social authority; see "Love and Consanguinity in Richardson's Novels," *Studies in English Literature 1500–1900* 24 (1984), 521.

Protean Lovelace   Jocelyn Harris

W hen Clarissa calls Lovelace "a perfect Proteus," more variable
than the chameleon,[1] she points to him as a very icon of the
mutability that once meant man's paradoxical potential for creation
and destruction. To Erasmus, Vives, Pico della Mirandola, Ariosto,
Montaigne, Burton, Spenser, and Shakespeare, the shape-changing
sea-god Proteus was at once lawmaker and lawbreaker. As Spenser
says in the *Mutability Cantos*, men "their being doe dilate" by their
changes.[2] Civilization itself results from their restless aspirations to
learning and the creative arts. But when, like Proteus in his other
manifestations, men hide malignity behind a benvolent mask, creative art turns to illusion, verbal distortion, acting, deception, rape,
and chaos in civil society.[3] Lovelace, who parodies Richard III's most
famous line (3:421), might boast like him:

1 Samuel Richardson, *Clarissa. Or, The History of a Young Lady*, ed. Florian Stuber, 8 vols,
  The Clarissa Project (New York: AMS Press, 1990), 3:141–42. References are to this edition. Other Richardson references are to: *Pamela or, Virtue Rewarded*, ed. T.C. Duncan Eaves
  and Ben D. Kimpel, Riverside edition (Boston: Houghton Mifflin, 1971); *The History of Sir
  Charles Grandison*, ed. Jocelyn Harris, 3 vols (London: Oxford University Press, 1972, reprinted in one volume, 1986). "Protean Lovelace" was first published in *Eighteenth-Century
  Fiction* 2:4 (1990), 327–46.

2 *The Poetical Works of Edmund Spenser*, ed. J.C. Smith and E. de Selincourt (London: Oxford
  University Press, 1912, reprinted 1959), *Mutability Cantos*, 7.58.

3 See A. Bartlett Giamatti, "Proteus Unbound: Some Versions of the Sea God in the Renaissance," *The Disciplines of Criticism: Essays in Literary Theory, Interpretation, and History*, ed.
  Peter Demetz, Thomas Greene, and Lowry Nelson, Jr (New Haven and London: Yale University Press, 1968), pp. 437–75.

> I can add colours to the chameleon,
> Change shapes with Protheus for advantages,
> And set the murderous Machiavel to school.
> (*III Henry VI*, 3.2.191–93)

To identify the exuberant Lovelace, who is "so light, so vain, so various, that there is no certainty that he will be next hour what he is This" (3:158), with the sinister shape-changer Proteus and various of his avatars goes some way to explaining the powerfully ambivalent responses he gives rise to.

In his masterpiece, *Clarissa*, Richardson opposes the Protean flux of Lovelace to the fixity of Clarissa. To do so, he draws on two vigorously competing world-views of his time, Hobbism, which perceives a materialistic universe based on restlessness, power, corruption, and self-interest, and Christian Platonism, which assumes the universe to be spiritually informed. Hobbist attitudes lie behind everything that Lovelace is and does, whereas ideal visions of an immanent being, expressed on earth in the power of law, sustain his victim and antagonist, Clarissa. The philosophy of Hobbes was expressed most clearly for the age by that "perfect hobbist" John Wilmot, Earl of Rochester,[4] and details from Rochester's life, works, and reputation flesh out Richardson's emblem of mutability, Lovelace. Rochester-Lovelace merges with other Proteus figures to whom he is explicitly linked in the novel, Jupiter (1:237; 3:163), Faust (5:310), Shakespeare's Proteus, Richard III, Shadwell's Don Juan,[5] Satan, and Macheath. Their changing natures confirm that he is essentially a Proteus.

To Hobbes the Protean nature of man is self-evident. His philosophy of flux begins in Galileo's theories of motion, and his own notion of physiology. Man, he observes, is naturally restless, and out of his imperative motion comes desire, from desire power, from power

---

4 Antony à Wood, *Athenae oxoniensis* 3:229, cited by Dustin H. Griffin, *Satires against Man: The Poems of Rochester* (Berkeley: University of California Press, 1973), p. 15. At the end of his life Rochester was said to have repudiated the philosophy of Hobbes, although Griffin points out that Rochester was attended at the time by noted anti-Hobbists who would have been putting pressure on him (p. 15n28).

5 For Lovelace as Proteus and as Don Juan, see my "Richardson: Original or Learned Genius?" in *Samuel Richardson: Tercentenary Essays*, ed. Margaret Anne Doody and Peter Sabor (Cambridge: Cambridge University Press, 1989), pp. 188–202, and my *Samuel Richardson* (Cambridge: Cambridge University Press, 1987), pp. 68–69.

war, and from war the obliteration of absolutes and restraint. He concludes that the commonwealth requires a central controlling power, if it is not to collapse into anarchy.

In Hobbes's materialistic universe there are no souls, only bodies. Hobbist man is a mechanical apparatus consisting of sense organs, nerves, muscles, imagination, memory, and reason, responsive but also self-moving because of in-built appetites and aversions which maintain motion and prevent death.[6] "Life it selfe is but motion," says Hobbes (p. 32). He characteristically figures the life of man in the similitude of a race: "continually to be outgone is misery: continually to outgo the next before is felicity: and to forsake the course is to die."[7] "To have no Desire," he says, "is to be Dead: so to have weak Passions, is Dulnesse" (p. 139). Men, though, demand different degrees of power, riches, and honour, depending on their complexions, customs, and education (pp. 32–33).

All desire may be reduced to "Desire of Power. For Riches, Knowledge and Honour are but severall sorts of Power" (p. 139). "Power simply is no more, but the excess of the power of one above that of another."[8] Desire for power rapidly becomes harmful and invasive, especially as some men's desires are without limit: "I put for a generall inclination of all mankind, a perpetuall and restlesse desire of Power after power, that ceaseth onely in Death" (p. 161).

There are many kinds of power: "to have servants, is Power: To have friends, is Power: for they are strengths united." Eloquence also is power (pp. 150–51), but above all, kings provide prime examples of the lust to conquer (p. 161). So Lovelace too will find.

It follows in Hobbes's "Warre of every man against every man" that "nothing can be Unjust. The notions of Right and Wrong, Justice and Injustice have there no place. Where there is no common Power, there is no Law: where no Law, no Injustice. Force, and Fraud, are in warre the two Cardinall vertues. Justice, and Injustice ... are Qualities, that relate to Men in Society, not in Solitude" (p. 188). Good and

---

6 Thomas Hobbes, *Leviathan*, ed. C.B. MacPherson (Harmondsworth: Penguin Books, 1968, reprinted 1971), p. 28. References are to this edition.

7 Hobbes's *Human Nature*, in *Works* (4:52–53), cited in Basil Willey, *The Seventeenth Century Background* (Harmondsworth: Penguin Books, 1934, reprinted 1962), pp. 100–101.

8 Hobbes, *Elements of Law* (part 1, chap. 8, sec. 4, p. 26), cited in *Leviathan*, p. 35.

evil, says Hobbes, are merely relative "to the person that useth them" (p. 120). Nor is there any right to property, "no *Mine* and *Thine* distinct; but onely that to be every mans that he can get; and for so long, as he can keep it." In a state of nature "every man has a Right to every thing; even to one anothers body" (pp. 188–90).

All that matters in a state of nature is self-preservation, and a man is entitled to do anything he considers the aptest means for it. Consequently, "the condition of meer Nature, that is to say, of absolute Liberty ... is Anarchy, and the condition of Warre" (p. 395). Hobbes knew from experience that civil war meant "that dissolute condition of masterlesse men, without subjection to Lawes, and a coercive Power to tye their hands from rapine, and revenge" (p. 238).

War within a household brings insurrection—quite literally— home. The family provides "a little Monarchy ... wherein the Father or Master is Soveraign" (p. 257), with all that monarchy's potential for disaster, as Hobbes saw when he wrote, "some have attributed the Dominion to the Man onely, as being of the more excellent Sex; they misreckon in it. For there is not always that difference of strength or prudence between the man and the woman, as that the right can be determined without War" (p. 253). So Clarissa's family and suitors will find.

To prevent anarchy, Hobbes proposes the Social Contract, in which men give up the right to invade others if others would do the same. To be successful, such a contract requires the transfer of rights to some sovereign power (pp. 40–45). Every man has a property in his own person, and the sovereign's job is to provide the conditions in which each man can make the fullest use of it (p. 48). "Of things held in propriety, those that are dearest to a man are his own life, & limbs; and in the next degree, (in most men) those that concern conjugall affection; and after them riches and means of living." Even a king must be subject to such a law as this (pp. 382–85).

Hobbes, then, as an empirical follower of Bacon and Descartes, describes what he saw at a time of civil war: men's irresistible propensity to bloodiness, avariciousness, violence, and conquest. He speaks as a dispassionate observer of "the characters of man's heart, blotted and confounded as they are, with dissembling, lying, counterfeiting and erroneous doctrines" (p. 83), and calmly proposes his solution, a sovereign power.

Lovelace's restlessness marks him as Hobbist man.[9] He has always to be doing, and not just in his own person. He acts multiple parts, he multiplies his restlessness through agents whom he animates to impersonate yet other characters again. Ovid, he boasts, "was not a greater master of metamorphoses than thy friend" (3:50). Dissatisfied with one scene, he creates many, the reflections of his own divided mind. A whirling restless man, he seeks variety and change. He abandons each conquest as soon as it is done, and puts off consummation with Clarissa so that love will not end. He fears that marriage weakens passion and leads to dullness (3:281), for like Shakespeare's Troilus (3.2) he acknowledges that desire is boundless and the act a slave to limit. He prides himself on his superior desires on account of his finer fashioning and kinglike aspirations, and justifies all he does from these vaster and more Faustian needs. But when he loses Clarissa, the object of his desire, his life and very motion are at an end.

Lovelace inhabits a state of nature, which for Hobbes is a state of war. His liberty is actually licence, as he boasts when he says, "I, who think I have a right to break every man's head I pass by, if I like not his looks" (3:122). He enjoys absolute power, even over the body of Clarissa. Lovelace believes he has a right to it when he abducts her, locks her up, deceives, drugs, and rapes her. He asserts his right to invade and possess, and though he says he will be honest in most affairs, "had I been a *bad* man in *meum* and *tuum* matters, I should not have been fit to live. As to the girls, we hold it no sin to cheat them" (4:321). He declares war on Clarissa and her family, he calls himself General, Emperor, Grand Signor. Families, says Richardson in *Sir Charles Grandison*, are "little communities ... so many miniatures [of the great community]" (1:25). The domestic civil wars in *Clarissa* are played out in a vocabulary of tyranny and slavery, power and subjection. Clarissa is indeed the woman Hobbes foresaw, whose su-

9 In *Virtue in Distress: Studies in the Novel of Sentiment from Richardson to Sade* (London: Macmillan, 1974), R.F. Brissenden remarks that the dominating motive in the world as portrayed by Richardson is a Hobbist lust for power (pp. 172–73), while Margaret Anne Doody explains just how Hobbist Lovelace and the Harlowes are, and notes a connection with Rochesters's *Valentinian*. See *A Natural Passion: A Study of the Novels of Samuel Richardson* (Oxford: Clarendon Press, 1974), pp. 119, 123–24, 342, 344.

periority in prudence forces her into war with her family and her lovers.

Everything is relative, to Lovelace. He typically analyses words away. Rape he says is not rape but a yielding reluctance; friendship is not friendship when it is between women (4:358; 5:254). He can talk his way out of any charge, like the lawyers in Westminster-hall who prove black white (6:212). He justifies his deceits by pointing to his Hobbist, Jonsonian world of knaves and hypocrites, lawyers, clergymen, doctors, relatives, and their gulls. All things seem to him corrupted by self-interest and the desire for power. Assuming even Clarissa to be tainted by humanity, he accuses her of avarice, her family's besetting sin, for mourning the loss of her virginity.

If the sexual transgression of a Proteus leads to civil destruction as Giamatti says, a libertine like Lovelace proves the need for a social contract. In assuming the right to physical and sexual conquest, tyranny, violence, anarchy, and defiance of the law, Lovelace has shaped his life by Hobbes. But Mr B. had argued that the law is above kings and queens (*Pamela*, pp. 355–56), and Lovelace must also learn that he has no *droit de seigneur*, no kingly rights, over a bourgeois girl whose family he despises. "Sprung up from a dunghil," he says scornfully, within every elderly person's remembrance (1:231). As a self-appointed king, he asserts his royal immunity; as a noble male, he claims special sexual privileges over Female Cits. To Lovelace, as to Congreve in the epilogue of *The Double Dealer*, the daughters of merchants are rightful prey. But, like Wycherley's Pinchwife, he will be cuckolded when Clarissa takes Death for her lover.

Richardson could easily have read Hobbes's own words, for *Leviathan* was very often reprinted. But Hobbist ideas were also to be found in many other works that Richardson obviously knew and drew upon for *Clarissa*, for instance Gay's *The Beggar's Opera*. As John Bender points out, Macheath was at once hero and highwayman, husband and adulterer, hanged and reprieved, great man and scoundrel. He was another paradoxical Proteus, and Lovelace often resembled him.[10]

10 John Bender, *Imagining the Penitentiary: Fiction and the Architecture of Mind in Eighteenth-Century England* (Chicago and London: University of Chicago Press, 1987), p. 87. For Richardson's use of Gay and Hogarth, see my "Richardson: Original or Learned Genius?"

But the impact of Hobbes on Richardson was surely enlarged by John Wilmot, Earl of Rochester, a man already mythologized in elegies, recollections, and fictional representations in plays as well as by the multiple self-projections of his works. Dead at thirty-three, Rochester epitomized wit and wickedness to the age. He was a true Proteus, combining high art with restlessness, licence, and destruction.

It is clear that the life and works of Rochester inspired the creation of Lovelace, as Margaret Anne Doody argues and James Grantham Turner confirms.[11] What could Richardson have known of him? In his playgoing apprentice days, he could have learned about Rochester's play *Valentinian* and about Mrs Barry, Rochester's mistress, whom he trained as an actress. Samuel Johnson's remarkably sympathetic life of Rochester was not published until 1779, but this · close friend of Richardson must have known of Rochester earlier and even spoken of him. Rochester's demonic reputation was in fact countered by his deathbed repentance, and Gilbert Burnet's account of it may have made Rochester's story seem safe even to Charlotte Brontë. Though brutal and amoral like Rochester, Lovelace is rarely so obscene as he, except for the startingly suggestive comment that if he had held Clarissa's and Anna's letters in his hand, "the Seal would have yielded to the touch of my warm finger [Perhaps without the help of the Post-office Bullet]; and the folds, *as other plications have done,* opened of themselves, to oblige my curiosity" (6:310–11). One is reminded of that nasty "soft, obstetric hand" in *The Dunciad* (4:394).

Rochester's role-playing, disguises, pranks, contradictions, high-spirited wit, promiscuity, obscenity, oaths, violence, despair, and abduction of his future wife made him a legend and a type. One might speak of "the Rochester" as we speak of "the Machiavel." Astonishingly, though, Richardson appears to have grasped Rochester's Protean personality in all its complexity, and created a character as brilliant and as destructive as its original.

11 See *A Natural Passion,* pp. 373–74n1. Turner, in "Lovelace and the Paradoxes of Libertinism," in *Samuel Richardson: Tercentenary Essays* (pp. 70–88), ascribes Lovelace's philosophy more generally to "the *mélange* of Ovidian seduction-theory and Epicurean philosophy that Richardson found in the court wits of Charles II and the seducer-heroes of Restoration drama and early eighteenth-century fiction."

Gilbert Burnet, *Some Passages of the Life and Death of the Right Honourable John Earl of Rochester* (London, 1680), frontispiece. Reproduced by permission of McMaster University Library.

When Rochester questioned and undermined authority in the ways described by Griffin[12] and dramatized in Lovelace, he was undoubtedly a lawbreaker. And yet his satire, its ferocity born of despair, proves him the one honest man in a corrupt world, a lawgiver attempting to restore society to civility. His *Advertisement* for his mountebank persona Alexander Bendo displays not only his Protean capacity to manipulate language by dazzlingly brazen word-play but also his courage in attacking "this Bastard-Race of Quacks and Cheats," and beyond that, the corrupt world. "So you see the *Politician* is, and must be, a *Mountebank* in State Affairs, and the *Mountebank* ... is an arrant *Politician* in Physick," he writes.[13] Rochester managed his dark vision through gaiety and the company of his merry gang, and wrote of himself that even when "half in the grave," he could not "leave off playing the fool and the buffoon."[14] Melancholic and filled with ennui, he claimed to be lashing the world of knaves and whores for its own good. Whenever he does so, he anticipates Lovelace's satirical and self-justifying condemnation of the world he lives in.

The grace and charm of Rochester's compulsive mutability were often remarked upon.[15] His restlessness proved Hobbes's physiological theories, as it would give life to Lovelace; it exemplified what Pascal described as man's condition, "inconstance, ennui, unrest."[16] Rochester attacked constancy on principle, as Burnet reports: "The restraining a man from the use of women, except one in the way of marriage, and denying the remedy of divorce, he thought unreasonable impositions on the freedom of mankind."[17] In his "Dialogue between Strephon and Daphne," he wrote, on the analogy of the birds: "Since 'tis Nature's Law to Change, / Constancy alone is

12 Griffin, p. 305.

13 *The Collected Works of John Wilmot Earl of Rochester*, ed. John Hayward (London: Nonesuch Press, 1926), pp. 155–57. References are to this edition.

14 *The Letters of John Wilmot Earl of Rochester*, ed. Jeremy Treglown (Oxford: Basil Blackwell, 1980), p. 202. References are to this edition.

15 *Rochester: The Critical Heritage*, ed. David Farley-Hills (London: Routledge and Kegan Paul, 1972, *passim*.

16 Pierre Pascal, *Pensées*, trans. H.F. Stewart (New York, 1950), p. 31, cited by Griffin, p. 18.

17 Gilbert Burnet, *Some Passages in the Life and Death of John Earl of Rochester* (1680; Folcroft Library Edition, 1973, reprint of 1878 edition), p. 67. References are to this edition.

strange."[18] Lovelace makes the same assumption in his Valentine's Day scheme to change partners every year, like the birds. Rochester believes in a state of nature, and sees relationships as brutal and rapacious. He portrays courtship as hawks hunting for prey, as does Lovelace. Rochester turned for security to male friendship and the rakish life, and discovered only "pain and perplexity, insecurity, and enslavement to the vagaries of passion."[19] The same might be said of Lovelace, dependent on friends and his own image. His passion traps, defeats, and finally silences him.

Rochester's early death shocked those who had known him into setting their recollections down in print, so that details from his life were widely available. Gilbert Burnet's account of his deathbed repentance in *Some Passages in the Life and Death of John Earl of Rochester* (1680) was many times reprinted, as was the sermon preached at Rochester's funeral. For instance, the preface to *Valentinian* remarks on his "publick chiding of his servants, which would have been ill-breeding and intolerable in any other man, became not only civil and inoffensive, but agreable and entertaining in him." The same is true of Lovelace. Rochester, like Lovelace, set his servants into disguises, ordering one dressed as a soldier to stand outside ladies' lodgings, while he himself was a renowned mimic, disguising himself as "a porter, or as a beggar, sometimes to follow some mean amours, which, for the variety of them he affected" (Rochester, *Works*, p. xxxix). Just so Lovelace pursues a lowly Rosebud for the sake of change. At other times, "merely for diversion, [Rochester] would go about in odd shapes, in which he acted his part so naturally, that even those, who were in the secret, and saw him in these shapes, could perceive nothing by which he could be discovered" (*Life*, p. 32). His most celebrated escapade was to present himself as an old itinerant quack, by which he gained the confidence of women. In his most elaborate guising, and with scrupulous attention to detail, Lovelace also dresses himself as an old man to gain access to Clarissa at Hampstead. Like Rochester, he pretends to age and impotence in order to seduce

---

18 *The Poems of John Wilmot Earl of Rochester*, ed. Keith Walker (Oxford: Shakespeare Head Press, Basil Blackwell, 1984), p. 13, lines 31–32. References are to this edition.

19 Griffin, p. 20.

Rochester was "able to adapt himself to all capacities and hu-
mours," and could "make himself good company to all kind of
People at all times," but soon tired of their "cramming and endless
invitations" (*Works*, p. xxxix). So too Lovelace wins over the bourgeois Harlowes while secretly despising them and planning to seduce
their daughter.

Rochester was also familiar through other people's dramatic representations of him. George Etherege drew him as Dorimant in *The
Man of Mode* (1676), the most famous of all stage rakes. Dorimant
is witty, violent, high-handed, and inconstant; takes many mistresses
including a whore; swears oaths; and ridicules other people—just
as Lovelace does. He is "the Prince of all the Devils in the Town,
delights in nothing but in Rapes and Riots."[20] Dorimant quotes often from Waller, as Lovelace would. Mrs Loveit explains something
of Rochester's appeal when she says, "I know he is a Devil, but he
has something of the Angel yet undefac'd in him, which makes him
so charming and agreeable that I must love him be he never so
wicked" (2.2). She gestures here to traditional representations of
Proteus as half-demon and half-angel, to the fallen angel Satan, and
to the Satanic Lovelace who was to come.[21] Nathaniel Lee represented this doubleness by means of two characters in his *Princess of Cleve*
(1689), "the Spirit of Wit" Count Rosidore, and the darker Duke
of Nemours, both based on Rochester. The appeal of the fallen angel was Richardson's frequent subject: Anna at the ball admires a
man she knows has destroyed her friend, a rake in whom humane
and demonic qualities oddly mix, and even Sir Charles Grandison
is portrayed as a rake in his address and a saint in his heart (3:93).
Richardson cited Medea in Ovid's *Video meliora proboque; Deteriora se-
quor* in *Grandison* (2:138) to describe the terrible dilemma of a rake,
uncontrollably and endlessly metamorphosing between angel and
demon. Perhaps Burnet's citation of the tag reminded him of it (*Life*,
p. 41).

20 George Etherege, *The Man of Mode, or, Sir Fopling Flutter*, pp. 183–287, vol. 2, *The Dramatic Works of Sir George Etherege*, ed. H.F.B. Brett-Smith (Oxford: Basil Blackwell, 1927),
3.2. References are to this edition.

21 See my *Samuel Richardson*, esp. pp. 66–67.

Thomas Shadwell's violent and vicious play *The Libertine*, which has often been thought to be based on Rochester, is most obviously influential for Lovelace. First produced in 1675, it played frequently thereafter to packed houses. Here another Proteus figure, Don Juan, closely prefigures Lovelace's worst violence. Lovelace's rapes, his murderous Isle of Wight plot, and his anarchic Valentine's Day plan all share many significant details with Shadwell's play.[22]

Richardson also seems to have known and used Rochester's own poetry, as Doody argues, especially his recognition of man's wanton destruction beyond necessity, compared to the animals, in "A Satyr Against Mankind." He probably knew Rochester's letters as well, as we may deduce from the similarities between the styles of Lovelace's and Rochester's heroical epistles.[23] Like his own merry monarch, Rochester rolled about from whore to whore ("A Satyr on Charles II"), and boasted to have taken ten thousand maidenheads in "The Imperfect Enjoyment." Lovelace too takes maidenheads, and turns his victims into whores. Both complain of impotence.

Rochester's despairing lines, "Hudled in dirt, the reas'ning Engine lyes. / Who was so proud, so witty, and so wise" (*Poems*, p. 92), are closely echoed by Richardson's account of rakes dying miserably in attics (6:325–26). Rochester's understanding that "all Men would be *Cowards* if they durst" (*Poems*, p. 95) reflects his special pleasure in Falstaff (*Letters*, pp. 96, 193), and Lovelace too becomes a Falstaff at the end when he meets his friends at Gad's Hill and plays the buffoon (8:185–90). In "A very Heroicall Epistle in Answer to Ephelia," Rochester shows his egotism when he writes "In my dear self I center ev'ry thing," his variety when he argues "For 'tis Natural to change, as love," and his lust to power when he says:

> Oh happy Sultan! ...
> Who envies not the Joys of thy Seraill?
> Thee like some God, the trembling Crowd adore
> Each Man's thy Slave, and Woman-kind, thy Whore.
> (*Poems*, pp. 112–14)

22 See my *Samuel Richardson*, pp. 68–69.

23 For details, see *A Natural Passion*, pp. 373n1, 341. For the letters, see Doody's *The Daring Muse: Augustan Poetry Reconsidered* (Cambridge: Cambridge University Press, 1985), p. 271n5.

All these qualities appear in Lovelace, the "Grand Signor" (4:183). And finally, Lovelace's whole aim seems summed up in Rochester's "Sab: Lost":

> Shee yeilds, shee yeilds, Pale Envy said Amen
> The first of woemen to the Last of men.
> Just soe those frailer beings Angells fell
> Ther's noe mid way (it seemes) twix't heav'n and hell,
> Was it you end in making her, to show
> Things must bee rais'd soe high to fall soe low?
>
> (*Poems*, p. 26)

Clarissa seems to have been equally inspired by Rochester's play *Valentinian* (1685), which is based deliberately and significantly, like *Clarissa* itself,[24] on the story of Lucretia, the Roman matron raped by Tarquin simply because she was good. The play tells of the Emperor Valentinian's rape of Lucina, wife to Maximus, but Richardson's version radically departs from its models because Clarissa is single, rejected by her family, friendless, imprisoned, and alone. This makes her resistance more heroic still.

Valentinian boasts of kingly power, as Lovelace will:

> Have I not Praetors through the spacious Earth
> Who in my Name do mighty Nations sway?
> Enjoying rich Dominions in my Right;
> Their temporary Governments I change,
> Divide or take away, as I see good;
> Am I not Emperor? This World my own?
>
> (*Works*, p. 170)

Lovelace itemizes his powers in similar terms: "Preferments I bestow, both military and civil. I give Estates, and take them away at my pleasure. Quality too I create. And by a still more valuable prerogative, I *degrade* by virtue of my own imperial will ... What a poor thing is a monarch to me!" (4:43). But the enormous difference is that he deludes himself. All his powers are illusory.

Valentinian is devotedly served by the "Dull, faithful, humble, vigilant and brave" general Aecius (*Works*, p. 176) rather as Lovelace

---

24 See Ian Donaldson, *The Rapes of Lucretia: A Myth and Its Transformations* (Oxford: Clarendon Press, 1982).

is befriended by Belford, whom he despises. The emperor instructs his servants to deceive, as Lovelace will:

> To tempt, dissemble, promise, fawn and swear,
> To make Faith look like Folly use your Skill
> Virtue an ill-bred Crosseness in the Will,
> Fame, the loose Breathings of a Clamorous Crowd—
> Ever in Lies most confident and loud!
> Honour a Notion! Piety a cheat!
> And if you prove successful Bawds, be great.
>
> (*Works*, p. 172)

Lucina (meaning moon) is imaged forth like Clarissa (meaning full of light) by light and by cold. She is "Cold as Crystal / Never to be thaw'd," modest, "but chaster than cold Camphire," a "Cake of Ice" (*Works*, pp. 177–79), with vestal fire shooting from her eye—Lovelace mutters "something of *Ice*" (4:105) when he cannot win Clarissa, the vestal woman (4:203). Valentinian constantly characterizes his passion as fire—Clarissa's ice is also vulnerable to fire, Lovelace's literal and figurative weapon. Fire reflects Lovelace's passion and his own aspiring motion; fire flushes her out of her room, in a bold attempt to melt her resolve. Lucina describes Valentinian's pursuit as that of the spider and the fly: "all the Nets you have pitcht to catch my Virtue, / Like Spiders webs I sweep away before me" (*Works*, p. 183), and Lovelace uses the same image (3:63). Claudia, Lucina's woman, thinks the world "a dreadful Wilderness of Savage Beasts; / Each man I meet I fancy will devour me" (*Works*, p. 191). Clarissa and Anna Howe learn to view their world in the same way.

Like Lucretia, like Clarissa, Lucina attracts because "She is such a Pleasure, being good" (*Works*, p. 177). She resists temptation by jewels and by ambition, only pointing to a Lucrece that hangs by. Later, Valentinian orders a masque of the rape of Lucrece to be played, so that any woman's shrieks can be said to be part of the play. As with Lovelace, his play-acting forms part of his counterfeiting (*Works*, p. 205). In order to "possess her chaster and uncorrupted," this Tarquin of an emperor sets up his "Masterpiece" of a plot (*Works*, p. 188). Using women whom Lucina calls devils rather than women (*Works*, pp. 181–83), Valentinian lures her into the palace by a trick, as Lovelace would use his satanic crew of whores to lure Clarissa into the brothel. Act 2 ends with a brief respite of tension, Lucina's release, swiftly followed by the announcement of the rape. Similarly Clarissa's return from Hampstead will only be described once the rape has taken place. Lucina understands she will be betrayed when she is surrounded by whores and bawds, and so does Clarissa in the brothel, just before the rape is accomplished. Proculus reports, "'Tis done Lycinus," just as simply as Lovelace writes, "The affair is over. Clarissa lives" (5:291). Lucina vows that as long as there is life in her body, "I'le cry for Justice," to which the Emperor replies, "Justice will never hear you; I am Justice" (*Works*, p. 207). Clarissa too will turn to the law, and Lovelace will respond by claiming all power to himself.

Rochester's protagonists fall to blaming each other. Valentinian accuses Lucina of "Witchcraft," of fair eyes and heavenly beauty, and for being good (*Works*, p. 208), just as Lovelace would charge Clarissa with being a witch, too beautiful, and too good for envious mortals to bear. Lucina says that he has murdered her honour, "And can there be a love in Violence?," "I am lost for ever, / And if thou let'st me live, thou'rt lost thy self too" (*Works*, p. 208).

> Gods! what a wretched thing has this Man made me?
> For now I am no Wife for *Maximus*;
> No Company for Women that are vertuous.
> No Family I now can claim or Countrey
> No Name but *Caesar*'s Whore ...
> (*Works*, p. 209)

Clarissa too refuses to marry the man who has violated her, and Lovelace knows damnation to be his purchase (7:424). After the rape her name is "*Wretchedness!*" (6:250). She is no longer Harlowe but harlot, having lost her name, her identity, her connections with her family. If Lucina sees that this is the end of goodness, remarking, "Why then I see there is no God—but Power" (*Works*, p. 210), Clarissa knows too that her reputation is gone.

Both women prefer death to that loss. Lucretia stabbed herself in public, but Lucina and Clarissa both die privately, of grief. Clarissa sinks her head down on her bosom like "a half-broken-stalked Lily" when she is brought back to the brothel (5:287), an image repeated in the lily on her coffin and her "hands, white as the lily" (7:412).

After the rape Maximus calls Lucina "Lilly," "Thou sweetly droop-
ing Flower" (p. 210), and in the masque written to accompany the
play, the moon throws down lilies, "arm'd for thy defence," "As white
and cold as Snow or Innocence." Lucina's tears fall like "chrystal
Fountains" (p. 210), like Clarissa's "charming fountains" of tears in
Lovelace's baroque speech (6:31).

Maximus asks why Lucina was chosen "among Millions of thy Sex"
(p. 210), the queston that Clarissa, in echo of Job, will ask herself. Lucina's remedy is death. Decius, like Belford, urges her to live
and draw "from that wild man a sweet repentance," but she replies
only that "his penitence is but increase of pleasure, and his prayers are said to deceive us" (p. 212). Like Belford promising to edit
Clarissa's papers and present them to the world, Aecius promises Lucina enduring fame, memory, a monument, and "The Praises of a
just and constant Woman" (p. 212). "The pleas'd expiring Saint" Lucina dies peacefully and gladly, "Choakt with a thousand Sighs," dead
of "Grief and Disgrace" (acts 4–5). She meets death as a lover. The
saintly Clarissa also dies of sighs and "grief," smiling, in serenity and
happiness, calling upon Jesus with her last breath (7:414, 425; 8:7).
Valentinian at first denies the fact of Lucina's death, as a limitation
on his power: Lovelace likewise will not "bear the word *dead* on any
account" (7:427). Chylax tries to comfort Valentinian by saying that
"All Women are not dead with her," as Lovelace's friend Mowbray attempts to comfort him with the question, "what was there in one
woman more than another?" (7:427). The emperor replies that Lucina was simply unique, explaining, "A common Whore serves you
...: / A meer perpetual Motion makes you happy," whereas for himself, "was there but one / But one of all the World that could content
me, / And snatcht away in shewing?" (p. 220). Lovelace learns the
same tragic lesson.

The epilogue to *Valentinian* by a "Person of Quality" curiously anticipates objections that would be made to *Clarissa*. Lucina turns to
the women in the audience with "Tell me ye fair ones, pray now,
tell me why / For such a fault as this to bid me dye?" Lovelace himself would argue the same. Many a critic too would remark unkindly
on the inflaming tendency of the work, as Lucina does:

Did you not pity me, lament each groan,

When left with the wicked Emperor alone?
I know in thought you kindly bore a part,
Each had a *Valentinian* in her heart.

In a masque written for the play by Sir Francis Fane, the gods are a cynical and vicious crew who gang up on Lucina, defended only by the moon. "None e'er was ravish'd, but with close consent," says Mercury, an idea echoed by Lovelace when he argues that women always give way "in a yielding reluctance; without which I will be sworn, whatever Rapes have been attempted, none ever were committed, one person to one person" (4:358). Richardson may then have noted even the addenda to Rochester's play.

Whenever Lovelace looks back to Hobbes, to Rochester himself, to the various theatrical representations of Rochester, or to Rochester's works, the consequences for him are fatal. Trapped in his own mechanistic world-view, he is "a machine at last, and no free agent," as Belford tells him (5:223). His body controls him, his heart chokes him, circumstances change him and modify his behaviour, his plots work on without him. Libertines, said Belford, are narrow-souled wretches who "move round and round (like so many blind millhorses) in one narrow circle" (6:403–4). When Lovelace loses all sense of free will, liberty, and choice, he foregoes his mutability, and with it, identity itself.[25] Like Rochester he has become a Signior Dildo, a sexual machine sundered from the thinking mind, a mere mechanical device. He rapes a body he has reduced to matter by an opiate, and can expect no return of love. Impotent at last, he is a debauchee disabled by the consummation of his wishes.

Rochester believed like Hobbes that if man has no soul, he must be set among the brutes. His animal imagery for humanity reflects it. Lovelace, who uses the same Iago-like imagery, makes the same charge: "Women have no Souls. ... And if so, to whom shall I be accountable for what I do to them?" (4:330). But just as Rochester

25 Margaret Anne Doody observes, "No one is a stable identity, nor can consciousness ever know a self; we are each a bundle of perceptions, and by looking within we catch only the perception of the moment," in "Disguise and Personality in Richardson's *Clarissa*," *Studies in the Eighteenth Century 7: Papers Presented at the Seventh David Nichol Smith Seminar*, ed. Jocelyn Harris, with the co-operation of Robert P. Maccubbin and David F. Morrill, a special issue of *Eighteenth-Century Life* 12 (1988), 18–39.

was persuaded at the point of death about the existence of souls (*Life*, pp. 28–29), Lovelace comes to see Clarissa as "Soul all over" (5:227). Having lost her even temporarily, he writes in despair, "my whole Soul is a blank: The whole Creation round me, the Elements above, beneath, and everything I *behold* (for nothing can I *enjoy*) are a blank without her!" (6:196). Without Clarissa, its informing soul, his universe of matter is meaningless.

Hobbes had said that in a state of nature the life of man is "solitary, poore, nasty, brutish, and short" (p. 186), a statement which Richardson proves by his closely corresponding image of rakes dying young, diseased, poor, and friendless, "Reduced, probably, by riotous waste to consequential want, behold them refuged in some obscene [obscure] hole or garret; obliged to the careless care of some dirty old woman, whom nothing but her poverty prevails upon to attend to perform the last offices for men who have made such shocking ravage among the young ones" (6:325–26).[26] Belford escapes from a brutish life to a life of reason, but Lovelace's other friends die hideously as Rochester's had done, and Lovelace himself turns mad and "brutish" at Clarissa's death. No longer the noble hawk he liked to call himself, he is now a dog, a puppy, chicken-hearted, creeping into holes and corners like an old hedgehog hunted for its grease (7:427–28). He dies young, in a duel, among strangers.

In Lovelace Richardson portrays the sheer *cost* of being a Rochester, that Hobbist example of the Protean potential in man. To a large extent Lovelace creates the corrupt world of change and illusion that he inhabits, shines in, and ultimately quits. Clarissa provides another world-view altogether.

What Lovelace longs for, has within his grasp, and loses, is the sovereign power that Hobbes recommends to prevent anarchy and meaninglessness. If Lovelace lives by reaction, Clarissa lives by absolutes. She represents that still centre in the material world proposed by Hobbes, as well as the spiritual peace for which Lovelace feels both appetite and aversion. To her as to the Cambridge Platonists,

---

26 Cf. Rochester's Corinna in "A Letter from Artemiza in the Towne to Chloe in the Countrey." A decayed and diseased *memento mori* scorned by all, forsaken and oppressed, she must lie all winter "in some darke hole," "And Want, and dirt endure" (*Poems*, p. 88).

God is immanent in all creation, a divine mover as well as an original creator. The task of the reasoning human being is to become as godlike as possible by imitating Christ in faith and works. Richardson signals this philosophy most clearly when Clarissa keeps Thomas à Kempis's *Imitation of Christ* in her room, the most widely read book in Catholicism after the Bible. A man like Sir Charles Grandison can imitate Christ by being godlike in daily life, but even a woman like Clarissa can still believe in her own inner light, conscience, and its outward manifestation, the law. Unlike Hobbes, she sees a spark of divinity in the soul of each human being, and spurns the riches, pleasures, and powers of the world for eternal life.

Her model may well have been Mary Astell, the feminist and Christian Platonist whose life and ideas resemble Clarissa's in so many respects—a life lived in imitation of Christ, charity, intense female friendships, longing for a Protestant nunnery, impatience with praise, belief in men as predators, and preparation for a better world to make up for the disappointments of this. She too kept a coffin in her room as she lay dying. Richardson could have known of her through their mutual acquaintances, the High Tory Atterburys, and when her life was to be published in George Ballard's *Memoirs of Several ladies of Great Britain* (1742), he subscribed to it and offered to advise Ballard on its publication through his friend Mrs Sarah Chapone in 1750. But Richardson may have already read Ballard's comment on Astell's modesty, that she was "as ambitious to slide gently through the world without so much as being seen or taken notice of, as others are to bustle and make a figure in it,"[27] because Anna writes in *Clarissa*'s first letter that she is "So desirous, as you always said, of sliding through life to the end of it unnoted ... tho' now, to your regret, pushed into blaze, as I may say" (1:2–3). He seems to have been familiar with Astell's treatises on women's education (1694) and on marriage (1700), and could have encountered her letters on the love of God written to John Norris, the last of the

---

27 *Memoirs of Several Ladies of Great Britain who have been Celebrated for their Writings of Skill in the Learned Languages, Arts and Sciences*, ed. Ruth Perry (Detroit: Wayne State University Press, 1985), pp. 382–92. I am grateful to Ruth Perry for sending me copies of letters in the Bodleian Library relating to Richardson's connections with Ballard and Chapone (Bodl. Ballard MSS 43:132, 106, 155).

Christian Platonists, which made her such a significant figure in the literary world of London by 1705.[28]

Wherever Richardson found Clarissa's philosophy, she believes in a fixed good. Against all the evidence of avaricious, violent, self-interested parents and siblings and society, the proven duplicity of Lovelace and his agents, and her betrayal by church and society, Clarissa trusts in God, in the social contract, the Leviathan, and the power of words to move. She believes that the law exists to protect her: "The LAW shall be all my resource: The LAW," she says (6:63). Men only succeed in vilest attempts "if they can once bring themselves to trample on the Sanctions which bind man to man" (7:68), she says, referring to the settlements, licences, provisos, and reparations that Lovelace presents to her, then annuls.

The contest between the two philosophies is expressed by light and dark. This is traditional enough, but frequently Richardson seems to be thinking of the Platonic meanings of Spenser in book 3 of *The Faerie Queene*, the book of Chastity. Richardson admired Spenser, and Harriet Byron refers to the first sighting of Florimell riding on a "milk-white palfrey" (3.1.15) in *Grandison* (1:285). Florimell represents cosmic beauty manifest in the sublunary world,[29] and Clarissa's Platonic beauty is also constantly imaged by light. Her very name suggests light, and images of light, of suns and stars, surround her. She is especially represented as a comet. This image of streaming, blazing hair leads her directly back to Britomart, an aspect of Gloriana, the Elizabeth to whom Clarissa is several times compared, and to Florimell. Britomart's shaken-out hair shines like an aurora; Florimell's

> ... faire yellow locks behind her flew,
> All as a blazing starre [comet] doth farre outcast
> His hearie beames, and flaming lockes dispred,
> At sight whereof the people stand aghast. (3.1.16)

28 See my *Samuel Richardson* for instances where Richardson seems to be drawing on Astell's life and ideas. See Ruth Perry, *The Celebrated Mary Astell: An Early English Feminist* (London and Chicago: University of Chicago Press, 1986), p. 75.

29 See Stevie Davies, *The Idea of Woman in Renaissance Literature: The Feminine Reclaimed* (Brighton: Harvester Press, 1985), p. 71.

The pattern of their stories is remarkably similar.[30] Florimell escapes into the boat of an old fisherman who defiles her garments with fish-scales when he attempts to rape her. Clarissa's old lover Solmes is equally characterized by images of smearing and spoiling. Florimell is delivered by the lustful Proteus to another captivity in an underwater Hades, just as Clarissa's deliverer imprisons her in a brothel. Proteus tempts Florimell daily "with this or that," and transforms himself to dreadful shapes, "But euermore she him refused flat." Like Clarissa, she would rather die (3.8.39–42). Clarissa's story follows the same path, with Richardson adding as if by natural association details from Pluto's abduction of Proserpina to Hades, as Perdita describes it in *The Winter's Tale* (4.4.119–27). Shakespeare's pale primroses, violets, and lilies recur in the hymeneal colour of Clarissa's pale primrose yellow dress, the violets embroidered on it (3:28), and the fleurs-de-luce, which mean light, the light of her name.

Not just one but two Protean artist-enchanters hold women in tormented captivity in book 3 of *The Faerie Queene*. Proteus's cruel analogue is Busyrane, guardian of a bound Amoret, whose breast is pierced and heart drawn forth, transfixed with a deadly dart (3.12.21). If he figures the "straunge characters of his art" in Amoret's living blood, one could equally say of Lovelace writing letters about his torture of Clarissa that his intention was

> ...all perforce to make her him to loue
> Ah who can love the worker of her smart?
> A thousand charmes he formerly did proue,
> Yet thousand charmes could not her stedfast heart remoue.
> (3.12.31)

Spenser makes his sexual meanings explicit by describing a tapestry of raped women from Ovid's *Metamorphoses* in the House of Busyrane in canto 11. Many of them recur in the web of allusion and significance that is *Clarissa*.

30 Roxann Wheeler first drew my attention to the similarities. I also gladly acknowledge the inspiration of Lynn Hall's MA thesis, "The Straying Fool: Division and Collapse in Rochester's Writing" (Auckland University, 1988), for renewing my interest in Rochester.

If Florimell, Britomart, Amoret, and Clarissa represent light, Proteus, Busyrane, Pluto, Satan, and Lovelace stand for darkness. Their demonic deceptions turn men away from God. "Beelzebub," says Hobbes, "is Prince of Phantasmes ... and these Daemons, Phantasmes, or Spirits of Illusions, signifie allegorically, the same thing. This considered, the Kingdom of Darknesse ... is nothing else but a *Confederacy of Deceivers, that to obtain Dominion over men in this present world, endeavour by dark and erroneous Doctrines, to extinguish in them the Light, both of Nature, and of the Gospel, and so to dis-prepare them for the Kingdome of God to come*" (p. 627). If Sir Thomas Browne saw Truth as "that obscured Virgin half out of the Pit,"[31] Clarissa dreams a hideously prophetic dream that Lovelace tumbles her into a deep grave ready dug, throwing the dirt and earth upon her, and trampling it down with his feet (2:264). Nothing, says Clarissa, not even rape, can be worse than Lovelace's falsehoods, forgeries, perjuries, and impersonations (6:126, 295). His deceptions test her belief in her own perceptions, his trials test her trust in God. Lovelace's real crime is his attempt to put out the light in Clarissa, his determination to destroy in her the candle of the Lord, the reason that leads her to heaven.

Silence falls at the end of *Clarissa*. The contest between fixity and flux ends with the deaths of their defenders, and we are left to judge. Belford, like Hamlet's friends, like Rochester's, must sense that all that was extraordinary has vanished from the world. All he can do is record, and pass his knowledge on. Lovelace abandons a world of matter without meaning, and ends transfixed by death; Clarissa exchanges her fixity for new life. Their conflict has been immense, on a scale unattempted yet in the English novel. Here in *Clarissa* Richardson the humanist explores man's Protean paradoxical capacity to create and to destroy.

---

31 Sir Thomas Browne, *Christian Morals*, in *The Prose of Sir Thomas Browne*, ed. Norman Endicott (New York and London: New York and London University Presses, 1968), 2:5.

Clarissa's Treasonable Correspondence: Gender, Epistolary Politics, and the Public Sphere

Rachel K. Carnell

In a letter to Lady Bradshaigh, Samuel Richardson emphasized the importance of generating active debate among his readers. He even went as far as to suggest that the readers themselves may become almost author-like in their participation in the public reception of his novels:

> The undecided Events are sufficiently pointed out to the Reader, to whom this Sort of Writing, something, as I have hinted, should be left to make out or debate upon. ... It is not an unartful Management to interest the Readers so much in the Story, as to make them differ in Opinion as to Capital Articles, and by Leading one, to espouse one, another, another, Opinion, make them all, if not Authors, Carpers.[1]

Richardson's fascination with the public debate about his novels and his empowerment of readers to participate in debates about

1 Samuel Richardson, letter to Lady Bradshaigh, 25 February 1754, in *Selected Letters of Samuel Richardson*, ed. John Carroll (Oxford: Clarendon Press, 1964), p. 296. "Clarissa's Treasonable Correspondence: Gender, Epistolary Politics, and the Public Sphere" was first published in *Eighteenth-Century Fiction* 10:3 (1998), 269–86.

their meaning place him squarely within the eighteenth-century social phenomenon that Jürgen Habermas has described as the public
sphere.

Although Richardson obviously did not employ the vocabulary
of a twentieth-century social critic, the rational debates and exchanges that his novels generated—through letters, periodical reviews, private conversations, and public discussion in coffee-houses—
correspond closely to Habermas's description of the bourgeois public sphere, in which private individuals participated in critical public debate through the universalizing capacity of rational thought.
Habermas even refers to the public reception of Richardson's novels,
in which "Richardson wept over the actors in his novels as much as
his readers did," as part of the cultural context that created the "family's self-image as a sphere of humanity-generating closeness." This
perception of shared humanity permitted rational men of different
ranks to engage in public debate "without regard to all preexisting
social and political rank."[2]

In Habermas's analysis, Richardson belongs not to the political
public sphere, in which opponents of the Whig government "raised
to the status of an institution, the ongoing commentary on and criticism of the Crown's actions and Parliament's decisions," but to its
somewhat tangential stepsister, the literary public sphere. Habermas acknowledges that these two spheres were interconnected and
"blended with each other in a peculiar fashion," but he never fully
explains how the literary public sphere is connected to the realm
of political debate. One of his few observations about the distinction between the two spheres is that "female readers as well as ap-
prentices and servants often took a more active part in the literary
public sphere than the owners of private property and family heads
themselves."[3]

Exactly in what way women and other dependents were active par-
ticipants in the literary public sphere remains opaque in Habermas's
analysis. Their role as readers seems limited to helping bourgeois

2 Jürgen Habermas, *Structural Transformation of the Public Sphere*, trans. Thomas Burger (Cambridge: MIT Press, 1989), pp. 50, 48, 54.

3 Habermas, pp. 60, 55, 56.

household heads conceive of themselves as humanized through the sphere of the family: literature and public discussions about literature enable private individuals to see themselves in the universalizing terms of "love, freedom, and cultivation—in a word, as humanity."[4] Habermas thus considers the role of literature apolitical, except in its humanizing influence on political players. This strand of thought in a work of social theory first published in 1962 should not surprise us, given that the political basis of the early British novel has only recently been reasserted.[5] If, however, we develop Habermas's provocative claims about the public sphere through an analysis of the political discourse of Richardson's fiction, we will comprehend the non-partisan but highly political nature of Richardson's work; we will also be able to appreciate the complex relationship between humanizing morality and political analysis that characterized the eighteenth-century literary public sphere.

The contrast between the eponymous narrator of Richardson's *Pamela* (1740), who at first expresses her oppression in the politicized terms of "tyranny" and "rebellion," and her "lord and master," Mr B., who wishes to present their relationship as "a pretty story in romance,"[6] underscores the novel's liminal position during the mideighteenth century: intrinsically political and yet definable as pure romance. Richardson himself repeatedly describes his novel as a warning to women not to marry rakes and a warning to parents not to force their children into marrying against their individual wishes. The novel's contemporary reception certainly reiterated this inter-

4 Habermas, p. 55.

5 See, for example, Nancy Armstrong, *Desire and Domestic Fiction: A Political History of the Novel* (Oxford: Oxford University Press, 1987); Michael McKeon, *The Origins of the English Novel 1600–1740* (Baltimore: Johns Hopkins University Press, 1987); Carol Kay, *Political Constructions: Defoe, Richardson, and Sterne in Relation to Hobbes, Hume, and Burke* (Ithaca: Cornell University Press, 1988).

6 Samuel Richardson, *Pamela; or Virtue Rewarded*, Shakespeare Head edition, 4 vols (Oxford: Basil Blackwell, 1929), 1:31. References are to this edition.

pretation: Edward Young, for example, described it as "The Whole Duty of WOMAN."[7]

This moralistic reception, however, belies the highly politicized discourse of Richardson's fiction. From the start of Richardson's first novel, Mr B. is concerned that Pamela's letters are "treasonable," because she "exposes" or makes public (through her letters to her parents) his "private" attempts to seduce her. Similarly in *Clarissa* (1747–48), Lovelace describes the "letters that pass between these ladies" (Clarissa and Anna) as "of a treasonable nature."[8] While both men represent versions of tyrannical patriarchs in the home, both also personify the state—Mr B. as a member of Parliament, Lovelace as a potential inheritor of his uncle's seat in the House of Lords. Further, by having Lovelace liken Clarissa's martyrdom both to that of Lucretia and to that of the Catalans after the English had reneged on their promise of a military alliance under the terms of the Treaty of Utrecht (1713), Richardson marks her tragedy as directly political in a way that challenges Habermas's view of the literary public sphere as merely humanizing.[9]

Notwithstanding the obvious political language in the novel, the bulk of twentieth-century criticism of *Clarissa* has focused less on the political context of the novel than on Richardson's skill in describing character or on the poststructural demeanour of the text.[10] In

---

7 Quoted in T.C. Duncan Eaves and Ben D. Kimpel, *Samuel Richardson: A Biography* (Oxford: Clarendon Press, 1971), p. 287.

8 Samuel Richardson, *Clarissa or The History of a Young Lady*, ed. Angus Ross (London: Penguin Books, 1985), p. 573. References are to this edition.

9 Richardson describes Clarissa holding "up to Heaven, in a speechless agony, the innocent licence (which she has in her own power); as the poor distressed Catalans held up their English treaty" (p. 887).

10 Cynthia Griffin Wolff focuses on Richardson's universal description of "character under stress" rather than the historical context that might have caused the structural development of complex novelistic characters. *Richardson and the Eighteenth-Century Puritan Character* (Hamden, Conn.: Shoe String Press, 1972). Lawrence Stone uses the example of *Clarissa* as "literary evidence" of "a prolonged public argument during the late seventeenth and eighteenth centuries about a child's freedom of choice of a marriage partner." *The Family, Sex and Marriage in England 1500–1800* (New York: Harper and Row, 1977), pp. 280–81. While Richardson's work accords with the sociological evolution that Stone describes, to consider domestic scenarios in literature merely as mirrors of actual life experience belies the rich interplay of symbolic nuance in any eighteenth-century discussion of family structure. Tony Tanner offers a Lacanian reading of the patriarchal Harlowe household

the last two decades, the need for a more specific political analysis of Richardson's work has become increasingly apparent. While Terry Castle and Terry Eagleton have pointed out that *Clarissa* must be understood in terms of the politics of rape, they do not provide the precise historical context through which to understand the novel's own discourses about gender and political power.[11] While Nancy Armstrong brilliantly analyses the ways in which Richardson's domestic fiction obscures its political comments about class differences as "gender came to mark the most important difference among individuals," her work does not fully address the fact that many political debates during this period would have occurred under the guise of domestic scenarios.[12] Although she does not specifically mention Habermas, Carol Kay nevertheless lays the groundwork for a Habermasian critique of Richardson's project through her analysis of Richardson in terms of Hobbes's and Hume's writings on government power and private counsel.[13] Similarly, Toni Bowers suggests

in *Adultery in the Novel* (Baltimore: Johns Hopkins University Press, 1979). The possibility that Lacan's theory offers for contextualizing family dynamics into their social and linguistic context is undercut, however, by the transhistorical concept of desire on which Tanner relies. *Clarissa* criticism moves away from psychology to textual play when William Beatty Warner describes the ambiguity of the text, concluding that "rape is the most cogent response to Clarissa's fictional projection of herself as a whole unified body." *Reading "Clarissa": The Struggles of Interpretation* (New Haven: Yale University Press, 1979), p. 67.

11 Terry Eagleton responds sharply to "the truly reactionary nature of this [Warner's] type of 'deconstructionist radicalism,' once divorced from the social and political contexts it so characteristically finds hard to handle." *The Rape of Clarissa: Writing, Sexuality, and Class Struggle in Samuel Richardson* (Minneapolis: University of Minnesota Press, 1982), p. 67. Terry Castle argues, in response to Warner's poststructural rhetorical analysis, that "the excruciating situation that Clarissa dramatizes is that a rhetorical system is not 'powerful' unless grounded in political power." However, exactly what sort of political power is being discussed and exactly who is wielding it remains obscure. *Clarissa's Ciphers: Meaning and Disruption in Richardson's "Clarissa"* (Ithaca: Cornell University Press, 1982), p. 25.

12 Armstrong, p. 4. Part of the difficulty may result from her reliance on Rousseau's *Du Contrat social* (1762), a work published two decades after the appearance of Richardson's first novel, rather than on the earlier British articulations of the social contract, which routinely analyse political authority in terms of questions of gender and authority in the household (pp. 30–34).

13 Published one year before *Structural Transformation* became readily available in English, Kay's work suggests the way in which Richardson routinely translates political criticism into a discourse of morality, thus anticipating the interconnection that Habermas makes between affective humanism and the public sphere (pp. 123–93).

that, in *Clarissa*, even motherhood is represented in the language of public politics.[14]

In her study of eighteenth-century epistolary fiction, Elizabeth Heckendorn Cook reiterates Armstrong's suggestion that Richardson's work plays a vital role in helping to construct what we will later assume to be natural differences between the public and domestic spheres; she also follows Kay's lead in analysing the connection between humanistic discourse and public power. In particular, Cook describes how epistolarity, or the letter form, helps to create the ideology of affective humanism that Habermas describes in his analysis of the public sphere:

An "inner realm" that follows its own laws and is inherently free from extrinsic purposes, especially from economic considerations or constraints, found its discursive mode in the familiar letter and its epistemological model in the idea of a universal, transparent language of the expressive body, which offers a window onto the heart.[15]

Cook also observes that although Habermas at times attempts to distinguish a literary public sphere from the political public sphere, his focus is in fact the political public sphere, while her focus is on "the transnational ideal of a *literary* public sphere."[16]

By contrast, I return to the specific politics of the British public sphere in the 1740s. Acknowledging that at this point in history, political discourse was inevitably connected to narratives about the domestic family, I develop and refine Habermas's theory about the relationship between the literary and political public spheres.

Although the family has been an analogy for the state since the time of Aristotle, the analogy was revived with enthusiasm during the seventeenth century as commentators from James I to James Tyrrell

14 Toni Bowers, *The Politics of Motherhood* (Cambridge: Cambridge University Press, 1996), pp. 196–224.

15 Elizabeth Heckendorn Cook, *Epistolary Bodies: Gender and Genre in the Eighteenth-Century Republic of Letters* (Stanford: Stanford University Press, 1996), p. 93.

16 Cook, p. 11.

sought to justify either the obligation to obey or the right to resist the monarch.[17] Thus a novel whose author claims in the preface to "caution parents against the undue exertion of their natural authority over their children in the great article of marriage" must be understood as having rich political resonance.

Since 1680, when Robert Filmer's *Patriarcha* appeared posthumously in response to the first Exclusion crisis, the hierarchical paternalistic household became aligned with attempts to keep the Stuarts on the throne; John Locke's *Two Treatises of Government* (1689) vindicated a parliamentary monarchy by correcting Filmer's interpretation of the first household: God did not grant dominion of the earth solely to Adam, but granted sovereignty jointly to Adam and Eve. Although this metaphorical dispute over shared power in the household may have seemed anachronistic by the 1740s, the Parliamentary Revolution of 1688 had neither eliminated traditional belief in divine right nor silenced debates about it in the public sphere.[18] In fact, discussions about the structure of the state continued well into the eighteenth century and were revitalized particularly when the Jacobite uprisings of 1715, 1719, and 1745 threatened the stability of the crown. When Clarissa describes Lovelace as a tyrant and when Mr B. refers to Pamela's letters as "treasonous papers," we should hear echoes not only of Jacobite cabals surrounding the final attempt of 1745, as Morris Golden has persuasively argued, but also of earlier debates over social contract theory which were marked by discussions of tyranny in the household.[19]

One obstacle to interpreting the specific political discourses that permeate *Clarissa* is that even in some of the more sophisticated

---

17 For full details of this evolution in political theory, see Constance Jordan's excellent article, "The Household and the State: Transformations in the Representation of an Analogy from Aristotle to James I," *Modern Language Quarterly* 54:3 (1993), 307–26.

18 Martyn P. Thompson, "The Reception of Locke's *Two Treatises of Government* 1690–1705," *Political Studies* 24:2 (1976), 189. Critical interest in Locke's *Two Treatises* did not begin in earnest until the first decade of the eighteenth century: the work itself did not sell particularly well in the 1690s but became increasingly popular throughout the eighteenth century (p. 184).

19 Morris Golden, "Public Context and Imagining Self," *SEL* 25 (1985), 575–98. Eaves and Kimpel refer to Richardson's thorough knowledge of Locke's theories of education and his at least cursory knowledge of Shaftesbury, Mandeville, Bolingbroke, Hartley, Hume, and Berkeley (p. 571).

twentieth-century criticism, it remains a commonplace to dismiss Anna Howe as a person; she is viewed "more as an extension of Clarissa herself than as a separate individual."[20] Yet, viewing Anna as merely the psychological dark side of Clarissa's own personality prevents us from taking seriously the political content of the highly rational exchange between the two women friends. While theirs is theoretically a private exchange of letters, it is also, rather unexpectedly, an exchange in which two women debate Clarissa's relationship to her family in language that recapitulates the public sphere exchanges from the 1680s and 1690s between the proponents of divine right and the proponents of social contract theory.

Richardson's own political stance, confusingly characterized by his bragging about his father's support for the Duke of Monmouth in a letter to Johannes Stinstra[21] and by his involvement in printing some Jacobite-influenced issues of the *True Briton*, is hard to locate within a standard binary distinction between Tory and Whig. As T.C. Duncan Eaves and Ben D. Kimpel suggest, he is opposed to any abuse of power that verges on tyranny, whether in the hands of Tories or Whigs.[22] Margaret Anne Doody has pointed out the difficulty of deciding whether Lovelace and Mr B. are portraits of Tory tyrants or Whig abusers of governmental control. Her conclusion is that Richardson's novels should be interpreted as "a discourse about power," particularly about the power of abusive, censoring government.[23] In so far as the abusers of power in Richardson's *œuvre* are not central figures in government, but private men and heads of household, it makes sense to turn to the political discourses that link state power to household power if we are to understand the precise criticism of power that Richardson's novels provide. Al-

---

20 Wolff, p. 131. Ian Watt and Terry Eagleton make similar observations.

21 Letter of 2 June 1753, *Selected Letters*, p. 228.

22 Richardson's suspicion of monarchs who might be tyrants and his support of the public's right to overthrow these is evident in the 1724 issue of the *True Briton*, for which Richardson was probably the printer and which resulted in a trial of treason for the publisher: "Englishmen would do well to beware of a 'future' possible king who, being easy and inactive, might 'permit every Man in his Court to be a Tyrant but Himself.'" For a summary of issues 5 and 7 (17 and 24 June 1724), see Eaves and Kimpel, pp. 26–29.

23 See Margaret Anne Doody, "Richardson's Politics," *Eighteenth-Century Fiction* 2 (1990), 119.

though Richardson's novels certainly nurtured the affective humanism that Habermas ascribes to the literary public sphere, they also
demonstrated how unresolved conflicts about gender and authority, disregarded by increasingly abstract political treatises, were being mediated and re-evaluated through the domestic scenarios of
eighteenth-century fiction.

Shortly after his marriage to Pamela, Mr B. explains to his Lincolnshire neighbours: "I think the Distinctions of *Whig* and *Tory* odious; and love the one or the other, only as they are honest and worthy
Men; and have never (nor ever shall, I hope) given a Vote, but according to what I thought was for the publick good, whether *Whig*
or *Tory* proposed it" (2:229). Like his reformed rake hero, Richardson was less interested in partisan politics than in a broader debate
about obedience and authority, a debate he returns to through the
domestic metaphors that had been implicated in political discourse
since the 1680s, when Richardson's father first pledged support to
the Duke of Monmouth.

As Golden has shown, anxieties and debates about the final Jacobite attempt on the English crown (1744–45) permeated London during the years when Richardson was drafting *Clarissa*. And while many
of the original tracts in support of social contract theory—by writers
such as James Tyrrell, Algernon Sidney, and William Atwood—had
ceased to be in print by the early eighteenth century, Locke's *Two
Treatises of Government* became increasingly popular as the eighteenth
century progressed, and the anonymous *Judgement of Whole Kingdoms
and Nations* (1710), an essentially plagiarized abridgment of Locke's
Treatises, became one of the best-selling pamphlets in eighteenth-
century Britain, as the country gradually came to accept the principles of parliamentary monarchy and contract theory.[24] It might be
logical, therefore, to propose that Richardson, as a loyal supporter of
the Revolution of 1688, was simply recapitulating the arguments of
social contract theory in order to assist popular understanding of it.

24 Richard Ashcraft and M.M. Goldsmith, "Locke and Revolution Principles," *Historical
Journal* 26 (1983), 773–800: 789.

His critique of power, however, is always multivalenced, and his novel provides as much a critique of social contract theory as a vindication of it.

In *Clarissa*, we can identify a recapitulation of an older formulation of the debate about obedience and authority, characterized specifically by a contrast between a patriarchal and a contractarian version of the domestic household. In the face of tyranny, Clarissa articulates an ideal of obedience traditionally espoused by proponents of absolute monarchy and by those retaining Jacobite loyalty during the final succession crisis in the mid-1740s. "My duty," she explains, "will not permit me so far to suppose my father arbitrary" (p. 95). Although this is delivered in a bitterly sarcastic speech, Clarissa does intend to follow the letter of patriarchal tradition—which means obeying her father, but not her increasingly tyrannical brother.

Her attitude does not mean, as Florian Stuber claims, that "Clarissa … clings to an idea of what her father should be … no matter what he actually does."[25] She is aware that her father is unjust or she would not consider escaping with Lovelace; however, the principle of divine right theory means that the monarch is always right, even when he acts tyrannically. Her deferential language corresponds to dicta in Robert Filmer's *Patriarcha*: "the Father of a family governs by no other law than by his own will." Filmer continues, "Kings keep the Laws, though not Bound by them."[26] Under this rule, which governs the whole Harlowe family, it would be treasonous for a daughter even to give the impression of disagreeing with her parents. After a negotiating session with Clarissa, in which they debate whether she should respond to one of Lovelace's letters, Mrs Harlowe, pleased with her daughter's honesty and compliance, shows her appreciation by agreeing to conceal Clarissa's original disagreement: "It shall not be known that you have argued with me at all" (p. 96). In this extremely literal version of patriarchal divine right, even voicing differences with authority is considered treasonous.

By contrast, Anna Howe espouses the recognizable tenets of social contract theory with such enthusiasm that she seems to have no

25 Florian Stuber, "On Fathers and Authority in Clarissa," *SEL* 25 (1985), 565.

26 Robert Filmer, *Patriarcha*, in *Patriarcha and Other Political Works of Robert Filmer*, ed. Peter Laslett (Oxford: Basil Blackwell, 1949), p. 96.

doubt about their relevance to the dependent situations of Clarissa and herself. In the epistolary exchanges between the two friends, she voices the same objections to arbitrary authority that were voiced by contract theorists in their arguments to exclude James II from the throne in 1688 and that were alluded to in every subsequent statement of social contract theory published in the eighteenth century. "AUTHORITY!" she declares, "what a full word is that in the mouth of a narrow-minded person, who happened to be born thirty years before one!" (p. 85). Anna is willing to disobey her own mother and order a carriage herself to help Clarissa escape, rather than see her friend fall into Lovelace's clutches. Clarissa, however, refuses this seemingly reasonable offer on the grounds that it would force Anna to disobey her own mother, a disobedience for which Clarissa could not countenance being responsible. Yet Anna continues to challenge Clarissa's perception of her own family: "Another would call your father a tyrant, if you will not" (pp. 132–33).

In structuring the exchange between Clarissa and Anna as a quasi-political debate, Richardson is clearly not interested in having either the divine right or the contractarian position triumph: each demands the reader's respect. On the other hand, in pursuing a political analysis through exchanges about domestic oppression, Richardson is able to call our attention to what is ignored in a binary political argument, that is, those voices which are simply omitted. As recent feminist critics of early liberal political theory have observed, the first proponents of a parliamentary monarchy seem consciously to have written women out of the discourses of civil liberty. Carole Pateman argues that the idea of translating power from a patriarchal monarchy to a fraternal or parliamentary sharing of power evolved in tandem with the exclusion of women from the new fraternal power structure and the reinforcement of their purely domestic responsibilities in the household. The newly articulated social contract therefore depended on a prior sexual contract. She explains that "the story of the social contract is treated as an account of the creation of the public sphere of civil freedom. The other, private, sphere is not seen as politically relevant."[27]

27 Carol Pateman, *The Sexual Contract* (Stanford: Stanford University Press, 1988), p. 3.

To understand Pateman's analysis, we need only consider that when John Locke defended the idea of the social contract in his *Two Treatises* and explained that when God granted dominion of the earth to Adam, he designated Eve as joint monarch: "as many Interpreters think with reason, that these words were not spoken till Adam had his wife, must not she be Lady, as well as he Lord of the World?"[28] British social contract theorists, while not concerned with the household *per se*, originally located their argumentative linchpin in an unexpectedly modern vision of shared power in the family. However, despite this frequent analogy with the family, social contract theorists never intended to challenge a wife's presumably "natural" subordination in the household, which Locke describes in a subsequent paragraph as "no other Subjection than what every wife owes her husband."[29]

In 1706, Mary Astell, a High Church Tory, responded to the original framers of the social contract by asking, in the preface to the third edition of her *Some Reflections on Marriage*, "if Absolute Sovereignty be not necessary in a State, how comes it to be so in a Family?"[30] Similarly, Daniel Defoe portrayed the heroines of his novels *Moll Flanders* (1722) and *Roxana* (1724) struggling valiantly against male heads of household (whether husbands or employers) who seduce and desert them. In the early 1740s, Eliza Haywood asserted that her domestic anecdotes were actually more political than were parliamentary squabbles, which she likened to "the Knots Children tye at School in Packthread."[31]

The contradiction surrounding women's position in the social contract may explain why, once each succession crisis was over, references to the family were less frequent in descriptions of the social contract. By the 1740s, David Hume was writing philosophical essays on the original contract between citizen and monarch

28 Peter Laslett, ed., *Locke's Two Treatises of Government* (Cambridge: Cambridge University Press, 1960), First Treatise, paragraph 29.

29 *Two Treatises*, First Treatise, paragraph 48. For further discussion of Richardson's complex attitude towards maternal authority, see Kay, pp. 166–67.

30 Mary Astell, *Some Reflections on Marriage* (London, 1706), in *The First English Feminist*, ed. Bridget Hill (New York: St Martins, 1986), p. 76.

31 Eliza Haywood, *The Female Spectator*, 4 vols (London, 1745), 2:124.

that do not mention the family. In his essay "Of Passive Obedience" (1752), Hume attempts to mediate traditional disagreements between rights-based and obedience-based models of government by suggesting that "*both these* systems *of speculative principles are just.*" His only reference to the familial basis of authority refers to the absurdity of believing "the consent of the fathers to bind the children, even to the most remote generations";[32] he overlooks the fact that since 1680 many arguments against passive obedience were grounded not in the rights of sons but in the rights of women to disobey tyrannical or abusive husbands. In 1767 Adam Ferguson refers to the family only once in his *History of Civil Society*, and then to a foreign seraglio. In striking contrast to the increasingly abstracted accounts of liberal political theory, Richardson and other eighteenth-century British novelists uphold the method of Tyrrell's *Bibliotheca Politica* (1694) and of Locke's still-popular *Two Treatises* by reasserting the metaphorical relationship between power relations in the family and power relations in the state.

The epistolary argument between Clarissa Harlowe and Anna Howe, then, may be viewed as responding to a discourse of civil liberty that by 1740 no longer routinely utilized the metaphors of the family on which it had originally relied (although such metaphors would later be reintroduced during the political tensions of the French Revolution, as, for example, in Burke's *Reflections on the Revolution in France*). Clarissa's highly traditional articulation of the theory of divine right rejects the fraternal sharing of power that Pateman describes as underlining the social contract. Rather like royalist proto-feminists Mary Astell in 1700 and Olympe de Gouges in 1791, Clarissa seems to recognize that a fraternal sharing of power will be of little benefit to the sisters in a family or to the dependent women in a nation.

As a conventionally moralistic thinker, of course, Richardson would not have challenged the logic of abstraction that limited public de-

---

32 David Hume, *Essays, Moral Political, and Literary* in *David Hume, The Philosophical Works*, 4 vols. ed. Thomas Hill Green and Thomas Hodge Grose (Darmstadt: Scientia Verlag Aalen, 1964), 3:444, 447.

bate to propertied men. In an oft-cited contribution to a *Rambler*, in 1751, he mocks the "ladies who frequent those publick places," who "are not ashamed to shew their faces wherever men dare go," or "who shall laugh loudest on the publick walks,"[33] leaving no doubt about his agreement with the relegation of women to the domestic sphere. At the same time, however, in his private correspondence, which was "chiefly with Ladies," he applauded the private contributions of women that are routinely excluded from public debate:

I am envied, Sir, for the Favour I stand in with near a Score of very admirable Women, some of them of Condition; all of them such as would do Credit to their Sex, and to the Commonwealth of Letters, did not their Modesty with-hold them from appearing in it.[34]

Cook calls attention to the fact that for all his solicitation of suggestions from his readers, Richardson rarely heeds the proffered advice: "Like Clarissa's God, Richardson is reluctant to permit his readers to depend for epistemological and moral certainty upon any but himself."[35] Nevertheless, despite his approbation of all that is modest in a woman and despite his reluctance to take the advice of the women whom he describes as a potential asset to the "Commonwealth of Letters," it is evident that Richardson is keenly aware of the loss that ensues from keeping women's superior rationality out of the realm of public debate.

If Richardson's female characters represent an ironic feminization of the masculine debate in the public sphere, Richardson's depiction of Clarissa's traditional paternalism helps us to understand and criticize what Habermas would describe as eighteenth-century affective mythology:

The status of private man combined the role of owner of commodities with that of head of the family, that of property owner with that of "human being" *per se*. The doubling of the private sphere on the higher plane of the

---

33 *Rambler* 97 (19 February 1751), reprinted in *The Works of Samuel Johnson* (New Haven: Yale University Press, 1969), 4:158.

34 Letter to Johannes Stinstra, 2 June 1753, *Selected Letters*, p. 234.

35 Cook, p. 28.

intimate sphere ... furnished the foundation for an identification of those two roles under the foundation of the "private."[36]

Habermas further explains that the sentimental doubling of the propertied bourgeois man for "man" in general may not have been mere capitalist ideology: "The rational-critical debate of private people in the *salons*, clubs, and reading societies was not directly subject to the cycle of production and consumption."[37] We see here how the literary public sphere contributed to the genuine sense of universal humanity that helped private individuals view their social relationships in terms other than hierarchical class relations.

Habermas does not, however, acknowledge that "man" may refer not only to men of superior rank but to citizens in general, male or female. In the case of gender difference, by contrast, the literary public sphere did not blur the distinctions between the sexes, but highlighted them. Rather than obscuring social differences caused by gender, eighteenth-century novels such as *Clarissa* specifically called attention to the difference that gender makes in relations of power. For all her espousal of paternal over fraternal rights, Clarissa emphasizes that there may be a greater power struggle between individual men and individual women in the household than there ever is between a propertied male and his representative in Parliament. When she cries to Lovelace, "permit me the freedom which is my birthright as an English subject" (p. 934), Clarissa emphasizes that as an Englishwoman she has been brought up to believe that the discourse of universal liberty applied to individuals in general, not to men only.[38] Lovelace's abuse of power is extra-familial, since he and Clarissa are not married, and yet the way in which their relationship echoes the characteristics of an abusive marriage (the confined physical setting, the arguments, the passive aggressive behaviour) calls

36 Habermas, pp. 28–29.

37 Habermas, p. 160.

38 This is consistent with Florian Stuber's observation that in a novel devoid of strong paternal figures, Clarissa becomes an example of prudent, mature masculine power: "In her Will, Clarissa uses power, but with restraint, and only for the purposes of love and nurture. She seems an ideal secular authority. The mind is father to the deed. Or, if I can break through the sexism inherent in the metaphor, Clarissa herself becomes a Father" (p. 574).

into question the capacity of family structure to guarantee the affective humanism that Habermas claims was generated by Richardson's
œuvre.

When Clarissa is emotionally alienated from both her mother and
her sister and desperately craves the affections of Lovelace's relations, he mocks the humanitarian ideal of the domestic family by
tricking her with paid counterfeits of his female cousins. Richardson's location of the supposedly private action between Lovelace and
Clarissa in the rented abodes of brothels and public houses further
suggests that there is no such thing as a family space of potential human contact not controlled by the legal and economic power that
males retain inside and outside the household. Clarissa's last will and
testament, which defines her rhetorically as a martyr to her family,
is calculated to call attention to the difference between her affective
loyalty to her family (to whom she legally wills most of her separate property, which her father and her brother had always retained
under their control) and the real emotional support provided by
her beloved Mrs Norton, whose care she describes as "seconding the
piety and care of my ever-honoured and excellent mother" (p. 1415)
and to whom she wills an unexpected (and subsequently contested)
six hundred pounds.

The ideal of a loving, caring family—fundamental to a Lockean
concept of liberal political theory and fundamental to Habermas's
notion of affective humanism—is pictured by Richardson not in the
image of the Harlowe family but in the union between Anna Howe
and her persistent lover, Hickman. Although Anna repeatedly insists
on her "aversion to all men: to him: to matrimony" (p. 1456), she
eventually marries Hickman, following both Clarissa's advice and her
own mother's wishes. In contrast to Clarissa's notion that family harmony can only be achieved through old-fashioned patriarchalism,
Anna's marriage proves that her modern contractarian principles
are the most plausible route to an equal union. The narrator tells
us that "there is but *one will* between them; and that is generally his
or hers, as either speak first upon any subject, be it what it will" (p.
1492).

In taking contract theory to its logical extreme, Anna Howe has
managed to rewrite Genesis so that Locke's hypothetically updated

version of the family (in which husband and wife share equal dominion in the household) actually applies to her own marriage. Furthermore, in establishing a strong contrast between "his" and "hers," this
passage undercuts the public sphere ideal of a genderless, universal individual and emphasizes instead that a true contract between
non-abstract individuals must grant as much weight to the female
will as to the male will. Thus even as the early British novel, according to Armstrong, was emphasizing the importance of gender difference over other political difference, and, according to Habermas,
was serving to generate affective humanism among propertied men,
it was also offering a corrective supplement to the abstract debates
of the political public sphere.

Unlike the monologic account of *Pamela*, in which Pamela's own letters provide the dominant voice, the thoroughly dialogic interplay
between Clarissa and Anna in Richardson's second novel represents
an exchange that might take place in a coffee-house debate about
politics; Clarissa herself even at one point challenges her brother to
a debate. Moreover, Richardson calls our attention to the extreme
rationality of Clarissa and Anna: neither ever yields to the sort of
passionate rage that marks Lovelace's letters to Belford; each expresses her position thoughtfully and dispassionately. Richardson's
choice then—to place the most rational debate in his novel in the
voices of politically powerless women—emphasizes the irrationality
of excluding women from public debate.

This is not to say that Richardson would want women running for
public office or otherwise avoiding their duties as wives and mothers.
If we follow the example of Pamela—providing her private letters for
public circulation and eventually, at the urging of her husband, writing a type of conduct-book for child-rearing—we can understand the
ways in which Richardson might have envisioned women entering
the literary public sphere through a commentary on the domestic
sphere. We must remember, however, that in the second part of the
novel, Pamela not only becomes a potential author but also enacts
a public courtroom scene when she cleverly puts herself on trial

for her husband's act of adultery against her. This scene, in which a woman in the domestic sphere manipulates a public figure (her husband) by a private, fictional dramatization of a public court, confounds the difference between the public and domestic spheres. Richardson ultimately shows how women could criticize the political sphere (or at least the adulterous dishonesty of a public member of the House of Parliament) through rational discourse within the domestic household.

Like those who today insist on the relevance to a politician's public career of "private" acts of sexual harassment, Richardson's heroines insist on the significance of a public man's private acts of oppression. In so doing, they challenge the separation of the literary from the political public sphere. Richardson obviously designated the emergent novel as a genre that could challenge the tacit underpinnings of the political public sphere and be undertaken equally well by women as by men.[39] Furthermore, his own novels challenge the assumption that the household should serve only as an arena that humanizes the bourgeois citizens' conceptions of themselves as human and not as a category that is itself worthy of public scrutiny.

Beyond the implicit debate about government structure that takes place in Clarissa and Anna's "treasonous" correspondence, Richardson has Clarissa go out of her way to make public what would otherwise have been seen as a personal or domestic crime—her rape. In Richardson's first novel, when Pamela taunts Mr B. with the possibility of her gaining revenge on him, Lucretia-style, should he succeed in raping her, she is probably more serious than he believes, but his quick allusion to the romance comedy he feels their story will tell erases the memory of Lucretia's tragic fate, just as it erases the political reference to the overthrow of the Tarquin monarchy that resulted from that earlier, presumably private, act of rape. By contrast, Richardson's tragic heroine, Clarissa Harlowe, rather than simply stabbing herself, as Lucretia did after mutely publicizing her violation, and as Lovelace fears she might do, allows herself to die

---

39 See notes on Richardson's encouragement of or influence on Charlotte Lennox in Duncan Isles's appendix to *The Female Quixote* (1752; Oxford: Oxford University Press, 1989), pp. 419–28.

gradually, as if willing her own slow physical disintegration while she readies the legal tenets of her last will and testament.

In tracing the history of eighteenth-century rape law, Frances Ferguson explains that while rape was theoretically considered a crime that should be prosecuted publicly, women did not often dare to prosecute rapists.[40] Yet, while Lovelace repeatedly stresses that Clarissa should save herself the shame of her rape's being known, she continues to publicize what, as in the story of Lucretia, has always been both a deeply personal and an essentially political offence. In Richardson's time, of course, the politics of rape would have been defined in terms of the violation of a husband's unique right to his wife. Richardson, however, redefines both the politics of rape and the significance of making such a crime public.

Clarissa talks candidly of her experience to the strangers from whom she rents a room during the last period of her life; she writes to Lovelace's female cousins, making public his actions. By thus publicizing the most intimate details of her private oppression, Clarissa expands the idea of the public sphere from periodical and coffee-house debates among propertied men to include gossip among neighbours and boarding-house keepers as well as epistolary exchanges between aristocratic women. In refusing to present her case in a public court of law, she implies that the public system of justice would not protect her rights as a rational citizen as well as would an expanded public sphere that included the voices of other concerned and empathetic women.

Clarissa not only expands the notion of who should be included in the public sphere, but she also enlarges the range of subject matter appropriate for discussion. By insisting on publicizing a crime that others want her to contain within the domestic sphere of the household, Clarissa suggests that domestic violence is as worthy of public scrutiny as is state tyranny. Anna Howe and Lovelace both believe that Clarissa should stop publicizing her rape and simply marry her rapist (thus containing Lovelace's criminal act within the *ex post facto* ceremony that legally nullified the crime). Lovelace believes that the tragic ending on which Clarissa insists could be avoided

40 Frances Ferguson, "Rape and the Rise of the Novel," *Representations* 20 (1987), 88–112.

through its containment either as domestic comedy or romance: "Is not *the catastrophe of every story that ends in wedlock accounted happy*, be the difficulties in the progress to it ever so great?" (p. 944). Both Lovelace and Anna wish to render the highly political tragedy of Lucretia into the domestic romance of *Pamela*. Clarissa, however, will write her own tragic story against the grain of romance convention, using the form of tragedy (traditionally about crises in the nation state) to thwart the domestic containment of a romance ending.

By publicizing her rape and making public, through her last will and testament, the hypocrisy of the supposed benevolence of her paternal family, Clarissa redefines the public sphere not merely as a means of criticizing tyranny in the state but as a means of protesting against abuses of power in the household as well.[41] By framing his critique of the public sphere within a work of fiction, Richardson thus insists on the political relevance of the literary public sphere. Ultimately, however, the novel's tragic ending contains Richardson's challenge to the political public sphere within a pessimism that would have paralysed real reform of women's position. Although Anna Howe's story allows for a certain optimism, its narrative subordination to the central tragedy guarantees the reader's focus on the fact that Clarissa has few morally viable options other than death. Richardson's *Clarissa* thus stands as testimony both to the contradictions inherent in the universalistic discourse of the bourgeois public sphere and to the social structures that would obstruct and delay its ultimate self-transformation.[42]

41 While I suggest ways in which Clarissa manages to make her story public, Cook focuses on Clarissa's failure to find "a narrative *agora*: an open public space where she can tell her story." For Cook, Clarissa is "transformed into a personification, one circumscribed by the more powerful narrative of eighteenth-century male literary authority." *Epistolary Bodies*, p. 112. While Clarissa's political message is ultimately subordinated to the message implied by her tragic martyrdom, her words nevertheless enter the public record through Richardson's novel. Certainly her twenty-first-century readers have been educated by their transgressive potential.

42 Habermas has recently described the potential for self-transformation inherent in "the universalistic discourses of the bourgeois public sphere." See "Further Reflections on the Public Sphere," in *Habermas and the Public Sphere*, ed. Craig Calhoun (Cambridge: MIT Press,

By resurrecting the highly gendered discourse of earlier debates about authority and obedience, Richardson has managed to challenge the emergent ideal of a public of letters that excludes the insights of the women of genius who compose the marginalized, but still viable, "commonwealth of letters." If Clarissa's discourse within the literary public sphere challenges the hegemony of the bourgeois public sphere only to be silenced by the tragedy of her demise, the novel's own potential for effecting social transformation founders on its reception (to which Richardson himself certainly contributed) as merely a conduct-manual about marriage. While Richardson's most famous tragedy interrogates the logic by which women were excluded from the political public sphere, it simultaneously helps, through the power of its moral discourse, to obscure the profoundly political foundation of both domestic fiction and the literary public sphere.

1992), p. 429. He does not fully explain, however, how a critique of the exclusionary tendencies of the public sphere was being scripted by the same writers whom he cites as helpful in constructing its affective mythology. Furthermore, simply acknowledging that the public sphere had a potential for self-transformation does not begin to acknowledge the role the novel might have played in both enabling and obstructing such a transformation.

Is *Clarissa* Bourgeois Art?

Daniel P. Gunn

A t the beginning of *Clarissa*, the social atmosphere seems dense, pregnant, thick with meaning. From the start, the heroine is entangled in her family's scheme to accumulate property through marriage and concentrate it on a single heir. Her situation is further complicated by Lovelace's distinguished family background and the mixture of deference and hostility he prompts in the Harlowes, by the ambiguous status and trajectory of her own estate, and by frequent explosions of social jealousy and resentment from everyone around her. With this much social conflict in the air, it is perhaps not surprising that critics should have concluded that the moral ideas put forward by Richardson in *Clarissa* are circumscribed and defined by their partisan character—in short, that they are revolutionary "bourgeois" or "Puritan" ideas, asserted against the interests of the ruling aristocracy. Although it has been persistent and influential, this "bourgeois" account of *Clarissa*'s ideology depends on a romanticized and probably misleading view of class conflict in the eighteenth century, and it tends to disguise both the equivocations in Richardson's position and the socially coercive force of his moral rhetoric. In this essay, I begin by questioning the claim that *Clarissa*'s values are bourgeois; I then go on to propose a different model of

Richardson's ideological position—one which can help to explain the ambiguities and contradictions in his treatment of moral issues.

The idea that *Clarissa* is an expression of militant bourgeois ideology has a distinguished history. In "Clarissa Harlowe and Her Times," the seminal essay in this line, Christopher Hill argued that Richardson's aim in *Clarissa* was "to assert the bourgeois and Puritan conception of marriage against the feudal-cavalier standards of Lovelace and the Harlowe emphasis on concentration of property." At about the same time, Dorothy Van Ghent claimed that, in *Clarissa*, "the aristocracy is put in its place" and that, by her death, Clarissa "symbolically ... makes great her class," the "prosperous bourgeoisie," and "gives supernatural sanction to its code." Finally, in *The Rise of the Novel*, Ian Watt found in Clarissa's virtue "an expression of the moral superiority of her class"; she is "the heroic representative of all that is free and positive in the new individualism." During the last thirty years, this general view of class and ideology in *Clarissa* has frequently been repeated, and it has never seriously been challenged. Terry Eagleton restates Hill's thesis at the beginning of *The Rape of Clarissa*, where he argues that *Clarissa* is "an agent ... of the English bourgeoisie's attempt to wrest a degree of ideological hegemony from the aristocracy," part of the bourgeoisie's attempt "to saturate the whole ruling ideology with its own influence."[1]

1 Christopher Hill, "Clarissa Harlowe and Her Times," *Essays in Criticism* 5 (1955), 335; Dorothy Van Ghent, *The English Novel: Form and Function* (New York: Rinehart, 1953), pp. 55–57; Ian Watt, *The Rise of the Novel: Studies in Defoe, Richardson, and Fielding* (Berkeley: University of California Press, 1957), p. 222; Terry Eagleton, *The Rape of Clarissa: Writing, Sexuality, and Class Struggle in Samuel Richardson* (Minneapolis: University of Minnesota Press, 1982), p. 4. Further references to Hill and Eagleton appear in the text. Hill follows the line of inquiry opened by H.J. Habakkuk in "English Landownership 1680–1740," *Economic History Review*, 1st series, 10 (1940), 2–17, and "Marriage Settlements in the Eighteenth Century," *Transactions of the Royal Historical Society*, 4th series, 32 (1950), 15–30. For the pervasiveness of this account in criticism of *Clarissa*, see, for example, T.C. Duncan Eaves and Ben D. Kimpel, *Samuel Richardson: A Biography* (New York: Oxford University Press, 1971), pp. 239–41; Mark Kinkead-Weekes, *Samuel Richardson: Dramatic Novelist* (London: Methuen, 1973), pp. 123–24; Angus Ross, Introduction to Samuel Richardson, *Clarissa or The History of a Young Lady* (New York: Viking, 1987), pp. 20–22; Siobhan Kilfeather, "The Rise of Richardson Criticism," in *Samuel Richardson: Tercentenary Essays*, ed. Margaret Anne Doody and Peter Sabor (New York: Cambridge University Press, 1989), p.

This kind of reading usually begins by opposing Clarissa's bourgeois moral sensibility to Lovelace's aristocratic background; the conflict between these characters is then read as a projection of political conflict between their respective classes.[2] It follows that Clarissa's persistent superiority over Lovelace—"My soul is above thee, man!"[3]—and her eventual triumph over him through death demonstrate Richardson's preference for the ideology of her class, the emergent bourgeoisie. Richardson's status as an "organic intellectual" of the bourgeoisie supports this reading, as do the conventional critical and historical formulations which link Puritanism, bourgeois individualism, and the rise of the novel.[4]

Unfortunately, this lucid initial picture cannot account for *Clarissa*'s sustained criticism of acquisitiveness and economic self-interest —traits usually associated with the bourgeoisie. Van Ghent seems not to have recognized this complication, and she consequently asserts that the "value-system of *Clarissa*" consists of "Puritanism in mor-

254; John Richetti, "Lovelace Goes Shopping at Smith's: Power, Play, and Class Privilege in *Clarissa*," *Studies in the Literary Imagination* 28 (1995), 24. Although he does not directly address the issues I raise in this essay, Michael McKeon departs from the standard historical account in *The Origins of the English Novel 1600–1740* (Baltimore: Johns Hopkins University Press, 1987). He reads *Pamela* traditionally enough, as a predominantly "progressive" text, which offers "the message that inherited social status is strictly 'accidental' and strictly uncorrelated with the 'natural' gifts of virtue and merit" (p. 365); by the end of the novel, "we and B. know that it is [Pamela's] terms that have prevailed, that her apparent linguistic assimilation masks a supersession of aristocratic honor" (p. 368). But his brief comments on *Clarissa* suggest something different that is closer to what I argue below: Clarissa is "a conservative heroine" who "resists assimilation to the progressive model of her predecessor"; Richardson "evinces the darker, conservative apprehension that the essence of utopia is that it is not to be found in this world" (p. 418). "Is *Clarissa* Bourgeois Art?" was first published in *Eighteenth-Century Fiction* 10:1 (1997), 1–14.

2 See, for example, Hill, pp. 319–20, 323–24; Van Ghent, pp. 55–56; Watt, pp. 221–22. Eagleton takes this kind of reading for granted: "It would be easy, and relatively unoriginal, to show how Richardson's novels are among other things great allegories of class warfare, narratives of alliance and antagonism between a predatory nobility and a pious bourgeoisie" (p. 4).

3 *Clarissa*, ed. Ross, p. 646; Samuel Richardson, *Clarissa. Or, The History of a Young Lady*, ed. Florian Stuber, The Clarissa Project, 8 vols (New York: AMS Press, 1990), 4:202. References to *Clarissa* are by page number to the Ross edition (based on Richardson's first edition, 1747–48), followed by references to volume and page number of the AMS edition (a facsmile of the expanded third edition, 1751). The passages I cite were not altered substantially by Richardson's revisions.

4 For the phrase "organic intellectual," see Eagleton, pp. 2–3.

als, parental authoritarianism in the family, and the cash nexus as the only binding tie for society at large."[5] Even if we leave aside the novel's troubled attitude towards parental authoritarianism, surely this last item has a false ring. The admirable characters in the novel—Clarissa, Anna, Mrs Norton, the reformed Belford—are conspicuously indifferent to their own financial interests, even when, as in the case of Clarissa or Mrs Norton, there is genuine distress, and they repeatedly show themselves willing to give up money or property for the sake of some perceived higher value, such as filial duty, friendship, charity, or moral integrity. Meanwhile, characters such as James Harlowe or Solmes, who insistently seek financial gain and define human relations accordingly, following the dictates of the "cash nexus," are severely criticized. The acquisitiveness and economic aggressiveness associated with a cash economy are seen in *Clarissa* as tyrannical and destructive, even as vulgar: by the novel's standards of cultivation and good manners, James and Antony Harlowe come off very badly, as does the horrible and nearly illiterate Solmes.

As they manœuvre to take this more conservative strand of *Clarissa's* moral rhetoric into account, even critics as subtle as Watt and Hill have a tendency to lapse into self-contradiction.[6] Thus Watt sees Clarissa as "the heroic representative of all that is free and positive in the new individualism" but nevertheless simultaneously in combat *against* "the economic individualism whose development was so

5 Van Ghent, p. 61. The phrase "cash nexus" derives from the *Communist Manifesto*: "The bourgeoisie, wherever it has got the upper hand, has put an end to all feudal, patriarchal, idyllic relations. It has pitilessly torn asunder the motley feudal ties that bound man to his 'natural superiors,' and has left remaining no other nexus between man and man than naked self-interest, than callous 'cash payment.'" Karl Marx and Friedrich Engels, *Basic Writings on Politics and Philosophy*, ed. Lewis S. Feuer (Garden City, NY: Doubleday, 1959), p. 9. The persistence of a stark and oversimplified feudal/capitalist opposition in English literary criticism can in part be traced to its importance in Marxist theory. See Norma Landau, "Eighteenth-Century England: Tales Historians Tell," *Eighteenth-Century Studies* 22 (1989), 208–18.

6 I recognize, of course, that ideological formations in literature are themselves characteristically riven by contradictions. But my concern here and on the following pages is with contradictions in the arguments of the critics themselves—in particular, the logically contradictory assertions they make about the position of the bourgeoisie in eighteenth-century English society and the degree to which *Clarissa's* values are to be identified with the class interests of the bourgeoisie.

closely connected with that of Puritanism."[7] Hill begins by defining *Clarissa* as a bourgeois critique of aristocratic "property marriage"; in this reading, the Puritan struggle for individual salvation is "of a piece" with bourgeois individualism, and both obstruct the constant efforts of aristocratic proprietors to consolidate property through marriage (pp. 320, 328–30). Eventually, however, Hill is forced to abstract Puritan values from their bourgeois economic context, in order to show how *Clarissa* can function as a criticism of capitalism as well as property marriage. "Clarissa's standards," it turns out, "are those of the Puritan *ideal*, not those of conventional market morality"; they are "high Puritan standards, not of this world"—in fact, "a *criticism* of this world's standards" (pp. 331–32; emphasis added). By making this turn, Hill undercuts his own earlier arguments about the class basis of Clarissa's moral code—it no longer seems fair to suggest that the novel is "bourgeois art" (p. 320) if it is in fact a criticism of the market mentality of the bourgeoisie—and it becomes very difficult to situate Clarissa's "high Puritan standards" in the class struggle Hill has described. It is not far from here to the position of the critics William Warner calls "humanists," who argue that *Clarissa* supports "human dignity" or "the human being's innermost self" against the depredations of both bourgeoisie *and* aristocracy.[8] But if we reach this point, at which it is necessary to imagine a disengaged sphere of timeless human value, opposed to eighteenth-century society as a whole and allied with none of its class interests, we must ruefully confess that we have left the history of ideological conflict behind.

7 Watt, p. 222.

8 William Beatty Warner, *Reading Clarissa: The Struggles of Interpretation* (New Haven: Yale University Press, 1979), pp. 219–58. See, for example, Arnold Kettle, *An Introduction to the English Novel*, 2 vols (London: Hutchinson's Library, 1951): "The conflict of *Clarissa* ... is the conflict of love (i.e. human dignity, sympathy, independence), versus money (i.e. property, position, 'respectability,' prejudice)" (1:66); and Kinkead-Weekes: "[We have learned from social criticism that] Clarissa's tragedy is an exposure of a materialist and acquisitive society; of the moral decay of both the aristocracy and the 'middle class'; of a view of human relationship grounded on money and property ... [Richardson's] imagination told him that what was really the issue in the situation he had created was the sacredness of the human being's innermost self—whether we use the new word 'psyche' or the old word 'soul.' What is really unforgivable about Lovelace ... is that he cannot conceive or respect the essentially private inner core of personality that each person has a right to dispose of as only he or she may wish" (pp. 124, 141).

The class basis of Clarissa's values remains elusive even in Eagleton's *The Rape of Clarissa*. At the outset of his argument, Eagleton characterizes "the emergent English bourgeoisie" (p. 8) of the eighteenth century, which Richardson "represent[s]" (p. 7), as a revolutionary class, out to "wrest a degree of ideological hegemony from the aristocracy" (p. 4). Richardson's novels are an "agent" (p. 4) of this struggle, "lynchpins of an entire ideological formation" (p. 5), part of the bourgeoisie's project of "curbing or uprooting [certain aristocratic values]" in order to "saturate the whole ruling ideology with its own influence" (p. 4). Although Eagleton complicates this picture by acknowledging that "no mortal combat took place between nobility and bourgeoisie" in England, since "the middle class was content to shelter peacefully behind the insignia of traditional society, negotiating an ideological alliance with its social superiors" (pp. 3–4), the language of his opening pages insists on the "virulent aggression" (p. 4) which was necessary for the creation of the alliance: a revolutionary class must "wrest the most cherished symbols from the grip of its rivals" (p. 2), "challenge" and "oust" its "oppressors" (p. 1) in the cultural sphere, and "challenge the dominant ideology" (p. 2); by helping to shape and articulate the ideology of the bourgeoisie, Richardson "played a key role in the English class struggle" (p. 3).

In his opening pages, Eagleton associates the values of *Clarissa* with the interests of a revolutionary bourgeoisie in its struggle against aristocratic oppressors. But he also wants to read *Clarissa* as "arguably the major feminist text of the language" (p. viii), and, as his argument develops, this causes him to reimagine the enemy as the more generalized "patriarchal tyranny" (p. 16) or "ruling-class patriarchy" (p. 16). Since it is not at all clear that terms such as "ruling class" or "patriarchy" should be associated with the aristocracy in contradistinction to the bourgeoisie, the conflict between classes drawn so sharply in Eagleton's opening pages begins to dissolve. Later, Clarissa's dying is "a surreal act of resignation from a *society* whose power system she has seen in part for what it is," "a negation of *society*," and "documentary evidence against a *society* where the rape of Clarissa is possible"; it is an inconvenience for "the ruling class" or "the patriarchs" (pp. 74–75; emphasis added). But who constitutes "society" or "the ruling class" here? In what sense are the interests of these groups opposed to those of the bourgeoisie whose ideology Richardson is said to articulate? The original definition of class conflict no longer seems to carry any weight in these new formulations, and, three-quarters of the way through the book, not surprisingly, the bourgeoisie is *itself* defined as the power against which Richardson is struggling: "Bourgeois ideology is made to stand shamefaced and threadbare in the light of its own doctrines. ... It is not only that Clarissa exposes the rift between bourgeois pieties and bourgeois practice; it is also that those pieties themselves, once submitted to the pressures of fictional form, begin to crack open" (p. 77).

At the end of his analysis of *Clarissa*, Eagleton returns to the conflict between the aristocracy and the bourgeoisie, but the picture he gives is now more complicated, and the class basis of the novel's ideology has become obscure. Because he recognizes "the primacy of class struggle," Richardson affirms "the coherent bourgeois subject" against "ruling-class rapacity" (p. 85); Clarissa's death is "the triumph of bourgeois patriarchy" (p. 89) and "the strongest conceivable affirmation" (p. 90) of its ideology. But this death also "mutilates" the Harlowes, leaving the novel with "no where to turn but to Clarissa herself" (p. 89). Thus Clarissa's death "encompasses both aristocracy and bourgeoisie, revealing their true unity of interests" (p. 89)—they are "part of the same ruling-class power bloc" (p. 88), "two wings of the eighteenth-century ruling class" (p. 89)—and Richardson's novel embodies a Utopian wish to resolve "the deathly contradictions of patriarchal and class society" (p. 93) by means which are not yet historically available. It is difficult to see how, at one historical moment, the "bourgeoisie" can logically be characterized both as asserting itself against "ruling-class rapacity" and as constituting a "wing" of the "ruling-class power bloc." Even more conspicuous here, though, in the light of Eagleton's opening pages, is the gradual detachment of *Clarissa*'s values from any recognizable class interest. If, as Eagleton asserts, the moral rhetoric of *Clarissa* exposes the bourgeoisie's patriarchal repression of women and its dominant position in an exploitative society, this rhetoric cannot at the same time serve a struggling, revolutionary bourgeoisie. What class interests, then, does it serve? What does it mean, if we do not postulate classless and transhistorical moral values, to "turn ... to Clarissa herself"?

Like the critics I have been discussing, I want to examine the relationship between *Clarissa*'s moral rhetoric and class interests in eighteenth-century England.[9] However, I do not think the novel's principal ideological effect is likely to have been felt through allegorical representations of social or political conflict.[10] Nor do I think the traditional picture of a struggle between the aristocracy and the bourgeoisie offers much help in the effort to historicize *Clarissa*, regardless of how the project is conceived. As historians have frequently pointed out, the English aristocracy persists stubbornly throughout the early modern period, even when, after centuries of "rising" and "emerging," the bourgeoisie might be expected to have triumphed at last.[11] This persistence alone ought to sug-

9 I want to stress, however, that I do not think that *Clarissa* is in any sense *about* class conflict or the expression of class interests. I am not trying to "read" *Clarissa*, or elucidate its rich and varied aesthetic texture; I am trying to propose an alternative historical model for commentary about its ideological resonance.

10 There has recently been some interesting discussion of the ways in which contemporary political issues might have been represented in *Clarissa*. In *Richardson's "Clarissa" and the Eighteenth-Century Reader* (Cambridge: Cambridge University Press, 1992), for example, Thomas Keymer sees the conflict between Clarissa and her father as alluding to "the conflict of people with prince" (p. 120), while Lovelace's villainy carries suggestions, from a Whig perspective, both of "the historical example of the Protectorate and the contemporary menace of Jacobite autocracy" (p. 173). There is additional evidence of Richardson's support for Whig principles in John A. Dussinger, "*Clarissa*, Jacobitism, and the 'Spirit of the University,'" *Studies in the Literary Imagination* 28 (1995), 55–65. By contrast, Margaret Anne Doody sees Richardson as a Tory and hears an echo of Walpole in Lovelace's first name: see "Richardson's Politics," *Eighteenth-Century Fiction* 2 (1990), 113–26. See also Morris Golden, "Public Context and Imagining Self in *Clarissa*," *Studies in English Literature* 25 (1985), 575–98 and Jocelyn Harris, *Samuel Richardson* (Cambridge: Cambridge University Press, 1987). While explicit political references like these may very well have been present in *Clarissa*, they would have been minor suggestions, at best, in comparison to Richardson's treatment of personal morality. The challenge for ideological criticism, I think, is to investigate the ways in which seemingly *non*-political material furthers class interests—indirectly, by subterranean means.

11 For a summary of some key arguments on this question, see McKeon, pp. 157–69. As McKeon notes, the "orthodox view" among historians of the early eighteenth century now suggests "political, social, and economic stability," with the classic argument about "the rise of an 'entrepreneurial' and 'middle class' gentry" now "replaced by a thesis of the persistence

gest that conventional ideas about class conflict during the period
are displaced or askew. Literary critics have been particularly mistaken in associating capitalism, as a mode of production, solely with
the interests of an urban bourgeoisie—people like Richardson—
and opposing these interests to those of a feudal aristocracy in the
countryside. Following E.P. Thompson, I want to propose a different model, in which capitalism has already begun to predominate in
both rural and urban areas at the time of *Clarissa*, leaving England
in the hands of the relatively small and predatory class of people in
possession of substantial land, substantial capital, or both, with the
position of the landed proprietor remaining central as the tangible
manifestation of power and the goal of nearly all wealth.[12] In this
model, capitalism has become the dominant mode of production,
both for landed proprietor and City magnate, with both operating
according to a logic of investment, production, and improvement,
seeking the best return possible on their property. The principal
class opposition, then, and the site of ideological tension, is not
between the aristocracy and an urban, professional bourgeoisie—
for Thompson and many other historians, the latter can hardly be

of the aristocracy" (p. 167). Although he is sceptical about this consensus, McKeon reaches
a conclusion consistent with the view I outline below: "Nevertheless we may get closer to
the heart of this extraordinary alliance if we stress not its 'aristocratic' character but the
way in which capitalist or 'middle class' values have transformed the aristocracy: how individualistic and class criteria are eating away, as it were from within, at a social structure
whose external shell still seems roughly assimilable to the status model" (p. 167).

12 See E.P. Thompson, "Patrician Society, Plebeian Culture," *Journal of Social History* 7 (1974),
    382–405, and "Eighteenth-Century English Society: Class Struggle without Class?" *Social
    History* 3 (1978), 133–65. In these essays, Thompson's principal concern is to allow a sep-
    arate sphere of cultural activity for the poor during what he calls "a predatory phase of
    agrarian and commercial capitalism" ("Eighteenth-Century English Society," p. 139). The
    picture he draws is of an exploitative gentry and aristocracy, already capitalist in orienta-
    tion, intent on maximizing profits and accumulating money through agriculture, commer-
    cial speculation, government office, marriage, and any other available means, and existing
    in a relation of tension with the plebeians, who, while not yet conscious of themselves as
    a working class, still had begun to struggle against the domination of their oppressors.
    While it differs in tone and in its emphasis on struggle, this polarized model of eighteenth-
    century society is similar in key respects to the models offered by Peter Laslett in *The World
    We Have Lost* (New York: Scribner's, 1965), pp. 22–52, and Harold Perkin in his chapter
    on "The Old Society" in *The Origins of Modern English Society, 1780–1800* (London: Rout-
    ledge and Kegan Paul, 1969), pp. 17–62. For discussions of these and other views of class
    in eighteenth-century English society, see W.A. Speck, *Society and Literature in England 1700–
    1760* (Atlantic Highlands, NJ: Humanities Press, 1983), pp. 41–45, and R.S. Neale, *Class in
    English History* (Oxford: Oxford University Press, 1981), pp. 68–84, 96–98.

said to exist, as a class, until the end of the eighteenth century—but rather between the powerful, who own property, control production, and seek to maintain their privileged position, and the great masses of the dispossessed.[13]

If we imagine *Clarissa* as an ideological statement in this kind of society, it seems quite misleading to invest it with the energy of a revolutionary class, struggling to overthrow its oppressors. The novel's surface action depicts a conflict within the ruling class—a disagreement between rival predators—rather than a conflict between representatives of different classes. Despite the differences in their origins, Lovelace's family and the Harlowes are both clearly part of the privileged élite, and both, characteristically, have their property concentrated in landed estates. Although Lovelace grumbles that Harlowe Place is "sprung up from a dunghill within every elderly person's remembrance" (161;1:231), this kind of movement into and out of the ruling class had been a regular feature of English life for centuries, and there can be no doubt about the Harlowes' status at the time of the novel. Taken together, the family's estates are enough to make "a noble fortune" for James, giving him "such an interest as might entitle him to hope for a peerage" (77;1:73). James has, in his own right, "a considerable estate" in Scotland and "one as considerable in Yorkshire" (41;1:6); he also apparently has had an Oxford or Cambridge education, in the same college as Lovelace (48–49;1:19–20). In a society in which substantial proprietors made up as little as one or two per cent of the population, it would seem ludicrous to suggest that the distinction between Lovelace's and Clarissa's family backgrounds represents a *class* distinction; they are, on the contrary, both members of the small and privileged ruling élite.

Nor does it seem plausible, in this model, to argue that Clarissa's moral values represent the *interests* of the bourgeoisie in its struggle

13 On the bourgeoisie as a class, see Thompson: "Thus for at least the first seven decades of the century we can find no industrial professional middle class which exercises an effective curb on the operations of predatory oligarchic power" ("Eighteenth-Century English Society, p. 143), and "Patrician Society," p. 395; Laslett, pp. 36–37; and Perkin, pp. 61–62. On the central importance of the relationship between the powerful and the dispossessed, see Fredric Jameson, *The Political Unconscious* (Ithaca: Cornell University Press, 1981): "for Marxism class must always be apprehended relationally, and ... the ultimate (or ideal) form of class relationship and class struggle is always dichotomous. The constitutive form of class relationship is always that between a dominant and a laboring class" (p. 83).

against the aristocracy. In critical discussions, the term "bourgeoisie" seems to have two possible senses; in neither can its interests be imagined as opposed to those of the aristocracy in eighteenth-century England. In its first, more proper sense, "bourgeoisie" refers to an urban financial, mercantile, and professional class: townspeople, business people, lawyers, and doctors. But in the mid-eighteenth century, Thompson suggests, this group was extremely small and allied in a "client relationship" to the nobility and gentry, whose younger sons it recruited and whose interests it served in exchange for patronage and support. It certainly was in no position to challenge the authority of the ruling class or supplant it. In a second, looser sense, influenced by Marxist theory, "bourgeoisie" has come to mean "ruling class under capitalism" or "those in control of the means of production in a capitalist economy"; this is the sense which Thompson has in mind when he refers to the eighteenth-century nobility and gentry as "an agrarian bourgeoisie."[14] But as Thompson's usage will itself suggest, the "bourgeoisie" in this second sense cannot be seen as struggling against the nobility and gentry; they *were* the nobility and gentry, who controlled virtually all England's productive resources, whether in agriculture, mining, industry, or trade. There was no one for members of this class to challenge or oust but themselves.

The nobility and gentry did, however, have to modify their relation to the exploited majority in order to *become* a bourgeoisie, in this second, looser sense—and it is here, in the means by which the ruling class maintained its power over the dispossessed, that we should look for the ideological significance of *Clarissa*. Even if the ruling-class oligarchy was constituted more or less as it always had been, the new economic and social forms associated with capitalism demanded new forms of ideological control; the eighteenth-century English ruling class can be seen as exploring, in Fredric Jameson's words, "various strategies of the *legitimation* of its own power position."[15] This was especially true in the area of morality, the novel's preferred ideological sphere, where some strategies, such as orthodox religious

14 "Eighteenth-Century English Society," pp. 142–42, 162.

15 Jameson, p. 84.

doctrine or the myth of subordination, were traditional, while others, such as the emphasis on individual integrity and judgment, were new.[16] The gradual shift to capitalism made for a heterogeneous mixture of moral norms, all of them designed to serve the interests of the ruling class in different ways. If the novel assisted in the development of capitalism in eighteenth-century England, it did so not by supporting the revolutionary aspirations of a "rising" class of shopkeepers and tradespeople against aristocratic oppressors, but rather by mediating between these heterogeneous ideological modes within the ruling class to produce a new and seemingly coherent system of mystifying ideas. In *Clarissa*, Richardson's moral rhetoric did precisely this kind of work, drawing disparate and even contradictory ideological strands together into a powerful and reproducible aesthetic form—a new myth for the ruling class.

What would this ideological work have looked like in practice? To answer this question, we should turn, I think, not to *Clarissa*'s explicitly social and political content, but to its attempt to shape its readers' ideas about conduct and personal morality. At this level, one finds not militant "bourgeois" ideology but rather a collection of inchoate and historically inconsistent ethical postures. Consider, for example, Richardson's treatment of the moral status of passion. In the conservative and overtly Christian strand of *Clarissa*'s moral rhetoric, human passion is a temptation, a hindrance to salvation, which must be renounced in the interests of virtue. As she draws close to death, Clarissa exhibits an eerie and unworldly calm, unbroken even by longing for Anna; she recognizes dreamily that "the thought of death, and its hoped-for happy consequences ... in a manner annihilates all other considerations and concerns" (1306;7:313).

16 In distinguishing between these competing strategies of legitimation, I am describing a conflict similar to that which McKeon sees in the contrast between "conservative" and "progressive" ideologies in the middle of the eighteenth century (for example, pp. 174–75.) My contention, however, is that even what McKeon calls "progressive" ideology was finally coercive in its effect, since it set up myths of individual freedom and meritocratic fluidity which legitimated social division, and since it tended to deflect moral attention away from economic practice and into a sexually charged feminine and domestic sphere.

Richardson expects us to endorse this posture of extreme renunci-
ation, just as he expects Aaron Hill to admire Clarissa's "exemplary"
efforts to "subdue" and "prevail over" her passion for Lovelace.[17] The
utter annihilation of the world and its attendant passions is, he implies, the final goal of Christian devotion.[18] But he simultaneously
presents *susceptibility* to passion as an index of moral worthiness. The
note of Lovelace's villainous "hard-heartedness" is struck repeatedly;
he boasts that he is, when faced with the "distresses" he has caused,
"seldom betrayed by tenderness into a complaisant weakness unworthy of himself" (601;4:109).[19] By contrast, Clarissa claims that her
"benevolent heart" would make her "fly to the succour of ... a poor
distressed" like herself (893;5:307), and she is regularly overcome
by her emotions as she resists Lovelace's stratagems and advances.
A truly good human being, Richardson suggests, will have a tender
and susceptible heart, like Clarissa's.[20] The contradiction is stark: in
one formulation, what rises naturally from the heart, "inclination,"
"passion," "resentment," even the longing for friendship and happiness on this earth, should be repressed and overcome by the pious
Christian; in another, the heart's emotional impulse towards others,
towards pity and sympathy, is the mark of Christian virtue.

These conflicting ideas about the relation between virtue and
strong feeling are drawn from traditional and progressive ruling-
class ideologies, respectively. Richardson's attack on desire and the
passions is deeply conservative; it descends, as critics such as Margaret Anne Doody and Carol Flynn have suggested, not so much

17 Richardson to Aaron Hill, 24 October 1746, in *Selected Letters of Samuel Richardson*, ed. John
   Carroll (Oxford: Oxford University Press, 1964), p. 73.

18 For an analysis of Clarissa's meditation on death and the rejection of the flesh it entails,
   see Allan Wendt, "Clarissa's Coffin," *Philological Quarterly* 39 (1960), 481–95.

19 See, for example, Clarissa's reflections on Lovelace's response to *Venice Preserved* (640;4:188)
   and Morden's account on the character of a libertine (564;4:33). Morden's references to
   the unmoved hardness of the libertine, even when faced with "prayers, tears, and the most
   abject submission," echo Lovelace's self-characterization.

20 For a reading sympathetic to this suggestion, see Henry Fielding's letter of praise to
   Richardson: "God forbid that the man who reads this with a dry eye should be alone with
   my daughter when she hath no Assistance within Call." Fielding to Richardson, 15 October
   1748, printed as an appendix to [Sarah Fielding,] *Remarks on Clarissa* (1749), Augustan Reprint Society no. 231–32, ed. Peter Sabor (Los Angeles: William Andrews Clark Memorial
   Library, 1985), n.p.

from militant Puritanism as from a Roman Catholic and Anglican tradition of self-denial and meditation, with roots going back to the middle ages.[21] As ideology, this position looks backward towards a pre-capitalist system of domination, based on order and degree, emphasizing strict deference and the repression of self-interest. By contrast, the exaltation of each person's "benevolent heart" as a moral guide suggests a less deferential social system, one which places a premium on individuality and authenticity. This second, progressive vision of morality supports the interests of the propertied class just as vigorously as asceticism, but in a different (and more forward-looking) ideological context. Simply put, a morality which grants the individual her own intuitive authority encourages the myths of freedom and openness—anyone can rise, anyone can prosper— which, under capitalism, replace the myth of security as a justification for the common people's dispossession and a disguise for their exploited condition.

These two visions of morality and passion in *Clarissa* are fragments from parallel and historically discontinuous ruling-class ideologies, superimposed on one another in the construction of Clarissa's character. Interestingly enough, they are alike in one respect: they define morality as an inner state, abstracted from the world and powerless to effect change, and they thereby render morality less likely to inhibit economic development. As R.H. Brissenden has pointed out, a key feature of the sentimental moral response is the powerlessness of the observer, who can, it seems, do nothing, when faced with distress, but experience an agreeable *frisson* of individual sensation.[22] By individualizing morality and associating it with a feeling of detached powerlessness, the cult of "virtue in distress" drew morality out of the sphere of public affairs and discouraged any moral scrutiny of social practice. In the middle of the eighteenth century, the Christian ethic of repression and self-denial epitomized by Clarissa's death seems to have had something like the same effect. By the time Richardson wrote *Clarissa*, this kind of moral rhetoric had begun to lose its

---

21 Margaret Anne Doody, *A Natural Passion: A Study of the Novels of Samuel Richardson* (Oxford: Clarendon, 1974), pp. 175, 178–79; Carol Houlihan Flynn, *Samuel Richardson: Man of Letters* (Princeton: Princeton University Press, 1982), pp. 26–28.

22 R.F. Brissenden, *Virtue in Distress: Studies in the Novel of Sentiment from Richardson to Sade* (London: Macmillan, 1974), p. 8.

practical ideological connection with actual social arrangements—
the hierarchical system of deference which produced it had long
been in the process of transforming itself—but it persisted, in the
textual condition described by Jameson as "sedimentation," continuing to emit outmoded messages from its buried position.[23] Under
the nascent capitalism of the mid-eighteenth century, the effect of
those messages was, as Raymond Williams has pointed out, to deflect
attention away from social practice entirely. "Though [*Clarissa*] engages with the current acquisitiveness and ambition of the landown-
ing families," Williams writes, "it is in the end not a criticism of a
period or of a structure of society, but of what can be abstracted
as 'the world.'"[24] When Clarissa's decision to set aside the "world"
is held up as an example of the moral life for young women readers and built into one of the principal moral myths of English culture, it ratifies the implicit assumption that the moral life can have
no effect on what happens *out there*, in the corrupt universe of economic transactions. In *Clarissa*, as elsewhere, it is the *female* subject
who is particularly identified both with virtue and with this separation from "the world"; confined to the newly articulated domestic
sphere, the eighteenth-century heroine becomes the locus of moral
concern, while the world of men carries on according to its own un-
scrutinized logic. In this context, it is perhaps worth noting that even
Clarissa's transcendent virtue is unable to prevent the duel between
Lovelace and her cousin Morden.

On the subject of passion, then, the assertion that Richardson's
morality supported the interests of a revolutionary bourgeoisie is undermined both by the inconsistency of his views and by their convenience for anyone attempting to *maintain* a position of power. Richardson's achievement, as an ideologue, was to equivocate between two
repressive moral ideologies, disguising their inconsistencies and incorporating them both into his ideal of human conduct. In doing
so, he helped the eighteenth-century ruling class to reimagine itself,
during a period of economic change, without breaking sharply with

23 Jameson, pp. 140–41.

24 Raymond Williams, *The Country and the City* (New York: Oxford University Press, 1973), p.
65.

its most valued traditions. Because so many of Richardson's readers still wanted to believe in the efficacy of conservative moral ideas—came, indeed, out of a settled tradition which had *always* believed in them—Richardson performed a valuable service by inscribing such ideas into his moral system. But he also responded to the need for a more atomized and individualistic morality, appropriate for the fluid and openly exploitative world which was coming into being. His characteristic narrative strategies—an intense concentration on the particular and the local, obsessive repetition and moral insistence, and a tremendous capacity for equivocation—made it possible for him to assimilate contradictory moral assumptions into his myth of idealized female conduct.[25] And Clarissa's vivid presence both as a character and a symbol of moral integrity in turn made this myth crucial for the development of moral ideology in Austen, Eliot, and other novelists.

If the view I have outlined here is accurate, *Clarissa* is neither as simple nor as radical as the critical tradition which imagines it as "bourgeois art" would suggest. Its moral rhetoric is layered and inconsistent, complicated by the slow and uneven adaptation of England's ruling élite to capitalism. It may endorse values which can very loosely be called "bourgeois," but these are signs of a privileged group's continuing struggle to maintain power over common people, and they coexist with more traditional ruling-class values, which have a parallel coercive force. Like most novels, *Clarissa* is

---

25 On Richardson's equivocation regarding the crucial moral question in the novel, see Keymer, pp. 85–141. In treating Clarissa's conflict with her father, Keymer argues, Richardson employed the "subtle and endlessly modulating discriminations of casuistry," with the intent "not to instruct the reader in the answer to a problem ... about which he is, as a novelist, quite literally equivocal," but "instead to put the problem to a reader in such a way as to enact the troubling unavailability of resolution" (pp. 122, 123). In my account, the "subtle and endlessly modulating discriminations" characteristic of Richardson's text allowed him to incorporate competing and inconsistent ideological constructions without collapsing into overt incoherence. McKeon's vision, in *Origins*, of the dialectical relation between progressive and conservative ideologies may also be relevant here; if, as he suggests, "progressive ideology has an inherent tendency toward the conservative" (p. 420), we should perhaps not be surprised to find elements of both emerging in a complex text like *Clarissa*.

more an instrument of subtle control than a manifesto; it helps to formulate and disseminate a powerful ideological program which maintains the position of the privileged. At a moment of poise, suspended between old and new ruling-class ideologies, Richardson seems to have been fluent in both idioms: aspiring and prosperous, a man of the City, but also deferential, with a mysterious gentleman friend in his youth and connections here and there with the great in later life. His ideological position is perhaps best represented by the famous Joseph Highmore painting which shows him standing in front of a portrait of Lady Bradshaigh and her husband on their Lancashire estate.[26] The portrait within the portrait is a traditional country-house picture, an image of power and settled proprietorship; Richardson looks out at us from beneath its aegis.

---

26 The painting hangs in the National Portrait Gallery, London, and is reproduced in colour on the jacket of this book and in black and white facing the introduction (p. 3). For a discussion of the circumstances surrounding its composition, see Eaves and Kimpel, *Samuel Richardson*, p. 525.

Abuse and Atonement: The Passion of Clarissa Harlowe

Peggy Thompson

While still at Harlowe Place, Richardson's title character is tormented by the choice her family forces her to make: either she must enter a marriage that is physically, ethically, and spiritually repugnant to her or she must abandon the dutiful obedience by which she has always defined herself. Once Clarissa makes the agonizing decision to leave her father's house, Lovelace exacerbates the pain of her ostracism with deception, manipulation, confinement, threats, harassment, and, finally, rape. Richardson scholars have discussed this narrative of relentless suffering in scientific, Sadean, iconographic, and biblical contexts, as well as in relation to the literary traditions of tragic drama, the seduction narrative, and the literature of holy dying.[1] This essay will focus on the intersection of two additional interpretive contexts for Clarissa's suffering:

---

1 For discussions of Clarissa's suffering in scientific contexts, see R.F. Brissenden, *Virtue in Distress: Studies in the Novel of Sentiment from Richardson to Sade* (New York: Barnes and Noble, 1974), pp. 34–35; Ruth Perry, *Women, Letters, and the Novel* (New York: AMS Press, 1980), pp. 22–23; and especially Ann Jessie Van Sant, *Eighteenth-Century Sensibility and the Novel: The Senses in Social Context* (Cambridge: Cambridge University Press, 1993), who cites Brissenden and Perry as precedents for her argument that Richardson's (and Lovelace's) method has "much in common with the investigative methods of science, particularly the sensibility experiments, which ... combine invasive entry with provocation of pain" (p. 64).

her identity as an eighteenth-century woman and her identity as a Christ figure. More specifically, I will argue that three classical theories of Christ's atonement preached widely in eighteenth-century London and evoked in the characterization of Clarissa reinforce an eighteenth-century social construct of woman as passive, defenceless moral martyr. Ellen Pollak provides a powerful summary of this construct:

Woman was a creature whose intellectual deficiencies and emotional instability made her unfit to govern herself even as they especially suited her to a passive mode of spiritual martyrdom in which her "virtue" consisted in the "art" of regulating herself according to the demands of an arbitrary masculine desire. ... An emblem of the other world, her role would be— like that of the original incarnation of perfection—to rectify human lack by means of beatific suffering. By bearing the burden of all deficiency in herself, she would vindicate the sufficiency of men.[2]

Rita Goldberg has demonstrated how such a burden informs the profoundly ambivalent relationship between Clarissa and Lovelace,

Van Sant also provides a list of others who have explored the influence of Sadean eroticism on the novel (pp. 64–65n20): Mario Praz, *The Romantic Agony* (Oxford University Press, 1970), pp. 97, 99; John Traugott, "An Essay to Find the Reader," *English Literature in the Age of Disguise*, ed. Maximillian Novak (Berkeley: University of California Press, 1977), pp. 181–82; Ian Watt, *The Rise of the Novel* (Berkeley: University of California Press, 1965), pp. 231ff.; and Leopold Damrosch, Jr, *God's Plot and Man's Stories: Studies in the Fictional Imagination from Milton to Fielding* (Chicago: University of Chicago Press, 1985), p. 219. Clarissa's identification with Job is explored by Tom Keymer, "Richardson's Meditations: Clarissa's *Clarissa*," *Samuel Richardson: Tercentenary Essays*, ed. Margaret Anne Doody and Peter Sabor (Cambridge: Cambridge University Press, 1989), pp. 99–109; Jonathan Lamb, *The Rhetoric of Suffering: Reading the Book of Job in the Eighteenth Century* (Oxford: Clarendon Press, 1995), pp. 226–47; and Robert A. Erickson, *The Language of the Heart, 1600–1750* (Philadelphia: University of Pennsylvania Press, 1997), pp. 216–26. Doody discusses Clarissa's suffering in several additional contexts: tragic drama, seduction narratives, the literature of holy dying, and iconographic traditions; see *A Natural Passion: A Study of the Novels of Samuel Richardson* (Oxford: Clarendon Press, 1974), pp. 99–240. "Abuse and Atonement: The Passion of Clarissa Harlowe" was first published in *Eighteenth-Century Fiction* 11:3 (1999), 255–70.

2 Ellen Pollak, *The Poetics of Sexual Myth: Gender and Ideology in the Verse of Swift and Pope* (Chicago: University of Chicago Press, 1985), p. 46. Pollak's focus is on Swift and Pope, but I quote her here because this description of the construct is so direct and succinct and because, as we shall see, it is clearly applicable to Richardson's character. For economic and legal implications of this construct, see Laura Brown, "The Defenseless Woman and the Development of English Tragedy," *SEL* 22 (1982), 438–41; and Susan Staves, *Married Women's Separate Property in England, 1660–1833* (Cambridge: Harvard University Press, 1990), pp. 224–27.

both of whom act on a double-edged belief in the "possibility of an extraordinary woman's redeeming or damning power."[3] But frequently critics have resisted seeing Clarissa primarily as a moral or spiritual martyr. Goldberg herself, for example, argues that while carrying tremendous mythological weight as a potential saviour, Clarissa struggles towards an identity that is more than symbolic, exemplary, or objective.[4] Others deny that Richardson's heroine is essentially passive. Margaret Anne Doody, for example, insists that Clarissa "refuses to be a mere victim," while Elizabeth Bergen Brophy has outlined many ways that Richardson, "a radical social critic," takes issue with the heroic ideal of the passive woman in all of his novels.[5] Most important, Clarissa herself repeatedly insists on distinguishing the virtue to which she aspires from the submission it often appears to be. She claims, for instance, "that although I wished to be thought *meek*, I would not be *abject*; although *humble*, not *mean*."[6] The character herself, then, resists primary definition as one who suffers at the hands of and for the sake of others. But such an understanding of Clarissa, and implicitly of woman, is reinforced in the novel by the identification of Clarissa with Christ, particularly by eighteenth-century assumptions about what Pollak refers to as the "beatific suffering" of "the original incarnation of perfection."

Among the diverse scholars who have discussed Clarissa as a Christ figure,[7] John Dussinger has demonstrated that Richardson himself unequivocally embraced suffering like Clarissa's as the way of Christ. More specifically, Dussinger identifies in Richardson an "introspective Anglican religion, which traditionally stressed the authority of

3 Rita Goldberg, *Sex and Enlightenment: Women in Richardson and Diderot* (Cambridge: Cambridge University Press, 1984), pp. 93, 106–7.

4 Goldberg, pp. 106–7.

5 Doody, pp. 101–2; Elizabeth Bergen Brophy, *Samuel Richardson* (Boston: Twayne, 1987), p. ix.

6 Samuel Richardson, *Clarissa or The History of a Young Lady*, ed. Angus Ross (New York: Penguin, 1985), 193; 1:291. References are to this edition, which is based on the first edition, followed by references to the third edition, ed. Florian Stuber, 8 vols (New York: AMS Press, 1990). See also 307; 2:196.

7 See, for example, Goldberg, pp. 108, 126–7; Allan Wendt, "Clarissa's Coffin," *Philological Quarterly* 39 (1960), 488–89; Damrosch, p. 259; Terry Eagleton, *The Rape of Clarissa: Writing, Sexuality and Class Struggle in Samuel Richardson* (Minneapolis: University of Minnesota Press, 1982), p. 62; and Erickson, pp. 216, 224, 226.

conscience and the burdens of following Christ's example."[8] Such a faith assumes a subjective theory of atonement carrying great sway among Richardson's friends and contemporaries: each individual must choose to accept and emulate the gift of Christ's sacrifice. This theory is articulated by John Tillotson, Robert South, and John Sharp, whose sermons, Dussinger points out, are in Clarissa's library at Sinclair's establishment.[9] In the churches of London, however, this was just one of three classical theories of atonement preached widely in the twenty years prior to the publication of *Clarissa*. Indeed, it was not uncommon for two or even all three theories to be evoked within individual sermons, most of which lack the sophistication and self-conscious consistency of those written by Richardson's (and Clarissa's) favourites, but which are valuable nonetheless for revealing deep-seated and widely held assumptions about the meaning of Christ's suffering. These assumptions extend to and mediate the novelist's and his characters' understanding of Clarissa's Christlike suffering—significantly, in ways that reinscribe and reaffirm woman's identity as ideally passive, suffering, and salvific.

The early church fathers characterized the atonement achieved through Christ's passion as a divine conflict with and victory over evil. The emphasis was on God's triumphant power in reconciling himself with his imperfect creation, as Robert Wright preached in a sermon in 1740: with his death, Christ "hath laid a Foundation for the Reconciling of a sinful World unto God" (1740).[10] This theory—widely known as *Christus Victor*—reduces human suffering to a transient point in a cosmic drama. Henry Read, who like Wright was preaching to benefit a charity school in London, used the familiar image of a journey to convey the ultimate insignificance of earthly

8 John A. Dussinger, "Conscience and the Pattern of Christian Perfection in *Clarissa*," *PMLA* 81 (1966), 236–45.

9 Dussinger, p. 236n3.

10 Robert Wright, *Scripture Knowledge and Practice necessary to Salvation, A Sermon Preached for the Benefit of the Charity School in Gravel-Lane, Southwark, on New-Years-Day, 1739–40, in St. Thomas's, Southwark* (London: Printed for Richard Hett, 1740), p. 10. See also Gustaf Aulen, *Christus Victor: An Historical Study of the Three Main Types of the Idea of Atonement*, trans. A.G. Hebert (New York: Macmillan, 1954), pp. 4–7.

suffering: "Tho I meet with Losses and Disappointments, and injurious Treatment, I am but a Stranger on Earth, and will not fret and be dejected because I meet with Traveller's Fare" (1739).[11] Others preaching at this time minimize human pain by stressing the profound difference between this life and an afterlife. John Cennick, for example, said that life with God will be more "solid" and "perfect" (1744), while George Lavington, Chaplain in Ordinary to His Majesty, referred to our future life as "most substantial" (1746).[12] The Curate of the Tower in London, Thomas Broughton, took a different tack; he exhorted his audience of soldiers to holy thoughts so that "all your Watchings, Labours, and Pains ... may, in the End, turn to your own great and everlasting Good: and that your very want of Ease, Riches, and Happiness, in this World, may, thro' Submission and Resignation to the Will of God become so many Glorious Preparatives for Rest, Honour, and Felicity, in the World to Come" (1737).[13] In a kind of theological alchemy, then, earthly labour and pain become the stuff of eternal felicity, and are, therefore, to be welcomed, not lamented.

In the *Meditations* printed privately after the novel was published, Clarissa applies an identical theology of suffering to her own tribulations: "I was graciously enabled to look back upon those distresses which had been so grievous to me, as so many mercies manifested by the Divine Goodness to draw me to Himself."[14] Clarissa's creator

11 Henry Read, *This Year shalt thou die, A Sermon Preached for the Benefit of the Charity-School in Gravel-Lane, Southwark, on New-Years-Day, 1738–39, in St. Thomas's, Southwark* (London: Printed for Richard Hett, 1739), p. 22.

12 John Cennick, *The Good Samaritan, Being the Substance of a Sermon Preach'd at the Tabernacle in London in the Year 1744* (London: Printed for the author, 1744), p. 13; and George Lavington, LL.D., Rector of the United Parishes of St Mary Aldermary, and St Thomas the Apostle; Residentiary of St Paul's, and Chaplain in Ordinary to His Majesty, *A Sermon Preached in the Parish-Church of Christ-Church, London, On Thursday May the 1st, 1746* (London: Printed by J. Oliver, 1746), p. 14.

13 Thomas Broughton, A.B., Fellow of Exeter College, Oxon, and Curate of the Tower in London, *The Christian Soldier; or, the Duties of a Religious Life, Recommended to the Army: in a Sermon Preach'd Before His Majesty's Second Regiment of Foot-Guards in the Tower-Chapel, on their leaving the Garrison, On Sunday, October 23, 1737*, Published at the Request of the Officers of the Army then present, and of several of the Tower Inhabitants (London: Printed for C. Rivington at the Bible and Crowne in St Paul's Churchyard, 1738), p. 23.

14 Samuel Richardson, *Meditations Collected from the Sacred Books* (1750; reprinted New York: Garland, 1976), p. viii.

also explicitly adopts the language and assumptions of the *Christus Victor* theory of atonement. In his postscript to *Clarissa*, for example, Richardson wonders: "And who that are in earnest in their profession of Christianity but will rather envy than regret the triumphant death of CLARISSA?" (1498; 8:289). We find a similar focus on what Clarissa wins, not on what she suffers, in critics such as Cynthia Griffin Wolff, whose final chapter on the novel is entitled "Clarissa Triumphant," and Lesley Berry, who characterizes Clarissa's death as "the culmination of ... [her] triumph as a Christian martyr."[15] Lovelace is stunned by Clarissa's victorious demeanour during their first meeting after the rape, but he recognizes immediately its Christian derivation: "my present account, to which she unexpectedly called me, seemed, as I then thought, to resemble that general one to which we are told we shall be summoned, when our conscience shall be our accuser" (900; 5:322). Acknowledging his confused and powerless response, he exclaims to his confidant, "Oh Belford! Belford! whose the triumph now!" (901; 5:324). Although his state of mind, like Clarissa's return to her "Father's house," is not without subsequent circumlocutions, Lovelace never regains the advantage. Hoping to reduce Clarissa to absolute dependence on him through the rape, he instead ensures her inexorable movement from him—much to his chagrin, frustration, and ultimate madness.

In his controversial reading of *Clarissa*, William Beatty Warner also focuses on the transformation of Clarissa's torment into triumph. "The rape," he acknowledges, "is the genuine catastrophe of Clarissa's personal history. But it gives Clarissa this advantage ... [Lovelace's] artifices can now be reinterpreted to be a succession of the darkest contrivances, designed expressly to destroy her."[16] The rape becomes a sort of wrestling hold that backfires; Clarissa now has her rapist "*hypped*," as Lovelace himself complains (888; 5:300).

15 Cynthia Griffin Wolff, *Samuel Richardson and the Eighteenth-Century Puritan Character* (Hamden, Conn.: Archon Books, 1972), pp. 152–73; Lesley Berry, "'Anfractuous Ways,'" *Samuel Richardson: Passion and Prudence*, ed. Valerie Grosvenor Myer (London: Vision Press, 1986), p. 118. Wolff acknowledges that Clarissa's triumph, "if viewed in strictly psychological terms, is less than complete" because Clarissa's obsession with her father, though appropriate perhaps in religious terms, reflects, in psychological terms, "the limitations of this religious system" (p. 247n14).

16 William Beatty Warner, *Reading Clarissa: The Struggles of Interpretation* (New Haven: Yale University Press, 1979), pp. 72–73.

Warner accuses Clarissa of using a Christian "textual system to recuperate every loss, by making it part of the history of triumphant
virtue."[17] That textual system is the *Christus Victor* theory of atonement, which, as we have seen, Clarissa does indeed invoke, as does
Richardson himself, not only in the postscript, but also in his correspondence where he claims, "Clarissa has the greatest of triumphs in
this world. The greatest, I will venture to say, even *in* and *after* the
outrage, and *because* of the outrage, that ever woman had."[18] Ironically, Warner himself adapts a similar system, the notion of a larger
conflict in which all battles are mere episodes, to redefine a brutal and cynical rapist as a stalwart combatant in a "war of meaning."[19]
More significantly, the *Christus Victor* theory of atonement serves as
a congenial interpretive context for the rapist himself. Near the end
of the novel, Lovelace defends himself: "A *jest* I call all that has
passed between her and me; a mere jest to die for!—for has she not,
from first to last, infinitely more triumphed over me than suffered
from me?" (1308; 7:317). Lovelace's remark, weighing Clarissa's ultimate triumph against the "mere jest" he plays on her, is disturbingly
similar to both Warner's critique and Richardson's admiration of
Clarissa's response to her rape. All three exemplify the dangers of invoking the *Christus Victor* theory of atonement (consciously or not)
as an interpretive paradigm for the central conflict in the novel: in
focusing on Clarissa's victory, it denies the reality of her suffering.[20]
To borrow language from the sermons Richardson's contemporaries
were hearing, this paradigm implies that the rape, details of which
are notably absent in the novel, is less "substantial" and "solid" than

17 Warner, p. x; see also pp. 56–74. Citing Job rather than Christ as Clarissa's model, Keymer makes a similar point about Clarissa's *Meditations*: "From the earliest meditations, a
narrative begins to emerge, in which her suffering ceases to be arbitrary, and takes on the
character of a divinely sanctioned trial" (pp. 96–97). Erickson would agree, but he adds
that by "heroically translat[ing] herself into her own scripture," Clarissa indicts "patriarchal
and libertine authority in eighteenth-century literature" (pp. 224, 226). However, Lamb argues that Clarissa uses, not the exemplary prescription of Job, but its "non-normalizable"
particularity and intensity in her power struggle with Lovelace (pp. 226–47).

18 *The Correspondence of Samuel Richardson*, ed. Anna Laetitia Barbauld, 6 vols (London: R.
Phillips, 1804), 4:224–25.

19 Warner, p. 49.

20 See Joanne Carlson Brown and Rebecca Parker, "For God So Loved the World?" in *Christianity, Patriarchy, and Abuse: A Feminist Critique*, ed. Joanne Carlson Brown and Carole R.
Bohn (New York: Pilgrim Press, 1989), pp. 6–7.

the afterlife Clarissa is promised. It trivializes her agony as a mere stage in an extended struggle, a portion of the "Traveller's Fare" which she as a "Stranger on Earth" must expect before reaching her heavenly destination. In the context of this first theory, then, characters and critics who read Clarissa as Christ reinforce her identity as that of the passive woman whose suffering is justified by her role as "emblem of the otherworld."

In the eleventh century, Anselm of Canterbury (1033–1109) articulated a new theory of atonement, based on medieval law, which emphasized God's demands for justice and honour. According to Anselm, God could not forgive human sin "out of mercy alone, without any payment of the honor taken away from Him."[21] But because humanity was innately sinful, it owed God a debt it could not pay; hence the need for a human God, one who both owed and could pay the debt, just as John Tottie, Fellow of Worcester College in Oxford, preached at St Paul's in 1735: "the Person engaged in the great work of attonement and reconciliation ... united the Divine Nature to the Human, that he might by the one be the proper representation of those for whom the redemption was wrought, and by the other, give a price to those stripes by which all mankind were to be healed."[22] Tottie thus answers Anselm's question "Why Man Became God?" just as Anselm himself did centuries before. Robert Wright, who, we have seen, articulates the *Christus Victor* theory of atonement, also echoes Anselm's theory as he describes human need for divine salvation: the "misery of fallen Man is great in this, that he is wretchedly weak and Impotent, unable to recover himself out of his fallen State; ... he hath no ransom to give" (1740). God, therefore, must provide that ransom in the death of his child: "The Word of God shows the Lamb of God slain; his Death a solemn Sacrifice for Sin; his precious Blood a real Propitiation, and the Law and Justice of God fully satisfied

21 Anselm of Canterbury, *Why Man Became God and The Virgin Conception and Original Sin*, trans. Joseph M. Colleran (Albany, NY: Magi Books, 1969), p. 85.

22 John Tottie, *A View of Reason and Passion, as in their original and present State, A Sermon Preach'd before the Right Honourable The Lord-Mayor, Aldermen, and Sheriffs of the City of London, at the Cathedral-Church of St. Paul, On Sunday, December 21, 1735* (London: Printed for C. Rivington, at the Bible and Crown in St Paul's Church-yard, 1736), p. 24.

with what he hath done and suffered."[23] Wright is complacent about the justice of this arrangement, but many of his contemporaries betray a defensiveness about God's demand that he be appeased only through the sacrificial suffering of his child. Joseph Trapp, preaching for the Lord Mayor at St Paul's in 1729, and itinerant Congregational preacher Alexander Forrest, preaching on Christmas Day in 1737, used identical language to insist that punishment may be inflicted on one "for the sake of another" "without the least Impeachment of his [God's] Justice." Addressing a society devoted to evangelism, John Thomas flatly asserted God's "clear and undoubted Right to convey his Blessings to Mankind in his own Way." Even a God who had not offered salvation through Christ could never be called "unjust," the renowned George Whitefield argued. "No," he continued, "as for GOD, His Ways are perfect, and his Dealings with his Creatures are *holy, just and good*" (1738).[24] These defences of God's demands for satisfaction are all finally simple reaffirmations of God's absolute authority, which is the foundation of Anselm's theory as well. But Anselm not only reaffirmed God's authority to demand Christ's sacrifice; by basing this theory on medieval law, he reinforced the existing social order and justified the suffering of those called to make sacrifices in its name. Analogously, Richardson's evocation of Anselm's understanding of atonement, with its emphasis on appeasing a tyrannical God, reinforces the patriarchal order in Clarissa's society.

The "justly incensed" James Harlowe, Sr, is very similar to Anselm's God, who demanded that a perfect child atone for all his incapable,

23 Wright, pp. 8, 11.

24 Joseph Trapp [Minister of Christ-Church and St. Leonard's Foster-Lane, London], *A Sermon Preach'd before the Rt. Honourable The Lord Mayor and Aldermen of the City of London at the Cathedral Church of St. Paul; Friday, January 30, 1729, Being the Fast-Day for the Execrable Murder of the K. Charles I* (London: Publish'd at the Request of the Lord Mayor, and the Sheriffs; Dublin: Reprinted by N. Husser on the Blind-Key, 1729–30), p. 11; Alexander Forrest, Itinerant Preacher of the Christian Doctrine, *False Brethren forfeited, A Sermon Preached in Petticoat-Lane, White-Chapel, London; Sabbath the 25th of December, 1737 and in Substance, formerly in North Britain* (London: Printed for the Author; and Sold by A. Cruden, J. Robinson, and J. Graham, 1738), p. 14; John [Thomas], Lord Bishop of Peterborough, *A Sermon Preached before the Incorporated Society for the Propagation of the Gospel in Foreign Parts; At Their Anniversary Meeting In the Parish Church of St. Mary-le-Bow, on Friday, February 15, 1750* (London: Printed by Edward Owen, 1751), p. 10; and George Whitefield, A.B. of Pembroke College, Oxford, *On the Justification by CHRIST, A Sermon Preached at the Parish Church of Saint Anthony, &c.* (London: Printed by W. Bowyer, for James Hutton, 1738), pp. 19–20.

Portrait of George Whitefield (1714–1770), *London Magazine* (1770), opposite p. 549. Reproduced by permission of McMaster University Library.

sinful human brothers and sisters and did "not will the world to be reconciled in any other way."[25] Clearly this paradigm is deviously appropriated not only by Clarissa's unyielding father, but also by her decidedly imperfect siblings in their demands that Clarissa sacrifice herself to Solmes, ostensibly to appease the honour of the outraged parent, but actually to satisfy their own selfish passions. James, for example, cloaks his jealous resentment of Lovelace with concern for his father's authority: "My father supposing he has the right of a father in his child is absolutely determined not to be bullied out of that right. And what must that child be who prefers the rake to a father?" (223; 2:36). Similarly, Arabella, who has just been enraged by an allusion to her own failure to win Lovelace, constructs Clarissa's dilemma as a simple choice between the daughter's and father's wills. "And who ... is to submit," she asks her aunt sarcastically, "her father or she?" (205; 1:323). Whereas James and Arabella thus hide their self-interest behind respect for a father's authority, other characters implicitly reject the absolute authority entailed by Anselm's theory of atonement by criticizing Harlowe's demands that his daughter "sacrifice" herself to his wishes. For example, in language highly evocative of Anselm's God's insistence that only Christ's death could ransom sinful humanity, Anna Howe accuses Clarissa's mother of acceding to Harlowe's tyranny, of giving up "the most deserving of her children, against her judgement, a sacrifice to the ambition and selfishness of the least deserving" (133; 1:177).[26] Clarissa, who herself repeatedly characterizes the proposed marriage with Solmes as a sacrifice (123; 1:159; 125; 1:163), reports to Anna that Lovelace, too, has used this construction of the marriage to pressure Clarissa into dependence on him: "They [her family] had made it impossible (he told me, with too much truth) to oblige them any way but by sacrificing myself to Solmes" (167; 1:241). But when, just two letters earlier, he refers to Rosebud, a likely victim of Belford's seduction, as an unsuspicious lamb whose "throat will hardly shun thy knife" (162; 1:233), Lovelace reminds us of how similar he and the Harlowes are; both assume a patriarchal system that justifies abuse

---

25 Anselm, p. 79. See also Rita Nakashima Brock, "And a Little Child Will Lead Us: Christology and Child Abuse," *Christianity, Patriarchy, and Abuse*, pp. 51–53.

26 Anna repeatedly refers to the proposed union with Solmes as a "sacrifice" (67, 84–85; 1:54, 87).

of women as sacrifices to the demands and desires of men. Clarissa's grandfather, of course, is an exception to this generalization. Indeed, he subverts the Harlowe patriarchy by willing his Dairy House to the descendant who merits it—despite her gender and place in the birth order and despite the opportunity the family has to consolidate its property in James, Jr. But the surviving patriarch and his many agents rightly recognize that this posthumous attempt to reward and nurture Clarissa's virtue is profoundly subversive, and they violate the grandfather's will as brutally as they do its deserving beneficiary.

Acknowledging the abusive patriarchy in which Clarissa lives, Florian Stuber has argued that the "inadequacy of earthly authorities does not prevent Clarissa, or us, from imagining an ideal, personified in the image of Divine Authority, a power operating with mercy and justice to effect changes which nurture life." The crucial distinction Stuber makes between Harlowe, Sr, the abusive father and false god, and a merciful, nurturing Divine parent is, however, extremely fragile in the novel.[27] Stuber looks, not to Clarissa's grandfather, but to another character, Dr R.H., as an image of the true, loving God, but this minor figure is utterly inadequate to counteract the powerful image of Anselm's God provided throughout the novel in Clarissa's earthly father. James Harlowe, Sr, is introduced in Richardson's list of "The Principal Characters" just as Anselm describes his God: both are "despotic, absolute, and when offended not easily forgiving" (37).[28] Richardson further encourages the identification of the earthly and divine fathers by reducing the characterization of Harlowe to an authoritarian voice, speaking through his progeny.[29] Most important, Clarissa herself never succeeds in making the distinction absolute, exhibiting instead great ambivalence towards both her father and the unsettling concept of authority he exemplifies.[30] Her refusal to call her father "arbitrary" (95; 1:108)

27 Florian Stuber, "On Fathers and Authority in *Clarissa*," *SEL* 25 (1985), 572. Damrosch makes a similar point: "If Harlowe is a dreadful parody of the Augustinian God, the parody comes uncomfortably close to the original" (p. 235).

28 Richardson's third edition does not include this description of Harlowe, Sr.

29 Stuber points this out, but he does not comment on how it further identifies Harlowe, Sr, with a supernal father (p. 560).

30 Erickson, who claims that Harlowe, Sr, conveys "the anger of a superlatively jealous god," also argues that Clarissa is ambivalent towards her father's authority (p. 212).

implies that such authority is unacceptable to her, but she reserves her anger for his surrogates: her uncles, her sister, and especially her brother. She directly defies her father only at the cost of great personal anguish and eventually repents both the forbidden correspondence with Lovelace and, of course, her flight from her father's house. Her last earthly goal is the removal of her father's curse, and she wills him the financial legacy that could have allowed her to escape his power. In short, despite his unforgiving despotism, she can never bring herself to renounce her father or to stop trying to appease him. As a false authority, Harlowe, Sr, may be chastened by his daughter's suffering and death. But Clarissa's enduring wish for her father's approval perpetuates his presence as Anselm's irreproachable God, who finally gets the atoning sacrifice he demands. From this perspective, one cannot finally distinguish clearly between "the father's house" to which Clarissa returns as a beloved child and that to which she returns tormented to death. The merger of the two houses and two fathers in Richardson's novel reinscribes the invidious eighteenth-century assumption, part of the myth of passive womanhood, that appeasement and satisfaction are reserved for the man (the Father) while the agonizing sacrifice that makes them possible is assigned the Christlike woman.

The third major theory of atonement evoked in the novel originated with Abelard (1079–1142), but was popularized by the pietist movement of Richardson's own day. It was the theory of which Richardson was most conscious—especially given his close association with two of its most ascetic exponents, William Law and George Cheyne.[31] This theory shifts the emphasis from God's power and demands to Christ's gift as it is offered to save individual sinners. Personal acceptance of Christ and a decision to live in his spirit replace the sacraments as the means to salvation.[32] Such a theory is implied in

31 See Dussinger, pp. 241–44; Damrosch, pp. 230–31; and Rosemary Belcher, "'Triall by what is contrary': Samuel Richardson and Christian Dialectic," *Samuel Richardson: Passion and Prudence*, pp. 94–96.

32 Dussinger explains the close relationship between the religious imperative to live according to Christ's example and spirit and the thriving theories of a moral faculty in the eight-

countless sermons of the day exhorting listeners to follow Christ's example. For example, Henry Read tells his listeners in 1738 that to do good is to "imitate the perfect Example of the Redeemer." Christ's atonement is the pattern for all Christian charity, as Alexander Forrest explains: "This Christian Charity hath for its Principle, the Love of God shed in the Hearts of Believers, to make them one Heart and one Soul; and for its Patern, the Example Christ, who, by his Sufferings, hath Restored his people to the Favors of God, that they should Love one another, as he hath loved them" (1737). In another charity sermon, James Wood also interprets Christ's suffering not simply as the means to make Christian love possible, but as the form that love should take: the Christian "endeavors to tread in his [Christ Jesus'] Steps, and to walk even as he walked, to copy after his magnificent and sympathizing Temper, of whom it is said, that in all of Afflictions he was afflicted; that he bore our Sorrows and Griefs" (1731–32). George Whitefield is even more explicit in insisting that we suffer as Christ did: "*his* Doctrine was a Doctrine of the Cross; and their [his Disciples'] ... professing themselves to be his followers would call them to a constant State of voluntary Self-suffering and Self-denial" (1737).[33]

Clarissa's well-known adherence to Puritan conduct-books exemplifies a life lived in the spirit of Christ as called for in this interpretation of atonement. But by so living, Clarissa not only follows his example, she becomes an exemplar herself, thus reinforcing her identification with Christ. Anna Howe refers to her as "our pattern" (175; 1:256), and Joseph Leman remarks on her ability to convert others: "she goes nowhere, but saves a soul or two, more or less" (386; 2:345). Anna's and Leman's unadulterated admiration is unusual,

eenth century (p. 239). Eagleton further attests to the complex interrelatedness of the contexts in which meaning accrues to Clarissa's suffering by describing the "transitional point" at which *Clarissa* was written in terms remarkably similar to those used to describe the contemporary shift in understanding Christ's atonement: this was a time, Eagleton explains, when "a growing regard for the free affections of the subject deadlocks with a still vigorous patriarchal tyranny" (p. 16).

33 Read, p. 3; Forrest, pp. 35–36; James Wood, *Readiness to good Works, and Largeness of Mind in them, Recommended in a Sermon Preached in Gravel-Lane, Southwark, for the Benefit of a Charity-School there, January 1st 1731–2*, Published at the Request of the Managers (London: Printed for R. Hett, at the Bible and Crown in the Poultry, 1732), p. 9; George Whitefield, *The Nature and Necessity of Self-Denial, A Sermon preached at the Parish Church of St Andrew, Holborn, on Sunday, October 9, 1737* (London: Printed by W. Bowyer for James Hutton, 1738), p. 1.

however; the reactions of the Harlowes and Lovelace reveal the difficulties attending the concept of a personal saviour.[34] Clarissa's family reject the reproaching example in their presence and resent her for confronting them with their sins. As Anna Howe's opening letter seems to recognize, the more irreproachable Clarissa is, the more trials she must undergo from those who cannot emulate her: "You see what you draw upon yourself by excelling all your sex" (40; 1:4).[35] Or, as she bluntly reminds Clarissa later in her struggles, "Your merit is your crime" (237; 2:61). Lovelace is similarly honest, voicing what Clarissa's family will not admit: "She is so greatly above me! How can I forgive her for a merit so mortifying to my pride!" (734; 5:14). Just as the Harlowes disown her, Lovelace tries to annihilate her offending merit through the rape,[36] which is horribly foreshadowed in his metaphorical throttling of his feminine conscience:

I seized her by the throat—*There!*—*There*, said I, thou vile impertinent!— Take *that*, and *that!*—How often have I given thee warning!—And now, I hope, thou intruding varletess, have I done thy business!
   Puling and *in-voiced*, rearing up thy detested head, in vain implorest thou *my* mercy, who, in *thy* day, hast showed me so little!—Take *that*, for a rising blow!—And now will *thy* pain, and *my* pain from *thee*, soon be over!—Lie there!—Welter on!—Had I not given thee thy death's wound, thou wouldst have robbed me of all my joys. (848; 5:224)

Murderous resentment of her virtue is only the most obvious threat Clarissa's role as personal saviour presents to her, however. Lovelace is equally fearful of her failure; Clarissa can redeem him only if she resists him. Hence, the ambivalence he reveals towards his mighty effort to prove Clarissa's weakness.

   In his manipulative role of honourable lover, Lovelace veers impulsively towards a sincere marriage proposal (492; 3:220–21). But when Clarissa refuses, he pushes his vicious plot forward, even as

34 See Goldberg, pp. 35–36, and Rachel Myer Brownstein, "'An Exemplar to Her Sex': Richardson's Clarissa," *Yale Review* 67 (1977), 30–47, who both discuss how Clarissa's identity as exemplar is profoundly problematic.

35 In her analysis of Anna Howe's first letter, Goldberg explains how "unexamined praise" itself is "another version of Clarissa's persecution" (pp. 66–69).

36 Brophy argues that through the rape, Lovelace attempts to reverse the terms of his relationship with Clarissa, by making himself her "only possible savior" (p. 68).

he expresses contempt for his compulsive diabolism: "As I hope to live, I am sorry at the present writing, that I have been such a foolish plotter, as to put it, as I fear I have done, out of my *own power* to be honest. I hate compulsion in all forms; and cannot bear, even to be *compelled* to be the wretch my choice has made me!" (848; 5:223). His need for redemption by another is never more clear, but even acceptance of Clarissa's graceful virtue, Lovelace implies, will require her suffering: "For I am now awakened enough to think that to be forgiven by injured innocents is *necessary* to the Divine pardon" (1185; 7:86). The "awakened" Lovelace's logic is chilling: personal saviours, like Clarissa and Christ of the third theory of atonement, achieve the emotional and psychological power necessary to move others to repentance only by suffering at the hands of those they would save.[37] This is George Whitefield's assumption as he wonders at those who are unmoved even by the crucifixion:

What, can they see their Savior hanging on a Tree, with Arms stretched out to embrace them, and yet, upon their True Repentance, doubt of Acceptance with him? ... Look on his Hands, bored with Pins of Iron; look on his Side, pierced with a cruel Spear on purpose to unloose the Sluices of his Blood, *and open a Fountain for Sin*, and for Uncleanness;—And then despair of Mercy if you can![38]

To save Lovelace, Clarissa must not only suffer, but suffer horribly. To avoid such suffering is to refuse Christ's call that she walk the Way of the Cross for the sake of another.

Clarissa, then, is in a double-bind that appears even more insidious when we remind ourselves that in Clarissa's world sinners and saviours are divided along gender lines; it is no coincidence that Lovelace's murdered conscience is feminine. Goldberg summarizes: "there are evil male principles and good female principles. Once a woman is tainted with evil, the man who has violated her is polluted too. The violated (that is, sexual) woman is a reproach to mankind, and the road to repentance is closed anew by every victim."[39] In justifying the test to which he plans to put Clarissa, Lovelace recalls: "I

37 See Brown and Parker, p. 12.

38 Whitefield, *On Justification by CHRIST*, p. 24.

39 Goldberg, p. 84.

have read in some place [1 Corinthians 11] *that the woman was made for the man,* not *the man for the woman.* Virtue then is less to be dispensed with in the woman than in the man" (429; 3:84). Lovelace thus casts Clarissa in a dual role: she is servant of man and guardian of virtue, the same dual role attributed to the idealized passive woman and to Christ as suffering servant and messiah. As such, Clarissa is caught in an excruciating and inextricable trap implicitly justified by her identification with Christ, the personal saviour.[40] Thus, not only does this subjective view of Christ's passion—that he "died *for me*"—deflect interest from the suffering saviour; like the construct of the salvific woman, it can—and does in Lovelace—promote victimization in the name of salvation.

Identifying Clarissa with Christ does not settle crucial questions about the significance of her suffering. As evidenced by the multiple theories of atonement preached in Richardson's day and surviving in twentieth- century criticism, Christ's own suffering is problematic.[41] Is it primarily a triumph, an appeasement, or an example? Feminist theologians have raised new issues in recent years by articulating the dangers—for women especially—of confusing Christ's passion with passive suffering, some going so far as to deny that the crucifixion was redemptive in any sense.[42] This same distinction between

40 Brown and Parker's recent feminist critique of the third, personal theory of atonement is uncannily apt in describing Clarissa's dilemma: "We [women] must be viewed as vulnerable to victimization and loved not because of who we are but to save another from the guilt of being himself with us. If a man is himself, he destroys us. If he saves us, he must contradict his own nature" (p. 13), or, as Lovelace puts it, he must be "robbed ... of all [his] joys."

41 Among the many related issues that preclude a stable Christian doctrine of suffering are the distinction between suffering that results from personal sin and that which results from faithfulness; the importance (some would argue the necessity) of martyrdom; the sense in which Jesus can be both messiah and suffering servant; the meaning of the incarnation apart from the crucifixion; the need for others to suffer after Christ's passion; the question of whether God suffers; and the degree to which we can or should try to understand earthly suffering. See Jack Bemporad, "Suffering," *The Encyclopedia of Religion,* ed. Mircea Eliade (New York: Macmillan, 1987), 14:99–104.

42 See Brown and Parker, Brock, and other essays in *Christianity, Patriarchy, and Abuse*; and Mary Grey, *Feminism, Redemption and the Christian Tradition* (Mystic, Conn.: Twenty-Third Publications, 1990). For a recent attempt to recover the redemptive significance of the cross in a feminist context, see Sally B. Purvis, *The Power of the Cross: Foundations for a Christian Feminist Ethic of Community* (Nashville: Abingdon Press, 1993).

principled suffering, on the one hand, and rationalized abuse, on the other, is at the heart of the complex reactions Clarissa evokes. Without denying the perspective from which Clarissa's pain is a passion—purposeful and redemptive[43]—we can recognize how the three classical theories of atonement evoked in the novel (and its scholarship) contribute to Clarissa's identity as a passive woman who derives meaning and importance only from her victimization by men. Those men meanwhile assume the roles of moral combatant who does no real harm, incensed father whose demands for sacrificial appeasement cannot be questioned, and needy sinner whose salvation entails another's pain. Richardson, his characters, and his critics have all at times imposed these problematic paradigms on the novel. Thus, far from stabilizing this notoriously unstable text, viewing Clarissa as an atoning Christ raises new questions about interpretive strategies used both within and outside its pages.[44]

43 Doody's book provides the best development of that perspective.

44 Without mentioning Clarissa's identity as a Christ figure or the theories of atonement, Terry Castle, *Clarissa's Ciphers: Meaning and Disruption in Richardson's "Clarissa"* (Ithaca: Cornell University Press, 1982) makes a similar point. The "moral dimension" of *Clarissa*, she argues, is anything but "programmatic." Rather, "by tracing so searchingly the patterns of abuse and exploitation which occur when meanings are routinely and arbitrarily inscribed and reinscribed by interpreters, it invites us to examine the grounds of our own hermeneutic activity. ... It returns us to the matter of human suffering—the pain expressed by Clarissa" (p. 29).

"Written in the Heart":
Clarissa and Scripture

Robert A. Erickson

Theas rene sjel var i den bok. [Thea's pure soul was in that book.]
Ibsen, *Hedda Gabler*

Hearts are not had as a gift but hearts are earned.
Yeats, "A Prayer for My Daughter"

Discerning contemporaries well read in Richardson's fiction established what has come down to us as one of the most frequently invoked clichés of eighteenth-century literary history. In his novels Richardson provided a masterly representation of human "nature," and he was applauded particularly for his "delineation of the human heart."[1] The association of the heart and the writing process was always a close one for Richardson. It begins with the heart as

---

1 See the survey of responses in chap. 12, "The Reception of *Clarissa*; Richardson and Fielding," in T.C. Duncan Eaves and Ben D. Kimpel, *Samuel Richardson: A Biography* (Oxford: Clarendon Press, 1971), pp. 285–321. To Fielding's and Johnson's well-known appreciation of Richardson's knowledge of the human heart may be added this from the Marquis de Sade: "'The example of Richardson', wrote Sade, teaches that one must explore the heart, not virtue, 'because virtue, however beautiful and necessary it may be, is still only one of the modes of this amazing heart, the profound study of which is so necessary to the novelist and which the novel, faithful mirror of the heart, must necessarily map out in all its windings.'" Jay Clayton, *Romantic Vision and the Novel* (Cambridge: Cambridge University Press, 1987), p. 27. My ensuing comment on Richardson and the heart is based in part on his letter to Sophia Westcomb [1746] on "the converse of the pen." *Selected Letters of Samuel Richardson*, ed. John Carroll (Oxford: Clarendon Press, 1964), pp. 64–67. "'Writ-

memory, an exceedingly sensitive instrument for receiving, recording, preserving, and expressing human experience. In an analogy with the physiological operation of the circulatory system as it was understood after Harvey, in which the heart both receives and discharges the blood, the cultural ideal of the good woman or good man, for Richardson and many of his contemporaries, is represented by a friendly, undesigning, innocent, worthy, feeling heart (adjectives drawn from Richardson's correspondence), a heart capable of receiving the most refined impressions, but a heart which also hides nothing and which expresses itself with uncommon openness, spontaneity, and lucidity, whether speaking or writing—especially writing. The supreme goal for the Richardsonian correspondent was to transform human absence into presence by translating faithfully the life blood of intimate, natural, spoken conversation into written conversation. The intense epistolary correspondence Richardson describes is intimately connected with the receptive and expressive nature of the hearts of the writers and readers within his fictions and with the hearts of the outside readers of the fictions. Hence familiar letter-writing is an ongoing expression of the heart of the writer and an impression on the heart of the reader, a circulatory system of receiving, expressing, and receiving again those impressions and ideas closest to the hearts of the individual correspondents.

Richardson was acutely aware of impressions. For almost forty years he worked intimately with the process and business of printing and book-making—the messy literal business of print impression— before he wrote the first of his three novels. It is hard to imagine a more bookish writer than Richardson. He wrote books, he printed books, he collected books—he once even characterized himself as a book "taken up and laid down" by the ladies.[2] He was the only major English writer who made his living solely as a printer. Printing, reading—and eventually writing—books was his life work, so it is not at all surprising that given his acute religious sensibility he should see

ten in the Heart': *Clarissa* and Scripture" was first published in *Eighteenth-Century Fiction* 2:1 (1989), 17–52.

2 Richardson to Hester Mulso, 15 Aug. 1755, *Selected Letters*, p. 321.

172 ROBERT A. ERICKSON

his own life—and that of the fictional creation closest to his heart[3]—as part of God's Book of Life, the register of those names enrolled for salvation at the last day.

Talking about the heart and nature was a way for Richardson and his contemporaries to express an awareness of his having provided in his fictions a new representation of inner experience, most notably the "Passions," centring on love. "All the Letters are written," Richardson says in his preface, "while the hearts of the writers must be supposed to be wholly engaged in their subjects" so that the descriptions of "critical Situations" as they arise are "brought home to the breast of the youthful Reader."[4] It was customary in the eighteenth century to describe someone's being in love by saying his or her heart was "engaged," and we still use the term "engaged" in a similar sense. But obviously the connection with love is not the only sense in which the heart can be engaged. Readers of Richardson's novels have perhaps for too long made a simple association between the heart and love. There is much more to the metaphor of the heart than that.

If ethical and religious experience, in the Protestant tradition especially, is also taken to be an expression of the inner life, Richardson's stress on inner experience is also a way of exploring certain religious states of mind and being. He first put this idea explicitly in the postscript to the first edition: the work "is designed to inculcate upon the human mind, under the guise of an amusement, the great lessons of Christianity."[5] As he kept rereading and revising *Clarissa* through the first three editions (and all its "impressions"), the idea that the narrative had great religious import seems to have

---

3 Richardson was fond of referring in his correspondence to Clarissa as "my girl," and as her literary father he must have felt that after her demise he was suffering as much as her fictional father, whose own death from grief and remorse occurs shortly after Clarissa dies. Richardson once wrote to an acquaintance: "But, Sir, my nervous infirmities you know—time mends them not—and Clarissa has almost killed me." Richardson to J.B. Freval, 21 Jan. 1751, *Selected Letters*, p. 174.

4 Samuel Richardson, *Clarissa or, The History of a Young Lady*, Shakespeare Head edition, 8 vols (Oxford: Basil Blackwell, 1930), 1:xiv. References are to this edition, which is based on the revised third edition. Parallel references (where they exist), by page number, are provided to the edition of *Clarissa or The History of a Young Lady*, ed. Angus Ross (Harmondsworth: Penguin, 1985), which is based on the first edition. P. 35.

5 Penguin, p. 1495.

continued to work on him, but he came to express this idea more subtly. For example, in the preface to the third edition of *Clarissa* (1751), where after characteristically expressing his deeply felt sense of the work's monitory function, he notes that "above all" he aimed in *Clarissa* "to investigate the highest and most important Doctrines not only of Morality, but of Christianity, by shewing them thrown into action in the conduct of the *worthy* characters" and "the *unworthy*" (1:xv). Again, in the postscript to the third edition, in tones reminiscent of an Old Testament prophet, he amplifies in this age of "general depravity, when even the Pulpit has lost great part of its weight" (8:308), the "great end" he had in view in *Clarissa*. English divines of the later seventeenth century—Thomas Watson, John Norris, Robert South, John Tillotson, for example—seem closer to him in temperament than those of his own day, with a few exceptions such as his visionary friends Edward Young and William Law.[6] The "author thought he should be able to answer it to his own heart [if] ... he could *steal in* ... and investigate the great doctrines of Christianity under the fashionable guise of an amusement" (8:308).[7]

6 See Rosemary Bechler's discussion of Richardson and his "Brethren" of the 1740s in "'Trial by What Is Contrary': Samuel Richardson and Christian Dialectic," *Samuel Richardson: Passion and Prudence*, ed. Valerie Grosvenor Myer (London: Vision Press, 1986), pp. 94–98. On Richardson's overtly religious views, see Eaves and Kimpel, pp. 550–56.

7 The ambivalent word "investigate," which Richardson uses twice in describing his aim, does not occur in the preface or postscript to the first edition. For Johnson, to investigate means "to search out; to find out by rational disquisition"; investigation is "the act of the mind by which unknown truths are discovered" (*Dictionary*, 1755). The sense for both Richardson and Johnson seems to be in part a quasi-legal inquiry; it is a curiously scientific word for Richardson to use, and with it he can appeal to his more philosophical readers, even deists. But the word also has the older etymological sense of "to trace or find out by steps, to search or inquire diligently," to trace (*vestigium*, track) something back to its source in order to achieve an original meaning or state of being which has been lost or forgotten. See Nathan Bailey, *Dictionnarium Britannicum: Or a more Compleat Universal Etymological English Dictionary Than any Extant*, 2nd ed. (1736), s.v. "Investigate." This work was printed, in part, by Richardson. In one sense, the history of Clarissa Harlowe is the tracing of her *vestigia*, of the tracks of her pen, translated into print, signifying the pure remembrances of trial and transcendence which her author, who chooses this way to walk in the ways of the Lord (Psalm 119:1–3), wishes to impress upon his reader. Cf. Lovelace on Clarissa's "*vestigia*" (5:381; 916). Richardson's entire literary career might be seen as a recapitulation (and repetition) of the evolution from script to print. On the question of the meaning of the terms "Anglican" and "Puritan" as they relate to English Protestant doctrine and practice, I am following the lead of Horton Davies, who stresses the Puritans' preponderant concern with the individual's personal interpretation of holy scripture and "interiority," with intense self-examination, with preaching, and with recording the intervention of divine grace in

Richardson may have been an orthodox, conservative Anglican with strong Puritan traits in the conduct of his day-to-day life, but when he was writing *Clarissa* in the mid-1740s, his imagination transformed his conventional religious ideology into a radical exploration and reworking of the main doctrines of Protestant Christianity. In this visionary, even apocalyptic enterprise, Richardson has more in common—possibly through the influence of William Law—with the author of "The Marriage of Heaven and Hell" (another self-educated English tradesman and part-time printer) than with his conventional Christian contemporaries. What were the doctrines Richardson wished to investigate? Whether he thought his program through in a systematic way or not (and Richardson the novelist is certainly not the religious ideologue Terry Eagleton makes him out to be), *Clarissa* was to emerge as the most profound and disturbing exploration in English fiction of the major religious issues in the Protestant tradition, primarily those of the meaning and nature of evil, the significance of the Fall, the conflict between the fallen world and the individual soul, the meaning of regeneration, the nature of Christian forgiveness, and the question of God's ultimate relationship to humankind. In this essay I shall focus particularly on Richardson's representation of the human heart as figured forth in Clarissa's experience—her "heart-workings," to borrow a term from the Puritan divines—in the context of representations of the heart in scripture and devotional works which have the greatest bearing on his fiction. I shall argue that the central dynamic of this enormously comprehensive novel is a parable of the redemption of the heart, a new version of the traditional Christian account of how the Old Testament law of the father God gives way—in a regenerative process of unexampled trial and suffering for the new Christian hero,[8] a woman and a writer—to a new covenant echoing the one first articulated by

one's life, that is with "witnessing," orally and in writing. The Puritan must have been one of the most discursive of all religious beings. See Davies, *Worship and Theology in England* (Princeton: Princeton University Press, 1961–75), 1:40–56, 64–75, 255–324, 428–35; 2:117–32, 137–42, 161–84; 3:19–34, 94–113.

8 Trial is at the centre of heroic narrative, secular and religious, in the dynamic of journey, quest, ordeal, travel and travail, new birth, self-overcoming, transcendence. The word "trial" (which Richardson uses often in relation to Clarissa's experience) derives from *terere*, to rub, to thresh grain, the original gesture of rubbing the hands together to grind, sift, separate the wheat from the chaff. In heroic literature, the hands of the god or the fate fig-

Jeremiah in the apogee of Hebrew prophecy and reformulated by St Paul in 2 Corinthians, a covenant written not in stone but in the tables of the heart.[9] The evidence for this discussion will come from Richardson's own writing and reading, in so far as we know what he read, and from works that helped shape his religious milieu. In his correspondence Richardson cultivated the pose of the non-reader, but we know that he read the Bible—frequently, carefully, devotedly, and in such a way as to make it a creative element of his fiction.[10] His reading of the

ure test the mettle of humankind through trial—"that which purifies us is trial, and trial is by what is contrary," in Milton's indelible phrase in *Areopagitica.* Bailey, in his *Dictionarium,* guesses that trial is related to "tentatio," and to the notion of trial as "experiment" he adds the definition, "a temptation."

9 In Jeremiah God will make a new marriage with his bride Israel, not like the old covenant with "their fathers" (31:32) when the law was written only on stone tablets and the onyx stones of the fallible male priests; instead "I will put my law in their inward parts," with the suggestion also of a new generation in the womb and loins, "and write it in their hearts," the deepest of all inward parts, the seat of regeneration. In the Gospels, the "iniquity of the fathers" continues to be embodied in Pharisaic and apostolic "hardness of heart" (Mark 3:5, 16:14), but there is still the good ground of those who are of "honest and good heart," hearing the word, keeping it, and bringing forth fruit with patience (Luke 8:15), so that St Paul can say to the Corinthians, "Ye are our epistle written in our hearts, known and read of all men. Forasmuch as ye are manifestly declared to be the epistle of Christ ministered by us, written not with ink, but with the Spirit of the living God; not in tables of stone, but in fleshy tables of the heart" (2 Cor. 3:2–3). The present commentary on Clarissa's heart suffering is meant to complement and extend my discussion of her spiritual progress, under the metaphor of the "womb of fate," in *Mother Midnight: Birth, Sex, and Fate in Eighteenth-Century Fiction (Defoe, Richardson, and Sterne)* (New York: AMS Press, 1986), pp. 105–92. See also Lois A. Chaber, "'This Affecting Subject': An 'Interested' Reading of Childbearing in Two Novels by Samuel Richardson," *Eighteenth-Century Fiction* 8 (1996), 193–250.

10 *Clarissa* has become a test-case text for a variety of critical approaches to the eighteenth-century novel. Brilliant but erratic poststructuralist studies of *Clarissa*—William Beatty Warner, *Reading Clarissa: The Struggles of Interpretation* (New Haven: Yale University Press, 1979); Terry Castle, *Clarissa's Ciphers: Meaning and Disruption in Richardson's "Clarissa"* (Ithaca: Cornell University Press, 1982); and Terry Eagleton, *The Rape of Clarissa: Writing, Sexuality and Class Struggle in Samuel Richardson* (Oxford: Blackwell, 1982)—largely neglect the religious aspects of the novel. The important interpretations which do consider them—the early essay by John Dussinger (mentioned below); Cynthia Griffin Wolff, *Samuel Richardson and the Eighteenth-Century Puritan Character* (Hamden, Conn.: Archon Books, 1972); Mark Kinkead-Weekes, *Samuel Richardson: Dramatic Novelist* (Ithaca: Cornell University Press, 1973); Margaret Anne Doody, *A Natural Passion: A Study of the Novels of Samuel Richardson* (Oxford: Clarendon Press, 1974); Jean H. Hagstrum, *Sex and Sensibility: Ideal and Erotic Love from Milton to Mozart* (Chicago: University of Chicago Press, 1980), chap. 8; Carol Houlihan Flynn, *Samuel Richardson: A Man of Letters* (Princeton: Princeton University Press, 1982); Rita Goldberg, *Sex and Enlightenment: Women in Richardson and Diderot* (Cambridge: Cambridge University Press, 1984), chap. 1; Linda S. Kauffman, *Discourses of*

Bible was more characteristically Anglican than Puritan; Richardson should in this be counted with Swift or Arbuthnot—the literary generation of Tory Anglicans in eclipse during the period of his full creative maturity. Richardson thought the "Wisdom" books a "treasure of morality," notably Proverbs and two books, the Wisdom of Solomon and Ecclesiasticus, from the Apocrypha—still accepted as "inspired" in its moral instruction by many eighteenth-century Christians. Other books of the Bible particularly important to him in the composition of *Clarissa* are Genesis, the Psalms, the Gospel narratives, the Pauline epistles (particularly First and Second Corinthians), Revelation, and, above all, the book of Job.

There is no question that Richardson, despite his weak eyesight and modesty about his limited learning, was a diligent reader. We know he read in the line of duty many of the works that were produced by his press, and as William Sale long ago showed us, "The clergy constituted the largest single group for which he printed."[11] And we know Richardson read himself. In the whole course of the tortuous evolution of *Clarissa*, he put himself through the same protracted physical writing and reading efforts he inflicted on his main

Desire: Gender, Genre, and Epistolary Fictions (Ithaca: Cornell University Press, 1986), chap. 4; Margaret Olofson Thickstun, *Fictions of the Feminine: Puritan Doctrine and the Representation of Women* (Ithaca: Cornell University Press, 1988), chap. 4; and especially Leopold Damrosch, Jr, *God's Plot and Man's Stories: Studies in the Fictional Imagination from Milton to Fielding* (Chicago: University of Chicago Press, 1985), chap. 6—do not pay enough attention to the specifically scriptural dimensions of the novel, starting with the most obvious one, that *Clarissa*, in the first edition, is not much shorter than the King James Bible (with the Apocrypha), and moving to such shared features as (1) the narrative as a collection and series of smaller books (*ta biblia*/letters); (2) the stress on narrative progression through dialogue and the working out of a kind of "historicized didacticism"; (3) the profound early depiction of "family history"/"family tragedy"; (4) the role of editor/redactor (shared by the author and his "editors" in the novel, Clarissa and Belford); (5) the epistemological challenge to the reader. The "new" literary-historiographical approach to the Bible, especially in Robert Alter and Meir Sternberg, *The Poetics of Biblical Narrative: Ideological Literature and the Drama of Reading* (Bloomington: Indiana University Press, 1985), has exciting possibilities in relation to a text like *Clarissa*. Though Eagleton has some valuable things to say about "writing" in *Clarissa*, much poststructuralist criticism has over-emphasized "reading" *Clarissa* at the expense of the powerful "writing" motif. A useful exception is Christina Marsden Gillis's exploration of "literal space" in *The Paradox of Privacy: Epistolary Form in Clarissa* (Gainesville: University of Florida Press, 1984). See also the discussion of Richardson's rhetoric of the heart in John Mullan, *Sentiment and Sociability: The Language of Feeling in the Eighteenth Century* (Oxford: Clarendon Press, 1988), pp. 62–69.

11 William Sale, *Samuel Richardson: Master Printer* (Ithaca: Cornell University Press, 1950), p. 125.

characters—including constant revising, transcribing for friends, re-transcribing, rereading both aloud and silently passages in the novel itself, and rereading his previous writing—and he did all this while attending to the business of his press, which was another way in which he read himself, or his own output.[12] Richardson loved to read himself but almost always with a view to revision, correction, and the additional sharpening of critical passages. It is hard to imagine Richardson reading anything without pen in hand, at his desk, proofreading.

Richardson seems to have thought that his main contribution to the novel, his "new species of writing," was his representation of "writing to the moment," a talent for engaging his reader's heart by creating the illusion of the writing character's immediate and unfolding consciousness. In an age preoccupied with the artistic representation of "critical moments"—an attitude exemplified in the engravings of Hogarth—Richardson is the literary master of momentary narrative.[13] But all "moments" are by definition ephemeral. Richardson *did* finish the long labour of *Clarissa*, and with a finality many of his friends could hardly bear. For he never lost sight of the final version of God's narrative for humanity in the last judgment, and its bearing on his heroine's spiritual transformation.

Richardson's religious sensibility was especially attuned to the Puritan emphasis on the primacy of the word of God in scripture and the necessity for the Christian "professor" to read the Bible properly and to *write out* his or her relationship with God, from the simple activity of copying in a journal passages in scripture particularly relevant to one's sense of one's own spiritual needs (or those of others) to

12 "The number of hours in which he withdrew from [his business] to write, revise, and excise the text of his novels must have been extraordinary" (Sale, p. 33).

13 For Richardson's own commentary on this phenomenon, see *Selected Letters*, p. 316, and Lovelace's "I love to write to the *moment*" (4:385; 721). Cf. Eaves and Kimpel, p. 597. On the possible connection between Richardson's practice here and its relation to biblical narrative practice, cf. Northrop Frye's comment on the word *kairos* ("a crucial moment in time") in the context of concrete "words of power." *The Great Code: The Bible and Literature* (New York: Harcourt Brace Jovanovich, 1982), p. 7. See also Alter's assertion that "biblical narrative characteristically catches its protagonists only at the critical and revealing points in their lives" (Alter and Sternberg, p. 51). On the "critical moments" of birth, sex, and death in relation to eighteenth-century fiction, see *Mother Midnight*, esp. pp. 11, 40, 153, and 191.

the writing of extensive spiritual autobiographies, almost all of which could be described as conversion narratives.[14] (One recalls Richardson's observation to Stinstra that as a boy he "collected from ye Scripture Texts that made against" a certain backbiting widow.)[15] The Puritan, more than any other Protestant believer, stood in a "writing" posture with God and was supposed to be a living imitation of the Word made flesh, a living book of the Word, having transcribed him or herself into the proper relationship with God through scripture. Now Richardson saw himself as a "common reader" of the Bible, not as an expert in "opening" the text to elucidate doctrine. Because of his ill health and nervous disorders he was an infrequent church-goer, but he read many sermons in the course of his professional career, and he was familiar with a wide range of both Anglican and Puritan devotional literature.

A good introduction to the sense of God as author of human-kind and the Puritan emphasis on the centrality of God's word, attitudes I believe Richardson shared, may be found in the import-ant seventeenth-century Puritan divine Thomas Watson. For Wat-son, the Bible is a familiar letter, God's "golden epistle," sent ex-pressly to mankind, and he gives explicit directions on how readers should "prepare [their] hearts" for receiving this "love-letter" from the Lord. "How doth one delight to read over his friend's letter! The word written is a divine treasury, or storehouse ... to adorn 'the hidden man of the heart.'" One should labour to remember God's word, to get the scriptures "by heart," virtually to *become* the Bible. The Roman lady Cecilia "made her breast *bibliothecam Christi*," the lib-rary of Christ, and all "Christians should be walking Bibles."[16] John

---

14 See G.A. Starr, *Defoe and Spiritual Autobiography* (Princeton: Princeton University Press, 1965) and J. Paul Hunter, *The Reluctant Pilgrim: Defoe's Emblematic Method and Quest for Form in Robinson Crusoe* (Baltimore: Johns Hopkins University Press, 1966). For a more detailed study of the subgenre itself see Owen C. Watkins, *The Puritan Experience: Studies in Spiritual Autobiography* (New York: Schocken Books, 1972). There has been surprisingly little discussion of Richardson's reimagining of spiritual autobiography in *Pamela* and *Clarissa*.

15 *Selected Letters*, p. 230.

16 *Puritan Sermons 1659–1689*, ed. James Nichols, 6 vols (1844; reprinted Wheaton, Ill.: Richard Owen Roberts, 1981), 2:64, 58, 68. For a useful discussion of English and Amer-ican "preparationists" of the sixteenth and seventeenth centuries, see Norman Pettit, *The Heart Prepared: Grace and Conversion in Puritan Spiritual Life* (New Haven: Yale University Press, 1966), pp. 1–21, 48–124.

Tillotson himself (whom Richardson quotes at the end of *Sir Charles Grandison*) had said that "No man can write after too perfect and good a copy," and the most perfect of all fair copies was thought to be Christ.[17] As Richard Steele (the divine) puts it in his sermon on the mutual duties of husband and wife, Christ "'loved the church, and gave himself for it' ... The husband must write after this copy. Not to love his wife in word and tongue only, but in deed and in truth; that if his heart were opened, her name might be found written there." The true imitation of Christ is proper and virtuous "writing" after his example. "The purest love is written in prayer" and writing in the heart is the only sincere writing because it is the true union of word and deed—the writing of true virtue.[18]

Since the Bible is "the heart and soul of God" given to humankind, Watson implies that one should literally copy out the word of God by hand, especially those parts that point directly to one's condition, putting a "special star" beside them, so that one can give the proper answer to these questions: "Are your hearts, as it were, a transcript and counterpane [a legal copy] of scripture? Is the word copied out into your hearts?" Watson's culminating exhortation, "Get the word transcribed into your hearts. ... Never leave till you are assimilated into the word," suggests that to the Puritan sensibility the best Christians are those who have best experienced God's word as readers, transcribers, and writers.[19]

The Heart, Woman, and Scripture

Richardson read the Bible with the eyes of a master printer and with those of the young women characters—all writers—he so brilliantly

17 In attempting to justify his representation of a good man some readers had found simply too good to be credible, Richardson quoted these words from Tillotson's sermon, "Of the Divine Perfections." See *The History of Sir Charles Grandison*, ed. Jocelyn Harris, 3 vols (London: Oxford University Press, 1972), 3:466 and note. References are to this edition.

18 *Puritan Sermons*, 2:284, 281. In discussing the duties of parents and children, Richard Adams points out, "we should take notice of those fair copies they have set us, and imitate whatsoever is good, commendable, and virtuous in our parents." *Puritan Sermons*, 2:312. Cf. Damrosch's citation of Ames on parents' bearing the "image of God" in regard to their children (p. 234).

19 *Puritan Sermons*, 2:63, 68, 66, 70.

impersonated in his writing. In what follows, I ask the reader to help me "read" Richardson and scripture with a similar act of sympathetic impersonation. We shall turn first to the Old Testament. How would a Clarissa have read it? There is no more striking indication of Richardson's appeal to scriptural authority over a father's dealings with a daughter than Clarissa's invoking of Numbers 30 to rescind her promise to throw herself on the protection of Lovelace's family and meet him outside the garden door of her "*Father's house.*" Richardson the editor appends a note (in all editions) pointing out that "the vows of a Single woman, and of a Wife, if a Father of the one, or the Husband of the other, disallow of them as soon as they know them, are to be of no force" (2:320; 361).[20] This matter is so "highly necessary to be known; by all young Ladies especially" that the editor even quotes the four verses which particularly specify how the father's silence will affirm the vow by which the daughter "*hath bound her soul,*" or how his breaking his peace will override and cancel her vow. Only the father's voice is authentic. These verses may reinforce Clarissa's extraordinary deference to—and terror of—her father's voice.[21] Clarissa closes her "indigested self-reasonings" on her rash promise to Lovelace ("rather an *appointment* than a promise," 2:320; 361) and her strong bias against the odious Solmes by appealing to the authority of the heart: "the *heart* is, as I may say, *Conscience.*" She bases this appeal as well on scriptural authority, the "wise man" of Ecclesiasticus: "Let the counsel of thine own heart stand; for there is no man more faithful to thee, than It" (2:322; 362). Here then is a telling and poignant indication of Clarissa's early moral quandary. Asserting "the privilege of my sex" to change her mind, she can invoke, by way of scripture, her father's authority to absolve her of a confirmed promise (2:320; 360), while at the same time heroically defying his will that she marry Solmes and then justifying her action, again on scriptural authority, on the grounds

20 Sir Charles Grandison alludes indirectly to this passage when kindly admonishing his sister Charlotte for her unconsidered promise to Captain Anderson (1:408).

21 For all his gout-ridden debility, James Harlowe, Sr, possesses one commanding attribute, "a terrible voice when he is angry" (1:44; 60), a voice which will resonate in Clarissa's consciousness till the end. See Florian Stuber, "On Fathers and Authority in *Clarissa*," *Studies in English Literature* 25 (1985), 560, and Damrosch's discussion of Clarissa's father "as a dreadful parody of the Augustinian God" (pp. 234–36).

that she is following the counsel of her own heart. If Clarissa can invoke a rather obscure passage from Numbers to support her position that she is a daughter making every dutiful obeisance to her parents short of self-sacrifice, we may accept that her reading of the rest of the Bible is at least attentive.

Bernard Salomon, *Illustrations pour l'ancien Testament* (Lyon, 1554; 1961), woodcut, folio 25, *Moïse brise les tables de la Loi*. Reproduced by permission of the Thomas Fisher Rare Book Library, University of Toronto.

Inveterate Bible-readers and letter-copiers like Richardson (or Clarissa, or Anna Howe, or Pamela) would be unlikely to overlook the industrious scribal activities of Moses in Exodus, who, it will be recalled, breaks the original tablets of the Law written by "the finger of God." Returning to the top of Mount Sinai, he spends forty days and nights rewriting the Law (at God's dictation). Moses is also aware that God himself has written a book (Exod. 31–34). In "the literature of generation"—those works in English from about 1550 through 1750 which discuss human conception and birth (mostly midwife manuals and treatises on reproduction)—one encounters frequent allusions to Psalm 139:

Holy Bible (London, 1726). Reproduced by permission of the Thomas Fisher Rare Book Library, University of Toronto.

For thou hast possessed my reins: thou hast covered me in my mother's womb. I will praise thee; for I am fearfully and wonderfully made: marvellous are thy works; and that my soul knoweth right well. My substance was not hid from thee, when I was made in secret, and curiously wrought in the lowest parts of the earth. Thine eyes did see my substance, yet being unperfect; and in thy book all my members were written, which in continuance were fashioned, when as yet there was none of them. (13–16)[22]

This passage might be taken as the paradigm for the way in which our ancestors, at least up to the nineteenth century, viewed the postlapsarian creation of human life. In trying to read the passage in something like the way Richardson (or his creation the writer and reader Clarissa) might have read it, we would stress that all persons are originally "written," member by member, in God's book (at other points in the Old and New Testaments called the "book of life") even before they come into being.[23] God thus "writes" humankind "to the moment" (the members "in continuance were fashioned"), before, during, and after conception. The reader pictures God writing people into his book as if it were a narrative, or to readers in the 1740s, a novel.[24] God then presides over a manufactory operation that results in a human artifact, the body "wrought" in the secret workshop of the womb. Richardson, modest as he appears to be, saw himself as part of a literary tradition (which included Chaucer, Spenser, and Milton) in which the author or "maker" is at times an interpreter of God's word by means of his fictional creations. As such, he is a finite imitator of the Creator. Hence in Richardson's unique iteration of the divine creative process, his characters are

---

22 See the discussion of this psalm in *Mother Midnight*, pp. 13–15.

23 Some other examples of the "book of life" especially relevant to this essay: after the golden calf of the Israelites is destroyed, Moses implores God, "Yet now, if thou wilt forgive their sin—; and if not, blot me, I pray thee, out of thy book which thou hast written" (Exod. 32:32). This book is the one referred to by the Psalmist when he says of his enemies, "Let them be blotted out of the book of the living, and not be written with the righteous" (69:28). St Paul singles out "those women which laboured with me in the gospel ... whose names are recorded in the book of life" (Phil. 4:3), and the writer of Revelation, invoking the authority of Jesus in Luke 12:8, has the Lamb say, "He that overcometh, the same shall be clothed in white raiment; and I will not blot out his name out of the book of life, but I will confess his name before my father, and before his angels" (3:5).

24 Cf. Damrosch's relevant commentary, pp. 2–5.

first "written" in his manuscript and then "wrought" into books in the workshop of his printing press.

Besides the intricate stories of Moses and the Lord as writers of books, the overall movement of God's word, written or spoken, entering ever deeper into the verbal texture of human experience, has other climactic representations in the Bible especially relevant to the heart experience of Clarissa. The story of Hannah, for example, had particular interest for Richardson, I believe, partly because of his intense preoccupation (not uncommon in the eighteenth century) with perpetuating his own given name. Six sons were born to the Richardsons (Richardson was married twice); all died in childbirth or early childhood, and four were named Samuel.[25] Richardson's more than ordinarily paternal interest in the experience of childbirth is evident all through his novels, and he was undoubtedly aware that scripture repeatedly recognizes the unique inward experience of women, an experience related to their bearing of children. This sense of woman as the preserver and nurturer of human seed is related to women's experience of the heart. From Genesis onward, the representation of women in the Old Testament has a close and recurring association with the heart. The creation of woman was occasionally pictured in the seventeenth century as beginning with an actual incision in Adam's breast; in Milton's words, woman began as "a Rib, with cordial spirits warm, and life-blood streaming fresh; wide was the wound" (*Paradise Lost*, 8.466–67). Eve was thought to come from the breast region because woman was meant to be man's companion, the two sharing the emotional tribulations and comforts of life. The dark aspect of this mode of creation was that woman would also be regarded *as* man's wound, as the primary cause of his recurring heart misery—woman as "Wo to Man."[26] The Lord's dynamic of creation in Genesis almost always works from the inside out, and

25 "Perhaps the gravest disappointment of Richardson's life was the death of four sons and one nephew by whom he hoped to see his press perpetuated. ... In a desperate attempt to perpetuate the name of Samuel, [Richardson and his first wife, Martha] had named three of their infant boys after their father" (Sale, p. 11). The fourth Samuel, by Richardson's second wife, Elizabeth, was baptized on 26 April 1739 and died less than a year later (Eaves and Kimpel, pp. 48–50).

26 Bailey, *Dictionnarium*, "Woman." One of the features of Bailey's dictionary was the insertion of illustrative proverbs, including under this entry "*Women, Wealth, and Wine, have each two Qualities, a good and a bad. That is, they are either a blessing or a curse, according to the*

Genesis 2 stresses the *process* of this creation, a moment by moment account, similar to the one we noticed in Psalm 139.

God's unique relation to Eve is carried over to her childbearing. It is God who gives her her first son; Adam is almost incidental. This sense of the Lord's special intimacy with the womb and his role as the supreme arbiter of its fertility is evident in the stories of Sarah, Rebekah, Rachel, and Hannah. Hannah and Sarah are both advanced in years and barren; unlike Sarah and the other barren women, Hannah prays directly to the Lord for a man-child: "she spoke in her heart; only her lips moved"; she was communing with God in her heart, the deep spiritual domain within all humankind. She, not Eli, is the true priest. No voice is heard in that place; the words are only thought. God alone hears what she says and only she knows what she has asked for in the spiritual realm of the upright heart and pure preferred by God before all temples. To outward appearance, to the imperceptive Eli, she is drunk: "No, my lord, I am a woman of a sorrowful spirit: I ... have poured out my soul before the Lord" (1 Sam. 1:15). She opens her heart to God, asking him for a son (according to a gloss at verse 20 in the authorized version, "Samuel" means "Asked of God"), and dedicates him as a loan to the Lord, to do the Lord's work. Richardson's talent for discerning the workings of the human heart recalls his namesake Samuel who selected "the Lord's anointed." Samuel learns to distrust appearances and follow God's direction to the inward truth, "for the Lord seeth not as man seeth; for man looketh on the outward appearance, but the Lord looketh on the heart" (1 Sam. 16:7). In our contemporary concern with the unquestionably patriarchal cast of the entire Bible we ought not to lose sight of the scriptural representation of woman as the sacred living temple in which God enacts the mystery of the generation of life. Woman is the nurturer of God's all-potent seed and word, embodied in the children of God, humankind. This makes scriptural woman profoundly different from scriptural man. She has two sources of inward communion with God, her womb and her heart, for heart also includes mind. Man has only one.

use we make of them," a definition which betrays the conventional view of woman as mere instrumentality, like language itself. In this view "woman" is shaped and defined by language as if she were a piece of woven stuff. Cf. Bailey's derivation of "woman" from *wan* (Welsh), "a *Web* and *Man*, q.d. a weaving person."

New-historicist literary interpretation has been concerned, in part, with the representation of images and figures of the human body in literary texts of the seventeenth and eighteenth centuries, but not enough attention has been paid to how various internal organs—the tongue, the liver, the spleen, the kidneys or "reins," the "bowels" as the seat of compassion, the womb, and especially the heart—are made to reflect the most complex expressions of the interior human condition. The heart is the primary symbol of the ambivalence of human existence because scripturally it is the fountainhead of all wickedness as well as the source of truth and sincerity.[27] In the seventeenth and the first half of the eighteenth centuries, the representation of the heart took on new and more positive meaning as the source of circulatory power and vital equilibrium. The heart, physiologically as well as in the sense of mind, emotion, sincerity, courage, commitment, integrity, inner religious conviction, and above all—by the mid-eighteenth century—compassion, comes to stand for the essential core of humanity. The heart becomes what it means to be human. When Clarissa says that Lovelace "wants a *heart*: and if he does, he wants everything" (1:296; 184), she sums up in one simple phrase this evolving network of rich associations against which her own heart experience must be measured.

The Letter Killeth

The overall structure of *Clarissa* may be seen as a religious narrative drama in five acts progressing through an English house of five

27 With Gen. 6:5 as his text ("And God saw that the wickedness of man was great in the earth, and that every imagination of the thoughts of his heart was only evil continually"), Stephen Charnock shows how this evil fountain may be cleansed (*Puritan Sermons*, 2:386–420). This passage may be set beside David's representation of the deep inwardness of God's domain in the heart and of his plea to God to prepare the heart for his reception in 1 Chron. 29:17–19. Pehaps the most succinct expression of this inwardness, and the one most relevant to the portrayal of the preparation of Clarissa's heart for grace and redemption, is the psalmist's fusion of the motifs of the "book of life" and the writing in the heart: "in the volume of the book it is written of me, I delight to do thy will, O my God: Yea, thy law is within my heart" (40:7–8). This formulation suggests that the writing in the heart may be translated into the book of life, or even that one's final "writing in the heart" may be one's place or passage in the book of life itself.

enormous rooms.[28] Act 1 takes place almost entirely in Clarissa's father's house (to 2:339; 370). Acts 2 (2:339–5:16; 370–736) and 3 (5:16–6:101; 736–967) occur largely in the house of the demonic Mother Sinclair, the London bawd with whom Lovelace lodges Clarissa until her final successful escape. In act 4 (6:101–8:5; 967–1362), Clarissa, after sojourning in various London lodging houses, returns, in act 5 (8:5 to the end; 1362 to the end), to her father's house in her own "house," her carefully inscribed and embellished coffin. The Clarissa of act 5, though dead, is a more powerful and influential character than she was alive. Clarissa's literal progress through these houses has a larger figurative and religious dimension. Within the overall movement of the novel, beginning and ending in her father's house (in the temporal and spiritual senses of the term), the heroine, after undergoing the loss of her chastity (her "honour") under the influence of a figurative second "mother" (the world as represented by the interlocking complex of London, Mother Sinclair, and her diabolic "son," Lovelace), and finally reclaiming her soul by achieving the religious single life she has wanted since the Solmes affair, is virtually defined in terms of the experiences of her heart.

The "History (or rather Dramatic Narrative) of Clarissa" (8:309; cf. 1495)—to use Richardson's words—may be understood, in large part, as the story of assaults on her heart. In the first part of the novel, the word "heart" is used most often in particularly emotional and crucial encounters between the heroine and her mother and father in neo-scriptural contexts of blessing and cursing. When her mother says "I charge you ... on my blessing, that you think of being Mrs. Solmes," the change from "Clarissa" to the hiss of "Mrs. SOLMES" has the impact of a verbal blow, almost a curse ("what a denunciation was that!"), and Clarissa faints. "*There* went the dagger

28 Castle sees Mrs Sinclair's "huge, quaggy carcase" as "a great summarizing image of Richardson's own problematic text," a suggestive assertion of the very real influence of Sinclair in the novel (p. 37; cf. *Mother Midnight*, pp. 138–47). Eagleton sees Richardson's novels "as *kits*, great unwieldy containers crammed with spare parts" (p. 20). The two views are conveniently summed up in Angus Ross's sense of the "shifting quality" of the text (introduction, p. 16). Many other readers have been impressed with the massive stillness of the book. But the text is both stable and unstable, a living drama of voices within its house-like printer's frame. Cf. Gillis's discussion of Mrs Sinclair's house (chap. 2).

188 ROBERT A. ERICKSON

to my heart, and down I sunk" (1:104; 89). Her mother later says, "as you value your Father's Blessing and mine ... resolve to comply" (1:108; 91). Clarissa faints because, as a remarkably dutiful Christian daughter with a keen awareness of the Old Testament force of blessings—and withheld blessings—she places the highest value on her parents' verbal approval of her marriage, whenever it should come about. Charlotte Harlowe's revealing response to Clarissa's tears and anguish—"The heart, Clary, is what I want" (1:131; 103)— tells us she craves (for a complex of reasons) Clarissa's complete submission, not her sincerity. Her words also convey that profound equation in the English language between desire and nothingness in the word "want": Mrs Harlowe says she herself lacks a heart. In good Puritan fashion, Clarissa examines herself: "is not Vanity, or secret Love of praise, a principal motive with me at the bottom?—Ought I not to suspect my own heart?" (1:134; 104).

The conflict in the Harlowe family now has overtones of an ancient religious war. Uncle John Harlowe, speaking for the family, puts the situation squarely from the point of view of the three elderly Harlowe males and their sense of the binding force of the patriarchal word: "our promises and honour were engaged before we believed there could be so sturdy an opposition ... we are an *embattled phalanx*" (1:226; 150). Behind this plaintive assertion lies the notion that once the paternal word has been formed and uttered there can be no drawing back. After reminding her daughter that her refusal may shorten her father's already diseased life, Mrs Harlowe asks her climactic question: "Are you determined to brave your Father's displeasure? ... Do you chuse to break with us all...?" and Clarissa phrases the central issue: "is not my sincerity, is not the integrity of my heart, concerned in my answer? May not my everlasting happiness be the sacrifice?" (1:150; 112). Invoking the language of the Old Testament (the phrase "integrity of heart" is used in Genesis and 1 Kings), she knows that marrying Solmes will violate her deepest sense of right and wrong and her self-respect; acceding to her parents' demands in this case is to commit a sin which may imperil her immortal soul. Hence Clarissa, for the first time, links the integrity and purity of her heart with the preservation of her soul, her guiding religious principle to the end, however difficult it may be to follow.

Not long after Clarissa is tricked and frightened into leaving her father's house with Lovelace, her spiteful sister Arabella sends a letter describing how her "Father ... on discovering your wicked ... Elopement, imprecated, on his knees a fearful Curse upon you. ... No less, than 'that you may meet your punishment, both *here* and *hereafter*, by means of the very wretch, in whom you have chosen to place your wicked confidence'" (3:282; 509). After receiving this letter, Clarissa writes to Anna Howe: "O my best, my *only* friend! Now indeed is my heart broken! It has received a blow it never will recover" (3:280; 508). She has heard about parental curses and she attributes great weight to them. The immensely wealthy house of Harlowe in the England of 1730 would seem to have its roots in Puritan culture, and the Harlowes are a picture of the Puritan family gone terribly wrong.[29] What little we know about the background of James Harlowe, Sr, and his two unmarried brothers suggests that the three sons were brought up on the Bible, and there are indications that James, the paterfamilias, made much of the traditional paternal role of personally instructing his children in the moral lessons of the Bible, especially the Old Testament. Long after receiving her father's written curse (every syllable of which she carries like a weight upon her heart), Clarissa, still suffering from the after-effects of the violence done to her head and to her heart in the rape, will recall the story of Rebekah's cheating Isaac and the father's misplaced blessing: "My Father used, I remember, to enforce the Doctrine deducible from it, on his children, by many arguments" (6:214). This doctrine would seem to be the irrevocable power of a father's blessing (or curse) and the rightness of God's will even in apparently unjust cases. In

---

29 On the nature of the Puritan family in relation to the Harlowes, see L.L. Schücking's still relevant *The Puritan Family: A Social Study from the Literary Sources* (1929; reprinted New York: Schocken Books, 1970), pp. 56–95, 145–58, and Christopher Hill, "Clarissa Harlowe and Her Times," reprinted in *Samuel Richardson: A Collection of Critical Essays*, ed. John Carroll (Englewood Cliffs, NJ: Prentice-Hall, 1969), pp. 102–23. More recent studies of the evolution of the family during and after the eighteenth century—Edward Shorter, *The Making of the Modern Family* (New York: Basic Books, 1975); and Randolph Trumbach, *The Rise of the Egalitarian Family: Aristocratic Kinship and Domestic Relations in Eighteenth-Century England* (New York: Academic Press, 1978)—have little commentary on Puritan and religious elements in English family life. Even Lawrence Stone's comprehensive work, *The Family, Sex and Marriage in England 1500–1800* (London: Weidenfield and Nicolson, 1977), is not particularly illuminating for *Clarissa*.

other words, James Harlowe, Sr—though exceedingly benevolent to his younger daughter until the Solmes affair—was one of those family tyrants who would resort to scripture to uphold any of his actions. Clarissa's mother, bringing to mind the jealous God of the Old Testament, once reminds her daughter that she has "a jealous Father, needlessly jealous ... of the prerogatives of his Sex ... and still ten times more jealous of the authority of a Father" (1:117; 96). The old man is biblical to the last. His final message to Clarissa, not long before her death, is an extract from Ecclesiasticus (often regarded in the eighteenth century as the most virulently anti-feminist book in Scripture) about a father's grief caused by a shameless daughter got with child in her father's house (chap. 42).[30] The passage has all the more impact on her since it was from Ecclesiasticus, the very book that, as we have seen, Clarissa cited to justify her opposition to her father. This letter, like the curse, is also conveyed by another hand, here the officious Uncle Antony Harlowe, an old bachelor intimately conversant with Ecclesiasticus, especially the anti-feminist passages. He exhorts his niece "to lay it to your heart," and provides a stinging commentary on each verse he cites (7:113; 1196).

After learning from her Aunt Hervey that her father would have knelt to her to prevail upon her to marry Solmes, Clarissa responds, "I had deserved annihilation, had I suffered my Father to kneel in vain" (3:277; 506). Now from her sister she learns that he got down on his knees in the ritual posture of prayer to imprecate this horror on her head, and the worst of it is, "the Curse extends to the life beyond This" (3:281; 508). In the carefully circular balance of its parts, the curse seems to be formulaic, as if her father had learned it by heart from a book.[31] To someone so extraordinarily sensitive

30 The phrase "Father's house" (like "Father's curse") resonates throughout *Clarissa* and recalls the biblical repetition of the phrase in such passages as Deut. 22:21: "Then they shall bring out the damsel to the door of her father's house, and the men of her city shall stone her with stones that she die; because she hath wrought folly in Israel, to play the whore in her father's house."

31 The mortal condition imposed by God on Eve in Genesis 3:16 was taken in the eighteenth century to be God's curse on woman and, like Clarissa's father's curse, it also has two parts. Any intelligent young woman of Clarissa's time might be expected to have felt anxiety when reading the first part of this verse, and the ambiguity of "multiply thy sorrow and thy conception" seemed to imply repeated conceptions and repeated agony, as was indeed the case with nearly all fertile wives; as for the second part, she might well have been

to the spoken and written word (almost superstitiously aware of the mysterious self-fulfilling power of language, especially of scriptural invocation), so highly verbal and articulate herself in all her dealings with others, so well instructed from an early age in the Bible by the "learned Divines" with whom she corresponded (8:225) and by her nurse and spiritual mother, Mrs Norton (the daughter of a divine, 7:54; 1167), such a curse, coming at a moment when Clarissa is attempting to collect all her fortitude and will power to cope with her dangerous situation, has an actual physical impact on her. She is "*unhinged*" (3:291; 513), and except for the ability to write, almost immobilized. Her response here prefigures her even more shattering collapse after the rape.

Behind Clarissa's "Now indeed is my heart broken!" (3:280; 508) and the cliché (tired even in the eighteenth century) of the heart broken for disappointed love, stands the far more vital and immediate religious significance of the image of the tables (i.e., stone writing-tablets) of the heart, and within that image the breaking of the tables of the Law. We have noted Clarissa's ambivalent adherence to a father who, "according to the Old Law," has "the *right* of *absolving* or *confirming* a child's promise" (2:320; 361). Later, with Lovelace, she speculates, "how shall I behave when got from him ... if, like the Israelites of old, I shall be so weak as to wish to return to

troubled about the idea of apparently inexorable "desire" for her husband-to-be, and the notion that he would "rule over" her seemed to imply a master-servant relationship as well. Clarissa's cruel brother remarks on her "high notion of the matrimonial duty" (2:35; 223), playing upon the proverbial sexual debt ("due benevolence") the wife owes the husband. He has already reminded his sister that she too is part of "the animal creation" (2:26; 218), alluding to Dryden's translation of *Amor omnibus idem* in Virgil's third *Georgic* ("Thus every creature, and of every kind, / The secret joys of sweet coition find: / ...For love is Lord of all, and is in all the same"). Until her decline, Clarissa is represented in the novel as a nubile young woman of extraordinary beauty and sexual attractiveness. She makes clear her physical revulsion for Solmes, but we can infer that she also finds Lovelace attractive physically and in other ways and she holds a traditional sense of a wife's subordination to her husband (1:147; 110, and cf. Damrosch's remarks, p. 228). Nearly all the great curses by a father on a daughter in earlier English literature have sexual force or implication, and this, though muted, is not absent in Clarissa's father's curse. Besides Brabantio's curse on Desdemona and Lear's curse on Goneril, Richardson seems to have had in mind Priuli's curse on his daughter Belvidera in *Venice Preserved* (1.1). Lovelace's "*Oh, for a curse to kill with!*" when Clarissa makes her first escape from Mother Sinclair's (5:16; 736) is a self-conscious echo of Jaffeir's curse on Priuli and the senators of Venice (2.2). Lovelace and Clarissa had attended a performance of *Venice Preserved* in London.

my Egyptian bondage?" (4:161). From the very first it is her father, not Lovelace, who is Moses to Clarissa's Israel. Not Moses, the leader who brought the chosen people out of the wilderness, but the Moses who conveyed the anger of a superlatively jealous god. The tablets of her heart are now broken within her, as were the tables of the Law in Exodus, by the wrath of a father incensed at the disobedience of his children. "Don't let them break your heart," Anna Howe implores her friend (3:288; 511).[32] But the damage has been done. From here to the end, Clarissa's broken heart can be mended only through spiritual restoration.

There is much cursing in scripture, but no human father ever curses his daughter. If Miriam's father "had but spit in her face, should she not be ashamed seven days?" (Num. 12:14). The power of a father's curse would be almost unspeakable in its effect. Stoning would seem to have been a preferable alternative. A son or daughter who curses his parent is put to death (Lev. 20:9). "None but God can curse" (3:285), and Clarissa's father is not God, but a father who speaks with the sanction of the Lord, and in the early eighteenth century, a father's word still had the reputed power of that sanction. It was a truism that, as the Puritan Richard Adams puts it, obedience "is the parents' due as in the place of God: they bear his image in their parental authority and relation."[33] Recalling the customary feminine gesture of holding a letter to the bosom, or inserting it into the bosom, Arabella says to her sister, "If all this is heavy, lay your hand to your heart, and ask yourself, Why you have deserved it" (3:284; 510). Bella tells Clarissa to take her crime and the words of this curse and press them down—seal them—into her heart, but there is little need to reinforce their impact with a physical gesture: "The contents of my Sister's Letters had pierced my heart" (3:298–99; 517), and Clarissa falls gravely ill. Clarissa's father's curse shatters and pierces her heart

---

32 Anna comes to her friend's aid with consolatory advice and passages from the Gospels and Romans: "None but God can curse," "*bless and curse not*," "*pray for them that persecute and curse us*" (3:285); it is equally significant that at this point she also sends Clarissa her personal copy of Norris's *Miscellanies* (which Clarissa returns) to help assuage her friend's grief. This popular book, by a prolific seventeenth-century Neoplatonist divine, was a cherished favourite of Richardson's. See also note 39.

33 *Puritan Sermons*, 2:321; see Noah's curse on Canaan, the son of Noah's son, Ham (Gen. 9:25).

in a combined evocation of the breaking of the Law and the Crucifixion before Lovelace completes the breaking of her heart in her madness as a result of the rape.

The Fortified Heart

In "the depth of vapourish despondency" (3:281; 508) after receiving her father's curse, Clarissa's relation to her broken heart becomes increasingly more complicated. Anna Howe is aware that all along in Clarissa's relationship with Lovelace, her friend has attempted to remain truthful to her, and to preserve the integrity of her heart: "I know the gentleness of your spirit; I know the laudable pride of your heart" (4:85; 588). But Anna senses, though even she cannot say it outright, that she is not now simply trying to save her friend's peace of mind, or her reputation—she is trying to save Clarissa from destruction. Too much time has elapsed since she left her father's house. Clarissa must not stand on her delicacy and punctilio now, but "Give him the day" (4:86; 588). The advice of her friend prompts in Clarissa, despite her despondent spirits, a firm and clear reassertion of her sense of the integrity of her heart and the real meaning of her delicacy with regard to Lovelace. She will explain to her friend, once for all, that the motives for her behaviour to Lovelace "arise principally from what offers to my own heart; respecting ... its own rectitude, its own judgment of the *Fit* and the *Unfit*. ... Principles that *are* in my mind; that I *found* there; implanted ... by the first gracious Planter" (4:102–3; 596). Clarissa here enunciates Richardson's version of "right reason"—another version of the *imago dei*—adapted from Milton. But she is all too well aware that "the heart is very deceitful" (4:103; 596), and she asks Anna not to spare her, but to help her rectify what might be amiss in her heart. Clarissa is becoming more deeply aware of the ambivalence of her heart (and not just in love matters), an ambivalence rooted in the scriptural representation of the heart. As she looks within herself now, Clarissa feels caught up in a dilemma from which she can never fully escape as she attempts to reconcile the claims of a just and laudable pride of heart with a deceitful pride, the equally sincere emotions of loving and despising someone, strong prophetic givings and misgivings about her fate, impulses of counsel and reproach, of forgiveness and self-justification.

On Sunday 23 July, the last day of her eighteenth year, Clarissa writes to Anna Howe the most important letter in the history of her heart suffering. Much earlier, she had identified herself with Israel in its wanderings (4:161). Now she identifies herself with David, and Anna with Jonathan, as she reaffirms the sacred ties of pure friendship and explains to her friend for the last time why she cannot marry Lovelace. She will humbly attempt to imitate the "sublimest Exemplar," Christ, in his resignation to the will of God, persuaded that she will not live much longer. The strong sense of her error, the loss of her reputation, the resentment of her family, and Lovelace's barbarous usage of her, culminating in her rape while drugged with laudanum, all have "seized upon" her "heart ... before it was so well fortified by *religious considerations*," as she hopes it now is (6:412; 1118). In other words, before the rape her heart was not strong enough, in a religious sense, to enable her to survive the temptations and afflictions that were visited upon it. Here is a tacit admission that, as good a person as she knew herself to be, she was not good enough, in these terrible circumstances, to survive and live on her own high moral terms in the world in which she finds herself. That is the real tragedy of Richardson's Clarissa.

For the sympathetic reader, who considers Clarissa a moral exemplar to her sex, this is perhaps the most difficult moment in the entire history. But the novel is not telling young eighteenth-century women who have been wronged to curse men, forgive them, and die. Clarissa's welcoming of death is no more an example to be followed than Griselda's obedience to the Marquis Walter is meant to be an example in Chaucer's "Clerk's Tale."[34] It is not simply Clarissa's fate, but the fortitude, piety, and heroic resignation with which Clarissa dies that are meant to be exemplary. For in this passage Clarissa also implies that between the rape and her writing of this letter, she has been able to fortify and restore her broken heart.

Even before she has fully regained her senses, Clarissa—unable to speak—engages successively in two separate and distinct acts of writ-

---

34 Cf. E. Talbot Donaldson on Griselda, *Chaucer's Poetry: An Anthology for the Modern Reader* (New York: Ronald Press, 1958), p. 920.

ing. In terms of her spiritual survival, this is her "critical moment" in the novel. When she has lost almost everything—her honour, her speech, her senses—she still has the capacity to write. All along, we have been aware that Clarissa's primary act of life is writing. For her, to live is to write.[35] From Genesis, she has learned that woman is created out of an act of mutilation, God's rebuilding or revising of Adam's rib into Eve. God anatomizes Adam and creates Eve. From Psalm 139, she learned that humankind is written in God's book before being wrought in the womb. God writes humankind into being; writing precedes living. Clarissa is a new Eve for eighteenth-century woman—not an Eve who bears sons but an Eve who writes—and a new Mary, not the one who bears the child-redeemer but the woman-writer who bears a new female version of the Word, a womanly hero of virtue and wisdom who combines in herself qualities of the two chief moral exemplars of scripture, Job and Christ, with more of the former in her composition than the latter. Partly as an act of revenge—on Clarissa, on her family, on womankind—Lovelace wounds her irreparably. Clarissa is comatose for at least forty-eight hours after the rape, an act which Lovelace justifies by a medical analogy as a kind of surgery necessary in "acute cases" (5:339; 896). As she gradually attains intermittent consciousness, she attempts to write, but "what she writes she tears," throwing the fragments under the table, then trying to write again (5:326; 889). These acts of writing are like the desperate survival gestures of a drowning person, the victim flailing about, attacking the destructive element. It is as if Clarissa goes back to the origin of writing itself—writing as a hostile act. The word "write" comes from a word for tearing, wounding. But it is herself she is marking and tearing. Clarissa begins life after the rape by a kind of self-mutilation in her mad papers, torn fragments of her own written self. But shortly after the composition of the mad papers she begins a *new* kind of writing. This new writing is available to us both within and without the text of the novel

35 "By turning in her confusion to the written word," Clarissa is "clearly trying to reinstate order. In a sense, to go on writing is to go on living." H. Porter Abbott, *Diary Fiction: Writing as Action* (Ithaca: Cornell University Press, 1984), p. 92. Though "raped and in one sense broken, Clarissa still writes. That is the important point. Writing sustains existence and affirms existence" (Gillis, p. 53).

in the book of Clarissa's *Meditations* Richardson had privately printed for friends. Clarissa seems to be tearing up the old raped self
and beginning a new one *in writing*. The mad papers all refer to
her own immediate experiences in relation to members of her family and to Lovelace, and contain almost no biblical echoes; the new
writing is an explicit transcription of scripture. It is no longer writing as tearing but writing as ordering; one might call it Clarissa's new
covenant written out of her own suffering.

Clarissa's little book of *Meditations* has a place of central importance in our experience of the novel. In adherence to good Puritan
practice Clarissa makes transcripts of those parts of the Bible she
feels are especially relevant to her spiritual condition. But these are
not simply copies—they are "collections," small anthologies, usually
half a page in length, of selected verses put into the writer's own order. Clarissa says, in her own preface to the collection, "*In some places
I have taken the liberty of substituting the word* her *for* him, *and to make
other such-like little changes of words.*"[36] These little changes are nothing less than a revision of patriarchal scripture into her own person
and gender. According to the "Editor of the History of Clarissa," in
his "Advertisement to the Reader," thirty-six such meditations were
composed, four of which are inserted in the "history" (there are actually five). Richardson clearly implies in this "Advertisement" that
he did not insert more of the "Meditations" for fear of not engaging the attention of those readers (the light, the careless, and the
gay) who stood most in need of instruction. Moreover, Richardson
is remarkably sparing of scriptural allusions throughout *Clarissa*. He
does not want the novel to sound like a tract, and his artistic restraint and skill in this respect are admirable. It is taken for granted
that the heroine knows her Bible; it is her wide reading in literature and history that is stressed at various points in the novel (for
example, 8:238). The main thing is that after the rape, at the moment of deepest personal crisis, Clarissa really begins to read the

---

36 *Meditations Collected from the Sacred Books; And Adapted to the Different Stages of a Deep Distress;
Gloriously surmounted by Patience, Piety, and Resignation. Being those mentioned in the History of
Clarissa as drawn up by her for her own use* (1750; reprinted Garland Press, 1976), p. viii. See
also John A. Dussinger, "Conscience and the Pattern of Christian Perfection in *Clarissa,*"
PMLA 81 (1966), 240–41; Eaves and Kimpel, pp. 311–12. Cf. *Mother Midnight*, pp.180, 257,
282; and Tom Keymer, *Richardson's "Clarissa" and the Eighteenth-Century Reader* (Cambridge
and New York: Cambridge University Press, 1992), pp. 112, 212, 225.

Bible most deeply—to become truly "engaged" in it, perhaps for the first time—as she transcribes and transforms it into her own spiritual autobiography, her own scripture.

In the first three-quarters of the novel, Clarissa alludes to the Bible, directly or indirectly, only about fifteen times. Of these allusions, four are to the New Testament, and one of these already shows Clarissa wittily adapting the Bible (1 Cor. 13:7) to her immediate needs. In her surprise meeting with Lovelace near the woodhouse, defending in great agitation her decision to remain in her father's house, she tells him "that it became me, ill as I was treated at present, to *hope* every-thing, to *bear* every-thing, and to *try* every-thing" (1:261; 167). Of her remaining allusions, most are to the Old Testament, with Job predominating, and five are to Ecclesiasticus. Lovelace (who can almost always quote scripture to his advantage) is not far behind Clarissa with about ten allusions. Again the Old Testament predominates, with his error in attributing the adage "*no wickedness is comparable to the wickedness of a woman*" to either Socrates or Solomon caustically pointed out by the editor (3:115; 441). In the last quarter of the novel, the balance of allusions naturally tips towards Clarissa largely because of her five "Meditations."

The first "Meditation" (not in the text of the novel), dated "June 18," would have been written only five days after the rape and the self-mutilation of the mad papers when Clarissa, having been stopped by Mrs Sinclair herself from escaping the house, retreats to her chamber (5:345; 898, "*Sunday Afternoon, 6 o'Clock [June 18]*"). The editor notes that here, "in the anguish of her soul, she transcribes and adapts the curses of Job on his birth-day" ... "Let the day perish wherein I was born, and the night in which I was conceived." She substitutes a second "I" for "there was a man child" (Job 3:3).[37] She writes herself into the book of Job and thereby into her own scripture, but by so doing she allows scripture to influence her living

---

37 *Meditations,* p. 2. Cf. Michael Ragussis's discussion of how Clarissa's "pronominal transpositions displace the male from the center of language ... and unname him." *Acts of Naming: The Family Plot in Fiction* (New York: Oxford University Press, 1986), pp. 32–33; Cf. Kauffman, p. 155. See also John Norris, "*The Third Chapter of Job Paraphrased,*" *A Collection of Miscellanies* (London, 1687), pp. 20–22; and Richardson's friend Edward Young's "A Paraphrase on Part of the Book of Job," *Edward Young: The Complete Works. Poetry and Prose,* ed. James Nichols (1854; reprinted Hildesheim: Georg Olms, 1968), 1:245–59.

experience in the most immediate form of writing to the moment. She must begin with a curse in which Job, innocent of intentional fault, brings down on himself what Clarissa's father has brought down on her. Everything in *Clarissa* comes back to that curse. The heroine unknowingly begins the restoration of her heart with a passage which in effect uncreates, undoes the old Clarissa (a parallel to her self-mutilation in the mad papers) as she begins her new role— the one most compatible with her author's modest sense of his own talents as writer and printer—as copier, "collector," and composer of extracts, and *"when collected, the frequent recourse I had to them ... gave me still greater comfort."*[38] By collecting the biblical extracts, she re-"collects" herself—"writes" herself on paper and composes herself in person—so that she is supremely prepared for her encounter with Lovelace and the women after the rape. Again, writing precedes speech for Clarissa at the beginning of her restoration and her triumph. Then follows her assessment of the hierarchy of evil authority poised against her. Her sacred "compact" is opposed to Lovelace's evil one: "Tell me ... whether thou hast entered into a compact with the grand deceiver, in the person of his horrid agent in this house [i.e., Sinclair]; and if the ruin of my Soul, that my Father's curse may be fulfilled, is to complete the triumphs of so vile a confederacy?" (5:349; 900). It is clear from this passage that Clarissa does not finally equate Lovelace with Satan, as so many have argued. The rhetorical series of "whether ... if ... if" suggests that Clarissa already knows that the combined demonic power of "the grand deceiver" Satan acting through his agent Sinclair, and their Faustian victim, Lovelace, cannot destroy her soul (the equivalent of the "second death" or being blotted out from the "book of life" in Revelation 20:14–15) so long as she chooses to accept God's forgiveness through grace. Clarissa in this great scene challenges Lovelace to speak and he is almost entirely incoherent (5:350–51; 901). Her oral presence prevails over

---

38 *Meditations*, p. vi. Clarissa's collecting and composing herself in this fashion recalls her creator's life work as an orderly "compositor," "collector" of extracts, and ultimately "composer" of fictions, and one wonders further just how much Richardson's "mystery" as master printer enters into the whole "mystery" of his particular kind of narrative creativity. See Eagleton's speculation on the ironies of the master printer (*The Rape of Clarissa*, pp. 40–41). Robert Alter's discussion of "composite artistry" (*The Art of Biblical Narrative*, chap. 7), has interesting implications for Richardson's creative practice; Clarissa herself might be seen as engaging in a kind of *midrash* in the composition of her *Meditations*.

his, just as the "written mind" of her scriptural *Meditations* will prevail over his despairing correspondence.

The book of *Meditations* is especially important to an evaluation of the novel's religious meaning because, as Belford points out, Clarissa performed these exercises "to take off the edge of her repinings at hardships so disproportioned to her fault. ... We may see by this, the method she takes to fortify her mind" (7:99; 1189). This remark would seem to be Richardson's most pointed indication in the text of the significance of Clarissa's scriptural and scriptive activities in the heart-fortifying process. She eventually bequeaths the book of *Meditations* to her dear Mrs Norton (8:118; 1417) and her mother finally wants to possess the book. Moreover, our concern with the significance of the actual book of *Meditations* outside the novel is further testimony to the sense of many readers that one is never finished with this novel (or with any great novel but especially *Clarissa*)—one has never fully *read* it. But the *Meditations* are not meant finally for Clarissa's "friends"; they are written primarily for the God who alone can read the heart. Running throughout the *Meditations* are several allusions to "the great day of account," and Clarissa clearly has the Day of Judgment—and her ultimate and final Reader—in mind as she reaps the comforts of transcribing the Wisdom books, concluding her *Meditations* with the fourth and fifth chapters of the book of Wisdom itself. Her title, "*An Early Death not to be lamented*," alludes to Enoch (Gen. 6:24): "living among sinners, he was translated." Almost her last transcribed words in the "Meditation" are "And when they cast up accounts of their sins, they shall come with fear: and their own iniquities shall convince them to their face."[39]

Clarissa warns Lovelace in her posthumous letter to him to take care lest he have "Not one good action in the hour of languishing to recollect, not one worthy intention to revolve, it will be all reproach and horror; and you will wish to have it in your power to compound for annihilation" (8:136; 1426). As the Puritan clergyman Thomas Watson points out in his "The Day of Judgment Asserted," two books will be opened at the trial of doom. The first is "*the book of God's omnisciency*" in which God has registered all of humankind's actions.

39 *Meditations*, pp. 75–76.

200 ROBERT A. ERICKSON

This is God's "book of remembrance" (Mal. 3:16), the "book of life." The second book is the one each man and woman brings to be unclasped at the trial, one's "book of conscience" or one's writing in the heart, the trial testimony of word, thought, and deed. Watson puts his emphasis on the crimes which will be revealed: "The sins of men shall be written upon their foreheads with a pen of iron," but a divine like the Anglican Robert South notes that the book of life registers "all good and evil, whether done, spoken, consented to, or imagined."[40] In language which recalls the creation of woman out of the wound in Adam's breast, Watson represents Christ as "*kardiognostes*," "a Heart-Searcher" or "Heart-Knower," virtually a cardiac surgeon: "it is not the most shining profession [which] Christ is taken with, unless he see the curious workmanship of grace in the heart, drawn by the pencil of the Holy Ghost. ... Christ will at the day of judgment make a heart-anatomy; as the surgeon makes a dissection in the body ... nothing then will stand us in stead but sincerity," Clarissa's chief virtue and Lovelace's chief failing with respect to her.[41] When one recalls that it was Christ who was imagined as the divine person actually creating woman in the original heart-anatomy of Adam, womankind is seen to be a crucial element in the entire anatomizing process—one which involves creating, analysing, writing, judging—from the First Day to the Last. Although her heart is mortal, Clarissa's scriptural writings will, through the transformative power of divine grace, survive in the book of the heart—her "book of conscience," her "name"—which Christ will "open" and "confess"

40 *Puritan Sermons*, 5:464, 462; Robert South, *Sermons Preached upon Several Occasions* (London, 1845), 2:548 (Lovelace had supplied Clarissa's closet at Mrs Sinclair's with copies of South's and Tillotson's sermons, 2:194). In a richly suggestive passage likening "*Mans nature to a Book, or law to itself*" in *The Resurrection of the Dead*, Bunyan discerns four books that will be opened at the last day. *Christian Behavior, The Holy City, The Resurrection of the Dead*, ed. J. Sears McGee (Oxford: Clarendon Press, 1987), pp. 252–85. Cf. also Warner's stimulating comment on Clarissa and the "book of life" (pp. 69–71).

41 *Puritan Sermons*, 5:462–65. Cf. Starr, p. 6n. Watson's emphasis on "the anatomy of the heart" is central to all representations of the heart in seventeenth- and eighteenth-century narrative. Clarissa's allegorical letter to Lovelace about embarking for her "father's house" might seem to qualify her sincerity, but see Damrosch's justification of the letter in the light of Baxter on the necessity of at times speaking "darkly" (p. 237). Cf. the Gospel precedent: "Jesus ... said unto them, Destroy this temple, and in three days I will raise it up. Then said the Jews, Forty and six years was this temple in building, and wilt thou rear it up in three days? But he spake of the temple of his body" (John 2:18–21).

aloud at the last day when the elect are named (Rev. 20:12; 3:5). Adversity was Clarissa's "shining-time," but her radiant heroism was an expression in the visible world; all of her final scriptural activities are devoted to fortifying her heart, the inward realm and record of the spirit.

As Clarissa transcribes herself into scripture, scripture helps to guide her into the proper way to Christ. As she rewrites the Bible, it rewrites her. This ongoing process might best be described as one of mutual "translation," a more complicated version of what happens to Enoch. Clarissa is now doing what her beloved Thomas à Kempis advises concerning spiritual consolation. Unfortunately, she was unable to heed this advice properly in order to save her life in the time of trial, but it is not now too late to save her soul. Thomas's Lord, represented as a "reader" of lessons, speaks to the faithful soul:

Write my words in thy heart, and ponder them diligently; for they will be very necessary in time of temptation. What thou understandest not when thou readest, thou shalt know in the day of visitation. I am wont to visit my elect two several ways, to wit, with temptation and comfort; and I daily read two lessons unto them, one reprehending their vices, and another exhorting them to increase of virtues. He that hath my words, and despiseth them, hath one that shall judge him at the last day.[42]

In the light of these passages concerning the "book of life" and the Last Judgment, we might say that Clarissa, like all humankind, is originally "written" by God in his book and "wrought" by God in the womb. As William Beatty Warner has said, "the Christian interpretive system gives Clarissa the idea of the self as a continuously unfolding history," or a book in the making.[43] Clarissa, fashioning the book of her works as the substance of her personal history, seeks to be recorded in God's book of life, and she uses the Bible to aid her in that endeavour. In God's final judgment, Clarissa hopes to be one of those

42 *Works of the Reverend and Pious Thomas à Kempis ... Vol. I ... The Imitation of Christ* (Edinburgh, 1801; the Keith translation of 1774), pp. 90–91. When her sister Arabella asks Clarissa for her "Thomas à Kempis," Clarissa replies, "Here it is. You will find excellent things, Bella, in that little book" (2:188; 296). There were several translations of *The Imitation of Christ* in small duodecimo editions in the eighteenth century (see Penguin, p. 1514).

43 Warner, p. 71. Cf. Clarissa the day before her death on "the winding-up of our short story" (7:438; 1345).

names called out by Christ in the absolution, as Robert South represents it, "Come, ye blessed of my Father," and not one of those in the denunciation, "Depart, ye cursed."[44] (It is not apparent that Clarissa would presume to be enumerated with the 144,000 martyr-witnesses in the first resurrection of Revelation 20:5.) Clarissa's letters, brooding as they often are with a spirit of intense self-examination and the discovery of a "secret sin"—guilt-ridden and guilt-written—with an acute concern over the fallible body, with a sense of foreordained and individually signalized doom, are written almost daily, again like a Puritan diary or spiritual autobiography.[45] Moreover, Clarissa, like her author, is represented as constantly reading, re-reading, and above all, transcribing copies of her own letters, and those of her correspondents. We think of the enormous expenditure of time that goes into the first draft of a typical letter in *Clarissa* and into all those copies, each of which becomes a little "better" as it goes through the transcription process. What happens to one who keeps making copy after written copy of her own experience? Something rich and strange—even terrible, perhaps. One turns into a Pamela, or a Clarissa, or a Lovelace, or a Richardson. Depending on how seriously we take it, a letter diary *does* become another self, an externalized self to which one may go for confirmation and authorization of who one is, or was. Clarissa's constant preoccupation with reading, transcribing, collecting, and recollecting her own book comes to exert a powerful influence on the self who does the writing. Something similar happens to Lovelace. His constant preoccupation with writing and reading about his stratagems assists in entangling him ever more securely in his own devices. Clarissa and Lovelace are their own individual scribes. The very act of transcribing or copying something tends to validate, authorize, valorize it.

---

44 South, *Sermons*, 2:548. Cf. Clarissa's impassioned plea to her mother, on her knees, for a last blessing *in writing*, "that I may hold it to my heart in my most trying struggles, and I shall think it a passport to Heaven" (7:82; 1180).

45 Although she cannot "prove" that Richardson was steeped in Puritan devotional literature, Wolff (pp. 4–53) is right in seeing Clarissa's affinity with the writers of such works. She notes that the seventeenth-century Puritan diarist represents himself in three primary roles—self-examiner, virtuous example, and saint. Clarissa represents herself, and is represented by others, in all these roles, and it is interesting that "participation in the Community of the Elect in Heaven" is another way of becoming recorded in the "book of life," a connection that Wolff passes over. Cf. Gillis (p. 46) and Damrosch (p. 220).

We recall that Clarissa is physically unable to transcribe the letter from her sister conveying her father's curse, and even Lovelace is incapable of transcribing Clarissa's mad papers after he has had all the torn bits and pieces collected in an effort to put her back together for himself. In the authority with which it becomes endowed as the *true* record of her experience, the expanding letter-diary dictates to the mortal Clarissa. She believes what she has written. And in the reciprocal process of being written by her story as well as writing it—an activity centred on the *Meditations*—Clarissa becomes what she has written.

Early in act 2 of the drama, Clarissa had described to Anna Howe why it was necessary for her to keep on writing *even if she were not to send her letter to anyone.* She has found, she says, that writing down "every-thing of moment" that happens to her may be of "future use" to her, and that by writing things down she entered into a "*compact*" with herself, "having given it," she goes on, "under my own hand to *improve,* rather than to go *backward,* as I live longer" (3:221; 483). She has made a written "compact" or covenant with her future self to improve herself. In the culminating fourth act of the drama, this "compact" comes to fruition. It replaces the "wretched composition" she once thought it might be necessary to arrange with Lovelace, a marriage of convenience to "save" her reputation, and she chooses a better salvation. Clarissa asks Belford to assemble her story because she will be "too much discomposed by the retrospection ... to proceed with the requisite temper in a task of *still greater* importance which I have before me" (7:67; 1173). This task is the new compact with God, a process of self-correction and restoration through writing, which we have traced in the *Meditations* and their reliance on the wisdom literature of the Bible. It is to the books of Job and Ecclesiasticus that Clarissa's Bible opens naturally in her harrowing stay at the Rowlands' debtors' prison (6:289–90; 1061). It would appear then that the wisdom literature of the Bible, not the New Testament, entered most deeply into Richardson's literary imagination in the composition of *Clarissa,* partly, no doubt, because of its proverbial nature, partly because of its apocalyptic fervour (no less intriguing to Richardson), but most important, because these books—especially Job—spoke most directly to the willed preservation of the integrity of one's heart—in writing—in the experience of tragic suffering and loss.

John Belford, as Clarissa's future executor, editor, and virtual apostle, begins reading the Bible in earnest under the influence of Clarissa's example and her "Meditation" of 15 July. He collates the individual "Meditations" he has access to with the original text, and the language he uses to characterize holy scripture—"the clear, the pellucid fountain-head" of the Bible, "this all-excelling collection of beauties" (6:428, 429; 1125, 1126)—is much like the language he uses to describe Clarissa and the style of her letters. In Belford's eyes, Clarissa is being fused with her "Meditations" and the original scriptural text. For Belford she becomes scripture personified, a "*bibliothecam Christi*" or "walking Bible," in Thomas Watson's words. She is the "Lady from the Scriptures" (7:99; 1189). For Belford and for Richardson's Christian readers, the chief impact of Clarissa as a suffering Job and Christ in one heroic female writer is that she translates herself into her own scripture, that she is the flesh made word.[46]

The developing divergence between Belford and Lovelace is nowhere more apparent than in their separate readings of the scriptural Clarissa. Lovelace responds to Belford's new-found edification with characteristic wit, reminiscent of Swift on Partridge. Lovelace is reminded of how scriptural enthusiasts will take the most far-fetched passages for "gospel" which seem to have any reference to the case at hand, so that "once, in a pulpit, I heard one ... vehemently declare himself to be a *dead dog*; when every man, woman, and child, were convinced to the contrary by his howling" (7:5; 1144).[47]

In his very next letter, however, Lovelace becomes his own scriptural enthusiast in the case of Clarissa by assuming for himself the

---

46 If we were to take Richardson's apparent transformation of the New Testament into fiction in its broadest sense, and were to see the Gospels as four separate narrative interpretations of the life of Christ, as the first "novel" (a new thing, good news) incorporating multiple points of view, and the letters of Paul as the first epistolary narrative (or "novel") of the gospel, it could be said that *Clarissa* combines both narrative techniques to extraordinarily complicated effect in representing the fate of Clarissa.

47 Cf. Bickerstaff on the gentlemen who bought Partridge's almanacs: "at every Line they read, they would lift up their Eyes and cry out, betwixt Rage and Laughter, *They were sure no Man* alive *ever writ such damned Stuff as this*." "A Vindication of Isaac Bickerstaff, Esq." in *The Writings of Jonathan Swift*, ed. Greenberg and Piper (New York: Norton Critical Edition, 1973), p. 439.

patriarchal role of the Old Testament God who presides over female fertility. He interprets the lines from Clarissa's "Meditation," *"For the arrows of the Almighty are within me; the poison whereof drinketh up my spirit. ... For the thing which I greatly feared is come upon me!"* (6:426–27; 1125), as veiled indications of what Lovelace hopes for: "in plain English, that the dear creature is in the way to be a Mamma" (7:13; 1147). He further declares that it would be the pride of his life "to prove, in this charming frost-piece, the triumph of nature over principle, and to have a young Lovelace by such an angel" (7:13; 1147). Lovelace epitomizes for Richardson all the power of amoral, unregenerate nature in one exceptional man, as Clarissa, with her affirmation to Anna Howe of the "Ties of pure Friendship" over the "Ties of Nature" (6:405; 1114), epitomizes—in her stress on principle—the exceptional woman. Lovelace finally realizes and accepts that, whether or not she is "in the way" he would have her be, she is going to die, and the final outcome of the history of Clarissa's responses to Lovelace's heart (as he and the reader both know) is now wholehearted rejection. As Lovelace claimed Clarissa's womb, so will he now claim her heart, but his rhetoric of the heart has become more and more violent, parodic, literal, insane:

My heart is bent upon having her ... tho' I marry her in the agonies of death. ... I will overcome the creeping folly that has found its way to my heart, or I will tear it out in her presence, and throw it at hers, that she may see how much more tender than her own that organ is. (7:89–90; 1184)

Finally, after her death, Lovelace the natural man reveals to Belford the full state of his manic desperation in a way appropriately reminiscent of the behaviour of Clarissa's mother in the early part of the novel ("The heart, Clary, is what I want"), as well as defining himself as the demonic counterpart to Thomas Watson's depiction of Christ as "Heart-Searcher" and "surgeon":

I think it absolutely right that my ever-dear and beloved Lady should be opened and embalmed. ... Every-thing that can be done to preserve the Charmer from decay, shall also be done. ... But her *heart*, to which I have such unquestionable pretensions, in which once I had so large a share, and which I will prize above my own, I *will* have. (8:47–48; 1383–84)

In the "Advertisement" to the *Meditations*, Richardson gives a poignant—almost wistful—further indication of his final intentions in *Clarissa* in a bald restatement, with a new twist, of the notion that some people have good hearts and some bad:

The History of Clarissa must be owned to be carried into length. But the subject was pregnant. All bad nature was endeavoured to be set forth in the principal Men: All good in those of the two principal Women: so that the whole compass of human nature ... was aimed to be taken into it.[48]

Richardson's use of "compass" in this context may be set beside Jeremiah's "for the Lord hath created a new thing in the earth, a woman shall compass a man" (31:22). However powerful the scriptural heroine might be in her traditional roles of helping to provide food, shelter, nurture, and comfort for man, in all the literal and figurative expressions of that kind of compassing—and however close she might be to God in the inner experience of womb and heart— no woman in Scripture is depicted as an important writer.[49] This role is reserved exclusively for men, from Moses on through Ezekiel, Job, St Paul, the gospel narrators, and the St John of Revelation—often prophetic figures concerned with apocalyptic eschatology. Clarissa is represented in her own scripture—that is, virtually all of her own writing and the writing about her after the rape—in the traditional role of suffering female saint and martyr, but now as a female Job and Christ combined, and her creator's new thing is the woman hero with her own weapon—mightier than the proverbial sword, mightier even than all of Lovelace's phallocentric power—the crow-quill pen of a modern prophet aimed as an arrow to probe and prove the hearts of her family, of Lovelace, of herself, and finally of her reader. But Clarissa's ultimate role as prophet comprehends and enlarges

---

48 *Meditations*, p. iii.

49 In the book which comes just before Job, however, the powerful Queen Esther is represented as in effect "unwriting" Haman's letter to destroy the Jews when King Ahasuerus authorizes her and Mordecai to write new letters (Esther 8 and 9). Esther's power over written language here has interesting affinities with Clarissa's "unnaming" and vanquishing of Lovelace and his writings. Cf. also Jezebel's letters written in Ahab's name to effect the stoning of Naboth in 1 Kings 21:8–11. Both examples show royal women usurping the traditionally masculine mode of royal correspondence.

her role as a writer whose life story inscribes the most comprehensive literary indictment of patriarchal authority in eighteenth-century
culture.

All of her last writings, diverse appeals to the head and the heart,
work to justify Clarissa to an almost completely corrupt and inimical
world and to an all-judging God, from the most literal expressions to
the most figurative. There is the collection and collation of her true
story drawn from her correspondence and Lovelace's, a task entrus-
ted to Belford. There is her Last Will and Testament (reminiscent of
the traditional deathbed blessing in the Old Testament, as in Gen.
27), an extraordinary aural emblem meant to be read aloud (as it
is by Colonel Morden), and her last letter heard in all its poignant
nuances by her devastated family and their friends, of whom only
Hickman and Morden saw her before her death: "my body ... shall
not be touched but by those of my own Sex"—nevertheless, "as I am
Nobody's," Lovelace may view "*her dead,* whom he ONCE before saw
in a manner dead" (8:106–7; 1413). Such sentiments brought forth
admiration, sighs, tears, then execrations from all assembled (8:125–
26; 1420–21). This moving appeal to the ears of her assembled aud-
itors will later be published for a second perusal by their weeping
eyes. There are her eleven posthumous letters to her family, friends,
and Lovelace (eleven epistolary apostles to join Belford), which take
seriously the injunction of Proverbs 25:21–22, "If thine enemy be
hungry, give him bread to eat; and if he be thirsty, give him water to
drink: For thou shalt heap coals of fire upon his head, and the Lord
shall reward thee," advice reiterated approvingly by the apostle Paul
in his Epistle to the Romans (12:20) in support of the Deuteronomic
doctrine, "Vengeance is mine; I will repay, saith the Lord." Since
Clarissa, in these posthumous letters, believes she is now in the presence of the Lord, the enormous unspoken bitterness and implied
reproach underlying her "forgiveness" in them seems to have the divine approval. As so often happens in biblical narrative, the implicit
meaning takes precedence over the explicit: Clarissa *knows* that her
parents are not going to be made happy by their two remaining children, that they will *not* forget their youngest child—that she was the
very centre of their life (8:25; 1372). To her brother she implies, despite "your rigorous heart," I know you are not such a monster that

now I am dead you can refuse to forgive me; after all, what will it cost you? I hope when you have children there will not be one Clarissa among them (8:26–29; 1373–74). Clarissa now believes herself to be beyond recrimination, and this is in a sense true, but the terrible energy released when her "*best self*" (6:115; 974) was lost, destroyed, sacrificed, becomes transformed into a kind of divine condemnation. With such power, what is the most certain way of having them avenge her against Lovelace? By begging them not to. The posthumous letters are an expression of the inhuman power of Clarissa's new divine self, and at the same time they are perfectly sincere in their forgiveness.[50] Clarissa's *writing* self became progressively weaker: in these letters particularly we hear the full intensity of the *written* self, a power directed at those she has left behind. Clarissa in these letters has gone beyond the sphere of the most awesome of all satirists—the prophet with divine sanction—to the prophet deified.[51]

Counterbalancing the aural influence of her will is the impact of her coffin in the funeral procession, an extraordinary memorial emblem. The coffin-desk upon which Clarissa wrote her life out to the end has become the final "book" whose cover now shields her corpse. The coffin is an object charged with tremendous talismanic power (a counterpart in Clarissa's scripture to the ark of the covenant) as it comes, the hearse drawn by horses, the church bell solemnly tolling, into the presence of the crowd of neighbouring men, women, and children, and is then carried into the hall of her father's house by six maidens. Clarissa is no longer a person but her own religious force emanating from this terrific object, a power capable of rewriting her relationship to all of her family, including her inflexible brother, who stands—a final Richardsonian impression—with "marks of stupefaction imprinted upon every feature" (8:77; 1398).

50 Cf. Flynn on Clarissa's "infernal forgiveness," pp. 42–45.

51 As Richardson was composing *Clarissa*, the great age of English satire—according to traditional literary history—had come to an end with the deaths of Pope and Swift. Fielding is usually thought of as the heir to the satirical tradition. But Richardson was not immune to the influence of the Tory satirists in verse or prose, nor to the satirical *Zeitgeist*. *Clarissa* in its protracted and massive social sweep is at least as powerful a condemnation of the errors of mid-century English culture as is *The Dunciad*. Richardson's unique accomplishments as a social satirist, in this novel particularly, but also in *Pamela* and *Grandison*, have gone largely unrecognized.

At the extreme limit of Clarissa's writing is the non-verbal appeal of the Old Testament prophet's symbolic object, the linen girdle or potter's vessel of Jeremiah, the engraved brick of Ezekiel. The hieroglyphically inscribed coffin functions this way as a memorial sign of the martyr-prophet, but Clarissa is also careful to impress her waning but no less vivid physical presence itself as a memorial emblem upon the mind and heart of her auditor or reader when (of the many examples that could be cited) she writes to her mother on her knees for a "Last Blessing" that never comes (7:77; 1178), when she stitches a "Meditation" to the bottom of her Uncle John's barbarous letter demanding to know if she thinks herself with child by Lovelace (7:106–7; 1192), when she drops to one knee, with clasped hands and uplifted eyes, imploring Anna Howe's Hickman to remember "that in this posture you see me, in the last moment of our parting, begging a blessing upon you both" (6:440; 1131). And over all of this hovers the powerful sense, in Clarissa's mind and gradually the reader's, that God has intervened in her life to help write the book of her fate as one of his elect, one of his specially called prophets; that by writing her "Book of Meditations" (virtually her "book of life"), she is writing her "name" in his book too, for eternity. Put another way, by allowing Clarissa to write, like Jeremiah, her own "Book of Consolation" and vanquish her enemy Lovelace, God writes her, member by member, in his own.

The Gnostic *Clarissa*

Margaret Anne Doody

Such a Sun in a family, where there are none but faint twinklers,
how could they bear it! ... The distance between you and them is
immense. Their eyes ake to look up at you. What shades does your
full day of merit cast upon them!

(Anna to Clarissa, 9 March)

Do they not act in character?—And to whom? To an Alien. You
are not one of them.

(Anna to Clarissa, 25 March)

O nce upon a time there was a Virgin Maid who lived in bliss surrounded by the light in which she participated. In her happy
home some say she was placed just below her Mother, in freedom
and felicity. But in making a false and deadly contact with an inimical element, whether out of inadvertence, curiosity, or desire,
this Virgin Maid lost her happy place. She was deceived and beguiled; she confused the low with the high, the false simulacrum
or reflected light with the reality. The arrogant and destructive deceiver who beguiled her brought about her fall. The Lady of Light
was nearly quenched by his arrogant power. But she, seeing the truth
at last, turned back, and repenting her error returned, slowly and
not without trials, through the unhappy chaos back to her place of
light.

Simply put, this summary gives us what we will, I think, recognize as a possible plot summary of Richardson's *Clarissa*—although we will all immediately protest against it, saying that Clarissa's place in her "original family" the Harlowes is far from truly happy. The plot summary I have just given *is* a justifiable, if greatly shortened, version of the Gnostic story of Sophia or Heavenly Wisdom. For centuries, the main source of information about the chief Gnostic versions of cosmic events was St Irenaeus of Lyons, who, in an all-out treatise *Against Heresies*, left the most accessible versions of the beliefs he attempted to refute; his work was widely known to learned Christian divines of various persuasions in the Renaissance and the Enlightenment. Texts more recently translated, such as *Pistis Sophia* (which was not translated into English from Coptic until the nineteenth and twentieth centuries), have added greatly to our own knowledge of these cosmologies and theologies, even before the discovery in this century of the Nag Hammadi manuscripts.[1]

Various forms of Gnostic beliefs can be traced in the thinking of some Renaissance groups such as the Family of Love which flourished in the environment of Renaissance print culture.[2] It would not be especially surprising if Richardson had come upon versions and variants of Gnostic thought fairly often, even in hostile citations in

1 St Irenaeus of Lyons writing *Against Heresies* about 180 AD left valuable information about the sects he was trying to combat, particularly the followers of Valentinus who began to flourish about the middle of the second century AD. Irenaeus summarizes what he takes to be the beliefs of various Gnostic groups, and is still the chief source of information about Gnostic thought in the early Christian era. *Pistis Sophia* was discovered, if not edited, in the eighteenth century; it was in the possession of Dr Anthony Askew, a divine at Cambridge. The discovery in the mid-twentieth century of the Nag Hammadi library of Gnostic texts buried in Egypt has greatly amplified our knowledge of Gnosticism. "The Gnostic *Clarissa*" was first published in *Eighteenth-Century Fiction* 11:1 (1998), 49–78.

2 Christopher W. Marsh, in a recent study, *The Family of Love in English Society 1550–1630* (Cambridge: Cambridge University Press, 1994), notes as others have done that the Family of Love on the Continent flourished chiefly among the Antwerp humanists and had a special connection to the printing house of the Plantins. New material was brought to England in "the wholesale transposition of a collection of mystical Dutch writings from the Low Countries to England during the 1570s" (p. 28). Among the works that came in were works of personal piety such as *The Imitation of Christ* (mentioned in *Clarissa*). Richardson's association with the printing fellowship might have put him in touch with the various strains of thought associated with the Familists in England. Richardson uses the phrase "family of love" to describe the Grandisons: see *The History of Sir Charles Grandison*, ed. Jocelyn Harris, 3 vols (Oxford: Oxford University Press, 1972), e.g., 1:133.

sermons and in antagonistic tracts. Richardson's age was full of religious controversy.[3] The atmosphere of the 1720s and 1730s was conducive to attacks upon "heresy," which means, of course, that heresies had to get some kind of airing. The endeavour on some sides to turn Christian theology into deistic moralizing—a tendency so visible in the eighteenth century—may actually have stimulated a kind of oppositional interest in inner-light doctrines of various kinds, as the rise of Methodism would seem to indicate.

My point is certainly not to say that Richardson was a Gnostic. Nor is it to argue that we can pin Richardson down to one ascertainable set of beliefs in a systematic and categorizing manner. Anyone who considers a religious matter intently and over a period of time and with imagination is quite probably going to be subjected to accusations of inconstancy or inconsistency, if not of heresy—or simple folly. What I want to do is to draw attention to the presence of the Gnostic story within *Clarissa,* and the significance of that presence. One of the reasons for the endurance of Richardson's story—and for the respect one has to accord the novel when one reads it in entirety—is the rich density of its material, its intellectual challenge and its symbolic depth. The symbolic depth is not achieved by setting down a simple linear moralistic story—even if efforts to make *Clarissa* into precisely that kind of story date from its own time.[4]

There are two symbolic systems I want to look at. I want to emphasize that I prefer to use words such as "symbol" and "symbology" rather than "allegory" or "allegorical." I take it that allegory refers to a hidden but not-so-hidden meaning that the reader is (in some sense) supposed to "get." I am not at all sure that the reader is meant

---

3 Anthony Collins, to take but one example, remained a controversial figure from *The Discourse of Freethinking* (1713) through the publication of *The Grounds of Christian Religion* (1724) and *The Literal Scheme of Prophecy* (1726). The Bangorian controversy had attracted numerous disputants, including William Law, as early as 1717. The deistic views of Dr Samuel Clarke, Queen Caroline's favourite philsopher, were eagerly disputed by many antagonists, including Dr Joseph Trapp. As well as the disputes between the upholders of Christianity and the deists and freethinkers, or the bitter disagreements between Churchman and Dissenter, there were frequent arguments within Anglicanism regarding the meanings of "Church" and "sacrament."

4 This is visible not only in the remarks of some commentators, but also in some overt simplifications such as the chapbook redactions told in the third person, with the moral made plain and obvious, produced for the uneducated in the late eighteenth century.

to "get" the lively symbolic system working within the narrative—although some readers must surely have done so. Richardson's "Gnostic *Clarissa*" within his *Clarissa* is not "the" *Clarissa* or "the answer" to our puzzles about the text. But its presence—if I am right—raises the ante about the novel's meaning, or what it is saying to us.

The novel *Clarissa*, more than any other eighteenth-century mainstream work, is about not being at home in the world. A great deal has been written by orthodox Christians about not being at home in the world, but the less orthodox have had even more to say about it. Some such works are openly and clearly allegorical—"The Hymn of the Pearl" or "The Song of the Soul" associated with the apocryphal text *The Acts of Thomas*, for example. In this (presumably) second-century "Hymn," the soul is represented as the child of a Great King who has been sent on away on an important errand:

> When I was an infant too young to talk, in my father's palace,
> Reposing in the wealth and luxury of those who nourished me,
> My parents equipped me with supplies and sent me out from the East,
>   our country, on a mission. ...
> They took away from me the jewel-studded garment shot with gold
> That they had made out of love for me
> And the robe of yellow color (tailored) to my size,
> But they made an agreement with me,
> Impressed it on my mind (so that) I might (not) forget it, and said,
> "If you go down to Egypt and bring from there the one pearl,
> Which resides near the ravenous dragon,
> You shall put (back) on that jewel-studded garment and the robe."[5]

---

5 *The Gnostic Scriptures*, trans. with notes and and introduction by Bentley Layton (New York: Doubleday, 1987), p. 371, lines 1–14. "The Hymn of the Pearl," also entitled "The Hymn of Jude Thomas the Apostle in the Country of the Indians," is of unknown authorship. It appears in *The Acts of Thomas*, probably written in Edessa in the third century, and has sometimes been attributed to the Syrian Christian Gnostic poet and philosopher Bardaisan (b. 154 AD). Although there are a number of manuscripts of *The Acts of Thomas*, only one manuscript in Greek and one in Syriac contain "The Hymn of the Pearl." But ideas from it seem to flow into a number of later works, including perhaps the medieval English poem *Pearl*.

The wandering soul forgets its mission and its true identity, taken up with the delusions of the place to which it travels, the false and shadowy "Egypt." It is an alien, but tries to conform too readily: "So I put on their style of dress, so that I might not look like one who was foreign." At last it is reminded of its true home: "And I snatched the pearl, and turned to carry it away to my parents. / And I took off the dirty clothing, and left it behind in their land."[6]

"The Song of the Pearl" is a relatively simple Gnostic tale, the emblematic story of one life, though an Everyman life. Other Gnostic narratives tell more dramatic stories about cosmic conflict between mighty and antagonistic entities. The substance of the Gnostic myths, particularly as outlined by St Irenaeus, was well known in Richardson's time; references (albeit disparaging) are to be found in the works of orthodox writers. For example, John Alexander in *The Primitive Doctrine of Christ's Divinity* (1727) produces an outline of what Irenaeus said the Gnostic Valentinians believed:

Their supream God and Father of all they called *Bythus*, i.e. *the Depth*, or *incomprehensible Being* ... him they supposed ... long before the beginning of the World, to have produced a glorious *Æon*, equal to himself, and capable to comprehend him: whom they called the *only-begotten* ... and *the Mind* (*nus*) [i.e. *nous*] they coupled him with another Female-*Æon* emitted at the same time, termed (*Alethia*) *Truth*. These soon propagated. ...The last Female-*Æon*, called *Sophia, Wisdom*, thro' an immoderate desire to search out and comprehend the unknown Father, had almost lost her Place in the *Plerôma* of the *Æons*.[7]

The Gnostic story of the Fall and Rise of the Virgin Sophia (in its various versions) is a story of supra-mundane significance. The important acts happen outside time and matter—time and matter are aspects of the fallen world, the dead world. Sophia herself is begotten by a drop of light falling downward into matter from the left hand of the true unchanging God. Thus was Wisdom born. Her counterpart, emanating from God's right hand, is Christ, who is complete light, with no admixture of matter. Sophia is light-fluid; she

---

6 *Gnostic Scriptures*, line 29, p. 372; lines 61–62, p. 374.

7 John Alexander, *The Primitive Doctrine of Christ's Divinity; Or, A Specimen of a Full View of the Ante-Nicene Doctrine. In An Essay on Irenaeus* (London, 1727), p. 20.

has been caught up in and given form by the mother-waters, the original *hylē* or matter. Beautiful as such a form is, she is anxious to rid herself altogether of the hylic and return to her sphere. References to such a system sparkle throughout literature of the Enlightenment. Cowley refers to the mother-waters in *Davideis*, "Where their vast *Court*, the *Mother-waters* keep," a line memorably parodied by Dryden in *MacFlecknoe* as "Where their vast Courts the Mother-Strumpets keep."[8] In the Gnostic system, the mass of the four original elements (Water, Darkness, Abyss, and Chaos) was brooded over by the Universal Mother. The Gnostic story is a series of falls—all of which explain the existence and dysfunction of matter, time, death, and the things of this world, including earthly powers. Irenaeus explains what the Gnostics said happened when the drop of light fell into the waters:

It absolutely sank into the waters ... set them in motion, recklessly proceeding all the way to the lowest depths, and it assumed from them a body. For—they say—all things rushed toward the secretion of light that it contained; clung to it; and enveloped it. ... Bound, therefore, by a body composed of matter, and greatly weighed down by it, this (power) recovered its senses, and attempted to escape from the waters and ascend to its mother. But it could not do so, on account of the weight of the enveloping body. But greatly suffering, it contrived to conceal that light, which was from above, for fear that the light too might be injured by the inferior elements, just as it had been.[9]

---

8 See the essay by A.L. Korn, "*MacFlecknoe* and Cowley's *Davideis*," *Essential Articles for the Study of John Dryden*, ed. H.T. Swedenberg (Hamden, Conn.: Archon Books, 1966), pp. 170–200.

9 *Gnostic Scriptures*, p. 174. This is from a section in Layton's book entitled "'Other' Gnostic Teachings According to St. Irenaeus." Compare G.R.S. Mead, "An Anonymous System from Irenaeus": "The *Universal* Mother brooded over the Waters; enamoured of her beauty, the First and Second Man produced from her the third Great Light, the Christ. ... But a drop of Light fell downwards to the left hand into chaotic matter; this was called Sophia, or Wisdom, the *World*-Mother. The Waters of the Æther were thus set in motion, and formed a body for Sophia (the Light-Æon), *viz.*, the Heaven-sphere. And she, freeing herself, left her body behind, and ascended to the Middle Region below her Mother (the *Universal* Mother), who formed the boundary of the Ideal Universe." G.R.S. Mead, with an introduction by Kenneth Rexroth, *Fragments of a Faith Forgotten* (New York: University Books, 1960), p. 188. The universal Mother is a puzzling character. Ioan Couliano points out that she is sometimes Sophia, "also called *agapē* or Love and elsewhere Silence ... a universal Mother, *protogeneteira* (first begetress), multiplying herself." In other versions of the scheme, such as that apparently produced by the Sethians, "the universal Mother is an androgynous entity who fecundates herself. She must be concretely represented as a womb endowed with a

Sophia's contact with what G.R.S. Mead terms "the Space-Waters" caused the generation also of a son, "the chief Creative Power of the Sensible World."[10] Sophia herself becomes by parthogenesis a "Mother Strumpet," conceiving by her descent a most imperfect offspring. This troublesome son in many Gnostic texts is named Ialdabaoth. Ialdabaoth is a tyrant, arrogant and assuming. He is the false God, the *Demiourgos* or Demiurge who creates Adam and Eve— but even Ialdabaoth can breathe life in them only by imparting some of the true light-fluid he received from Sophia.

The tyrant pseudo-creator we know from Blake as old Nobodaddy, Urizen.[11] Freethinkers also refer to this delinquent tyrant-power as "Jehovah," indicating that the biblical bossy deity, the jealous and angry God worshipped by ignorant Christians and Jews, is a perversion of the true serene light. We do not, of course, have to go far in *Clarissa* to look for bossy and unreasonable men who insist that their system of things is the height of reason. The two male Harlowes, the two Jameses, both named for a failed king, come to mind. But Lovelace above all is the representative of Ialdabaoth. He thinks of himself as the sun: "Knowest thou not moreover, that Man is the Woman's Sun; Woman is the Man's Earth?—How dreary, how desolate, the Earth, that the Sun shines not upon!"[12] But this is comic posturing, defying the truth of the novel, which is that Clarissa—whose name means "most light," "most bright," and also "most sparkling,"

phallus." Ioan Couliano, *The Tree of Gnosis: Gnostic Mythology from Early Christianity to Modern Nihilism*, trans. H.S. Wiesner and the author (New York: HarperCollins, 1992), pp. 80–81. This is not only a translation but a revision of the earlier *Les Gnoses Dualistes d'occident* (1990).

10 Mead, p. 188.

11 In speaking of William Blake, we might remember that Blake's "O rose thou art sick" owes something to one of Clarissa's "mad papers" (paper 3, 5:306) in Richardson's novel. Blake was evidently attracted to Richardson's work and found it (in some respects at least) congenial.

12 Samuel Richardson, *Clarissa. Or, The History of A Young Lady*, ed. Florian Stuber, The Clarissa Project, 8 vols (New York: AMS Press, 1990), 4:230. References are to this edition by volume and page number. Parallel references (where they exist), by page number, are provided to the edition of *Clarissa or The History of a Young Lady*, ed. Angus Ross (Harmondsworth: Penguin, 1985), which is based on the first edition, modernized in incidentals. The Penguin edition is referred to with no remark, save in exceptional cases, on differences in wording and accidentals. For the citation just given, cf. p. 660.

"most glaring," "most shining," "most famous"—is the sun. Anna
Howe says this, with emphasis, very early in the novel:

Such a Sun in a family, where there are none but faint twinklers, how could
they bear it! ...The distance between you and them is immense. Their eyes
ake to look up at you. What shades does your full day of merit cast upon
them! (1:170; 129)

Lovelace vividly likens Clarissa to the sun several times, most strik-
ingly perhaps when at Hampstead he sees his lost Clarissa once again
and feels like the man born blind in the story of Christ's healing—
or like the dreamer brought out of the cave in Plato's Parable of the
Sun in the *Republic*.

Then my Charmer opened the door, and blazed upon me, as it were, in a
flood of light, like what one might imagine would strike a man, who, born
blind, had by some propitious power been blessed with his sight, all at once,
in a meridian Sun. (5:83; 772)

When truly facing and *seeing* Clarissa, Lovelace must always yield his
own pretence to be the light.

Lovelace behaves as Ialdabaoth's true representative most strik-
ingly in his oft-announced arrogation to himself of the right to create:

I have changed his name by virtue of my own single authority. Knowest
thou not, that I am a great Name-father? ... Quality too I create. And by a
still more valuable prerogative, I *degrade* by virtue of my own imperial will,
without any other act of forfeiture than for my own convenience. What a
poor thing is a monarch to me! (4:43; 569)

Lovelace is supreme ruler, above all law: "The Law was not made for
such a man as me" (4:44; 569). He can, however, create only pseudo-
realties, weak fictions, *simulacra* and gimcracks. But we should not
make the Gnostic Lovelace too pathetic an antagonist, or too simple
a rake-villain. Once we bring this symbological system in, we must
be willing to face the suggestions of a more complex relationship
between the two protagonists on the supra-mundane sphere.

If we apply the Gnostic cosmological system to *Clarissa*, we can
play with the idea that in a super-narrative, a supra-narrative untold,

Ialdabaoth (Lovelace) is the child of Sophia herself, the offspring of Clarissa's eternal principle before she was born of flesh and blood. Clarissa's very birth into flesh and blood strikes Lovelace himself as odd: "Her nurse Norton boasts of her maternal offices ... So that there is full proof, that she came not from above all at once an angel!" (1:201; 145). He makes a comic show of repudiating the idea that Clarissa the divine could truly belong to her earthbound family: "She takes the man she calls her Father ... the fellow she calls her Brother ... to *be* her Father, to *be* her ... Brother ... Mere cradle-prejudices!" (1:201; 145). Most of the more extreme statements of Gnostic views in the novel are, as we might expect, made by Lovelace (the author could readily repudiate them at need). But not all are made in a totally jocular manner. When Clarissa falls ill after receiving her father's brutal curse, Lovelace says

I will tell thee—I was *in danger of losing my Charmer for ever.*—She was soaring upward to her native Skies. She was got above earth, by means, too, of the *Earth-born.* (3:276; Lovelace's emphasis; 518)

The "*Earth-born*" Harlowes are thus hylic mud-people, mere *simulacra* of human beings, without the divine spark, in contrast to the heavenly Clarissa. Anna has said practically the same thing, in a Gnostic shorthand, when she says that the Harlowes, in treating Clarissa so badly, act in character: "And to whom? To an Alien. You are not one of them" (2:61; 237). Clarissa, the "Alien," comes from above, from the Plerōma, from the light world, and has descended to the dull matter that the Harlowes occupy.

Despite his half-serious insistence that Clarissa is divine, Lovelace longs to impregnate her, which means (to him) using her to reproduce himself. But he also yearns towards her as a maternal being. In the "love-story" of Lovelace and Clarissa, Lovelace often imagines himself with his mother, or with Clarissa as mother—her breasts fascinate him. He wants to be perpetually loved and forgiven by Clarissa, a mother-figure who is to give unconditional and steady regard. He wants to have "a young Lovelace" by her, thinking (rightly) it would be a triumph to make "such an angel" give birth. Strangely, Lovelace in his mid-twenties seems to be suffering from a state of orphanage. He appears to have lost to death a most indulgent but pious mother (see, for example, 3:107; 441), and he never once alludes to his father. There is in the novel one allusion to this missing parent. After the rape, Clarissa reproaches Lovelace "Thou hadst a Father, who was a man of honour" (5:345; 912). It is natural, or at least realistic, that she should believe he did, but Lovelace's own psychological picture entirely lacks the father. It is striking that *only* in the case of Lovelace does this novelist present us with a major character who has no male parent in his psychic background. Richardson, who takes a great interest in family dynamics, gives a good glimpse of Mr B.'s original family, and Pamela of course has an important father as well as a mother. Clarissa's earthly parents are rendered for us in great detail. Sir Charles Grandison's relations with his parents, including his recently deceased father, Sir Thomas Grandison, as well as a mother who died when he was seventeen, are very important in shaping his development and attitudes. Lovelace refers to his mother several times in the narrative, but we tend to think of him as he does, as having, curiously enough, no father. This deficiency is eminently suited to his role, as defined by Karen L. King in her discussion of an archetypal bad boy and rapist:

The chief Archon (Samael, Sakla, Yaldabaoth) is characterized as blind, ignorant, or mistaken, and arrogant, the source of Envy and the Father of Death. He is androgynous and formed like a beast; his mother is the Abyss; he derives from Matter—no father is mentioned. Though he himself has no father, he is the world creator: the creator of a fatherless world like its fatherless father.[13]

The blind and arrogant Archon or Ruler is (as in the Gnostic text *The Hypostasis of the Archons*, discussed here by King) a cruel yet oddly ineffectual rapist, desiring, despising, yet curiously subjected to the female principle. In the dynamic of Richardson's novel, Lovelace remains an ignorant bastard, a pseudo-creator who is the product of a peculiar parthogenesis. In all his Ialdabaoth boasting, Robert Lovelace never boasts of his own paternity.

Lovelace-Ialdabaoth implicitly makes the vaunt of hubristic Ialdabaoth: "It is I who am the parent and god; and there is none above

13 Karen L. King, "Ridicule and Rape, Rule and Rebellion," *Gnosticism and the Early Christian World*, ed. James E. Goehring *et al.* (Sonoma, Calif.: Polebridge Press, 1990), pp. 8–9.

me."[14] He wants to drive his Clarissa-Sophia into the position of forgetting the higher heaven and worshipping only himself, trembling at his frown. But the light principle, however much she suffers, cannot do that. Indeed, it is by the Lady of Light's retention of the principle of light, however dimmed and unsteady in her lowest traverses of the lower world, that the power to love remains. That love is what sustains and creates in the universe— "Flowers, and Knots, and Trees, and the Sun, and the Moon, and the Seven Stars," a creation joked about by Lovelace when he says Clarissa made them by stitching them in her sampler (6:102; 971). But they are an original creation of Light and Love working in or with the material.

In the Gnostic cosmological narrative, Sophia can hardly simply *hate* Ialdabaoth or "son of Chaos" because he is, after all, her child. In the Gnostic system, such an "angel" has already given birth to an infant Lovelace. But if she is seduced by this imperfect offspring to make him momentarily her lover, and to mistake the cunning false system of mirrored lights for the true light, she has to escape. In the Gnostic narratives, the Virgin escapes by means of divine help from the first or real Heaven, not from any spectral imitation of the realm of Ialdabaoth. Christ is sent to help Sophia. Christ "clothed his sister Sophia with the Light-vesture and they rejoiced together."[15] In the "mystical marriage" they mount together to the Incorruptible Æon. According to *Pistis Sophia*, the Arrogant One seduced Sophia, deceiving her into taking the low for the high, imagining that the lower regions were the genuine Light. "And so in ignorance she descended into matter, saying 'I will go into that region, without my consort, to take the light ... so that I may go to the Light of lights, which is in the Height of heights.' ... But all the material emanations of Arrogant surrounded her, and the light-power of Arrogant set to work to devour all the light-powers in Sophia."[16] Only after going through a series of repentances, even descending altogether into Chaos, does Sophia, still yearning for the Light, move back to her origin. The stages of repentance set out in ancient Gnostic works such

14 *Gnostic Scriptures*, p. 175.

15 Mead, p. 191.

16 Mead, "The *Pistis Sophia*," *Fragments*, p. 470.

Pistis Sophia link their visions of the world to Egyptian apocrypha and Hermetic works. (Egyptian thought is much attached to numerical evolutionary stages of a progress; the Egyptians seem to be the ultimate progenitors of all twelve-step programs.) After the thirteenth repentance, Christ aids Sophia, sending her light-power:

Then, while Sophia pours forth hymns of joy, the power becomes a "crown to her head" and her *hylē* (or material propensities) begins to be entirely purified, while the spiritual light-powers which she has succeeded in retaining during her long combat, join themselves with the new vesture of light which has descended upon her.[17]

In the scheme of Richardson's novel, Clarissa, the fallen Sophia, descends into chaos. The first descent is a descent prehistoric as it were, the descent into the dunghill world of matter, figured as the world of the Harlowes and their Harlowe Place. (It is Lovelace who correctly identifies Harlowe Place as "sprung up from a dunghil," 1:231; 161). The light shineth in the darkness—and the darkness nearly comprehends it. Lovelace knows the Virgin carnally against her will, nearly destroying the light of reason in her. She goes into the depth of Chaos in the sheriff's officer's prison room, a totally hylic enclosure, decorated with dead and dying plants. The short sequence of scenes in which Clarissa is imprisoned represents the universal light being nearly overpowered by the darkness of the material world and by the absence of light-spark—an absence we know as human evil. The prostitutes taunt her with her change of state: "Methinks, *Miss*, said Sally, you are a little *soily*, to what we have seen you" (6:265; 1060).

Yet Clarissa's light is not overwhelmed by dirt, darkness, or despair even during her one day of unrecorded dereliction and agony in the three days in the prison room—although despair comes close to her. Clarissa has enough light still to enlighten this abode of death and darkness:

When I survey'd the room around, and the kneeling Lady, sunk with majesty too in her white flowing robes ... spreading the dark, tho' not dirty,

17 Summary of the ending of *Pistis Sophia*, Mead, p. 473.

222 MARGARET ANNE DOODY

floor, and illuminating that horrid corner. ... (Belford to Lovelace, 6:274; 1065)

Clarissa, as we see later, will sell her clothes to buy a coffin; like the King's child in "Hymn of the Pearl" she "took off [her] dirty clothing and left it behind in their land." She also confronts and subdues the "ravenous dragon": "And I subdued it by calling out my father's name."[18] Mrs Sinclair—in whom *sin* is *clear* (Richardson through Lovelace's allegorizing witticism does here get very close to the allegory direct)—is "the old dragon" (6:36; cf. 935; the "dragon" does not appear in the first edition). We might remember, however, that in one version of the cosmic Sophia-myth, one which could have been known to Richardson, Mrs Sinclair is also Sophia-Clarissa's child:

[Sophia] had almost lost her Place in the *Plerôma* of the *Æons*: And tho' recover'd after some time, yet produced a monstrous birth, called Mother *Achamoth*, a blind, shapeless *Æon*, made up of Ignorance and Passion, cast forth without the *Pleroma*, and yet under some Influence and Management of those within it: She produced the *Demiurgus* or Creator, who made the World.[19]

Achamoth, "a corruption from the Hebrew," is a word meaning "Wisdom" (*hokma*) and "Death" (*moth*).[20] Mrs Sinclair is Wisdom's Death, or Death-Wisdom. "Mother Sinclair," whose monstrous birth arises from Sophia's original error, is the true Mother of Lovelace, and it is thus hardly strange that he should so often term her "mother." In the supra-mundane drama, Clarissa-Sophia has a spiritual responsibility for both her monstrous children, a responsibility which she works off by living and suffering with and through them. But we can also say simply that on the mundane level Clarissa's imprisonment is brought about by the aggressively hylic fat bawd and her minions, emanations of the dark and angry powers of the cosmos, who when they come to taunt her come as projections of tyrannical Ialdabaoth.

18 "Hymn of the Pearl," line 59, *Gnostic Scriptures*, p. 374.

19 Alexander, p. 20.

20 *The HarperCollins Dictionary of Religion*, ed. Jonathan Z. Smith (New York: HarperCollins, 1995). "The distinction is clear in the *First Apocalypse of James* ... where Achamoth is an inferior and ignorant entity produced by Sophia" (Couliano, p. 81).

Once we say that, we begin to see (uneasily, perhaps) that if Ialdabaoth's avatars are James Harlowe Sr, James Jr, and (most powerfully and fully) Lovelace, then the attribution of the salient qualities of these wilful, jealous, and tyrannical males to the Judeo-Christian Deity is—just as Gnostics held—a blasphemy. If we follow the Gnostic clues, we will entertain the proposition that when Clarissa—in her own greatest exercise in allegory—speaks of "setting out with all diligence to my Father's House" (7:175; 1233), what is really meant is not a departure for the first time to the heavenly Father's house—"going up to heaven," as we may read it—but more truly a *return* to the Primal Light. The King and Queen of the Pearl-child are not found in the limited and earthbound Harlowes; the senior Harlowes are reflections of the dragon-force who would keep Clarissa, "the Alien," imprisoned with them, forced to conform and do as they do. We know, as Lovelace obtusely does not, that when Clarissa refers in her riddling letter to "my Father," she is not speaking of James Harlowe. But if we read her as the Gnostic Lady of Light, she is not speaking either of the Urizen Jehovah-God, whose representative on earth James Harlowe Sr took himself to be. If we take Clarissa in that sense, then even Lovelace the bad interpreter is partly right in believing that she refers to *returning.* The wise reader knows that Clarissa in her metaphorical letter cannot mean going back to live under the power of the Harlowes. But she is not going back either to the house of Nobodaddy, the petulant rule-maker and tormentor whose avatars are James Harlowe and Lovelace. The wise Gnostic reader may suspect that Clarissa in going to her *true* Father's house is returning to the Heavenly Sphere to which she belongs—what Lovelace himself calls (in what appears at first glance to be merely a lover's hyperbole) her "native Skies." This is the home from which she fell—in an original fall only echoed and really cured within the novel. The Harlowes are non-beings, each (as Lovelace said of Arabella) "a *mere mortal*" (1:197; 143). The Harlowes are emanations of the distorted and wintry cosmos of fallen and dead matter.

To begin to say such a scandalous thing is to challenge that other aspect of Richardson's story—the moralizing about what young ladies should do, about "good" behaviour, about obedience and propriety. All that becomes so much chopped straw. We observe the pretences by which chaos tries to legitimate itself. Here, I think, we come upon a partial explanation of the novel's enduring appeal. Only by incorporating such a powerful choke-pear as the Gnostic symbolic system could Richardson's work resist the pressure of what convention and custom had made of Christianity as a set of rules for nice and successful people, a set of rules making the poor and women know their place. Richardson himself, like any wise father and good citizen of the time, is attracted, on his worldly (and journalistic) level, by the very view that another part of him steadily resists, even though the attractive and easy opinions look like certainties and constitute almost everything that his contemporaries could recognize as "the moral." Had he not incorporated the conventional concerns (often using some very conventional viewpoints, as we see almost always in Morden and occasionally in Belford), Richardson could not have appealed to his public. Moreover, he could not even have been comprehensible to himself. But he sets up also this powerful resistance, this cosmic counter-story that fights against translating spiritual light into repressions defined as "duty." The novel's own radicalism begins in its own dialectic.

You may feel that I have overdone the matter in suggesting that the Gnostic story lies at the heart of *Clarissa*. But it may not have seemed entirely radical or unfamiliar to Richardson's own contemporaries. After all, one of Richardson's most intelligent readers was another novelist who named his own heroine "Sophia," perhaps in witty rebuke of Richardson's heroine and her status. We might refuse to entertain the presence of Gnosticism in *Clarissa* under the supposition that such ideas lie at some distance away from good solid Anglicanism, on the one hand, and from the scientific Enlightenment, on the other. But the "Enlightenment" itself was inspired by multiplex views of the true light, and how that light could be attained. A major influence on the thought of the late seventeenth and early eighteenth centuries is the work of Jakob Boehme (1575–1624; in English usually called "Behmen"), the mystic shoemaker whose series of tracts and treatises are at the foundation not only of modern theosophy but of much else in our thought.

Boehme is neither remote from nor inaccessible to Europeans of his time. His first work, *Morgenröte im Aufgang* (known in English as *Aurora*), appeared in 1612; Boehme's visions of the first flush of the dawn of spiritual light in himself were also appealing to many of his contemporaries and followers as an image of the cultural dawning of true enlightenment. A number of new works, clarifying and more fully setting out his system of thinking, appeared during his lifetime and just after his death; his writings were a major feature of Continental Protestant culture in the 1620s and 1630s. Boehme's treatises were soon translated into English, principally by John Sparrow (*Mysterium Magnum* in 1654, *Aurora* in 1656). Boehme's influence flickers through the poems of the later Metaphysicals, and is found in many places we might assume to be unlikely, including the physics of Isaac Newton.

Some of Boehme's works were translated in the mid-eighteenth century by William Law, best known to us as the author of the highly regarded and well-known devotional treatise, *A Serious Call to the Devout and Holy Life* (1728), a work known by, for instance, Samuel Johnson and Edward Gibbon. Law is not a peripheral figure. The fact that Law translated Boehme shows what a direct route Boehme had to the heart of Protestantism in England, including Anglicanism, although the German mystic philosopher may be seen as directly influential upon the Quakers and (even more) the Shakers. Boehme must also be considered a major and shaping presence within both the Enlightenment and the Romantic Age; he is certainly a powerful influence upon Blake, and on numerous successors including Hegel, Emerson, and Nietzsche in the nineteenth century and Heidegger in the twentieth.

We do not have to go far to look for connections between William Law and Richardson. John Dussinger has already commented on the connection between Law the moralist and Richardson, in his article "Conscience and the Pattern of Christian Perfection in *Clarissa*," and Rosemary Bechler's important article "'Triall by what is contrary': Samuel Richardson and Christian Dialectic" has underlined Richardson's "extraordinary circle" of mystically minded friends, including Law.[21] Richardson printed for William Law and also for John Byrom, the poet best known for his Christmas poem (later hymn) "Christians awake! Salute the happy morn."[22] Law's *Serious Call*, which does indeed call for Christian perfection, is a relatively early work representing rather the moral than the mystical side of Law, but the mystical works were well known to his contemporaries. In the mid-1730s William Law became engrossed in the writings of Jakob Boehme. Law got into a print controversy with Dr Joseph Trapp, a divine and a literary scholar, the first Professor of Poetry at Oxford, over issues of trusting inner light, and of world-despising and asceticism. Trapp's rebuke of Law in his *The Nature, Folly, Sin and Danger of being Righteous Over-much* (1739) was met by Law's *An Earnest and Serious Answer* (1740), and Trapp's *Reply to Dr. Law's Answer* (1741) was soon responded to by Law's *Some Animadversions*. Trapp highlighted what he considered the mystical and heretical beliefs in Law—"mystical" and "heretical" being one. Indeed, Law despises the created physical universe rather more even than Boehme, and his asceticism springs from a desire not to be tainted by the corrupt stuff of the world. Trapp argued that Law carried his hatred of matter so far as to make it wicked to smell a rose.

In *Grandison*, Richardson inclines a little more to Trapp's side of the argument.[23] Even in *Clarissa* he includes an implied compliment to Trapp, in incorporating in his narrative a sermon on Nathan's

21 John Dussinger,"Conscience and the Pattern of Christian Perfection in *Clarissa*," *PMLA* 81 (1966), 236–45; Rosemary Bechler, "'Triall by what is contrary': Samuel Richardson and Christian Dialectic," *Samuel Richardson: Passion and Prudence*, ed. Valerie Grosvenor Myer (London: Vision Press; Totowa, NJ: Barnes and Noble, 1986), pp. 93–113. Bechler points out the conection between Law and Boehme, and suggests possible influences of Boehme on Richardson's novel, taking her cue from Walter Benjamin, for whom Boehme was "one of the greatest allegorists" (p. 99).

22 Richardson certainly printed Law's *The Oxford Methodists* as early as 1733; see Willliam Merritt Sale, *Samuel Richardson: Master Printer* (Ithaca: Cornell University Press, 1950), pp. 126–27. Among Richardson's MSS is a passage of Boehme, evidently copied from Law. For Richardson's acquaintance with John Byrom, see T.C. Duncan Eaves and Ben D. Kimpel, *Samuel Richardson: A Biography* (Oxford: Oxford University Press, 1971), p. 459. Byrom wrote some manuscript poems to Richardson. Bechler's article deals with connections between Dr George Cheyne, William Law, and John Byrom.

23 It would take too long to argue here the many ways in which that is so. (The thematic differences are, broadly speaking, what I was driving at in *A Natural Passion*, though I did not realize then the extreme asceticism tugging at Richardson from the Cheyne-Law side.) Briefly, any reader can see that in *Grandison* Richardson goes out of his way to speak highly

rebuke to King David over the Bathsheba affair (3:325; 540), an obvious reference to Trapp's well-known sermon of 1738, *The Royal Sin; or, Adultery Rebuk'd in a Great King* (aimed at King George II).[24] But for the most part, in *Clarissa*, Richardson entertains Law's side of the argument.

As the London literary world entered the 1740s, writers could hardly help being aware of this controversy, or of the animating spirit of "Behmenism." Richardson we know had produced a first draft of *Clarissa* in 1742–44, and by January 1745 a revision of this version "in a series of vellum volumes" was ready to circulate to readers.[25] William Law produced an edition of Boehme (incomplete) as *Works of Jacob Behmen* in 1744; the preparation of this work thus coincides with the period in which Richardson was working seriously at getting *Clarissa* under way. Richardson may have been introduced to Law though his physician, Dr George Cheyne, with whom he was in touch in the period (he had printed works by both Cheyne and Law in 1733). It was Cheyne who had introduced Law to Boehme.[26] Cheyne's own belief in the necessity of putting the body under the rule of the spirit, the desirability of spiritualizing the too stout— the too clamorously hylic—body contributed to his success as a diet doctor. At Cheyne's advice, Richardson gave up all alcoholic drinks

of physical pleasures, of wealth and cheerfulness, and of worldly order. This novel is almost aggressively not world-despising. It is also more carefully orthodox in its Anglicanism in many important respects, and goes out of its way to discuss the coexistence of Catholicism and Anglicanism. This novel also contains the first attempts in Richardson's *œuvre* at drawing really good clergyman of the established churches, in the portraits of Dr Bartlett and Father Marescotti. Parson Williams in *Pamela* is rather a clot and a klutz, Parson Peters is a sycophantic worldling, and the Reverend Mr Lewen in *Clarissa* is a portrait of moral failure more serious than the greed and obtuseness of Brand. (I personally find *Sir Charles Grandison*'s Dr Bartlett disgustingly sycophantic, but I do not think Richardson means us to think so.) By the 1750s Richardson seems less than enthusiastic about Methodism. Methodism is mentioned in *Grandison* with at best only patronizing approbation, and Charlotte's pronouncement against "over-doers" is not really contradicted.

24 *The Royal Sin: or, Adultery Rebuk'd in a Great King.* Being a Discourse from the following text. And Nathan said unto David, Thou art the man, 2 Sam. xii.78. Deliver'd in the parish of St. Martin's, and published at the unanimous request of the congregation. Addressed to those whom it may concern. (London: J. Hoggonson, 1738).

25 See Florian Stuber, "Text, Reader, Writer, World," introduction to *Clarissa*, 1:6.

26 Bechler, p. 96.

and adopted a vegetarian diet—thus following much Gnostic and Hermetic practice.[27]

Jakob Boehme himself is an inheritor of many "heresies" including the Kabbala, Hermeticism, and the major forms of Gnosticism, though he gives them original expression in working out his salvation. Boehme is also endeavouring to incorporate the new science of the Renaissance, making his work harmonize with astrology as most "scientifically" considered, and also with the chemistry of Paracelsus, which gave a new view of the cosmos as mutable and transmogrifying. Boehme's imagistic mode of thinking has a great deal of literary appeal, and we should not be surprised to find it harmonized within Richardson's imagistic system in *Clarissa*, where its import helps to fill out and enliven the Gnostic side of the novel's meanings, while also tempering them.

In Boehme's system there is no emphasis upon a fiendish *Demiourgos*, but the world of matter is a bad and lowly thing. Man is a tripartite being: "Man only (among all the earthly creatures) hath

27 A certain apocalypticism is apparent in even the gently teasing (and repeated) advice given by Cheyne to Richardson to reduce: "You will fall away infinitely to what you are; every Atom and Fibre of your old Habit must be worn out; all must become new and you'll get to a moderate, Active gay Temper and Habit, and write Books without End." Letter of 2 February 1742, *Letters of Dr. Cheyne to Richardson*, ed. Charles F. Mullett, *University of Missouri Studies* 18 (1943), 83. The old body, the body of sin and death, is to be cast aside. Cheyne's regimen includes not only abstinence but frequent fasting, evacuation through purges and bleedings, and a determined bulimia in the use of what he unpleasingly calls "Thumb Vomits." If Clarissa is anorexic, bulimia would seem to be represented rather unfavourably in Lovelace, with his dramatic retchings after the self-administered dose of ipecac. Cheyne's advocacy of consistent vegetarianism was a reflection of a spiritual rather than pragmatic vision. Virginia Smith, in "Physical Puritanism and Sanitary Science," comments on the "two major outbreaks of 'serious' vegetarianism at the beginning and at the end of the eighteenth century": "Two mystic neo-Platonic phases can at present be identified. The first, in the 1720s and 1730s, was that surrounding the quietist natural philosophers George Cheyne (1671–1743) and William Law (1686–1761). While Law and his admirers such as John Byrom and John Wesley were conducting philosophic vegetarian experiments, Cheyne's influential advice book *Essay of Health and Long Life* (1724) laid the basis for the popular acceptance of the vegetable-based diet." *Medical Fringe and Medical Orthodoxy 1750–1850*, ed. W.F. Bynum and Roy Porter (London: Croom Helm, 1987), p.178. As Smith points out, "the right to manage the body for personal salvation was a special preoccupation closely associated with classical and Christian philosophic traditions and earlier magical practices" (p. 176). A movement towards systematic vegetarianism is always a move to greater purity, and to a more spiritualized, less gross, version of the physical being. It sits well with periods in which Gnosticism becomes, if not dominant, at least culturally important among the educated—a period like our own, in short.

a threefold body and spirit."[28] He has the fleshly self, an astral self, and an inner spiritual being which is God within. Angels and men alike "bear in themselves the great name of God" (*MM* 4:13, p. 15). For Boehme (as for Traherne) man has in his true self an angelical nature, and grows within an angelic world. Byrom's Christmas hymn has as its original last line "Of angels and of angel-men the King"; as Stephen Hobhouse notes, this "quaint expression" is "no doubt a reminiscence of the poet's study of Boehme."[29] Hobhouse is here commenting on William Law's statement: "If your will is angelic, you are an angel and angelic happiness must be yours."[30] Remembering that Law was an acquaintance and Byrom a friend of Richardson's, we should probably read all references to Clarissa as "an angel" a bit more carefully—noting too that Lovelace, through his self-disguising amorous language, consistently recognizes the spiritual reality.

According to Boehme, there is nothing that does not contain God, but the more material, the more imperfect and lumpish, the less there is of divine light. It is our duty and privilege to work with God— in a sense, *as* God—to redeem the whole labouring creation. Earth and stone are cold, hard, dark, and lifeless. The whole of Tellus is caught in dark matter and material will.

In *Mysterium Magnum*, Boehme distinguishes "the seven properties of the eternal nature, which make three Principles or worlds" (6:13, p. 26). The first property or "form" is the Astringent: "the concreting of the eternal nothing into something ... the cause of all essences ... a mother of all salts." The second "Form," the Bitter, is "compunctive," "a cause of all life and stirring, so also of the senses and distinction." The third "Form" is "Anguish, or the sensibility," "wherein the senses become active." The fourth "Form" is "Fire; Spirit; Reason; Desire" "wherein the holy powers of the free lubet are delivered from the astringent undigested roughness; for

---

28 Jakob Boehme, *Mysterium Magnum. Or an Exposition of the First Book of Moses called Genesis,* trans. John Sparrow (London, 1654), in modern reprint, ed. C.J.B. (London: John M. Watkins, 1965), chap. 11, section 20, p. 176. The reprint modernizes some spellings and removes italics. References are to this edition (*MM*) by chapter, section, and page.

29 Stephen Hobhouse, with a foreword by Aldous Huxley, *Selected Mystical Writings of William Law* (London: Salisbury Square, 1948), p. 272.

30 Hobhouse, p. 134.

the fire devoureth in its essence the dark substance of the impression; and works it forth out of itself ... into spiritual powers." (We
might feel here we are touching very closely on the realm of Hegel's
Phenomenology of Spirit, for Hegel defines making matter into spirit
as the great task of the human mind.) The fifth "Form" is Light,
Love, "the holy spiritual love-desire, where the holy will of God now
... brings itself forth through the fire in the light" (6:14–18, pp. 26–
27). The sixth "Form" is Sound, Voice, the divine Word, and the
seventh is "Essence, Being," "mansion and house of all the rest" of
the forms (6:19–20, p. 27). These seven forms or properties are not
to be understood as divided, but as mingling and interacting.

Yet at times Boehme separates them hierarchically, always making
the Astringent the lowest. In *Aurora* the scheme differs slightly from
that in *Mysterium Magnum*; but here too the Astringent is the base
note, the quality of Lucifer, *par excellence*, and of death and Hell, also
of salt and stone, ice and heart. The second quality in *Aurora* (as not
in *Mysterium Magnum*) is defined as the Sweet, which is the overcom-
ing of the Astringent. The Sweet is the fountain of the mercy of God,
the softening of the heart, the melting of ice, the divine water. When
Lovelace says "Anatomists allow, *that women have more watry heads than
men*" (6:31; 932), he makes an unwitting compliment, though he
is speaking physiologically and satirically. In Boehme's system to be
"more watry" is to be more compassionate and nearer the heavenly.

The third quality or "Form," according to *Aurora*, is the Bitter,
which penetrates and triumphs within the astringent and the sweet,
and allows for joy, triumph, and delight. The Bitter is the fundamental principle of motion, of stirring, "and is well called *Cor* or the
heart, for it is the trembling, shivering, elevating, penetrating spirit
... in the sweet quality the bitter is mollified, so that it becometh
very richly loving and joyful."[31] But when there is too much, or when
it has not enough of sweet to act upon, the bitter turns deadly, is
experienced as a poison, a tearing, pain and stench:

31 Jakob Boehme, *Aurora. That is, the Day-Spring. Or Dawning of the Day in the Orient Or Morning-
Rednesse in the Rising of the Sun*, trans. John Sparrow, in a modern edition "edited by C.J.B.
and D.S.H.," a reprint of the 1914 edition (London: Watkins and Clarke, 1960), chap. 8,
section 48, p. 157. References are to this edition by chapter, section, and page.

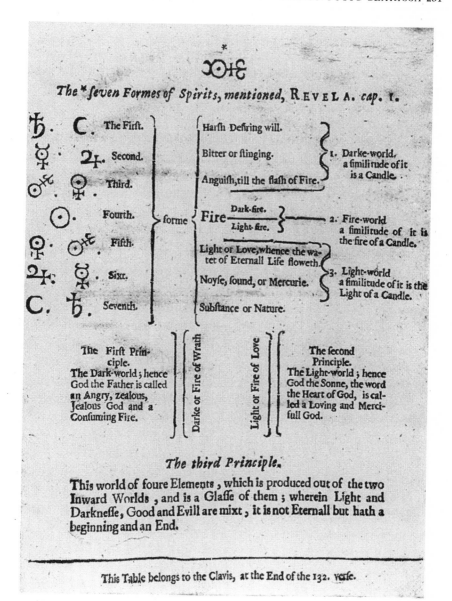

A diagram of Boehme's system, as given in *The Clavis, or Key, or an Exposition of some principall Matters, and words in the writings of J. Behmen.* Published with *XL Questions concerning the Soule* [trans. J. Sparrow] (London: Matthew Simmons, 1647). Reproduced by permission of The Bodleian Library, University of Oxford.

In the sour quality it causeth a *rankness* and brittleness, a stink, a misery, a house of mourning, a house of darkness, of death and of hell; an end of joy, which therein can no more be thought upon: For it cannot be quieted or *stilled* by anything, nor can it be enlightened again by anything; but the dark, astringent or harsh, stinking, sour, torn, bitter, *fierce* quality riseth up to all eternity. (8:52, p.157)

The scene in which Belford visits the brothel to see the dying Mrs Sinclair offers a good illustration of the total domination of "the Bitter," in Boehme's sense. We are made to imagine the close room, the stench of Mrs Sinclair's gangrene, the smell of the prostitutes after a long night, and their disordered appearance, their face-paint "lying in streaky seams," their hair indebted to "the black-lead comb." The tired whores surround the "huge quaggy carcase" of Mrs Sinclair: "her big eyes, goggling and flaming- red as we may suppose those of a salamander ... her livid lips parched, and working violently." She cannot be quiet but fills the house with lamenting angry cries: "she was raving, crying, cursing, and even howling, more like a wolf than a human creature" (8:50–55; 1387–90). Mrs Sinclair, cursing, blaming others, and speaking her own despair ("*I*, who can neither cry, nor pray!"), exhibits bitterness at its extreme.

James Harlowe Jr and Robert Lovelace both exhibit astringency at its extreme. Lovelace accuses Clarissa of astringency, when he says he must "steel my heart, that I may *cut thro'a rock of ice* to hers" (4:111; 602). If Clarissa is both "rock" and "ice" she combines two major images of the Astringent. Lovelace uses the very word when he deliberately takes what he calls "astringent medicine" (4:264; cf. 673; in the first edition the medicine is not "astringent" but "balsamic"). This medicine, the Eaton's Styptic, is to help him to recover from the ipecacuanha he took in order to make himself ill and thus to elicit some sign of Clarissa's love for him. Ironically, he gets Clarissa to administer the Styptic, this "astringent medicine," to him (4:277; 678). Lovelace does not need to be any more astringent than he already is. Clarissa embodies and represents sweetness—but with enough astringency to give her what we recognize as "will," to produce the friction or reaction of "*the flash.*"

All three of these qualities—astringency, sweetness, bitterness—as Boehme describes them, have their own colours:

Moreover it [the bitter] is the imaging or forming of all sorts of *red* colours in its own quality; in the sweet it imageth or formeth all sorts of *white* and *blue*, in the astringent, or harsh and sour, it formeth all sorts of *green*, *dusky* and mixed colours, with all manner of forms or *figures* and *smells*. (*Aurora* 8:47, p. 156)

We see the red predominate in Mrs Sinclair, her eyes "goggling and flaming-red." The sweet, almost always associated closely with Clarissa, is intimated in details of her clothing at the time of the abduction/elopement. Oddly enough, she does wear yellow, like the child in "Hymn of the Pearl": "Her morning-gown was a pale primrose-coloured paduasoy." But the dominant colors are white and blue: "Her head-dress was a Brussels-lace mob. ... A sky-blue ribband illustrated that." She wears a "coat" [or overskirt] of "white satten" and her shoes are "Blue satten." Above all, her sweetness is reflected in her own work, "cuffs and robings curiously embroidered ... in a running pattern of violets and their leaves" (3:28; 399–400). For Boehme, flowers, especially blue or white flowers, represent the quintessence of divine sweetness. When Clarissa is dying, her hands are seen "white as the lily, with her meandring veins more transparently blue" (7:412; 1351). Lovelace in his dream-vision in which he sees Clarissa ascending to the heavens catches at "her azure robe" (7:148; 1218).

Yet Clarissa is also constantly surrounded by images of the astringent, most remarkably in the emblematic scene in the prison room in the "horrid hole of a house" with its coarse and broken furnishings, its smoky ceiling, the windows "dark and double-barred, the tops boarded up to save mending," the only light the faint and irritating twinkling of a minute candle in "an iron shove-up candlestick." The pale fire of such a nearly lightless candle, a "faint twinkler" like a member of the Harlowe family, cannot enlighten. In the past, a dreary succession of such nearly useless candles has been used by other miserable prisoners, who, having "no other way to amuse themselves," have left the ceiling "smoked with variety of figures." Now even the coarse but vital element of visible fire itself has almost disappeared, its place being taken by smoke. In this nearly lightless room the power of light is rendered more feeble than anywhere else in the novel—because the light is denied, shut out by the boarded-up windows.

234 MARGARET ANNE DOODY

Darkness and stoniness announce the astringency of the place. The strangest element in the composition is the weird bouquet in the "large stone-bottle without a neck" which takes the place of the absent fire. This container is "filled with baleful Yew, as an Evergreen, withered Southernwood, dead Sweet-briar, and sprigs of Rue in flower" (6:272–73; 1065). Here indeed we have the mixture of the green and the dusky, with various figures and smells (yew and rue and southernwood have different kinds of bitter and sour odours). Richardson renders his scene dense with different kinds of ugliness, almost all attaching firmly to Boehme's category or form of the Astringent, or the inert and durable, the lifeless—even the violence of the bitter is absent, and sweetness has died with the "dead Sweet-briar."

The Astringent, according to Boehme in *Mysterium Magnum*, is a desire "self-conceiving ... substantial, wholly rough, harsh, hard and thick" (*MM* 3:9, p. 8). But in *Mysterium Magnum* the second "Form," compunction, is "constringency," an attracting which begins to torment the inert with desire. "For here ariseth the first enmity between the astringency or hardness, and the compunction or sting of stirring; for the desire maketh hard, thick and congealeth, as the cold stiffeneth and freezeth the water. Thus the astringency is a mere raw coldness" (*MM* 3:10, p. 8). The third property, defined in *Aurora* as "penetrating or triumphing," is in *Mysterium Magnum* defined as the distress caused by the relation of the other two; "anguish" makes possible life and the awakening of power. Anguish—distress, conflict—is a powerful if relative good. It is fire. In the low form (or to the low vision) this fire is a painful and terrible thing. God's love, that is, must be perceived as the fire of wrath from a certain point of view. God's love is the divine fire which emerges in the conflict of the cosmos between "the horrible astringent hard compunctive sharpness" and the "free lubet" which "is a great meekness" (*MM* 3:25, p. 11)— that is, between the imperfect will knowing itself as will, and the will as love and gentleness.

Now both these dash together in one another. The sharp will eagerly and mightily desireth the free lubet, and the lubet desireth the austere will; and as they enter into and feel each other, a great flagrat is made, like a flash of lightning. (*MM* 3:25, p. 11)

This is felt as both illumination and death, for "the astringent harsh darkness" which cannot be kindled retires into itself as the enmity to light, as the abyss (*MM* 3:26, pp. 11–12).

Boehme notoriously uses "fire" in several senses; at times it is good, as in divine fire, but that seems only a comparative good—for those who truly love the divine, there is no fire, there is only light. Fire is a low element bespeaking conflict. Fiery people are imperfect, the angry (like salamanders) live in fire. Some are "combustible spirits," as Lord M. (with some justification) complains is the case with Colonel Morden (7:266; 1282). In an important section of *Clarissa*, Lovelace tries to frighten his beloved into accepting him sexually by setting fire (under controlled circumstances) to part of his dwelling, turning the brothel's inner house into what it really is, a place of fire (with more smoke than fire, more dirt than purification). The fire expresses how Clarissa's light is felt within the brothel, felt *by* the brothel. Here she is a fiery tiger ("a Tyger of a Lady," 6:36; 935), like Blake's Tyger, burning bright.

Lovelace has a nightmare of return to the astringent harsh darkness, of falling into the abyss (one of Boehme's favourite images, the *Urgrund*), when he dreams of tumbling down "into a hole more frightful than that of Elden; and, tumbling over and over down it, without view of a bottom" (7:148). He is not going down into a place (like Dante's Inferno), but is in the Void, the bottomless emptiness of God's withdrawal. He has sought the *Urgrund* instead of the *Ungrund*, Boehme's word for the unconditioned and unconditional being of God. Lovelace is a victim of the gravity that he loves, that pulls him inward to the self-attracting and anti-vital low point, the point of nearly entire materiality, untouched by spirit, hence the true Void.

Hell for Jakob Boehme is not a place but a logical necessity, a first ground. He is not quite consistent about this, but in most of his writings it seems clear that Hell is not a "place" to which we "go," for each of us has within the spark of life eternal, which is God. Part of man's deepest trouble is his individual ego (in which even desire for heaven can also become entrapped), human individuation in a competitive and separating mode:

Now all men are proceeded out of this only man, he is the stem or body, the other are all his branches, and do receive power from their stem, and bring forth fruit out of one root, and each twig enjoyeth the tree's ens, also they do all alike enjoy the four elements and the astrum alike.

What folly is it then, that the twig willeth to be an own tree; and grows up of itself as a strange plant, as if its fellow-twig did not stand also in its stem. It is the Serpent's introduced ens which seduceth and divideth the branches on the life's tree of man from the only life of man, bringing each twig into a peculiar sundry hunger, desiring to be a tree by itself, in self-full power and domination. And therefore it desireth the muchness of this world for its own property, that it might greatly enlarge itself in the Serpent's ens, and be a great, thick, strong, fat, well-spread tree. ... In all self-hood and own-hood [annotated by Sparrow as "Selfish interests, mine-hood and thine-hood, meum and tuum"] there is a false plant; one brother should be the sovereign cure and refreshment to another, and delight or content his mind with the insinuation of his love-will. There were enough and enough in this world, if covetousness drew it not into a selfish property. (*MM*, chap. 24, "Of the Cause and Rise of the Curse of the Earth," 17–21, p. 161)[32]

This lesson of brotherhood and necessary connectedness Clarissa tries in vain to teach her family, but they cannot bear to hear it: "the World is but one great family. Originally it was so. What then is this narrow selfishness that reigns in us, but relationship remembred against relationship forgot?" (1:46; 62)

In Boehme's system, God's love is manifested in the flash of love-fire, but within the cosmos or the individual life any such flash is felt as pain. Clarissa, according to this scheme, is a representative not just of the light in its serene radiance but of "*the flash*," the sudden manifestation of love's fire—which must always be felt as pain to those caught up in the dark astringent world of cold hostility. The flash as the light comes is felt as pain both to "the Astringent" and to "the Sweet" whose conflict makes it happen.

When the flash riseth up in the heat, then first the sweet water *catcheth* or captivateth it, for therein it becometh shining. Now when the water catcheth the flash, that is, the *birth* of the light, then the sweet water is terrified. ... Now when the astringent quality, which is very cold, catcheth the heat and the flash, then it is *terrified*, as in a tempest of lightning; for when the heat cometh with the light into the hard cold, then it maketh a *fierce* flash, of a very fiery and light colour. ... And the flash in itself *keepeth* its fierceness, from whence existeth the bitter quality, or the bitter spirit,

---

32 This image is surely a source of Grimmelshausen's satiric vision of the tree in *Simplicissimus*.

which *now* riseth up in the astringent quality ... and the light or flash *drieth* itself in the hardness, and shineth clear and bright, *far brighter* than the light
of the sun. (*Aurora* 10:17–20, p. 211)

In the antithesis and union of the opposing but inevitable qualities
the sparkle is born. Distress—adversity—conflict—must be there to
make the shining. So Anna tells Clarissa, "the time of ADVERSITY *is
your* SHINING-TIME" (4:64; 579). A consideration of such a passage as
that just quoted from *Aurora* in connection with *Clarissa* makes a new
sense of Anna's words (which also present us with a new hyphenated
compound phrase, quite in the Boehme style). Boehme's image also
gives a new sense to phrases such as "two or three flashes of lightning
from her indignant eyes" (4:7; 553) and likewise to whole scenes,
such as that in which Lovelace sees Clarissa at Hampstead and she
"blazed upon" him—and to all the other references to her shining,
her blazing. We should probably note here that although in the plot-
story Lovelace is as full of lies as the Devil, as a spiritual visionary
he seems compelled to tell the truth, though with an affectation of
poetic fantasy and joke that may make the true appear false to the
unwary or too superficially knowing reader, who hears Lovelace's
fictions but cannot hear his truth. We are not good judges of voices.

In this present state of existence, says Jakob Boehme, we do not
even have our true voices—the sound is harsh, the notes are few:

For where the sound is gross, harsh and shrill, there it is strong in the dark
impression; and there the fire is vehement and burning. As we men after
the fall of Adam have so awaked and enkindled the fire of the dark world
in our vital essence, that our vital sound is gross and beast-like, resembling
the abyss; and the like is to be understood of the sound in the darkness.
For as the generation of the word is, in its manifestation in the light, in the
holy power, so also in the darkness: but altogether rigorous, harsh, hard
and gross. ... And this proceeds from the essence of the astringent hard
compunctive anxious generation, viz. from the original of the coldness, or
cold fire's source. (*MM* 5:19, p. 22)

Voices in *Clarissa* are often "rigorous, harsh, hard and gross."
Clarissa's father speaks "with a big voice" (1:93; 87)—*vox et praeterea
nihil.* There is not very much to Mr Harlowe, but he tries to make
himself *be*, to make his will all-powerful, through the thunder of his

voice. The Harlowes (except for Clarissa's mother) are an astringent, hard, and anxious generation who love laying down the law, and speaking coarsely; they are great interrupters of each other's sentences. Lovelace is overheard by Clarissa on the first evening of her forced elopement with him speaking harshly to the servants at the inn, cursing and swearing in the astringent and self-centred language of the low self, making sounds "gross and beast-like," as Clarissa rather too tartly reminds him in her satiric dig, pretending she mistook him for a low soldier, "Well do they make it a proverb— *Like a trooper!*" (3:21; 396).

Mrs Sinclair's wolf-like howling presents the low point of our earthly and bestial language. Another kind of abuse of speech, another species of dreadful language really quite as bad as Mrs Sinclair's, however, is represented in the quotation-sprinkled, minced, and pompous language of Parson Brand—about whom Howard Weinbrot has written so well.[33] Brand's perversions of the sacred, as well as his unstoppable gushing that would overrun all other voices, exhibit a great sin against the light, and he bears out Boehme's satiric view of professional ministers and learned schoolmen:

> *But who were they* that falsified and adulterated the right, pure Christian doctrine, and *always fought* against and opposed it? *Even* the learned doctors and scribes, popes, cardinals, bishops, and great dons or masters and teachers. *And why did the world* follow after them, and depend on them? But because they had great respect, were in great *authority* and *power,* lived stately, and carried a port in the *world.* Even such a *proud whore* is the corrupt, perished human nature.
>
> (*Aurora* 9:12, p. 190)

Brand, who is a marked or branded man in Richardson's system, initially thinks—or pretends to think—that he by his severe suspiciousness is rescuing a brand from the burning, prescribing a wholesome suffering for this "poor *limed soul*" (7:286; 1292–93). He favours exiling her to the colonies, in a quasi-penal manner. An interest in punishing others is presented throughout Richardson's novel, as it is throughout Boehme's work, as the mark of a low, self-regarding,

---

33 See Howard Weinbrot, "Clarissa, Elias Brand and Death by Parentheses," *New Essays on Samuel Richardson,* ed. Albert J. Rivero (New York: St Martin's Press, 1996).

and angry personality, a sign of defect, the encouragement of a devil within, sure to create anger and dissension in others. Lord M., hearing this man's name, exclaims *"Brand! Brand!* It should have been *Firebrand"* (7:282; 1291; this is one of Richardson's rare tributes to Fielding, to *Pasquin* in which the cleric Firebrand is a bad advisor to Queen Ignorance). Parson Elias Brand is governed by his own desire to get on the right side of John Harlowe—and to be connected with the family who may have gifts to offer. Although he at first reprobates Clarissa as a light woman and prevents her family from seeing her, in his later letter he hints that he would be willing, after her rehabilitation, to espouse her himself if the price were right (7:384–85). Brand himself is a whore, "a *proud whore*," and the equal of Madame Sinclair, of Sally and Polly—if less able to speak to the point than any of these.

This Elias (Elijah is coming?) is a symptom of the chronic sickness of his society, and of the chronic fatigue of a Church weakened from within by proud and self-centred men who do not love their fellow beings. The human word is sick. It may seem odd to say that *this* is the insight of an author who loved words as much as Richardson, but the full exploration of language within this text, though sometimes decried as "prolixity," is necessary for the complete illustration of the vanity and imperfection of most human language. I would draw the reader's attention in particular to the suspect language of Colonel Morden. Not utterly without reason does the self-defensive Lovelace comment on Morden's "trite manner" (7:262; 1280). More plausible than Brand because more nearly approaching the good, Morden is still bound up in astringency and death—and rightly named after death, *Mors, la mort.* He loves the righteousness of his own anger. His judgments are poor (look at his conventional misogyny for a start); he is almost always worldly, materialistic, conventional, and self-justifying. He is very easily turned into an angry gentleman. Morden is the active proponent of the offensiveness which he pretends to punish.

Sickness abounds throughout the novel—almost everybody is sick at some point or other, including those who are not going to die within the story. It is comically noticeable that Mr Harlowe and Lovelace's uncle Lord M. reflect each other, most obviously in the fact that each is a sufferer from that (fashionable and aristocratic but painful) disease, the gout. Within this naturalistic detail we may read Boehme's earlier joke, in *Aurora*:

The musician hath wound up his pegs, and tuned his strings; the Bridegroom cometh. When the round beginneth take *heed* thou dost not get the *hellish gout* in thy feet; lest thou be found incapable or *unfit* for the angelical dance, and so be thrust out from the *wedding*, seeing thou hast on no *angelical garment*. (5:33, p. 109).

The sidenote to "*hellish gout*" is the single word "Podagra," starkly in the margin. In the first edition of *Clarissa*, Lovelace jokingly refers to his uncle as "that noble podagra-man."[34] Yet Lovelace wants to be a "podagra-man" too; in his expedition to Hampstead, he makes himself up as a gouty old gentleman. Three of the leading male characters (Mr Harlowe, Lord M., and Lovelace) are rendered as "podagra-men," unready for the angelical wedding dance. (Not only so, but England is evidently being run by the podagra-men.)

The dance circle is a heavenly-right version or reparation of the dreary circles in which people are caught in the world below. Clarissa on her coffin incorporates the emblem of the *ouroboros*, the serpent with its tail in its mouth, known to the modern West as an Egyptian symbol of the universe since the publication of *The Hieroglyphics of Horapollo* (1505).[35] The circular is the image of immortal Eternity, the true Eternity. For George Wither this emblem is "Eternities wide

34 *Clarissa* (1747–48) 3:349; cf. first edition, ed. Ross , p. 557. Was Richardson persuaded to take the phrase out of later editions because it was too unkind to the gouty?

35 *The Hieroglyphics of Horapollo* offers a key to and an explanation of certain Egyptian hieroglyphics (the only important explanation of that kind until the Napoleonic era). It is supposedly the work of a Hellenistic Egyptian living in Alexandria in the fifth century AD. The Horapollo family were involved in trying to find the key to all mythologies, synthesizing all religious thought—a typically Alexandrian proceeding. A few of their readings of the Egyptian symbols have been confirmed, or partially confirmed, by the discoveries of modern Egyptology, but in many ways Horapollo was off the mark. The publication of Horapollo in the early Renaissance stimulated a great interest in hieroglyphs and emblems. See *The Hieroglyphics of Horapollo*, translated and introduced by George Boas (1950), with a new foreword by Anthony Grafton (Princeton: Princeton University Press, 1993). See the second emblem, "the Universe": "When they wish to depict the Universe, they draw a serpent devouring its own tail, marked with variegated scales" (p. 43).

round."[36] But Boehme, we should note, uses it differently. In his "Dialogue of the Two Souls" in *The Way to Christ Discovered*, the *ouroboros* becomes a symbol of the fire-wheel of cosmic life, the delusive wheel of things in which the unwitting soul is caught.

And this the Devill did present to the soule, the Mercury in Vulcan, that is, the fiery wheele of Essence ... in the form of a Serpent. *The Devil sayd,* Thou thy selfe also art such a fiery Mercury, if thou doest break thy will off from God, and bring thy desire into this Art, then thy hidden ground will be manifested in thee, and then thou mayst work in the same manner also ... and then thou wilt instantly be as the fiery wheele is, and so bring all things into thy own power and possesse them as thy own.[37]

Mercury and Vulcan are images of things being made in the dark world blended with the fire-world, as is the material cosmos. Lovelace several times alludes to Mercury and to Vulcan, though the crowning pun is made by Richardson, who lodges Clarissa in Covent Garden with a couple named "Smith," the artificers presiding over her painful transformation. Such a Smith is the higher artificer, not the lower, the Mercury-*Demiourgos* holding us within the wheel of things.

Clarissa in her designs for her coffin-plate places the lily within the serpent. She is the snapped lily, which is likewise the soul. For Boehme too, the soul is a lily planted within the field of this world. The inner divine spark is also likened to the lily:

A man must wrastle so long, till the dark center that is shut up so close, break open, and the spark in the center kindle, and from then immediatly

36 See this emblem reproduced and commented upon in relation to Clarissa's coffin in my *A Natural Passion: A Study of the Novels of Samuel Richardson* (Oxford: Clarendon Press 1974), p. 186.

37 Jakob Boehme, "A Discourse between a Soule hungry ... and a Soule enlightened" (London, 1648), p. 4. The running title is "The Way from Darkness." Four pamphlets are included in *The Way to Christ*: "Of True Repentance," "Of True Resignation," "Of Regeneration," "Of the Super-rationall Life." To these were added other works formerly published as individual tracts, the most important for our purposes being *A Discourse between a Soule hungry and thirsty after the Fountain of Life ... with a Soule unenlightened* (1624) (elsewhere called *Colloquium viatorum, or, A Dialogue between an Enlightened and an Unenlightened Soul*). In that dialogue we find the emblem of the serpent with the tail in its mouth used very negatively. All quotations from *The Way to Christ* are taken from this 1648 edition—or rather compilation.

the Noble * Lilly-branch (* *Or, Lilly-twig*) sprouteth, as from the divine grain of Mustard-seed, as Christ saith.[38]

According to a "Behmenist" reading, the design Clarissa makes for her coffin-plate signifies her penitence at having fallen into the earthly Mercury, the desires of the mind, the fire-wheel or wheel of things of earthly desire, false gratification, and frustration. But her design also expresses her confidence in escaping this wheel of fire, this serpentine karmic round, even when apparently fixed within it. Clarissa with her spark of life, her "*Lilly-twig*," triumphs over Lovelace, impersonator of the Devil who loves time, delay, and repetitive process, who brings the serpent to the soul.

In another scheme of the novel, however, Clarissa is herself the Divine Wisdom, and Lovelace is the Bridegroom to whom she tenderly appears. In this trope, Lovelace becomes the Soul, and Clarissa is the heavenly wisdom, the Virgin Sophia, who seeks to mate with her erring and confused betrothed. Clarissa could say to Lovelace what the Virgin says to her penitent lover in Boehme's allegory in "Of True Repentance":

My Noble Bridegroome ... thou couldest not see my light, for thou didst walke in the valley of darknesse: I was very neare thee, and intreated thee continually, but thy sinne held thee captive in death, so that thou knowest me not.

And the Soul, the humbled Bridegroom, joyfully recognizes the saving love:

The Soule sayeth againe to its Noble Sophia, its love, that is borne againe in the Soule. O my noble Pearle, and opened flame of my light in my anxious fiery life, O how thou changest me into thy joy; O beautifull Love, I have broken my faith with thee, in my fallen Adam, and, with my fiery strength have turned my selfe to the pleasure and vanity of the outward world, and have fallen in love with a stranger, and had been constrained to walke in the valley of darknesse in this strange love, if thou hadst not come to me into the house of my misery. ... I behold in thee the mercy of God, which was hidden from me before by the strange Love.[39]

38 *The second Booke treating of True Resignation ... Written in the German Language 1622* (1647), included in *The Way to Christ*, p. 114.

39 "Of True Repentance," *The Way to Christ*, pp. 60–63.

If we consider a passage such as this, we may be tempted to say that the role of Sally Martin within the novel is more fully explicable. There are a series of imitations or substitutes for Clarissa, starting with Arabella Harlowe. Of these, Sally is most fully and intelligibly the "strange love." We see this in the weird scene in which, after Lovelace has failed to see Clarissa at Smith's (he has actually seen her for the last time, although he is not aware of that terrible truth), he returns to the brothel where Sally offers him her representation of Clarissa:

Come, said she, what will you give me, and I'll be virtuous for a quarter of an hour, and mimic your Clarissa to the life?

I was *Belforded* all over. I could not bear such an insult upon the dear creature. ...

But the little devil was not to be balked; but fell a crying, sobbing, praying, begging, exclaiming, fainting, that I never saw my lovely girl so well aped. Indeed I was almost taken in; for I could have fansied I had her before me once more. (7:145; 1217)

This is the most astonishing, perhaps the saddest, statement of Lovelace's own love of being deceived; he falls into the *simulacra* he has pseudo-created. There is no earthly good, the reader has to realize, not subject to earthly repetition in earth's mirror world of imitation. There is no gesture on earth Clarissa could make that could not be parodied or mimicked. Lovelace in the brothel, if in one sense the lord of a harem, fulfiller of male fantasy, is in another sense an imprisoned soul, living in the house of misery he created, tempted by his own fictions. Yet, if Sally is the "strange Love," Clarissa herself, the true love, is also a "strange Love," a stranger, the Alien.

On the cosmic scale, Clarissa and Lovelace cannot die, neither can they be symbolically separated. In Boehme's "A Dialogue between a Scholar and his Master, concerning The Super-sensuall life," the Disciple asks the Master "Doth it [the soul] not enter into Heaven or Hell as a man entreth into a house, or as a man passes through a hole [doore or window: translator's addition in brackets] into another world?" The Master replies "No, there is no such kind of entrings, for Heaven and Hell are present everywhere; and it is but the turning in of the will either into God's love or into his anger; and this cometh to passe in this life."[40] Moralists of the eighteenth century and later want to say "Clarissa goes to heaven and Lovelace goes to hell," while twentieth-century critics wish to say that Richardson in his simplicity said so. But in the terms of Boehme's mysticism that is a ludicrous statement. All humankind are one, and Clarissa, in so far as she represents "*the flash*," the light, sweetness, grace, cannot hate Lovelace—as indeed, the character Clarissa says she does not (7:378; 1342). If Clarissa is of the divine, what we mistakenly call "her will" must prevail, and the erring and astringent incomplete soul of Lovelace will be saved. Such a system gives the erring one a lower but more hopeful place than that of the early Gnostics' Ialdabaoth.

I do not argue for this "Gnostic reading" of Clarissa as the only reading—the novel is in dialogue with itself, and this is but one strand (an important one, however) of its dialectic. If there are at least six important ways of reading *Clarissa*, this is one. We can see, too, that the Gnosticism of Richardson's text divides and ramifies. There are two strands that I have identified, an antique Gnosticism and Boehme's theosophic mystic Gnosticism, and they are in dialogue with each other. In the end, I believe, the text favours Boehme above the more pessimistic mysticism that dismisses most of humanity as not meant to be salvageable. Boehme's system has for Richardson the attraction of avoiding the harsh divisiveness of purest Gnosticism, according to which there are the divinely spiritual beings, true souls or spirits, and the merely hylic people, the material beings who have only enough soul or *psychē* to get through this life in a kind of imitation of being, but who have no real place in the divine world. These hylic creatures are stuck in matter, to perish utterly. In Boehme's (and Law's) vision, no place and no soul-being is totally deserted by the divine. In some (Byrom's "angel-men") the divine is truly and more fully present. Considered even as purely human character, Clarissa is theosophically a partial embodiment of Divine

40 "A Dialogue ... concerning The Super-sensuall life," *The Way to Christ*, p. 24.

Being: "How the God within her exalted her ... Divine creature! (as I *thought* her) I *called* her" (5:233; 853). But the Divinity is to some extent within every human being, and, that being so, there must be a limit to punishment, moralism, and reprobation.

Such a system as Boehme's allows us to think of the Harlowes more charitably than we do according to the stricter Gnostic systems also suggested within the novel. The Harlowes are not just mud-people, earthy and disposable *simulacra* of the higher reality; they too can be seen as possessing the divine spark, albeit very dimly—they are, as Anna observed early in the narrative, "faint twinklers." Nothing that we see is entirely abandoned by the divine. As Lovelace observes, the sun shines even upon Mrs Sinclair's: "For that impartial orb shines upon mother Sinclair's house, as well as upon any other: But nothing within me can it illuminate" (5:330; 904). (He errs, for the spiritual sun could indeed illuminate him if he would turn to the light.) Boehme's system, to which I believe Richardson very much inclined, allows for the ultimate salvation of all mankind, but it brings very sharply to the foreground the discomforts of life in the dark, discordant, and astringent world.[41]

41 An early version of a portion of this paper was given as a plenary lecture at the De Bartolo Conference, Tampa, Florida, in February 1998.

Sir Charles Grandison: Richardson on Body and Character

Juliet McMaster

W hen charms of *mind* and person meet, / How rich our raptures rise!" carols Sir Charles Grandison to his bride, while
he plays upon "a noble organ" (3:274).[1] The moment forms a climax to the novel, since it is the fullest expression of achieved felicity
for Harriet Byron, now Lady Grandison. The full praise of her mind
and body, delivered by the husband she loves and admires in the
midst of a harmonious gathering of the people most dear to her, is a
consummation of her happiness.

Tears of joy ran down my cheeks. ... I was speechless. ... I thought at the time,
I had a foretaste of the joys of heaven!—How sweet the incense of praise
from a husband! That husband a good man!—My surrounding friends en-
joying it! (3:275)

It is fitting that Richardson should place this climax at the moment
of the declared harmony between flesh and spirit, or body and mind,
as the tension between them has been a constant theme and a major
source of the drama and interest of the novel.

1 *The History of Sir Charles Grandison*, ed. Jocelyn Harris, 3 vols (London: Oxford University
   Press, 1972). References by volume and page number are to this edition. "*Sir Charles
   Grandison*: Richardson on Body and Character" was first published in *Eighteenth-Century
   Fiction* 1:2 (1989), 83–102.

In the long battle over Richardson's reputation and the quality of his novels, the moralizing in them has been constantly attacked and justified. And the reputation of *Sir Charles Grandison*, in particular, fluctuates according to this argument, since it is the most overtly moral of the novels, with the least in the way of compensating sensational action. Richardson himself, of course, would have us believe that the "moral" is what really counts, while the "fable" is there only as a regrettably necessary sugaring of the pill. His work is "designed to inculcate upon the human mind, under the guise of an amusement, the great lessons of Christianity," and the story "was to be looked upon as the vehicle only to the instruction."[2] The most dedicated fans of his own day may have professed a willingness to dispense with the fable and swallow the moral unsugared: Lady Echlin, for instance (telling Richardson just what he liked to hear), claimed she was "better pleased with musty morals than a pretty love-story."[3] But the modern reader, with less patience for the aesthetic of moralizing, has much ado to rescue the pearl of drama from the clammy oyster of didacticism. Mark Kinkead-Weekes focuses on Richardson as "Dramatic Novelist." Carol Houlihan Flynn finds that in his best work "His artistic commitment to his characters subverted his moral intention." And she jettisons *Grandison* from her study as too morally ponderous: "The deadly weighted character of Sir Charles stifles the dramatic action of the book." But Sylvia Kasey Marks rejoices in the morality, finding *Grandison* not so much a surprisingly boring novel as a surprisingly interesting conduct-book.[4]

Surprise seems to be characteristic of the modern reader who ventures on the now largely unread pages of Richardson's last novel. I think that the response of Mark Kinkead-Weekes is a familiar one. *Sir Charles Grandison*, he says, "has a curious energy that constantly surprises one, in the midst of irritations, with the knowledge that one

2 Samuel Richardson, *Clarissa or The History of a Young Lady*, ed. Angus Ross (Harmondsworth: Penguin, 1985), "Postscript" to *Clarissa*, pp. 1495, 1499.

3 *The Correspondence of Samuel Richardson*, ed. Anna Laetitia Barbauld, 6 vols (1804; New York: AMS Press, 1966), 5:54.

4 Mark Kinkead-Weekes, *Samuel Richardson: Dramatic Novelist* (Ithaca: Cornell University Press, 1973); Carol Houlihan Flynn, *Samuel Richardson: A Man of Letters* (Princeton: Princeton University Press, 1982), pp. xi, 48; Sylvia Kasey Marks, *Sir Charles Grandison: The Compleat Conduct Book* (Lewisburg: Bucknell University Press, 1986).

is by no means as bored as one had thought."⁵ Faint praise, perhaps, for a novel that in the nineteenth century was so enormously influential, and so much admired by Austen, Thackeray, Eliot, Ruskin, and others. But it is worth exploring that curious energy, that residual interest that still remains for the twenty-first-century reader as a vestige of what it was that earlier and more committed readers found in it.

The equivalent for me of the drama and the sensational interest that balance the overt moralizing is the felt presence of the body. These characters last as incarnations, fully realized, with their physical attributes specified and set in tension with the social and moral pressures that surround them. Margaret Anne Doody, in a fascinating analysis of the scene in which Clementina, despite a phobia against the process, undergoes bleeding by a surgeon for her malady, makes the point that here "The reader is ... made aware of her presence as a real physical object—literally of flesh and blood."⁶ Yes, this is so; and it applies, albeit less vividly, to the other major characters in the novel, who still step from the pages for us complete with body, dress, gesture, expression. These things are of constant concern to the characters themselves, and the different letter-writers provide descriptions that are minute and extensive. The major principle that the correspondents urge on each other as they take up and exercise their several pens is to be "particular"—specificity is the cardinal virtue in their epistolary aesthetic as in Henry James's. And they are particular not only about who said and did what on which occasion, but on what he did with his hands, on what was the sensation of faintness accompanying her utterance, how many tears shed, sighs heaved, blushes blushed. Richardson keeps all this before us as part of his constant concern with the consonance of character and appearance, and his theme of the individual's necessary achievement of a proper relation of mind and body.

The word "body," of course, occurs relatively seldom in *Sir Charles Grandison*. The much more common term is "person," which refers almost exclusively to physical attributes, and more particularly to

5 Kinkead-Weekes, p. 279.

6 Margaret Anne Doody, *A Natural Passion: A Study of the Novels of Samuel Richardson* (Oxford: Clarendon Press, 1974), p. 384.

sexual attractiveness. "Person," in this novel of constant courtship, is very much to the fore, and under constant discussion. "Lovely as Miss Byron's person is," we hear of the heroine at the outset, "I defy the greatest Sensualist on earth not to admire her mind more than her person" (1:9). So speaks Greville, who certainly has some claim of his own to the title of sensualist. And Sir Charles Grandison himself, who certainly does not claim the title (though his being passionately in love with two beautiful women at once argues an unusual degree of susceptibility), confirms Greville's prophecy when he formally embraces Harriet as his bride: "The man whose Love is fixed on the *mind* [he means himself], all loveliness as is the admirable person that thus I again press to my fond bosom, must be as happy as a mortal man can be" (3:330). (Sir Charles's commentary on his embrace while he performs it has its ludicrous sound for the modern ear. But Richardson could not resist reiterating a major theme at this moment.) "Person" can even be separated from the person it belongs to, as an abstract quantity. Harriet's grandmother congratulates her that her love for Sir Charles "has not so much *person* in it, as most loves" (1:304), by which she means, of course, sexual desire. The characters play often with the term. Charlotte Grandison, in discussing a suitor her brother proposes for her, whispers that "the *person* he cannot know" (1:399), although Sir Charles does know the man. But as a man he cannot be a judge of the suitor's sexual attractiveness to a woman. So the word "person," like so many other terms in Richardson, comes to have a particularly sexual meaning.

The proper relation of mind to body is as important to Richardson as the proper relation of moral to fable. And as he enlists his characters to do a good deal of his moralizing for him, so he appoints them commentators on mind and person, and exemplars of different aspects of the relation of the two.

He moves beyond the theoretical level of discussion of mind and person in the abstract to a full and dramatic realization of the flesh. The body is constantly and vividly a part of the way we perceive his characters, as of the way they perceive each other. *Grandison*, more than *Pamela* and *Clarissa*, although still epistolary, allows for long passages of descriptive narrative by the different correspondents, and they pay full attention to matters of appearance. Perhaps this was one of the reasons for *Sir Charles Grandison*'s strong appeal in the nineteenth century, when it was undoubtedly *the* Richardson novel. Certainly the scraps of reminiscences that have come down to us from its readers show that its characters are remembered most vividly as physical presences: Jane Austen, ordering a pretty cap for herself, remembers Harriet: "It will be white satin and lace, and a little white flower perking out of the left ear, like Harriot Byron's feather"[7]—a memory of detail that argues a wonderful intimacy with a huge text. George Eliot, a great admirer of the novel, did not like Harriet Byron, but was susceptible to young Sir Charles's "fine curling auburn locks waving upon his shoulders" (1:359),[8] which she remembered in *The Mill on the Floss* (vol. 1, chap. 4). Even Thackeray, who in general took Fielding's side against Richardson, thought of Sir Charles first as a physical presence: he said his hero Esmond was "as stately as Sir Charles Grandison,"[9] and he drew on the novel largely for gesture, manners, and tone.

To the satiated taste of the modern, who is used to texts fully explicit on physical processes, *Grandison* may seem like a stuffy and inhibited book. But for its own day, and for the nineteenth century too, it was remarkably explicit about the body, while still maintaining its own standards of delicacy. Gynecological experience is highlighted, and there are dramatized scenes or discussions, more or less explicit, on menstruation,[10] defloration, pregnancy, parturition, lactation. One heroine goes into a mental and physical decline that is likely to end in death and which does involve insanity. We hear also of

7 *Jane Austen's Letters to her Sister Cassandra and Others*, ed. R.W. Chapman (London: Oxford University Press, 1932), p. 322.

8 "Like Sir Charles Grandison?" she asked in a letter of 30 October 1852; "I should be sorry to be the heathen that did not like that book." *The George Eliot Letters*, ed. Gordon S. Haight, 9 vols (New Haven: Yale University Press, 1954–78), 2:65.

9 *The Letters and Private Papers of William Makepeace Thackeray*, ed. Gordon N. Ray, 4 vols (London: Oxford University Press, 1945–46), 2:815.

10 I take it that menstruation is one thing that is at issue in the long debate over "the Day" of a wedding ceremony. Though almost everything else, including the choice of husband, and whether she is to be married or not, may be done for her, the bride traditionally has the final say on the naming of the day, presumably to avoid the embarrassment, in the rather public ceremonies connected with the bridal night, of her being in mid-period. Even Clarissa, who is being forced to marry a man she loathes, is given some say about the naming of the day of the wedding: "This day fortnight we design it to be," writes her mother (for only another woman can negotiate this matter), "if you have no objection to make that I shall approve of" (letter 41).

characters, male or female, with gout, smallpox, palsy, fever, ague, cancer. We are treated to some rather ghastly detail about the treatment of Jeronymo's festering wound, which is lanced and reopened. Several characters die lingering deaths from wounds, one of which was apparently an attempt at castration. A young man loses three teeth in a violent encounter, and an old woman two more when she bites a fricassee. And yes, these characters of refined sensibility do a lot of weeping and swooning; but their tears and their faints are presented with a specificity that makes them more than just flourishes on the page: the tears are wet, the states of consciousness and semi-consciousness are finely discriminated. It is a novel that deals, indeed, with delicate refinements of sensibility; but it also presents a thoroughly physical world inhabited by characters who live very much in the flesh.

Sexuality is to the fore, as always in Richardson's novels. But *Pamela* and *Clarissa* present sensational and unusual situations, with the heroine abducted, confined against her will, and under constant threat of rape by the sexually rapacious villain-hero. In *Sir Charles Grandison* the situations are less extreme and closer to common experience; and a range of different kinds of relation between men and women is presented, so that the reader is aware of the many modulations possible. *Grandison* is a treatise on how "Love various minds doth variously inspire."[11] And various bodies likewise. We are given considerable detail on sexual play and sexual response. There is a good deal of kissing, besides the more routine "saluting" that keeps before us the very frequent body contact in genteel society. And a kiss is not just a kiss, but, like the various states of consciousness between fainting and recovery, is carefully particularized by its degree of emphasis and for the response it elicits. Miss Barnevelt, with lesbian tendencies, snatches a kiss, and Harriet is offended (1:57). Greville, who has oral-sadistic tendencies, bites her hand when he kisses it, and "made prints upon it with his teeth." "By my soul, I could eat you," he exclaims (1:101). And of course there are more welcome kisses too, of hands, cheeks, foreheads, lips.

11 Dryden, *Tyrannic Love*, act 2. Doody uses the maxim as an epigraph to *A Natural Passion*. Lovelace, who quotes the line in his first letter, declares he is not interested in the whining "various minds," but is himself one of the "tempestuous souls" who are invaded by "raging flames" (*Clarissa*, letter 31).

Other kinds of sexual approach are perhaps more particular to Richardson—especially the passionate mingling of tears, which as in Sterne suggests its own kind of orgasm. This is the only kind of consummation, a chaste mingling of bodily fluids, for Sir Charles's fervent relation with Clementina: "my cheek was joined to hers, and bathed with her tears," he records of the big scene where she declares she cannot marry him in spite of her love (2:567).

Though kissing and weeping are sometimes used as a synecdoche for intercourse, this does not mean that Richardson avoids the real thing. The subject is necessarily skirted with some delicacy, but it is there, and a matter of explicit import to surrounding characters as well as to the principals. Harriet, who has helped to push her rebellious friend Charlotte into a marriage with a man she does not love, maintains a vigil for her on her wedding hight, knowing that "one of the greatest events of one's life" will be a greater ordeal for Charlotte than for a woman who loves the man with whom she is going to bed (2:337). And Harriet herself, when it comes to her own wedding night, is followed by the narrator to the very chamber where her eager bridegroom attends her (3:236–37). Richardson, that is, can be as piquante and suggestive in a book about virtuous characters as he was in *Pamela* about the outrageous Mr B.

I have taken this space to prove that *Sir Charles Grandison* is a sexy book not only to redeem it from its reputation as merely didactic and boring, but also to outline the context for the major theme that I am discussing, the issue of the proper relation of mind to body. The major characters are tested and developed in the light of their reconciliation with their own physicality, and virtuous behaviour is judged according to whether it promotes this reconciliation in others.

Sir Charles, to his lasting artistic disgrace, we know to be a moral paragon. It is because his virtue is so perfect and admired that he is beyond temptation and therefore dramatically uninteresting. And Richardson has been tactless enough not only to make him irreproachable, but to surround him with characters who keep reiterating his praises. All this being granted, it remains of interest, for an exploration of the themes of the novel, what kind of paragon he is. If he is a model to be followed, what does his example induce us to do?

Sir Charles is not only good himself, but he induces goodness in others. Whereas it was the chosen role for Mr B. and Lovelace to corrupt or destroy innocence, Sir Charles is a kind of moral therapist. He has a technique of magnanimity, of doing more than his own duty and taking on the neglected duties of others, that inspires the other characters to shake off their moral turpitude. The Danbys are an envious and quarrelsome family who have forfeited their father's sympathy and lost his fortune, which is left to Sir Charles instead. He asks them what money they require. They cautiously name sums as high as they dare. He gives them more than they ask for, and they become generous, harmonious, grateful. His uncle Lord W. is stuck with a mistress he is tired of but will not decently pay off. Sir Charles pays her out of his own pocket and, moreover, arranges a respectable marriage for his uncle, although a new heir would end his own prospect of inheriting his uncle's fortune and title. Lord W. is likewise shamed into probity and gratitude. That is the progress of a number of the novel's many subplots: Sir Charles is morally efficacious not by lecturing and laying down precepts, but by setting the example of magnanimity. This is a consciously chosen technique, and not simple acting out of his nature. He is an accomplished manipulator.

As an agent for good, Sir Charles characteristically brings appearance to accord with essence. As the book constantly emphasizes, it is part of being good that you should *look* good too, as though by a law of moral physics. When this harmonious relation is distorted, Sir Charles is at hand to put it right. This is his role in the most sensational action of the plot, Sir Hargrave Pollexfen's abduction of Harriet. Sir Hargrave offends against the law of moral correspondences by being handsome in appearance but wicked in motive and behaviour, and so he is an appropriate villain for the piece. Sir Charles not only rescues Harriet from him, but by a sort of inevitable necessity he makes him ugly too. "Lord bless me, my dear!" Harriet writes after the crisis, "the man has lost three of his fore-teeth! A man so vain of his person! O how he must be exasperated!" (1:200). This is his appropriate and only punishment—nobody attempts to get legal redress for his crimes of kidnapping a woman, trying to force her to marry him, and threatening rape.

The servant William Wilson is a test case for the relation of mind to "person." When he applies for the position of footman we get some rather suspicious emphasis on him. Harriet says, "He is well-behaved, has a very sensible look, and seems to merit a better service.

... I have a *mind* to like him, and this makes me more particular about him. ... Hire him at once, Mrs. Reeves says. She will be answerable for his honesty from his looks" (1:97–98). The reader, who has hitherto proceeded safely on the novel-reader's assumption that looks are indicative of character, is alerted by all this emphasis to switch to another, equally familiar, convention, of appearance as delusive. Handsome is as handsome does; first impressions are not to be relied on; and so forth. And sure enough, the plausible William Wilson turns out to be in the employ of Sir Hargrave Pollexfen, and a chief organizer of Harriet's abduction. "Her servant is, must be a villain!" exclaims her distracted cousin (1:121). And when Harriet is safely home again, she reproaches herself for her gullibility. "One branch of my vanity is entirely lopt off. I must pretend to some sort of skill in physiognomy! Never more will I, for this fellow's sake, presume to depend on my judgment of people's hearts framed from their countenances" (1:150–51). So far the story of Wilson is a slap in the eye for the physiognomists, and an object lesson in appearance as deceptive.

It remains for Sir Charles to restore the credit of physiognomy, and to renew Harriet's ingenuous faith in appearance as true. He gets a full confession from Wilson, and instead of punishing him gives him enough money to marry a virtuous young girl who loves him; and being so trusted Wilson proves that he is not innately wicked, but was only temporarily led into "vile ways ... by excess of good-nature, and by meeting with wicked masters" (1:175). Once set in the way of being good, he gives reason to suppose that he will stay so, as his countenance denotes. His story becomes like the anecdote about Socrates that the physiognomists love to tell. The physiognomist Zopyrus, on the evidence of Socrates' countenance alone, characterized the great philosopher as a lecher and a drunkard, thus bringing his science into disrepute; but Socrates justified him, by confessing that lechery and drunkenness were indeed strong tendencies in him, which he counteracted only by the strenuous exercise of his philosophy.[12] Sir Charles likewise sets the record straight

12 The story, which originates in Cicero's *Tusculan Disputations*, is a favourite one with physiognomists, and is cited by Parson Adams in *Joseph Andrews* (2:17). See Graeme Tytler, *Physiognomy in the European Novel: Faces and Fortunes* (Princeton: Princeton University Press, 1982), p. 36.

and authenticates the science of physiognomy. And as with William Wilson, so with Sir Hargrave Pollexfen, he re-establishes the proper relation between appearance and reality. He is in pursuit of a classical harmony of form and essence.

It is in keeping with Sir Charles's role as moral therapist that he has a physician as his right-hand man. Mr Lowther to Sir Charles is like the Palmer to Sir Guyon in the *Faerie Queene*, the appropriate guide and enabler. Armed with his English health, his native integrity, written instructions from a psychiatrist, and Mr Lowther, Sir Charles goes back to Italy to straighten out the physical and psychological problems of the della Porretta family. His friend Jeronymo is like the other libertines, Pollexfen, Bagenhall, and Merceda, who all receive ugly wounds in encounters from which they are rescued by Sir Charles, the knight of continence. The wounds are generally in the genital area. Jeronymo's is in "the hip-joint," Merceda's is the result of an attempt at castration by a cuckolded husband (2:341). One suspects a delicate allegory here, and that the wounds are what Moll Flanders would call "an admirable description, by the way, of the foul disease." All but Jeronymo ultimately die of them. In bringing Mr Lowther to minister to Jeronymo, Sir Charles is saving his friend from the consequences of his own sin, which have become all too visibly manifest.

Sir Charles himself, we are made to believe, is completely in tune with his body. What he seems he is, and this is his pride, as well as a great part of his irresistible attraction to others. "My looks, my Lord, generally indicate my heart," he declares proudly, when challenged (2:464). And others confirm him as "carrying his heart in his countenance" (2:9). Naturally, since he is so good, he is very handsome. "Sir Charles Grandison, in his person," records Harriet rather breathlessly, "is really, a very fine man. He is tall; rather slender than full: His face in shape is a fine oval: He seems to have florid health; health confirmed by exercise" (1:181). And naturally the women fall for him. But to fall in love with Sir Charles, whose *person* is a true mirror of his noble mind, is almost a virtue in itself, since it shows a proper and rational admiration for virtue. And hence no less than two surpassingly worthy women, besides several others not so worthy, are passionately in love with him.

Sir Charles is not so modest as to be unconscious of his personal attractions. To *appear* virtuous when you *are* so is itself a virtue; and it is one that Sir Charles consciously cultivates. He is a connoisseur of appearance, in himself and others. He has made deliberate choices in his style of dress, for instance, on which he is ready to deliver a mini-lecture:

In my own dress, I am generally a conformist to the fashion. Singularity is usually the indication of something wrong in judgment. I rather perhaps dress too showy, tho' a young man, for one who builds nothing on outward appearance: But my father loved to be dressed. In matters which regard not morals, I chose to appear to his friends and tenants, as not doing discredit to his magnificent spirit. (3:124)

This tone has exasperated subsequent readers, including Leslie Stephen, who complained that Sir Charles "is one of those solemn beings who can't shave themselves without implicitly asserting a great moral principle. ... He could give an excellent reason for the quantity of lace on his coat, which was due, it seems, to a sentiment of filial reverence." (Terry Eagleton, similarly impatient, calls this preachifying Sir Charles "a Jesus Christ in knee-breeches.")[13]

Sir Charles is attentive to pose and gesture as well as dress. He is stately and deliberate about his frequent kneeling, bowing, kissing of hands, and so on. Even his most unstudied action—as when, finding the seats near Harriet occupied by the ladies in their hoops, he sits on the floor at her feet—seems to be artistically arranged. Harriet notes that he adjusts his conversation to his pose, "as if he must be all of a piece with the freedom of his attitude" (3:93). And he is studious of facial expression, other people's as well as his own. When he is pacifying the ill-tempered Lady Beauchamp, his strategy is first to rearrange her features. "But let me, madam, see less discomposure in your looks. I want to take my impressions of you from more placid features: I am a painter, madam: I love to draw lady's pictures. Will you have this pass for a first sitting?" (2:274). Having induced her to adopt a smile, he is half way towards inducing the good humour it signals. In this case he successfully manipulates the essence by adjusting the appearance.

---

13 Introduction to *Samuel Richardson: Works*, ed. Leslie Stephen, 12 vols (London, 1883), 1:xxxix; quoted in Flynn, p. 46. Terry Eagleton, *The Rape of Clarissa: Writing, Sexuality and Class Struggle in Samuel Richardson* (Oxford: Basil Blackwell, 1982), p. 96.

In Harriet Byron we have a much more engaging instance of the consonance of mind and body. She is a healthy and attractive character whose beautiful appearance is a true reflection of her goodness; so she constantly strikes others, who are apt to exclaim, Behold the first in virtue as in face!—or some equivalent. We early encounter Greville's encomium: "But who, Madam, can describe the person of Miss Harriet Byron, and her person only; animated as every feature is by a mind that bespeaks all human excellence, and dignifies her in every Air, in every Look, in every Motion?" (1:9). Sir Rowland Meredith has his own less formal expression for the same sentiment: "Then such sweetness of countenance ... such dove-like eyes, daring to tell all that is in the honest heart!—I am a physiognomist, Madam ... Ad's-my-life, you are a perfect paragon!" (1:38). Harriet like Sir Charles is conscious that it must be part of her moral endeavour to live up to her pretty appearance; but she is less solemn and didactic about it than he is, and also less confident of success. And she has a healthy allowance of vanity, and in the early part of the novel she takes frequent trips to the mirror, "making mouths" at herself (1:46), trying on different appearances, as though they were dresses. The reader is induced to like her appearance too.

In the eyes of others she is from the beginning a proper match for Sir Charles, since she presents the achieved harmony of beauty with goodness; in her own mind, however, she has a development to undergo in attaining the proper relation between mind and body. Harriet's task—and it is no easy one for a Richardson heroine—is to come to terms with her own sexuality.

The Richardson who wrote *Pamela* and *Clarissa* created the lasting stereotype of Man as the ravening beast, subject to his passions, driven by sexual appetite, and Woman as pure and chaste, immune from desire. A careful reading of these novels of course reveals that he exceeds those stereotypes, but still the impression lasts: the Pamela precedent suggests that desire in a woman, if it exists at all, is in a dormant state, awaiting the awakening of the man's declaration, like Sleeping Beauty being aroused by the prince's kiss. In a study of the English novel, David Skilton complains of *Clarissa*, "this study of injured female innocence and male rapacity shows the same fundamental pattern of thought as the much cruder *Pamela*—a fetishistic devotion to 'purity' in women, set against an almost demonic sexual drive in the evil man. ... The fear of sexuality Richardson's novels display surely reflects psychologically on him and on his contemporary admirers."[14] But of course the contemporary admirers had noticed the stereotypes too, and they urged Richardson to revise them: "I am teazed by a dozen ladies of note and of virtue, to give them a good man," he wrote, "as they say I have been partial to their sex, and unkind to my own."[15] Sir Charles Grandison, the model gentleman and a virgin to boot, was to be the answer to Mr B. and Lovelace. But Richardson has not always received due credit for Harriet Byron, the heroine who falls in love and suffers the pangs of unrequited passion, as the reversal of the chaste and unawakened Pamela and Clarissa. Skilton, for all his strictures about Richardson's fetishistic devotion to purity in women, has no time for *Grandison*. But Anna Laetitia Barbauld at the beginning of the nineteenth century could appreciate the extent of the change that *Grandison* represents in Richardson's vision of female sexuality: "Richardson had been accused of giving a coldness to his female characters in the article of love ... but he has made ample amends for the imputed omission in his *Grandison*, where he has entered into the passion with all the minuteness, and delicacy, and warmth, that could be desired, and shewn the female heart to be open to him in all its folds and recesses."[16]

In a rather curmudgeonly letter to the *Rambler* of 9 February 1751, just after beginning *Grandison*, Richardson announces: "That a young lady should be in love, and the love of the young gentleman undeclared, is an heterodoxy which prudence, and even policy, must not allow." It was a maxim that Jane Austen noted with irony as one which her own heroines could not always live up to (*Northanger Abbey*, chap. 3). But neither can Harriet Byron, who, contrary to all Richardson precedent so far, falls in love with a man who not only has made no declaration, but lets her know that he is committed to another woman. With all the weight of Richardsonian moral precept and precedent against her, and with her own sense of delicacy that is

14 David Skilton, *The English Novel: Defoe to the Victorians* (London: Barnes and Noble, 1977), p. 22.

15 *The Correspondence of Samuel Richardson*, 5:272–73.

16 *Correspondence*, 1:cxviii–cxix.

founded on them, she is helpless against her own love. Richardson deserves more credit than he has received from twentieth-century readers for his rendering of Harriet's predicament: her initially unconscious love, her gradual discovery of it, her hesitating revelation, her rueful acceptance.

For all this the epistolary technique is particularly appropriate. Harriet's discovery of her love is bound up with her expression of it. And the discovery is particularly difficult because according to the convention she accepts her love should not exist at all. The sprightly Harriet of the opening letters, universally beloved but herself heart-free, takes a pride in her frankness. She can speak out on everything that passes in her mind, and anybody may read all she writes, because she has nothing to be ashamed of. "It is my glory," she exults to her intimate friend Lucy, "that I have not a thought in my heart which I would conceal from any one" (1:66). And she has no scruple about her letters to her cousin being shown also to her aunt and uncle. But as she becomes gradually aware that her "gratitude" to her rescuer may be developing into love—unrequited, and so unjustified, love—she develops a reticence that is an embarrassment to herself. "Don't read it out in the venerable circle," she catches herself asking as she writes (1:279); and she devises little signals in her letters, pointing hands and square brackets, to mark the passages that Lucy may not read aloud to her parents (1:290). Her unfamiliar reluctance in expression alerts her to what it is she is reluctant to express; and the love and its utterance unfold together.

The proud and heartfree Harriet does not give in without a struggle. Constantly courted by strings of suitors herself, she hates the thought of joining the ranks of ladies languishing for Sir Charles. "But here, my heart is left free. And O, thought I, now-and-then, as I looked upon him, Sir Charles Grandison is a man with whom I would not *wish* to be in love. I, to have so many rivals! He, to be so much admired! Women not to stay till they are asked, as Miss Grandison once said" (1:209). She is determined that *she* will never be one to be "*entangled in an hopeless passion!*" (1:218). And she humorously throws off the insinuations of her aunt that she is "over head and ears in the passion" (1:217). This series of letters is as spirited and engaging as anything in Richardson, and it is easy to see that Jane Austen is remembering them as she chronicles the gradual awakening to love of Elizabeth Bennet and Emma Woodhouse. But like those spirited heroines, Harriet must be humbled, and lose some of the sprightliness as she gains in psychological depth. "I am so much humbled ... that I have lost all that pertness, I think, which used to give such a liveliness to my heart, and alertness to my pen" (1:210). And even as she confesses her love, she tries to assume an illogical unconsciousness of it. "It is, I hope, a secret to myself, that never will be unfolded, even *to* myself, that I love a man, who has not made professions of Love to me" (1:386).

To be one of the women who will not "stay till they are asked" is shameful to the standard Richardson heroine, because an unrequited love, one that is against "prudence, and even policy," declares the sexual motive. This must be a love that has plenty of "person" in it after all. And Harriet must not only recognize this herself, but admit it to her confidante, to Sir Charles's sisters (who almost literally squeeze the secret out of her), and even to a relative stranger like the Dowager Countess of D. That she does so, and does it with dignity and conviction, is a welcome triumph of her love and her frankness over her delicacy.

Her attraction to Sir Charles has all along been strongly physical. After her minutely detailed description of him "in his person"—his "manly sunniness," "fine teeth," the "sparkling intelligence" of his eye, the "something great and noble, that shews him to be of rank"— she is aware of having been carried away, and quips ironically, "what is beauty in a man to me? You all know, that I never thought beauty a qualification in a man" (1:181). But on the next page she relapses: "For, O my dear, women's eyes are sad giddy things; and will run away with their sense, with their understandings, beyond the power of being overtaken either by stop thief, or hue-and-cry" (1:182). Her response is more than visual. "How irresistibly welcome to me was his supporting arm, thrown round me," she records, as she describes his rescue of her (1:167). When, after all she has had to endure during his attendance on her rival Clementina, they are at last engaged, she is clearly strongly aroused by his passionate kiss: "And, dear Lady G. he downright kissed me—my lip; and not my cheek—and in so fervent a way—I tell you every-thing, my Charlotte" (3:142). She faintly feels she ought to be modestly outraged, but she is not. Instead she notes with satisfaction, "I don't remember any instance of the like freedom used to Lady Clementina." (In the circumstances, we can forgive and accept her assumption that what Sir Charles had not recorded of his relation with Clementina had not happened.) And as they discuss the marriage day, Harriet can—almost—announce her sexual longing in words: "My heart, Sir, is—*Yours!*—I would have said—Why would my tongue not speak it?—My, my, I stammered—Why did I stammer?" (3:190). She does not quite say, "my body is yours, and wants yours"; but she has gone far towards it, for a Richardsonian heroine. It took three more generations before another heroine, Jane Eyre, could be as explicit about sexual consummation on the eve of her wedding: "I am not, as you seem to think, troubled by any haunting fears about the new sphere, et cetera: I think it a glorious thing to have the hope of living with you, because I love you" (chap. 25). Jane Eyre is bolder in expression than Harriet; but Harriet, trained in the upper reaches of rarefied delicacy, has accomplished her own long journey in facing her own physicality. In spite of falling under the shadow of Sir Charles's paralysing didacticism, Harriet Byron is no slouch of a heroine.

Clementina, Sir Charles's other possible mate, does not represent, like Harriet, the achieved harmony of mind and person. She is torn by an irreconcilable conflict of flesh and spirit. She exists and is made vivid for us as a creature of flesh and blood, as Doody says; but her carnality is like that of St Theresa, a kind of eroticism of the soul. In fact there are some suggestions that Clementina is almost all soul, her body being an embarrassing appendage, like Yeats's "sort of battered kettle at the heel." Her name connects her with Mercy, the salient quality of Christianity as against Old Testament justice. And the men who court her recurrently invoke her and their souls in the same breath, as though they were in some measure identified. "My Soul, I own to you, is in the distresses of the family of Porretta," says Sir Charles (2:367). Clementina apparently regards him partly in the same light: her brother claims, "Your *person*, Chevalier, is not so dear to the excellent creature, as your *soul*" (2:183). And at the end, when Clementina is visiting Sir Charles and worshipped from afar by her faithful other suitor, we hear that *he* has come to recognize her as soulmate too. "The *person* of the poor Count of Belvedere ... is loitering in town, endeavouring to divert itself there; while his *soul* is at Grandison- hall" (3:416). Clementina and her men seem to interact with each other rather as souls than as bodies.

Sir Charles's two loves are sparked by two different episodes of well-proven erotic power, a rescue and a master-pupil relationship.[17] Harriet he rescues in the flesh, by trouncing her abductor and transporting her bodily to safety in his coach; Clementina he first engages at a mental level: he *teaches* her. Initially he teaches her English, and then Milton: and so he involves her in the related conflicts of Protestantism and Catholicism, male and female, flesh and spirit, and divine and human authority that are all implicit in *Paradise Lost*. He is appropriately wedded and bedded with the more physical Harriet, while Clementina, never fully located in her own body, would by her own choice be nobody's bride but Christ's.

Clementina proves to be a tragic figure who is unable to resolve the dichotomies of flesh and spirit. Like Harriet, she falls in love with a man who has not fallen in love with her, and she is forced to discover this love for herself, and to reveal it to others. But she cannot reconcile the craving of the flesh with the exaltation of the spirit. She loves a man who is morally admirable, but damned as a heretic. Her exalted love embarrassingly manifests itself as a physical condition, the diagnosed disease of love melancholy, and she is forced to undergo the humiliation of surgical treatment and even of strait-jacket and bonds. She is not one of Richardson's finer creations, partly because she is never allowed a firm grasp on the epistolary pen; but she is useful in his scheme of oppositions in the women who surround Sir Charles, as the one who, being a heroic soul, is unable to achieve Harriet's reconciliation of mind and body. Perhaps Richardson should have permitted her to enter the nunnery after all, as she wanted.

To balance the airy spirit of Clementina, and complete the pattern of Sir Charles's passionate admirers, is the other Italian lady, the fiery Countess Olivia. Richardson had intended to give her story at more length,[18] but that he had sufficient other business on hand. But her uninhibited passion and "violent spirit," signalled by her black hair

17 See Doody, p. 320: "Sir Charles acts as her tutor ... and Clementina is just the kind of young woman to be affected by the master-pupil relationship—a powerfully-charged one for a woman in any case." It's worth noticing that Jane Austen too dwells on the master-pupil relationship (Tilney and Catherine, Knightley and Emma) as well as the rescue (Willoughby and Marianne) as situations productive of love.

18 See Jocelyn Harris, "Introduction" (1:xi), and note (2:675).

and glittering black eyes (2:364), are clearly intended as a contrast with Clementina's meek submissiveness. She is rich, beautiful, independent, powerful. And she is ready to become Sir Charles's mistress if she cannot be his wife. She proposes to him, follows him to England, offers him herself and her fortune, and pulls a knife on him when he refuses. Such a figure is not likely to get moral endorsement from Richardson, but she is allowed a degree of sympathy. Her own full initiation in passion gives her an insight into other people's: she is able to divine Harriet's love and she is generous to her (2:366). (She emerges, incidentally, as a forebear of two other wicked and experienced women, Thackeray's Becky Sharp and Trollope's Signora, who are both in on the secret of the modest heroine's love, and act generously at crucial points.) Lady Olivia and Clementina, the one all flesh and unbridled passion, the other all saintliness and disembodied spirit, are the two extremes for Sir Charles. Harriet, who reconciles the oppositions, and presents a harmonious union of mind and body, is his golden mean.

But his sister Charlotte, Lady G., has her place in the pattern too, and a considerable place in the book. For many readers, particularly female ones, she steals the show: "Lady G. is the gem, with her marmoset," wrote George Eliot. Male readers, for reasons equally obvious, are more hostile: Alan Dugald McKillop dismissed her as merely "taking over the more objectionable traits" of Anna Howe in *Clarissa*.[19] In creating her, and dramatizing her independent spirit, her wit, and her rebellion against a patriarchal society, Richardson is an accomplished feminist. Of course in working out her story and taming her at last he ceases to be one. But even in the process of becoming reformed, Charlotte memorably articulates the exasperations and humiliations undergone by an individual of strong personality and bright intellect who must be relegated to the constricting roles of daughter, sister, wife, and mother. She is one of the earliest women in fiction to give voice to certain recurring issues of the women's movement: she fumes at the threat to her identity that the woman undergoes in losing her name at marriage (2:391);

---

19 *The George Eliot Letters*, 2:65. Carol Flynn, who has not much time for *Grandison*, is still sympathetic to Lady G. (p. 260). Alan Dugald McKillop, *Samuel Richardson: Printer and Novelist* (Chapel Hill: University of North Carolina Press, 1936), p. 212.

she volubly resents it that her husband should "make me his chattels, a piece of furniture only, to be removed as any other piece of furniture, or picture, or cabinet, at his pleasure" (2:501).

Charlotte is first made rebellious against male authority by her father, a male chauvinist of the first water. When she watches him brow-beating her sister, she mentally calls him *tyrant* (1:340)—strong word for a daughter, in a book that supports the proposition that "No provocation ... from a father, can justify a rash step in a child" (1:350). Partly in reaction against her father, she gets entangled in a clandestine correspondence with the unscrupulous soldier, Anderson, who meanly takes advantage of her, and turns out to be illiterate to boot. Later she explains, "the sorry creature Anderson, proving a sorry creature, made me despise the sex: And my brother's perfections contributed to my contempt of all other men" (2:340). But if both the bad example and the good conduce to a contempt for the whole sex, apparently the men cannot win. And here Richardson's judgment on Charlotte diverges from his sympathy for her.

As he presents Charlotte, he makes her a case of the woman whose strong mental development has put her out of step with the physical. She is cerebral, intellectually fastidious, sexually cool. Because she is more intelligent than Lord G. she cannot see his other claims to her respect. "The assiduities, of this trifling man are disgustful to me," she owns (2:320). And when she is pressured into marrying him she proceeds with a merry war that almost reduces him to desperation. She has a plan to make a good husband of him that sounds like a neat reversal of Petruchio's program in taming the shrew.

None of your grave airs, my dear [she tells Harriet, who takes his part]. The man is a good sort of man, and will be so, if you and Lady L. don't spoil him. ... I'll tell you how I will manage—I believe I shall often try his patience, and when I am conscious I have gone too far, I will be patient if he is angry with me; so we shall be quits. Then I'll begin again: He will resent! And if I find his aspect very solemn—Come, come, no glouting, friend, I will say, and perhaps smile in his face. ...

If he was ready to cry before, he will laugh then. (2:361–62)

Taming husbands is not likely to meet with as much approval from the surrounding society as taming wives, and Charlotte finds that not only her husband but her friends disapprove of her procedures.

She humorously resents their interference in her training program: "No such thing as managing one's own husband, when so many wise heads join together, to uphold him. *Ut*-ter-ly ruined for a husband, is Lord G." (2:498). No wonder that this lively lady has won some fans.

A modern reader cannot but feel that Sir Charles's haste in pushing Charlotte into marriage with a man she despises is a betrayal, although it is clearly not meant to appear so. But in the ensuing scenes of the marriage Richardson presents, with considerable delicacy as well as humour, a successful coming to terms between man and wife, and between Charlotte and her own sexuality. Initially she is offended by her husband's caresses (though she is never disgusted, as, say, Clarissa is by Solmes), and she objects when "throwing his arms about me as I sat, [he] joined his sharp face to mine, and presumed to kiss me" (2:392). She leads him a dance, but his obvious love that coexists with his resentment of her treatment makes her, to her own surprise, fond of him—"love" would not be her word. She is even moved to a caress of her own.

A few days ago, in a fond fit, I would have stroked his cheek; tho' he was not in a very good humour neither—*So, then! So, then!* said I, as I had seen Beauchamp do an hour before by his prancing nag; and it was construed as a contempt, and his bristles got up upon it. Bless me, thought I, this man is not so sensible of a favour as Beauchamp's horse. (2:498)

—and she is even a little wistful, in the midst of the playful provocation, in remembering that her offended husband, now so touchy about being treated like a horse, was once glad enough "to be admitted to press the same fair hand with his lips, on one knee" (2:498). She gives signs of an awakening sexual response to her husband, in spite of herself. When in high dudgeon he takes up a haughty pose, she admits, "Yet ... I thought his attitude very genteel; and, had we not been man and wife, agreeable" (2:438). But even after their happy reconciliation, she still claims, "I know not what Love is" (2:517).

Lady G.'s next ordeal is to be a mother, a role she contemplates as being almost as bad as that of wife. "The word *mother*, what a solemn sound has it to me now ... —But, come, the evil day is at a distance; Who's afraid?" (3:261). She is impatient of the baby clothes, and the whole paraphernalia of motherhood; and when the infant arrives she calls it "Little Leech," "brat," and "pug" (3:403). She is ashamed of being seen suckling it, especially by its father, and humorously casts herself in the role of chaste Diana to his inquisitive Actaeon. This comic conceit saves from sentimentality the scene in which he rapturously embraces his wife and their suckling daughter, her "Marmouset," as she is subsequently called. The scene is the consummation of Charlotte's story, the moment at which her wit and her biological roles as mate and mother are happily reconciled. Afterwards she can staunchly declare, "here I, Charlotte G. ... stand forth, an example of true conjugal felicity" (3:402). In setting out to justify an arranged marriage for an intelligent and rebellious woman, and to convince us that even such a woman may become happy in her male-dominated society through a full integration of her active mind with her own physical processes, Richardson took on a difficult task. On the whole, he succeeds rather well.

If we read *Sir Charles Grandison* as the letter-writers write it, with the emphasis on the women and the body, it is a much more lively and interesting novel than the one the title points to, with the emphasis on the relatively wooden hero and his moral precepts.[20] Sir Charles is structurally and thematically central, as the male over against whom the women are facing their separate crises, and as spokesman and exemplar of the proper relation of body to character; but the best drama, the finest psychology, and the most lively expression belong to the women.

Richardson's last novel is a highly visual work.[21] It does not abound with detailed description of setting, such as was to become the staple of the work of Radcliffe or Scott; nor is it minutely graphic about the peculiarities of face and figure in the manner of Smollett or Dickens; but it is vivid and explicit about the characters in their relations with one another—about their facial expressions, their expressive gestures, their poses, their positions and actions relative to one another in the same space. "What a pretty picture would they make,"

20 The lively treatment of the novel by Richardson's biographers, T.C. Duncan Eaves and Ben D. Kimpel, it seems to me, does the novel less than justice for the fact that they devote nearly all of their chapter to Sir Charles, while acknowledging that the other characters are much more successful. *Samuel Richardson: A Biography* (Oxford: Clarendon Press, 1971), pp. 387–400.

21 See Harris, Introduction, p. xv.

Harriet as narrator reflects of Sir Charles in conference with her grandmother. "Let me sketch it out" (3:91). The same process is at work throughout, if less explicitly. Richardson is a choreographer, and he designs his characters' movements. The story takes its shape through a close-up chronicling of physical motions, and relationships are partly defined and rendered in these visual and physical ways. We judge of emotion and mental response not just by explicit commentary on them, but by the projected actions: the characters declare themselves and their feelings by socially sanctioned signals, as when they bow, kneel, salute, kiss hands; they also express themselves in less voluntary ways as they tremble, blush, weep, feel faint; and there are signs more individual and particular too, but still visible and declarative: they tap snuff-boxes, twist diamond rings on their fingers, pick at handkerchiefs, tilt up their scabbards. Richardson and his deputed narrators are communicating in this network of visual signs at the same time as the words are explaining and lecturing. All this aptly matches his thesis, developed fully in the evolutions of his major characters, about the necessary consonance between mind and body. If Richardson was most concerned, according to his own declared purpose, with inward and spiritual grace, his readers can still be grateful that he successfully rendered it in outward and visible signs.

"Sufficient to the Day": Anxiety in *Sir Charles Grandison*

Lois A. Chaber

Sir Charles Grandison, aptly characterized by Sylvia Kasey Marks as "the stepbrother of Richardson's other novels,"[1] has suffered from its reputation as a foray into social comedy in which the novelist abandoned the religious profundity and the psychological complexity of *Clarissa*. Richardson's new approach allegedly entailed, at worst, a smug complacency, at best, an idealism and optimism— a stolid faith in the efficacy and benevolence of social institutions. Even sympathetic critics of *Grandison* have failed to challenge directly Alan D. McKillop's long-standing excoriation of the novel for its "complacent assumption that polite society can stand, when properly purged of vice and error."[2] Jean Hagstrum's discussion of the

---

1 Sylvia Kasey Marks, *"Sir Charles Grandison": The Complete Conduct Book* (Lewisburg: Bucknell University Press, 1986), p. 13. "'Sufficient to the Day': Anxiety in *Sir Charles Grandison*" was first published in *Eighteenth-Century Fiction* 1:4 (1989), 281–304.

2 Alan D. McKillop, *The Early Masters of English Fiction* (Lawrence: University of Kansas Press, 1956), p. 81. Similar views of *Grandison*, dismissing it for its complacence or superficiality, can be found in the following: T.C. Duncan Eaves and Ben D. Kimpel, *Samuel Richardson: A Biography* (Oxford: Clarendon Press, 1971), pp. 398, 615; Cynthia Griffin Wolff, *Samuel Richardson and the Eighteenth-Century Puritan Character* (Hamden, Conn.: Shoe String Press, 1972), pp. 176, 194, 225, 227, 233; Carol Houlihan Flynn, *Samuel Richardson: A Man of Letters* (Princeton: Princeton University Press, 1982), pp. xi–xii, 5, 48–49; Rita Goldberg, *Sex and Enlightenment: Women in Richardson and Diderot* (Cambridge: Cambridge University Press, 1984), pp. 25–26; Gerard A. Barker, *Grandison's Heirs: The Paragon's Progress in the Late Eighteenth-Century English Novel* (Newark: University of Delaware Press, 1985), pp. 13–

novel epitomizes the way in which even sympathizers generally turn a blind eye to its more sombre ambiguities; after generously praising its depiction of human love, he raises the possibility of "a potentially darker side" to the work only to dismiss this idea completely, retaining the conviction that *Grandison* "is unredeemed by the psychological depth one finds elsewhere."[3]

For a different perspective on *Grandison* we can take our cue from Gerard Levin, who warns, in a psychoanalytic study of Richardson's novels, that an exaggeratedly assured tone is actually "a sign of uncertainty or anxiety."[4] But while Levin's approach is orthodox Freudian, my own reading makes use of Anglican homiletic motifs from Richardson's own milieu, not for the sake of proving an influence, but for probing beneath the misleading surface pomposities of *Grandison* in order to expose and explore disquieting veins which both complicate and enrich the text. To be sure, there is a school of

52; James Grantham Turner, "Richardson and His Circle," *The Columbia History of the British Novel*, ed. John Richetti (New York: Columbia University Press, 1994), pp. 99–100; Margaret Anne Doody, "Samuel Richardson: Fiction and Knowledge," *The Cambridge Companion to the Eighteenth-Century Novel* (Cambridge: Cambridge University Press, 1996), pp. 110–14. More sympathetic readings of *Grandison*, on the other hand, may be found in Mark Kinkead-Weekes, *Samuel Richardson: Dramatic Novelist* (Ithaca: Cornell University Press, 1973), pp. 279–394; Margaret Anne Doody, *A Natural Passion: A Study of the Novels of Samuel Richardson* (Oxford: Clarendon Press, 1974), pp. 241–367; Jocelyn Harris, *Samuel Richardson* (Cambridge: Cambridge University Press, 1987), pp. 138–64; Margaret Anne Doody, "Identity and Character in *Sir Charles Grandison*," *Samuel Richardson: Tercentenary Essays*, ed. Margaret Anne Doody and Peter Sabor (Cambridge: Cambridge University Press, 1989), pp. 110–32; Juliet McMaster, "*Sir Charles Grandison*: Richardson on Body and Character," *Eighteenth-Century Fiction* 1 (1989), 83–102, and pp. 246–67 above; George E. Haggerty, "*Sir Charles Grandison* and the 'Language of Nature,'" *Eighteenth-Century Fiction* 2 (1990), 127–40, and pp. 317–31 below; Wendy Jones, "The Dialectic of Love in *Sir Charles Grandison*," *Eighteenth-Century Fiction* 8 (1995), 15–34, and pp. 295–316 below; Betty A. Schellenberg, *The Conversational Circle: Rereading the English Novel, 1740–1775* (Lexington: University of Kentucky Press, 1996), pp. 51–68. However, all these readings posit an optimistic vision of life in Richardson's last novel. In the past decade, feminist approaches to *Grandison* have criticized the novel on different grounds: see Carol Houlihan Flynn, "The Pains of Compliance in *Sir Charles Grandison*," *Tercentenary Essays*, pp. 133–45; Tassie Gwilliam, *Samuel Richardson's Fictions of Gender* (Stanford: Stanford University Press, 1993), pp. 111–60; Lois A. Chaber, "'This Affecting Subject': An 'Interested' Reading of Childbearing in Two Novels by Samuel Richardson," *Eighteenth-Century Fiction* 8 (1996), 193–250.

3 Jean Hagstrum, *Sex and Sensibility: Ideal and Erotic Love from Milton to Mozart* (Chicago: University of Chicago Press, 1980), pp. 214–16.

4 Gerard Levin, *Richardson the Novelist: The Psychological Patterns*, Costerus: Essays in English and American Language and Literature, n.s. 9 (Amsterdam: Rodopi, 1978), p. 117.

thought which eschews altogether the relevance of Christian themes to the eighteenth-century novel; nevertheless, not too long after the onslaught of poststructuralist criticism two decades ago, Leopold Damrosch, Jr, reasserted the significance of religious themes in *Clarissa*, a significance which, I suggest, may be extended to the rest of Richardson's canon. (The two approaches need not be mutually exclusive, as I hope to indicate.)[5] Moreover, I align myself with both Damrosch and Rita Goldberg, in their studies of *Clarissa*, in insisting on the complexity and tension within Christian ideas themselves and on the problematic—even subversive—fictional deployment of these ideas by Richardson.[6]

An investigation into the imputed smugness or "serenity"[7] of *Grandison's* social world leads eventually to theological concerns. It is true that Richardson offers no program of social reform. Even with regard to the grossly unfair anti–Roman Catholic laws, we hear from Sir Charles that "a great deal ... may be said on this subject. I think it sufficient to answer for myself, and my own conduct."[8] Yet this toleration is not complacency; rather, it constitutes the most radical criticism possible, one which, assuming the inevitable inadequacy of social institutions and the impossibility of meaningful change, judges society from above, not from within.

In *Clarissa* social justice is shown to be a farce; in *Grandison*, rather than relaxing his grim vision of the inefficacy of human law, Richard-

---

5 Leopold Damrosch, Jr, *God's Plot and Man's Stories: Studies in the Fictional Imagination from Milton to Fielding* (Chicago: University of Chicago Press, 1985), p. 213. The classic case for the pertinence of Christian themes to Richardson's novels is John A. Dussinger, "Richardson's 'Christian Vocation,'" *Papers on Language and Literature* 3 (1967), 3–19.

6 In Goldberg, see esp. pp. 18, 22–23, 28–38, 43, 71–78, 84, 87, 94, 118; in Damrosch, see esp. pp. 1–17, 213, 256, 258–59, 262; however, in this essay I diverge from these two critics in considering Richardson a mainstream Anglican Protestant, as described by Eaves and Kimpel (pp. 550–56), rather than a "Puritan" writer as they do. For reinforcements of this distinction, see Hagstrum, pp. 186–87, 214, and James Louis Fortuna, Jr, *"The Unsearchable Wisdom of God": A Study of Providence in Richardson's "Pamela,"* University of Florida Monographs: Humanities, no. 49 (Gainesville: University Presses of Florida, 1980), pp. 5–7, 11.

7 See Hagstrum, p. 216.

8 Samuel Richardson, *The History of Sir Charles Grandison*, ed. Jocelyn Harris, 3 vols (London: Oxford University Press, 1972), 2:531. References are to this edition.

son actually intensifies this critique.[9] Despite the positive depiction of some lawyers in the novel, much of *Grandison* is taken up in displaying the miscarriages—even the misuses—of the law. To be sure, many of the most flagitious crimes—the attempted assassinations of the merchant Mr Danby and of Jeronymo della Porretta, the imprisonment of the clergyman Dr Bartlett on false charges—occur on the reputedly more sinister terrain of the Continent; nevertheless, I find it odd that Cynthia Griffin Wolff can speak of *Grandison* as placing its "faith ... in British justice"[10]—that very British justice whose "delays and chicaneries" Sir Charles refers to with scorn (3:3). In England itself Sir Thomas Grandison, Sir Hargrave Pollexfen, and Mr Greville all defy the law by duelling or attempting to duel. Sir Thomas seduces his daughters' governess with impunity and the dishonest dealings of his own stewards go unpunished. If in Italy the jealous Olivia feels free to send bravoes to abduct Sir Charles, no concerns about British justice prevent her from stabbing him when she follows him to England. Not only do these felons escape the proverbial clutches of the law, but the dishonest manipulate that law to their own advantage. The disreputable Mrs O'Hara starts legal proceedings against Sir Charles to gain control of the inheritance of her daughter, his ward; Everard Grandison, Sir Charles's dissolute cousin, having seduced a flock of innocents with impunity, eventually suffers from the false accusations of a whore as tainted as himself; and the Mansfields, defrauded of their rightful inheritance, have been defeated in litigation by their opponents.

Far from displaying Richardson's faith in British justice, *Grandison* seems designed to dramatize its inadequacies—as did much Anglican homiletic literature of the day, with which Richardson was familiar.

9 See Goldberg's trenchant discussion of Richardson's derogatory depiction of the law in *Clarissa*, pp. 97–101. Richardson's attitude is epitomized by his epistolary admission to Eusebius Silvester: "I have so poor an opinion of the Practises of the Law in general, and of their Proceedings in their Profession," 20 July 1756 (Forster Collection, Victoria and Albert Museum, 14, 4, f. 25). Leah Price's analysis of Sir Charles's extensive testamentary dealings throughout the novel, in "*Sir Charles Grandison* and the Executor's Hand," *Eighteenth-Century Fiction* 8 (1996), 329–42, buttresses my general point here because she demonstrates how he rarely sticks to the letter of the legal will but rather imposes his own, more benevolent "will" upon the legal ones whether as heir, executor, or advisor (pp. 339–40).

10 Wolff, p. 228.

Divines such as Isaac Barrow traditionally offered the limitations of human justice as a proof of "The Reasonableness and Equity of a Future Judgement":

As for human laws, made to encourage and requite virtue, or to check and chastize vice, it is also manifest that they do extend to cases in comparison very few; and ... they are so easily eluded, or evaded, that without entrenching upon them ... or coming within the verge of their correction, men may be very bad in themselves, extremely injurious to their neighbours, and hugely troublesome to the world: so that such laws hardly can make tolerable citizens, much less thoroughly good men.[11]

Not only is this an apt description of what we see in *Grandison* but Sir Charles himself sermonizes in a similar vein:

The laws were not made so much for the direction of good men, as to circumscribe the bad. Would a man of honour wish to be considered as one of the latter, rather than as one of those who would have distinguished the fit from the unfit, had they *not* been discriminated by human sanctions? Men are to approve themselves at an higher tribunal than at that of men. (2:140)

Such sentiments underlie Richardson's scorn for the term "legal" in both *Clarissa* and *Grandison*, where he uses it ironically to condemn the "circumscribed" vision of his villains: Lovelace exposes himself when after the rape he declares that "My whole view at the present is to do her legal justice,"[12] as does Sir Hargrave, who hopes to prove he is "a moral man" by making the kidnapped heroine of *Grandison* "legally" his (1:152). Both remarks can be contrasted with Sir Charles's reproach to his sisters when speaking of the disposition of his father's housekeeper and mistress: "Shall we do nothing but *legal* justice?" (1:372).

Just as the laws prove inadequate to restrain the evil in society, so "punctilio"—the rigid code of manners, decorum, and civility which

11 Isaac Barrow, *Sermons and Expository Treatises* (Edinburgh: T. Nelson, 1839), 2:376.

12 Samuel Richardson, *Clarissa, or the History of a Young Lady*, ed. Angus Ross (Harmondsworth: Penguin Books, 1985), p. 907. References are to this edition. For a discussion of Lovelace's association with the law, see John B. Zomchick, "Tame Spirits, Brave Fellows, and the Web of Law: Robert Lovelace's Legalistic Conscience," *ELH* 53 (1986), 99–120.

is the equivalent of legal order in the polite world—fails to safe-guard the individual's integrity, as Harriet, like Clarissa, eventually discovers. Early in the novel Harriet glimpses the savagery underly-ing social façades:

I can deal pretty well with those, who will be kept at arms length; but I own, I should be very much perplex'd with resolute wretches. The civility I think myself obliged to pay every one who professes a regard for me, might subject me to inconveniences with violent spirits, which, protected as I have been ... I never yet have known. ... to what evils, but for that protection, might I not, as a sole, an independent young woman, have been exposed? Since men, many men, are to be look'd upon as savages, as wild beasts of the desert. (1:64)

Forgetting this insight, however, she optimistically comments on the success of her punctilious handling of Sir Hargrave on the very evening of the fatal masquerade: "you will now therefore hear very little farther in my letters of this Sir Hargrave Pollexfen" (1:115). Ironically, this letter is immediately followed by one in which her cousin Reeves frantically relates her abduction. It is indeed a favour-ite device of Richardson's to juxtapose such complacent statements as Harriet's with facts that mock them: Clarissa's confident declara-tion that "a steadfast adherence to that my written mind is all that will be necessary" (p. 370) to break off with Lovelace is, we know, shock-ingly succeeded by the letter posted from St Albans. To stress the point, Richardson depicts Sir Hargrave sarcastically taunting Harriet for her much-lauded "civility" throughout her nightmarish abduc-tion (1:152, 155, 165). Social mores provide only tenuous and fragile safeguards against the ever-present violence of human passions.

To be sure, most of the rampant villainy in the novel is eventu-ally checked, but by a higher agency which bypasses, transcends, and even occasionally conflicts with the inadequate social sanctions. This divine agency is symbolized by Sir Charles himself, who serves as a kind of providence surrogate (particularly in the subplots and flash-backs) while still performing his role as an embarrassed and passive mortal lover in the main story of divided love, thus fulfilling a dual function not uncommon in eighteenth-century fiction.[13] By means of deliberate epistolary strategies Richardson keeps Sir Charles aloof, mysterious, and suggestively abstract in order to prepare us for his quasi-allegorical role as an analogy to divine providence, admittedly at the expense of his verisimilitude and vividness in the central love story.[14]

It is difficult to believe that after having his letter-writers preach the virtues of being "particular" and of "writing to the moment" in every novel including *Grandison*, Richardson did not know what he was about when calling attention to the lack of these qualities in the representation of Sir Charles. The Reverend Dr Bartlett, from whose papers an account of Sir Charles's early adventures is "extracted," warns us we are reading about events on a different plane of reality when he apologizes to Harriet: the account "is not what it might have been; but mere facts, I presume, will answer your intention" (1:456). Moreover, for a good part of the novel, the adventures with which Sir Charles is connected, like the fabulous tales of the Old Testament, are set in the past and conveyed to us through a clergyman. Even when we have caught up to Sir Charles's present life, more often than not we see him but darkly, at second hand. His adventures in France are reported by Charlotte, who has heard them from others; we learn about the rest of his Continental journey through Mr Lowther, the surgeon. When, after Sir Charles's second trip to Italy (where he has written some letters directly), he arrives back in England—our geographical foreground—his actions are once again filtered through Dr Bartlett or Harriet. Accordingly, one must agree

13 See Elizabeth Deeds Ermarth, *Realism and Consensus in the English Novel* (Princeton: Princeton University Press, 1983), p. 140 and Martin C. Battestin, *The Providence of Wit: Some Aspects of Form in Augustan Literature and the Arts* (Oxford: Clarendon Press, 1974), pp. 209–10. For discussions of Sir Charles's function as providence surrogate, see Doody, *A Natural Passion*, pp. 270–71; John Sitter, *Literary Loneliness in Mid-Eighteenth-Century England* (Ithaca: Cornell University Press, 1982), pp. 207–8; Marks, p. 92; Harris, *Samuel Richardson*, p. 140; and Fortuna, pp. 34–41. Even Price, in "Executor's Hand," acknowledges Sir Charles's transcendent, symbolic role by her offhand reference to Sir Charles "play[ing] Providence" (p. 338).

14 Richardson's distancing process has been noted, but solely for its detrimental effects, as in Harris, *Samuel Richardson*, p. 134. Doody's extensive discussion of Sir Charles (*A Natural Passion*, pp. 241–77) incorporates both criticism and an apologetic dimension relating to the fact that "through him, Richardson creates a philosophical background" (p. 274), though it is with the putative optimism of this "background" that my essay takes issue.

at least in part with Levin's comment that "the novel throughout has the tone of parable," for the many minor episodes in which Sir Charles rescues characters stand out as pointed religious apologues in a work of otherwise fastidiously mundane texture.[15] Besides Harriet's rescue—"a providential accident" as Richardson referred to it in his synoptic table of contents[16]—there is (as one of many examples) Mr Danby's stated reason for making Sir Charles his residuary legatee: "he had been the principal instrument in the hand of providence, of saving his life" (1:448).

Perhaps the most significant indication of Sir Charles's role as a providence surrogate is his symbolic position as the lord of Grandison Hall, an estate "situated in a spacious park" (3:272), whose chief characteristics are its amplitude and variety (the multiple lawns and prospects, the vast spectrum of fruits and blossoms in the neatly graded orchard, and so on, 3:272–73), suggesting Creation itself, increasingly defined during this period by its plenitude as well as its order. In fact, Margaret Anne Doody asserts that the entire fictive universe of *Grandison* is characterized by an extraordinary "variety in unity," and "harmonized diversity."[17] Sir Charles's course of study has prepared him to serve this estate, as God does the world, in the dual capacity of a preserving and a governing providence: "for while he was abroad, he studies Husbandry and Law ... the one to qualify him to preserve, the other to manage, his estate" (3:288). Even his almost perpetual absence from his English estate imitates a deity at once transcendent and immanent: "Tho' absent, he gives such orders, as but few persons on the spot would think of" (3:288). Sir Charles as Godlike master is summed up by Mr Lowther: "For humanity, benevolence, providence for others, to his very servants, I never met with his equal" (2:448).

To stop here would be merely to replace social with religious complacency, but further consideration of the doctrine of providence reveals the potential for a religious complexity which Richardson developed and intensified, and suggests how the providential

15 Levin, p. 88.

16 Samuel Richardson, *The History of Sir Charles Grandison*, with an introduction by William Lyon Phelps (New Yord: Croscup and Sterling, 1901), 1:xxxix. The editorializing table of contents was not included in the first edition on which Harris's edition is based.

17 Doody, "Identity and Character," pp. 126, 130.

interpositions which Sir Charles enacts ultimately create anxiety within the world of the novel. Indeed, according to Maurice Wiles, who points out that "divine agency" has been a troubling issue throughout Christian history, "the notion of God's acting in the world is highly problematical."[18] For one thing, the moral order created by providential interpositions was never seen by theologians of Richardson's era as final and complete, but only as a palpable hint of what was to come. As William Sherlock explained in his popular late seventeenth-century tract on providence, the justice of providential intervention was the justice of government, not the justice of the final judgment, and had as its aim not execution but exemplary correction and reward:

And therefore, though every particular good man be not rewarded, nor every bad man punished in this world, yet the divine providence furnishes us with numerous examples of justice, in the protection and defense of good men, and in the punishment of the wicked.[19]

Archbishop Tillotson also distinguished between "miraculous and extraordinary judgments which are immediately inflicted by God for the punishments of some crying sins, and the example of the world, to deter others from the like," and everyday evils caused either by "a necessity of nature" which "can make no distinction between the good and the bad" or by the voluntary acts of men which "many times will make no difference between the righteous and the wicked."[20]

Richardson, moreover, clearly subscribed to the view that providential justice in this life is partial and provisional, and that perfect justice is yet to come. In his unpublished fragment "The History of Mrs. Beaumont," he justifies his refusal to account completely for the punishment of various evildoers by having Dr Bartlett assert:

I am not ... for inferring temporal Judgments upon Evil-doers from every unhappy Event that befalls them. This Life is not the Life of final Rewards

18 Maurice Wiles, *God's Action in the World: The Brampton Lectures for 1986* (London: SCM Press, 1986), pp. 2–4, 25. For a more general discussion of the traditional doctrine of providence, see Battestin, pp. 150–63, and Fortuna, pp. 14–23.

19 William Sherlock, *A Discourse Concerning the Divine Providence* (1694; Pittsburgh: J.L. Read, 1849), p. 138.

20 John Tillotson, "The Justice of God in the Distribution of Rewards and Punishments" in *Sermons on Several Subjects and Occasions* (London: C. Hitch and L. Hawes, 1742–47), 8:182.

and Punishments. The Righteous as often suffer in it as the Wicked: Perhaps more frequently. And it is no bad Proof of another, a better, that they do.[21]

Accordingly, the providential rewards and punishments that Richardson chooses to dispense in his novels may be seen as strictly selective and exemplary. Defending his treatment of Lovelace to Lady Bradshaigh, he insisted that he should not do well "if I punished not so premeditated a Violation; and thereby made Pity on her Account, and Terror on his, join to complete my great End, for the sake of *Example* and *Warning*."[22] Mrs Norton in the novel emphasizes the point by explaining that Clarissa's harsh punishment in this life was "for example's sake, in a case of such importance" (3:330). Providential intervention, then, was not guaranteed, but was seen by Richardson and his contemporaries as a didactic and fragmentary imposition of order upon a world of widespread depredation and suffering.

This understanding of providence has an ambivalent effect on human beings. On the one hand, it generates profound spiritual gratitude. Robert South, the famous Restoration divine, speaks for a whole Christian tradition when he exclaims in a sermon "On the Mercy of God": "We live by a perpetual deliverance."[23] An amplification of the same theme by a seventeenth-century English diarist, however, reveals a terrifying vision of human life fraught with danger on all sides, as the concomitant of acknowledging a merciful God:

Indeed, what is our whole life, but a continued deliverance? We are daily delivered, either from the violence of the creature, or the rage of men, or the treachery of our own hearts; either our houses are freed from firing, or goods from plundering, or our bodies from danger, or our names from reproaches, or our souls from snares.[24]

---

21 Quoted in Eaves and Kimpel, p. 555.

22 To Lady Bradshaigh, 15 Dec. 1748, *Selected Letters of Samuel Richardson*, ed. John Carroll (Oxford: Clarendon Press, 1964), p. 104.

23 Robert South, *Sermons Preached upon Several Occasions* (Philadelphia: Sorin and Ball, 1844), 1:366.

24 John Beadle, *The Journal or Diary of a Thankful Christian* (1656), quoted in William Haller, *The Rise of Puritanism* (New York: Columbia University Press, 1938), p. 97.

Commenting on the belief in providence produced by "some event of remarkable or unexpected character," Wiles emphasizes the deleterious psychological side-effects of such contingent deliverance: "A traveller lost in the desert and rescued in the nick of time by the unlikely and unforeseen arrival of some other traveller may come to see the rest of his or her life as lived on borrowed time."[25]

The doctrine of providential interposition, moreover, places humanity in a passive and helpless—that is, infantile—position. Appropriately, Emily Jervois exclaims to her guardian Sir Charles, the providence surrogate, when he has interposed to resolve her pecuniary and family problems: "O Sir, you made us all infants!" (3:171). It is no coincidence that earlier she has recited a poem comparing providence to a "fond mother incircled by her children," here a parent figure whose benevolent omnipotence is laced with gratuitousness: "So it watches over us; comforting these; providing for those; ... assisting every one: And if sometimes it denies the favour we implore, it denies but to invite our more earnest prayers" (1:432). Emily's poem grapples with what Wiles calls "the age old difficulties" of "why this prayer is answered and not that."[26] Hence, as Tillotson admits, this sense of human vulnerability, of total and precarious dependence on sporadic providential aid, could lead to "an anxious care about events, a care that is accompanied with trouble and disquiet of mind about what may befall us."[27]

The homilies of the Anglican divines, echoed by Richardson, then, bear out Damrosch's assertion that in this period "faith in ultimate justice is entirely compatible with a feeling, at any given moment, of helpless misery,"[28] and it is this double-edged view of the human condition rather than complacency or optimism that we find in *Grandison*. When Sir Charles has been threatened by Greville (another rejected suitor of Harriet's), the heroine affirms her grateful faith: "is he not the care of Providence?—I humbly trust he is"

25 Wiles, p. 68.

26 Wiles, p. 105.

27 Tillotson, "Success Not Aways Answerable to the Probability of Second Causes," *Sermons*, 7:140.

28 Damrosch, p. 254.

(3:181). Her friend Charlotte, however, on hearing the happy outcome of this menacing episode, articulates the disquieting correlative of Harriet's pious trust: "I tremble, nevertheless, at the thought of what might have been" (3:197). In fact, Richardson's narrative, despite the many rescues and escapes, engenders anxiety throughout, exposing the need for perpetual deliverance and dogging its characters with constant reminders of what they have been delivered from, by means of two key strategies.

The precariousness of human fate is dramatized first of all by the presence of *alter egos* that embody alternative options for the fortunate characters, a version of the "analogues" that Eric Rothstein finds a characteristic technique of later eighteenth-century fiction. In *Amelia* in particular, according to Rothstein, the "analogues" increase "the potentialities of danger" in the novel, darken the plot, and depict "a more menacing world"[29]—effects that may also be attributed to the doubles in *Grandison*. Richardson was well aware that the best of us bear within us a more sinister potential self; Charlotte Grandison, teased by her brother, says of that paragon, "Had he been a wicked man, he would have been a *very* wicked one" (1:297).[30] Richardson first experimented with the use of doubles in *Pamela*, where the effect of the Sally Godfrey story is to make Pamela realize how narrowly she has missed the same fate: "that I have had the grace to escape the like Unhappiness of this poor Gentlewoman."[31]

29 Eric Rothstein, *Systems of Order and Inquiry in Later Eighteenth-Century Fiction* (Berkeley: University of California Press, 1975), pp. 184–87. Other resemblances to Rothstein's paradigm which will be noted in this essay will, I hope, help to corroborate his "system" in the way in which he invited scholars to do (p. 265)—particularly as he excluded Richardson from his discussion for pragmatic reasons (p. 5).

30 See also Harriet's remark, "had he been a free-liver, he would have been a dangerous man" (2:272). Strictly speaking, Charles has no double within the novel, unless it be the shade of Lovelace, with whom he has been disapprovingly linked: see Morris Golden, *Richardson's Characters* (Ann Arbor: University of Michigan Press, 1963), p. 15; Flynn, *Samuel Richardson*, pp. 231–34; Barker, p. 518; Marks, p. 55. Mary V. Yates offers a re-evaluation of this much-lamented resemblance between Richardson's best and worst of men, arguing that it is both intentional and morally viable, and pointing out the conscious intertextuality with *Clarissa*. "The Christian Rake in *Sir Charles Grandison*," *Studies in English Literature, 1500–1900* 24 (1984), 546–51, 555–56, 560–61.

31 Samuel Richardson, *Pamela; or, Virtue Rewarded*, Shakespeare Head edition, 4 vols (Oxford: Basil Blackwood, 1929), 2:333; *Pamela; or, Virtue Rewarded*, ed. Peter Sabor (Harmondsworth: Penguin Books, 1980), p. 497.

There, however, Richardson made his point blatantly, appending Sally's story at the end like the finger-wagging conclusion to a sermon; in *Grandison* such parallels pervade the novel, affecting both major and minor characters. For instance, the Obrien girl, used by Sir Thomas Grandison's scheming steward to draw the baronet into a second marriage, has as her *alter ego* the steward Bolton's young whore, who succeeds in marrying old Mr Calvert in order to secure the inheritance rightfully belonging to the Mansfield family. Miss Obrien, a more innocent if equally weak young woman, was saved from her own worst self by the timeliness of Sir Thomas's death.

What generally makes Richardson's doubles so anxiety-producing and fictively unique, however, is his characters' verbalized self-awareness of them. Such self-awareness is close to the use of "overt" doubles, which Paul Coates associates with "the self-conscious narrators of modernist fiction"—as opposed to the "latent" doubles of traditionally realistic narrative.[32] Harriet, for example, cannot wait for the full account of Clementina's imbroglio before laying out a double-columned, nearly full-page "parallel between our two cases" (2:158) for her own readers. In addition, after her rash flight to England in pursuit of Charles, the passionate Olivia becomes an instructive "parallel" for both these heroines. Harriet "could not help reflecting, on occasion of this Lady's conduct," that she shares with Olivia the absence of parental guidance, which explains Lady Olivia's erratic behaviour and makes her own good conduct the lucky exception (2:368). Clementina, too, perceives both the similarity and the difference: "Olivia, Sir, ... reflects upon me. It was indeed a rash step which I took, when I fled to England: How has it countenanced the excursion *she* made hither? Tho', God knows, our motives were widely different: Hers was to obtain what mine was intended to avoid" (3:428). Through "reflections" such as these the larger cast of characters and the more varied incidents of *Grandison* are brought to serve the introspective psychological purposes that we associate with Richardson's other novels. Not only does the multiplicity of pairings

32 Paul Coates, *The Realist Fantasy: Fiction and Realism since "Clarissa"* (New York: St Martin's Press, 1983), pp. 120, 116, 114. Coates does not discuss doubles in Richardson, but his identification of *Clarissa* as the precursor of the modern novel (p. 11) is related to my observations here.

and connections fulfil the "ideal of discriminated variety" that Rothstein attributes to his "family of novels,"[33] but here it is the characters themselves who make the discriminations.

In a self-recriminating vein similar to that of Harriet and Clementina, Charlotte tells the story of a Miss Hurste, who, like herself, became infatuated with a callow military man. Unlike Charlotte, however, Miss Hurste marries her soldier, and Charlotte is very much aware of both the gratifying *and* the terrifying implications of this *doppelgänger.*

Somebody met with an escape! Yet now-and-then I blush for Somebody. Yet between this Somebody and Miss Hurste's cases there was this difference— A father's apprehended—*Tyranny*— ... impressing the one; a tindery fit the other. In the one a timely recovery; in the other, the first folly deliberately confirmed. (2:551–52)

The word "timely" anxiously underscores for Charlotte the sheer grace and the slender contingency of *her* "deliverance." The nexus between the consciousness of an *alter ego* and a state of apprehensiveness or anxiety is appropriately generalized by Harriet when she compares herself to her cousin Lucy: "How apt are we to recollect, or to *try* to recollect, when we are apprehensive, that a case may possibly be our own" (1:285).

Even when the character who has been graced with the happier of two potential fates does not voice his or her own self-awareness, another character intervenes, turning action into "reflection"—in both senses of the word. Mrs Giffard, the mistress of Charles's uncle, as Harriet is aware, is the dark double of Mrs Oldham, Charlotte's father's mistress, and Harriet analyses the subtle differences in their situation in an effort to justify the contrasting Grandisonian (and therefore providential) treatment each mistress receives:

When the poor children are in the world. ... When the poor women are penitents, *true* penitents—Your brother's treatment of Mrs Giffard was different. He is in both instances an imitator of the Almighty; an humbler of the impenitent, and an encourager of those who repent. (2:307)

33 Rothstein, pp. 20, 240.

In fact, however, the officious appositive, "*true* penitents," unconsciously introduces an element of uncertainty into the distinction being made. Richardson's mirror images, rather than removing the threat of evil from his positive characters, as John Sitter claims,[34] actually reassert that threat, because the differences that have led to more melancholy fates are not so evident to the unreflecting majority.

Anxiety is intensified by a similar, but even more original, technique that allows the many criminal attempts discussed earlier to have a psychological effect even when foiled by providential agency. The more Harriet dwells gratefully on her rescue, the more she is forced to acknowledge with a shudder the multiplicity of possible evils cancelled out by this one act of arbitrary deliverance: "My mind has been greatly disturbed by Sir Hargrave's violence; and by apprehensions of fatal mischiefs that might *too* probably have followed the generous protection given me" (1:284). Not only was there the danger of Sir Charles's being wounded or killed, but her very rescue on Hounslow Heath, a notorious resort of highwaymen, might have imperilled her further: "It would have been very hard, had I fallen from bad to bad; had the sacred name of protector been abused by another Sir Hargrave" (1:166).

Harriet's comments on her rescue epitomize the prevailing syntactical pattern of the Grandisonian world—the language of possibility, of conditionality, of statement contrary to fact. In a word, the subjunctive, in particular the retrospective or past perfect subjunctive, dominates the characters' reflections, ranging from brief parenthetical comments on darker possibilities, such as "O my good Lady Grandison, how might your choice [of husband] have punished your children!" (1:331); "Tho' vile, he [Harriet's suborned servant Wilson] was less vile than he might have been" (1:295); and "What an uncontroulable MAN would Lady Olivia have made, had she been a man" (2:642), to extended meditations on what might have been: at one point in Charles's relations with Clementina's bellicose brother, the General, an entire scene is devoted to recreating the more dangerous scenario that might have occurred. For two pages the conversation proceeds in the following manner: "[Charles:] Had you

---

34 Sitter, p. 204. Gwilliam, in *Fictions of Gender*, is also concerned with "doubling" in this novel (pp. 146, 156, 157), but in the context of gender analysis.

made demands upon me that I had not chosen to answer, I would have expostulates with you. ... If you would not have been expostulated with, I would have stood upon my defence" (2:250). Characters even project entire hypothetical lifetimes in the subjunctive mood. Sir Hargrave expands on an alternative chain of cause and effect which is entirely plausible:

> if he [Sir Charles] had not interposed so hellishly as he did on Hounslow-heath, I had been the husband of Miss Byron in two hours; and she would have thought it her duty to reform me: And ... I swear, it was my intention to be reformed, and to make her, if I could have had but her *Civility*, tho' not her *Love*, the best of husbands. ... what a happy man had I then been!— Then had I never undertaken that damned expedition to France, which I have rued of ever since. (3:144)

Significantly, these vexed speculations of Sir Hargrave overlap with the nervous conjectures of Harriet, the effect being to corroborate the *lack* of inevitability in the heroine's escape from marriage to Sir Hargrave: "Drawn in by his professions of love, and by 8,000 *l.* a year, I might have married him; and, when too late, found myself miserable, yoked with a tyrant and madman, for the remainder of a life begun with happy prospects" (1:97).

The precarious thinness of the line separating the actual and the possible is emphasized by an ambiguous *lapsus calami* made by Emily Jervois near the end of the novel, when she has gone to live with Harriet's family in Northamptonshire to recover from her girlish infatuation with her guardian: "It is true, I was, (or might have been, I should rather say) a forward girl with regard to [Sir Charles]" (3:442). The cumulative effect is that these hypothetical events, with their generally undesirable implications for the protagonists, begin to subvert the real providential ones, impairing the confidence of these characters in a benevolent future. "Your *realities*, thank Heaven, are more delightful than your *resveries*," says Charlotte to Harriet, adding apprehensively, "I hope you'll always find them so" (3:195). William Beatty Warner has argued persuasively that there lurks within *Clarissa* a potential for comedy; I would claim that tragedy hovers over the seemingly comic world of *Grandison*.[35]

---

35 William Beatty Warner, *Reading "Clarissa": The Struggles of Interpretation* (New Haven and London: Yale University Press, 1979) pp. 76–87.

But we may go even further, spurred by Harriet's provocative observation that "when realities disturb, shadows will officiously obtrude on the busy imagination *as* realities" (3:48), a remark which bears out Ruth Perry's insistence on "the potency of consciousness" in the epistolary novel.[36] The postmodern criticism—in the work of Warner, Terry Castle, and Terry Eagleton—that transformed our understanding of *Clarissa*, cannot fail to leave its mark on *Grandison* as well.[37] This "language-centered critical theory" or "critical radicalism"[38] found in Richardson's epistolary narrative, with its characters who are self-conscious readers and writers, the paradigm of a radically indeterminate, polysemous literary text, and critics have pointed out that *Grandison*, if anything, has even more epistolary self-consciousness than the earlier novels.[39] In *Clarissa*, we were told, the text has plenty of authors but no authority. Since none of the narrators is genuinely neutral or objective, we are left with a text that is an autonomous, reflexive fabrication rather than a mimetic representation of "real" events, and which profoundly undermines our traditional faith in Richardson's "realism."[40] In *Grandison* too, from this point of view, language is the only verifiable action, and the supposedly "real" providential occurrences reported in the nar-

---

36 Ruth Perry, *Women, Letters, and the Novel* (New York: AMS Press, 1980). p. 101.

37 Warner, *Reading "Clarissa"*; Terry Castle, *Clarissa's Ciphers: Meaning and Disruption in Richardson's "Clarissa"* (Ithaca and London: Cornell University Press, 1982); Terry Eagleton, *The Rape of Clarissa: Writing, Sexuality and Class Struggle in Samuel Richardson* (Oxford: Basil Blackwell, 1982). Coates subjects *Clarissa* to similar poststructuralist analysis (pp. 23–49). Patricia McKee, in *Heroic Commitment in Richardson, Eliot and James* (Princeton: Princeton University Press, 1986), extended this methodology to *Pamela*. In 1992, in *Richardson's "Clarissa" and the Eighteenth-Century Reader* (Cambridge: Cambridge University Press), Tom Keymer argued that this same radical indeterminacy of *Clarissa* and its "authorizing" of the reader was in fact a deliberate strategy on Richardson's part.

38 The terms are Warner's in "Reading Rape: Marxist-Feminist Configurations of the Literal" [review of Castle and Eagleton], *Diacritics* 13 (1983), 12; and Goldberg's (p. 10), respectively.

39 See Jocelyn Harris, "'As If They Had Been Living Friends': *Sir Charles Grandison* into *Mansfield Park*," *Bulletin of Research in the Humanities* 83 (1980), 382, 402; Castle, p. 155n4; and Sitter, pp. 209–11.

40 Cf. Margaret Anne Doody, "Saying 'No,' Saying 'Yes': The Novels of Samuel Richardson," *The First English Novelists: Essays in Understanding*, Tennessee Studies in Literature, no. 29, ed. J.M. Armistead (Knoxville: University of Tennessee Press, 1985), pp. 69–70, who bucked the trend by heartily reaffirming Richardson's "realism."

rative are subsisting on a ground as insecure as that of the alternative possibilities articulated by the characters; in other words, the
subjunctive and the declarative events are equally "real."[41]

In fact, Damrosch's definition of Richardson as "protomodern,"
and Harris's observation that "wherever we turn ... Richardson
has usually been there first,"[42] are borne out by the way in which
Grandison approximates "The Garden of Forking Paths," an imagin-
ary narrative that Jorge Luis Borges writes about in one of his own
"fictions":

the "garden of forking paths" was the chaotic novel. ... In all fictional
works, each time a man is confronted with several alternatives, he chooses
one and eliminates the others: in the fiction of Ts'ui Pen, he chooses—
simultaneously—all of them. He *creates* in this way, diverse futures, diverse
times which themselves proliferate and fork. ... In the work of Ts'ui Pen,
all possible outcomes occur: each one is the point of departure for other
forkings.[43]

This description provides a paradigm for the experimental cosmos,
with its fissiparous structure, which is created, in effect, by the in-
cessant use of the subjunctive in *Grandison*. We may note the way
Harriet, for example, beginning with a simple conjecture about her
relationship to her milque-toast suitor, Mr Fowler, ends by projecting
several contingent futures, the labyrinthine proliferation of forkings
described by Borges:

I think I never could love Mr. Fowler, as a wife ought to love her husband—
May he meet with a worthy woman who can! And surely so good, so modest
a man, and of such an ample fortune, easily may: While it may be my lot,
if ever I marry, to be the wife of a man, with whom I may not be so happy,

41 Given that the subjunctive is the "fiction" of the grammatical sphere, this phenomenon
in *Grandison* is a variation on McKee's thesis that in the two earlier novels of Richardson
"all realizations are recognized and accepted as equally fictitious or equally real" (pp. 38–
39; see also pp. 11, 48). As to whether such propositions violate Richardson's intentions,
Damrosch comments: "the inner logic of a fiction often goes beyond, or even contradicts,
what its author intended to 'say.' ... Moreover ... it is precisely the rifting and disturbance
in belief that give rise to great literature" (p. 8); see also McKee's own justification, pp.
55n10, 100–101n9.

42 Damrosch, p. 260; Harris, *Samuel Richardson*, p. 1.

43 Jorge Luis Borges, "The Garden of Forking Paths," *Labyrinths: Selected Stories and Other Writings*, ed. Donald A. Yates and James E. Irby (New York: New Directions, 1962), p. 207.

as either Mr. Orme or Mr. Fowler would probably make me, could I prevail upon myself to be the wife of either. (1:79)

Disentangled from the gamut of modal auxiliaries and the optative subjunctive it employs, the passage suggests that Harriet may or may not be able to love Fowler; if she does not, then there are the possibilities of his meeting or not meeting someone else who will. Harriet herself may or may not marry, and if she does, it could be Mr Orme, Mr Fowler, or somebody else, and if it is somebody else, she may or may not be as happy with that person as with either of the former two men. The more she explores the logical possibilities of any situation, the more she has to worry about.

As a model, however, the "garden of forking paths" differs from Richardson's narrative in two ways: Richardson is primarily concerned with hypothetically diverse pasts rather than "diverse futures," and the crucial "choices," as I have argued earlier, are usually made by a providential rather than a human agent. There is a passage in Richardson's own novel which can be read as a metaphor for the entire Grandisonian cosmos—the disturbing dream Harriet has before her wedding, when Sir Charles is being threatened by Greville. The long account of this dream is dominated by what Harriet calls "contradictory visions" (3:150):

I was married to the best of men: I was *not* married: I was rejected with scorn, as a presumptuous creature. I sought to hide myself in holes and corners. I was dragged out of a subterranaeous cavern ... and when I expected to be punished for my audaciousness, and for repining at my lot, I was turned into an Angel of light. (3:148)

In Italy, at one time, Jeronymo's wounds were healed; at another, they were breaking out afresh. (3:149)

In the features of this dream we can see analogies to the text of *Grandison*. The dream extends over the whole range of the novel's concerns, not just the current plight of Sir Charles; it presents its personages as passive as does the novel itself; and, like the "garden of forking paths" and the postmodernist interpretation of *Grandison*'s grammar offered above, the dream pairs happy and unhappy versions of each event without privileging one or the other. As such, Harriet's dream is not simply another version of the hypothetical mishaps I have already discussed, but rather is a microcosm which consists almost entirely of verbal alternatives of negative and positive import equivalent to those of the subjunctive and indicative moods encompassed by the novel itself.[44]

Harriet's account of the dream is part of a series of letters which are self-consciously sent off to Charlotte. From directions *"written in a small hand, under the Superscription of the inner Cover"* we learn that, although Harriet instructs Charlotte to read first her subsequent letter in which Sir Charles dismisses and defuses Greville's threats in actuality, she nevertheless has yielded to cousin Lucy's insistence that she also "send the whole of that [earlier] shocking Letter" (3:179) containing the dream sequence, as if Richardson is indicating that both texts equally deserve a "reading"—by Charlotte, and by us. The apprehensive dream sequence and the waking events are literally bound together—the "dreadful one" is "stitched to the Cover" of the more sanguine one. Since this dream is experienced as a nightmare—the epitome of anxiety—and yet does in these various ways approximate or parallel the surrounding text of the novel, it is scarcely accurate to describe *Grandison* itself as optimistic—a comedy of manners.

There is a literary precedent in Richardson's career which partly explains his predisposition to perceive life as a succession of binary oppositions. The "forking paths" of *Grandison* are on one level an application of techniques of rhetoric which Richardson exercised earlier in his *Familiar Letters*, where the genre demanded the exploration of alternative possibilities such as "The Lady's Reply in case of a Prepossession," and "The Lady's reply in case of no Prepossession, or that she chooses not to avow it."[45] I suggest that in *Grandison*, however, this rhetorical device, which undergirds the novel's use of the subjunctive, has an ontological foundation. Threatened by the rationalistic determinism emanating from Continental philosophers such as Leibniz and Spinoza, as well as from English Deists, the Anglican divines of Richardson's period were concerned to depict

---

44 For an alternative reading of Harriet's dream sequence, see Flynn, "Pains of Compliance," p. 135.

45 Samuel Richardson, *Familiar Letters on Important Occasions*, ed. Brian W. Downs (New York: Dodd, Mead, 1928), from letter sequence 132–36 (pp. 157–62).

a non-necessary universe, and to allow God meaningful scope for choice in his government.[46] Hence, we find the Reverend Samuel Clarke evoking an image of the universe *sub specie aeternitatis*, not as a fixed chain of events, but as a vast labyrinth of potentiality very much resembling Harriet's paradigmatic dream and, ultimately, *Grandison* itself. God's view, he tells us, encompasses "all the possible compositions and divisions, variations and changes, circumstances and dependencies of things; all their possible relations one to another, and Dispositions of Fitness to certain respective Ends."[47]

Divine liberty, however, necessitates human uncertainty. Indeed, a certain degree of anxiety was considered psychologically normal, spiritually healthy, and even ethically essential in a providential universe. Sherlock points out that if providence were predictable, it would nullify the significance of moral choice: to choose good would be to choose happiness—"but where the event is not certain there is room left for wise considerations, for hopes and fears which are the natural springs of a free choice."[48] Excessive or obsessive anxiety, however, became an insult to providence, and the divines warned against it, centring their injunctions on the biblical text "Sufficient to the day is the evil thereof" (Matt. 6:34), as in the following excerpt from a sermon by Isaac Barrow:

this is that which our Saviour cautioneth against, as the root of discontent and sign of diffidence: *Take no thought for the morrow, for the morrow shall take thought for the things of itself: sufficient to the day is the evil thereof.* ... Could we follow this advice, never resenting evils before they come, never prejudging about future events against God's providence and our own quiet.[49]

That Richardson piously subscribed to this homiletic advice is apparent from its frequent recurrence within his novels. In the continuation of *Pamela* old Mr Andrews reproaches his apprehensive

---

46 For a lengthier discussion of this development in Anglican polemics, see Lois A. Chaber, "'This Intricate Labyrinth': Order and Contingency in Eighteenth-Century Fictions," *Studies on Voltaire and the Eighteenth Century* 212 (1982), 188–92.

47 Samuel Clarke, *A Demonstration of the Being and Attributes of God, 1705, and a Discourse Concerning the Unchangeable Obligations of Natural Religion and the Truth and Certainty of the Christian Revelation* (Stuttgart–Bad Cannstatt: F. Frommann, 1964), p. 233.

48 Sherlock, pp. 98–99.

49 Barrow, "Contentment," *Sermons*, 1:382.

daughter with that very biblical text just before her first trip to London with Mr B.,[50] and in *Grandison,* just after Sir Charles's proposal of marriage, Harriet is both her own tempter and rebuker: "May nothing now happen, my dear Lady G. to overcloud—But I will not be apprehensive. I will thankfully enjoy the present moment, and leave the future to the All-wise Disposer of events" (3:80). And yet another anxiety attack of Harriet's, this time over Greville's threats to Sir Charles, is parried by Charlotte's dismissive rebuke, "*Sufficient to the day,* and-so-forth" (3:195).

Another instance in *Grandison,* however, vividly illustrates how Richardsonian technique subverts Richardsonian doctrine, transmuting it into a more profound and disquieting insight. In a passage that calls attention to the hypothetical evils we have been discussing, Richardson demonstrates the inevitability of human *angst,* despite the ecclesiastical remonstrances against it, by means of an exaggerated and extraordinarily self-conscious version of his "writing to the moment" almost worthy of *Shamela.* Richardson's most typical "writing to the moment" actually consists of successive accounts of events in the recent past, highly coloured by current hopes and fears. In the scene under discussion, however, Richardson breaks normal procedure and allows Charlotte to travesty his method by describing an event in a letter written concurrently with the event itself as it unfolds. Charlotte has just been writing a letter to Harriet in which she perversely encourages her friend's apprehensions about Clementina's "resolution," when her sister, Lady L., intrudes. The mischievous and sceptical Charlotte communicates, in her own erratic epistolary manner, the subsequent efforts of her pious sister to insert that same biblical injunction into the text of Charlotte's letter:

But here she comes.—I love, Harriet, to write to the moment; that's a knack
    I had from you and my brother. ...
I will read your Letter—Shall I? says Lady L.
Take it; but read it out, that I may know what I have written. Now give it me
    again, I'll write down what you say to it, Lady L.
Lady L. I say you are a whimsical creature. But I don't like what you have
    last written.
Charlotte. Last written—'Tis down.—But why so, Lady L?

50 *Pamela,* Shakespeare Head edition, 3:151.

Lady L. How can you thus teaze our beloved Byron, with your conjectural evils?
Charlotte. Have I supposed an impossibility?—But 'tis down—*Conjectural evils.*
Lady L. If you are so whimsical, write—'My dear Miss Byron'—
Charlotte. My dear Miss Byron—'Tis down.
Lady L. (Looking over me) 'Do not let what this strange Charlotte has written, grieve you:—
Charlotte. Very well, Caroline!—*grieve you.*—
Lady L. 'Sufficient to the day is the evil thereof.'
Charlotte. Well observed.—Words of Scripture, I believe.—Well—*evil thereof.* (3:24–25)

The struggles of Lady L.—we may as well say of Richardson—prove futile, because, although Lady L. eventually has the final word in the encounter—"Regard not the perplexing Charlotte" (3:26)—we cannot help *but* regard her because it is Charlotte who is writing those words and who has made the technique of the passage run counter to Lady L.'s advice. The biblical message—"regard the present only"—is negated by the time taken to deliver it, here exaggerated by Charlotte but actually true of all verbal communication. The injunction about living only in the present has itself been made to depend on futurity; an exhortation to suspend thought ("*Take no thought.* ...") has been evoked within the ongoing process of discourse and of time itself.[51]

Grandison's unresolved ending, in which Clementina's marriage to her long-suffering suitor Count Belvedere is left dangling as a future possibility, is surely appropriate to a novel whose text discloses the permanent insecurity bred of humanity's existence within this temporality, and is as philosophically justifiable as "the conclusionlessness of *Rasselas, Tristram,* and *Caleb*" and the other problematic endings that characterize Rothstein's group of later eighteenth-century narratives.[52] Indeed, on this one point at least I must disagree with Jocelyn Harris, who finds the looseness of *Grandison*'s

51 Although John Preston, in *The Created Self: The Reader's Role in Eighteenth-Century Fiction* (New York: Barnes and Noble, 1970), calls Richardson's epistolary form "a literature of the 'now'" (p. 52), Janet Altman, in *Epistolarity: Approaches to a Form* (Columbus: Ohio State University Press, 1982), more accurately observes that "the present of epistolary discourse is vibrant with future orientation" (p. 124).

52 Rothstein, p. 260; see also pp. 8, 58, 240–41, 259, *et passim.*

ending adventitious and distressing to "the tidy-minded reader."[53] Her judgment rests in part on the assumption that Richardson at his best provides us with a tight, inevitable plot, but Warner and McKee have challenged this notion by arguing the essential arbitrariness and contingency of the narrative in *Clarissa* and *Pamela*, respectively.[54] In fact Warner's debunking of the traditional Aristotelian plot with its necessary causality provides a clue to the valid thematic function of *Grandison*'s "untidy" ending: "'plot' overcomes ... doubts about the past and anxiety over the future."[55] We have already seen how Richardson suggests the non-necessary, gratuitous nature of the providential events in *Grandison* through his use of *alter egos* and of the subjunctive, and we may further infer his implicit concurrence with Warner's criticism of the delusive complacency of "plot" from a comment on the human condition made by Clarissa, writing to her godmother, Mrs Norton:

It will be a great satisfaction to me to hear ... that my foster-brother is out of danger. But why said I, *out of danger?* When can *this* be justly said of creatures who hold by so uncertain a tenure? This is one of those forms of common speech that proves the *frailty* and the *presumption* of poor mortals at the same time. (p. 1121)

It is precisely such human "presumption" that Clementina punctures at the end of *Grandison* when she chides the over-jubilant Belvedere after she has made a contract with her parents containing what Harris calls a "near-commitment" to marrying him:[56] "I mentioned, my

---

53 Jocelyn Harris, "The Reviser Observed: The Last Volume of *Sir Charles Grandison*," *Studies in Bibliography* 29 (1976), 1, 10, 25. We are indebted to Harris in this article as well as to Peter Sabor, "Richardson and His Readers," *Humanities Association Review* 30 (1979), 161–73, for shattering the myth that Richardson was impervious to his correspondents' critical suggestions, but the aesthetic value of such revisions—as well as their origin in some instances—would seem to be open to debate, as indicated by the diverging opinions of Harris, "A Note on the Text," in her edition of *Sir Charles Grandison*, 1:xxvii—xxxvii, and Robert Craig Pierson, "The Revisions of *Sir Charles Grandison*," *Studies in Bibliography* 21 (1968), 164–89, about many of the same minor revisions of the text (see, for example, Harris, "Note," p. xxxii, and Pierson, 171).

54 Warner, *Reading "Clarissa,"* pp. 77, 83–87, 105–6, and "Reading Rape," pp. 26–27; McKee, pp. 55, 74–75.

55 Warner, *Reading "Clarissa,"* p. 218.

56 Harris, "Reviser Observed," p. 25.

lord, that it was for *your own* sake, that I wished you not to depend upon a contingency" (3:452).

Harris's severe judgment is influenced by what she perceives as the aetiology of *Grandison*'s open ending—Richardson's indecision and his susceptibility to criticism, leading to hasty, compromised revising. Her chief evidence is Richardson's various epistolary proposals to Lady Bradshaigh for the "Catastrophe" of the novel; however, the rhetorical question she poses—"But why should he offer her such a range of alternatives if he had indeed decided upon every detail of the conclusion?"[57]—can be answered differently by comparing these proposals to the rhetorical and psychological patterns I have been tracing in the novel. The iconoclastic criticism of *Clarissa* once again sets a precedent, in this case, for rejecting a strict boundary between what is "inside" and what is "outside" the novel and for reading Richardson's correspondence, in particular, as an extension and a replication of his fiction.[58]

In his exchange of letters with Lady Bradshaigh, Richardson's employment of the past perfect subjunctive links him with his own speculating characters in *Grandison*: "But had Clementina been the Wife of Sir Charles, and Harriet had broke her Heart, who would not then have pitied, and even preferred her?"[59] Richardson's earlier teasing of Hester Mulso also corresponds to the subjunctive technique of the novel:

Think you not that Harriet can shine by her behaviour in some very deep distress? ... Would it not be right to remove him [Sir Charles]?—But shall we first marry him?—Shall we shew Harriet ... in her vidual glory?—Mother of a posthumous—son, or daughter?—Which— ... The case too, so common? Or shall we remove him by a violent fever—or by the treacherous sword of Greville. ... On the very day of the nuptials?— ... or the day before?— Which?[60]

57 Harris, "Reviser Observed," pp. 1, 3, 20–27.

58 See especially Warner, *Reading "Clarissa,"* pp. ix, 77, 144–80; Castle, pp. 16, 138, 182; Eagleton, pp. 11–13. Also relevant are the parallels drawn by Flynn in her chapter "A Man of Letters: The Private Letter in Life and Art," *Samuel Richardson*, pp. 263–89. The general predisposition for a continuum between "the fictional" and "the real, historical world" in epistolary narrative is discussed by Altman, p. 111.

59 8 Feb. 1754, *Selected Letters*, p. 276.

60 20 June 1752, *Selected Letters*, p. 216.

Here we find the same forking of alternatives within alternatives—son or daughter, married or unmarried, the day of the wedding or the day before—as well as the insistence on the plausibility of tragedy—"the case too, so common." Harris believes that Richardson was genuinely considering endings more sensational than the one we have now and gave them up only because Lady Bradshaigh did not take the bait,[61] but we can see that the sensational alternatives in the example above more precisely echo the "conjectural evils" which hover perpetually over the characters of *Grandison.* Moreover, in a later letter to Lady Bradshaigh, Richardson explicitly connects his "suggestion" of a childbed death for Harriet with his heroine's apprehensive nightmare in the novel—"Harriet's Dream admirably made out in the flitting Ghost-like Duration of her Nuptials"[62]—reinforcing my contention that Richardson's gambits in the correspondence are links to the anxiety mechanisms of *Grandison,* not serious proposals for a conventional plot.

Finally, it is most revealing to examine the self-portrait that emerges in yet another letter to the same lady, when Richardson sets out to prove that it is within his literary power to bring about a proposal of polygamy, the idea of which has shocked Lady Bradshaigh:

But how will you bring Clementina, her Friends, &c.—How!—Let me alone for that. Cannot the Marquis and the Marchioness opportunely die? ... Cannot a wound of Jeronymo's ... break out, and kill him? Cannot I make the Bishop a Cardinal, or Archbishop may do, and send him on a Mission to China. ... Cannot the fierce General be killed in a Duel, or suffocated by the sudden Change of Wind, in going too near Vesuvius ..? And cannot they all bequeath her to the Care of the Chevalier. ... And then comes Harriet with her Proposal. ... If I resolve, never fear but I make it probable, and glorious for both Ladies.[63]

Is this not Richardson the artist playing providence to his nescient and passive audience, asserting his arbitrary and omnipotent will? In fact, may we not compare the whole play of possibilities sketched by Richardson for his various correspondents as a simulacrum of "all

61 Harris, "Reviser Observed," pp. 12–14.

62 8 Feb. 1754, *Selected Letters*, p. 278.

63 8 Dec. 1753, *Selected Letters*, p. 253.

the compositions and divisions, variations and changes" suspended by Samuel Clarke's God in His synoptic vision of life? Richardson's circle of sensitive souls, then, like Sir Charles Grandison's, was elected to remain in a constant state of deferential anxiety.

I have argued that a certain amount of anxiety is inherent in an orthodox providential world-view, but this anxiety is exacerbated by the disturbing new individualism which was finding ambivalent expression in the novels of the period,[64] and of which the widespread criminal aggression I have noted in *Grandison* is just one symptom. For Richardson, society was impotent to resolve these new tensions. His career did not reach into the subsequent historical period in which Evangelicism sparked off a new faith in the possibilities of a social reform which could ameliorate life on earth for the individual; yet the quietistic opinions of an earlier age that Richardson's characters frequently express do not really ring true in the novel either. Rather, *Grandison* as a whole resounds more plangently with an obsessive anxiety emerging from the conflict between the conscious desire to submit piously to a cosmic plan and the burgeoning sense of self which cannot help but be concerned with the individual's fate in this life.

64 See J. Paul Hunter, "The Loneliness of the Long-Distance Reader," *Genre* 10 (1977), 455–84; Eagleton, pp. 3–4, 16; Damrosch, pp. 4, 13, 16–22, 27, 39, 257, *et passim*. The "affective individualism," described by Lawrence Stone, *The Family, Sex, and Marriage in England 1500–1800* (London: Weidenfeld and Nicolson, 1977), pp. 221–69, moreover, is specifically linked to Richardson's novels by Hagstrum (p. 216) and by Stone himself (p. 228). Cf McKee, however, for an explicit challenge to the importance of individualism in Richardson's novels, pp. 51–52, 66, 128–30, *et passim*.

The Dialectic of Love
in *Sir Charles Grandison*

Wendy Jones

Samuel Richardson's *Sir Charles Grandison* is structured around an event that seems to defy both the novel's insistent and pervasive moralistic tone and its characterization of Sir Charles as a moral paragon: Sir Charles is in love with two women at the same time. Love for more than one woman is precisely the quality that distinguishes the rake, the kind of man Sir Charles himself excoriates. How can the exemplar of English integrity, who is not merely another worthy hero but a "vision of Christ as a realistic eighteenth-century gentleman,"[1] be involved in what he himself rightly defines as a "divided or double Love"?[2] Why is this paradox necessary for Richardson?

Sir Charles suffers a divided love because Richardson wants to endorse competing and contradictory cultural ideals: what writers have called "companionate" and "sentimental" love.[3] English society's endorsement of married love generated a dialectic: a tripartite dynamic

---

1 Jocelyn Harris, *Samuel Richardson* (Cambridge: Cambridge University Press, 1987), p. 140. "The Dialectic of Love in *Sir Charles Grandison*" was first published in *Eighteenth-Century Fiction* 8:1 (1995), 15–34.

2 Samuel Richardson, *The History of Sir Charles Grandison*, ed. Jocelyn Harris, 3 vols (London: Oxford University Press, 1972), 3:76. References are to this edition.

3 See Lawrence Stone, *The Family, Sex and Marriage in England, 1500–1800* (New York: Harper and Row, 1977), esp. chap. 8; Jean H. Hagstrum, *Sex and Sensibility: Ideal and Erotic Love from Milton to Mozart* (Chicago: University of Chicago Press, 1980), p. 162 and chap. 7; and Erica Harth, "The Virtue of Love: Lord Hardwicke's Marriage Act," *Cultural Critique* 9 (1988), 123–54. I use these terms anachronistically to describe eighteenth-century modes of feeling on the assumption that the categories they describe were cultural ideals even if

of ideologies, motivated largely by class interests.[4] Companionate
love, espoused primarily by the middle classes, arose in response to
the need for a rational basis for married love. Comprising prudence
and judgment, it provided a suitable alternative to blindly impuls-
ive romantic attraction and pure physical desire, both associated
with the aristocracy. But this category was itself subsumed by "sentimental love," a dialectical resolution of reason and passion, which
also became an acceptable basis for marriage. This dialectic, which
Grandison represents, facilitated an alliance between the aristocracy
(identified with the landed interest) and the middle classes (identified with the moneyed interest). Such multiple origins and interests
give rise to conflicts within what can be called the ideology of love.[5]

contemporaries did not specifically identify them as such. Indeed, naturalized ideological
categories are frequently nameless to those who experience them.

4 I follow Michael McKeon in my use of the term "dialectic." See *Origins of the English Novel,
1600–1740* (Baltimore: Johns Hopkins University Press, 1987). McKeon's analysis and my
own bring up the vexed issue of whether we can talk about "class" in the eighteenth century, and if so, whether we can talk about a generalized middle class. On this subject, see
R.S. Neale, *Class in English History, 1600–1850* (Oxford: Basil Blackwell, 1981); W.A. Speck,
Society and Literature in England, 1700–1760 (Dublin: Gill and Macmillan, 1983), pp. 42–45;
and E.P. Thompson, "Eighteenth-Century English Society: Class Struggle without Class?"
Social History 3 (1978), 133–65. I use the term "class" to designate different hierarchical social groups, whose boundaries were not always clearly demarcated (e.g., the gentry and
professionals confused the boundaries between the upper and middle classes). Contemporaries saw their society as divided into social groups. For instance, Robinson Crusoe
speaks of a "middle station" between the "higher or lower Part of Mankind." Daniel Defoe,
Robinson Crusoe, ed.J. Donald Crowley (London and New York: Oxford University Press,
1972), p. 4.

5 This view assumes that ideology is a system of perceptions inextricable from and mutu-
ally generative with material and institutional aspects of culture and society. Literary critics
have often missed the complex and interactive nature of eighteenth-century ideals of love.
Some assume that love is a homogeneous phenomenon: O.J. Cockshut, *Man and Woman:
A Study of Love and the Novel, 1740–1940* (Oxford: Oxford University Press, 1977); Alan
Macfarlane, *Marriage and Love in England: Modes of Reproduction, 1300–1840* (Oxford: Basil
Blackwell, 1986). Those who acknowledge that there are "different sorts of [heterosexual]
Love," as the novel's heroine Harriet Byron says (3:302), overlook either the variety of
these "sorts" or the cultural forces which give rise to this variety: Stone discusses the categories of romantic and companionate love but does not recognize their crucial synthesis
in sentimental love (pp. 217–53); Joseph Allen Boone also neglects this category, viewing *romantic* love as the motive for *companionate* marriage. *Tradition Counter Tradition: Love
and the Form of Fiction* (Chicago: Chicago University Press, 1987); Hagstrum shows how sentimental love includes both passion and friendship, but then does not account for the
historical and ideological factors that generate these categories (pp. 160–85); Harth as-
tutely historicizes sentimental love, but neglects companionate love, which serves a crucial

The formal features of novels often provide an especially legible and self-conscious exploration of this ideology, while the artifice of plotting serves to resolve contradictions at the level of form that re-emerge when such categories are seen outside the mechanism of narrrative. *Grandison*'s double plot bisects the novel along the lines of Sir Charles's divided love; this legitimates and hierarchizes "different sorts of Love" (3:302) at the same time as the resolution of the plot masks the paradoxes inherent in such difference.[6]

The Rise of Married Love

The diversification of "sorts of love" is linked to the rise of the love-match. The Restoration and eighteenth century saw the emergence of the ethical imperative to marry for love.[7] The necessary linking of love and marriage was popularized by the Puritans, and found its

function within the very terms of class analysis which underpin her discussion.

6 Jocelyn Harris observes that Richardson introduced Clementina, and hence Sir Charles's double love, "to solve the problem of story" in *Grandison*, which was somewhat stalled after Harriet's kidnapping and rescue. Richardson later made revisions in the seventh volume to placate readers who were uneasy about double heroines and a double love (as he promised Lady Bradshaigh he would do). See Harris's introduction (pp. ix, xii) and her article "The Reviser Observed: The Last Volume of *Sir Charles Grandison*," *Studies in Bibliography* 29 (1976), 1–31. This complex novel yields more than one explanation, however, for Sir Charles's double love. The didactic character of *Grandison*, as well as Richardson's method of composition—the pattern of maxim, illustrative scene, and commentary (Harris, "Introduction," p. ix)—accords with the view that Richardson, having established an ideal type of love in the story of Sir Charles and Harriet, then went on to distinguish it from the next best alternative (companionate love), while using minor characters and subplots to make further distinctions among the varieties of love and attraction. Margaret Anne Doody offers a different but compatible explanation to account for Sir Charles's double love, which "serves to articulate the balance between the aesthetic and moral imperatives of stablity and variety. ... The principle of varying multiples [such as two loves] ... encourages the belief that the goodness valued by society can be maintained without sacrifice to oppressive conformity." "Identity and Character in *Sir Charles Grandison*," *Samuel Richardson: Tercentenary Essays*, ed. Margaret Anne Doody and Peter Sabor (Cambridge: Cambridge University Press, 1989), p. 126.

7 Lawrence Stone's argument for an epistemic shift in attitudes towards marriage has been widely accepted, even by scholars who disagree with his conclusions. See, for example, Harth, and Susan Moller Okin, "Patriarchy and Married Women's Property in England: Questions on Some Current Views," *Eighteenth-Century Studies* 17 (Winter 1983–84), 121–38.

most famous expression in Milton's writings.[8] But it became widely accepted in the course of the eighteenth century, especially among the middle classes. The affirmation of love as a basis for marriage was not new, of course, as the numerous happy weddings that conclude Shakespeare's comedies demonstrate. But before this time, the love-match had been viewed as a desirable but inessential option. The "promise to love" of the wedding ceremony is a literal promise, a declaration made to another person with respect to the future. What is lacking in literature before this period, and what we begin to see thereafter, is an insistence on premarital love. Evidence of this shift in *attitude*, if not in practice, can be found both in representational literature such as plays (especially Restoration comedy), novels (those of Fielding, Austen, and many others), and in conduct-books;[9] such works repeatedly advocate the love-match while criticizing, both explicitly and implicitly, the forced or interested marriage.

The ideal of married love was linked to class interests and politics. Marriage for love was in part the result of what can be called reciprocal hegemony between the traditional upper classes (aristocracy and gentry) and a newer middle-class élite, which had emerged

8 See, for instance, the famous apostrophe to wedded love in *Paradise Lost* (book 4, lines 750–75) and "The Doctrine and Discipline of Divorce," *Complete Prose Works of John Milton*, vol. 2, ed. Ernest Sirluck (New Haven: Yale University Press and Oxford: Oxford University Press, 1959), p. 235. and *passim*. On the rise of married love as a Puritan ideal see William and Maleville Haller, "The Puritan Art of Love," *Huntington Library Quarterly* 5 (1941–42), 235–72. Kathleen M. Davies, in "The Sacred Condition of Equality—How Original Were Puritan Doctrines of Marriage?," *Social History* 5 (1977), 663–80, denies that new ideas about marriage were Puritan, associating them instead with the bourgeoisie (but for overlap between these two groups see J.R. Gillis, *For Better, For Worse: British Marriage 1600 to the Present* (Oxford: Oxford University Press, 1985), p. 105. Margo Todd argues that marital love had been forcefully advocated by Renaissance humanists, especially Erasmus, *Christian Humanism and the Puritan Social Order* (Cambridge: Cambridge University Press, 1987). While marital love might not have been the invention or intellectual property of the Puritans, they arguably had the widest influence on novelists, via Milton's appropriation of some aspects of Puritan doctrine. For the relationship between Puritan ideals of marriage and *Clarissa*, see Rita Goldberg, *Sex and Enlightenment: Women in Richardson and Diderot* (Cambridge: Cambridge University Press, 1984), esp. chap. 1; and Christopher Hill, "Clarissa Harlowe and Her Times," *Essays in Criticism* 5 (1955), 315–40.

9 See, for instance, Daniel Defoe, *Conjugal Lewdness; or, Matrimonial Whoredom. A Treatise concerning the Use and Abuse of the Marriage Bed* (1727; Florida: Scholars' Facsimiles and Reprints, 1967), p. 101; and Richard Allestree, *The Ladies Calling. In Two Parts* (1673), part 2, p. 20.

in the course of the seventeenth century.[10] The latter consisted of members of respectable professions such as the military and the law, succcessful traders and bankers, wealthy agrarian capitalists, and men engaged in mining and other investments. While this newer élite did not directly pursue political power, their implicit challenge to the feudal triad of status, wealth, and leadership initiated an alliance between themselves and the traditional upper classes. The aristocracy and gentry continued to wield political power, but the middle classes gained ideological power that buttressed their economic gains. Middle-class values altered aristocratic values, but the outer trappings of gentility—its manners and way of life—still defined success and the good life. Sir Charles Grandison, a very "bourgeois" gentleman in aristocratic clothing, is emblematic of this process.[11]

The foundation of the middle-class recoding of aristocratic values is an appeal to Christian virtue. The reformation of the concept of "honour," carried out most famously in Richard Steele's *The Christian Hero*, various *Spectator* and *Tatler* papers (*Spectator* 356, 516; *Tatler* 25), and, of course, Richardson's novels, is a case in point. Aristocratic honour is based on an heroic, martial ethos that endorses bravery, aggression, and pride. Middle-class honour depends on an alternative form of heroism which, as Sir Charles observes, "Christianity enjoins," and which "recommends meekness, moderation, and humility, as the glory of the human nature" (1:263). Throughout

10 This concept relies on Antonio Gramsci's account of hegemony as rule by consent in *Selections from the Prison Notebooks*, ed. and trans. Quintin Hoare and Geoffrey Nowell Smith (New York: International Publishers, 1971), pp. 5–23 and on Terry Eagleton's application of this concept to eighteenth-century studies. See his *Rape of Clarissa* (Minneapolis: University of Minnesota Press, 1982), pp. 1–5; *The Function of Criticism from "The Spectator" to Post-Structuralism* (London: Verso, 1984), pp. 9–27; and *The Ideology of the Aesthetic* (Oxford: Basil Blackwell, 1990), pp. 31–33.

11 That middle-class hegemony depends on the revision of aristocratic codes and values is a fundamental claim of Nancy Armstrong, *Desire and Domestic Fiction: A Political History of the Novel* (Oxford: Oxford University Press, 1987), and of Michael McKeon. On the middle-class appropriation of aristocratic customs, see Lawrence Stone and Jeanne C. Fawtier Stone, *An Open Elite? England 1540–1880* (Oxford: Oxford University Press, 1984), p. 409. On Sir Charles's relation to "an older aristocratic tradition" see Sylvia Kasey Marks, *Sir Charles Grandison: The Compleat Conduct Book* (Lewisburg: Bucknell University Press, 1986), p. 70.

Grandison, Sir Charles undermines and "rewrites" aristocratic honour by performing spectacular feats of bravery and prowess, often under circumstances befitting a hero of romance, but always in the service of a middle-class code of Christian virtue.[12]

Marriage for love is also a central instance of this process of redefinition. The love-match opposed an aristocratic practice, the marriage of interest, which dictated that marriage be arranged by parents, kin, and family friends in order to further the social, political, or economic interests of a family. Middle-class moralists thought that marriage should be based on the Christian ethic of love, rather than the worldly criteria of wealth and status. While they did not aver that love was the only important factor in the marriage choice, it was in their view the *sine qua non* of marriage. Without love, the marriage was not a true union in the eyes of God. "Political views may make a marriage," writes Defoe, "but, in the sense of God and Nature, 'tis my Opinion they make no Matrimony."[13] The wide acceptance of the love-match thus represented a triumph of middle-class virtues and values.

Crucially important issues of class mobility also contributed to the rise of the marriage for love. Marriage was an obvious means by which to circulate England's new capitalist wealth, thereby rejuvenating the fortunes of the upper classes and incorporating the newly wealthy into England's ruling élite. This was recognized by contemporaries, as Erica Harth demonstrates in her discussion of the debates over Lord Hardwicke's Marriage Act of 1753, which outlawed most types of clandestine marriage and hence made marriage without parental approval more difficult.[14] Yet despite the wide-

12 Nancy Armstrong calls this ethical Christian ideal a "domestic" ideal. *Desire and Domestic Fiction* (Oxford: Oxford University Press, 1987). I use a different terminology to suit a different emphasis: "virtue" rather than domesticity is often the key term in contemporary discussions of class mobility and interclass marriage, the issues with which I am most concerned in this essay. The ethical qualities I am discussing, however, certainly comprise the domestic, which becomes increasingly important throughout the eighteenth and nineteenth centuries. On Richardson's use of romance conventions, see Harris, *Samuel Richardson,* pp. 162–63; Margaret Anne Doody, *A Natural Passion* (Oxford: Clarendon Press, 1964), p. 294n1; and Carol Houlihan Flynn, *Samuel Richardson: A Man of Letters* (Princeton: Princeton University Press, 1982), p. 100.

13 Defoe, *Conjugal Lewdness,* p. 103.

14 Harth; see also Christopher Lasch, "The Suppression of Clandestine Marriage in England: The Marriage Act of 1753," *Salamagundi* 26 (1974), 90–109.

spread belief in and endorsement of a limited form of class inter-marriage (between the upper classes and the élite of the middling ranks), the purely utilitarian marriage of wealth and status was unacceptable, at least in theory, to élites of both groups. Love emerged as the the only acceptable motive for marriages across class boundaries for several reasons.

Wealth had always been an important consideration in the marriage of interest. Indeed, the wealth of the moneyed interest would have been especially attractive to the upper classes at this time, since the practice of strict settlement forced heads of families to keep their estates intact, while also providing portions for their younger children and maintaining the lavish standard of living that signified their power.[15] Yet status was as important a consideration as money in upper-class marriage. For even though the marriage of interest continued to hold sway in aristocratic circles through the eighteenth and nineteenth centuries, the upper classes never sanctioned what might look to us like its close cousin, the mercenary marriage. Because the status barriers to powerful social circles ensured upper-class political sovereignty, it was not to this group's advantage to accept misalliance as a common practice; to do so would have been tantamount to legitimating social mobility. Furthermore, condoning the purely mercenary marriage would have involved overtly endorsing the values of the marketplace, scorned by this social group, despite their real participation in market practices. It was in contradistinction to such values that they distinguished their own sort of wealth from that of the moneyed interest. But if love were the basis of interclass marriage, it could function as the exception that proved the rule of stable class boundaries. Of course, the middle classes condemned loveless marriage on ethical grounds. In addition, they could not appear willing to barter wealth for status, for it was precisely such a desire, characterized as both offensive social climbing and an undignified interest in getting a bargain, for which they had been traditionally satirized. Only love could provide a proper motive

15 H.J. Habakkuk, "Marriage Settlements in the Eighteenth Century," *Transactions of the Royal Historical Society*, 4th series 32 (1950), 15–30.

for socially and economically advantageous marriages. But "love," for both groups, had to be love of the proper kind.

"A Voluntary Passion"

Before about the middle of the seventeenth century, love had been represented as either physical desire or romantic passion. Neither was a suitable motive for marriage. Following a well-established tradition in Christian thought, physical desire, often linked to male libertinism, was deemed immoral. Romantic love, generally associated with seventeenth-century French romances and their English imitations, could lead both to unhappiness by inspiring unrealistic expectations, and to morally questionable behaviour such as elopement. With the rise of married love other affective ideals more appropriate to marriage emerged: marital companionship, or "companionate love," and the blend of reason and passion that can be called "sentimental love." While these categories were inchoate rather than fixed, and varying degrees of friendship, passion, and folly are represented throughout the period, there was nevertheless a pronounced tendency within various traditions and genres to make distinctions of this kind. Most influential of all, Milton's depiction of fallen and unfallen love in *Paradise Lost* contrasts salacious desire or lust with pure desire or love "founded in reason, loyal, just, and pure."[16] French romances, which Richardson appropriated to his own ends, abound in discussions about the many forms and nuances of love, distinctions which are epitomized in Mlle de Scudéry's famous allegorical map, "La Carte de la Tendre."[17]

16 *Paradise Lost*, book 4, line 755. Although representations of sentimental love became prevalent in the novel, the concept of a reasonable passion, like married love itself, was influenced by Puritan thought. It is significant that Clementina falls in love with Sir Charles while he is tutoring her in English by reading *Paradise Lost*; such Edenic love is precisely the ideal embodied by sentimental love, which Clementina, like Harriet, feels for Sir Charles. On Miltonic ideals of love see Hagstrum, chap. 2 and James Grantham Turner, *One Flesh: Paradisal Marriage and Sexual Relations in the Age of Milton* (Oxford: Clarendon Press, 1993), esp. chaps 6 and 7. For Miltonic overtones in *Grandison*, see Harris, *Samuel Richardson*, chap. 8.

17 James S. Munro claims that Mlle de Scudéry's map was widely misinterpreted in her own time as an intellectual exercise in gallantry. On the contrary, Scudéry's writings about love serve to point out serious moral distinctions. She repeatedly distinguishes the "pays de

Richardson was preoccupied with the notion that tender passion took different forms. In a letter to Hester Mulso, likely written when he was beginning to compose *Grandison,* he plays the devil's advocate, refusing initially to agree with Mulso that love can be considered "noble" because in most instances it is an irresponsible and destructive passion, "a Moloch deity, which requires duty, discretion, all that is most valuable, to be sacrificed to it."[18] Friendship rather than love deserves the "epithet" because "Sense may predominate in the one [friendship]; it cannot in the other [love]" (p. 193). But by the last part of the letter, Richardson admits that there is a kind of love that embraces both passion and friendship: "Those will be found to be the most noble friendships which either flame between persons of the same sex; or *where the dross of passion is thrown out, and the ore purified by the union of minds in matrimony*" (p. 193, emphasis added). Passion remains but has been purified by reason, "the union of minds."

Not only does Richardson make distinctions among kinds of love, but he is also insistent on the need for such distinctions. He is "not willing that love, *indiscriminately taken,* should be called noble"; he "will not, *without discussion, without examination,* allow it an equal claim" with friendship (p. 193, emphasis added). It is just such discussion, examination, discrimination that gives his last sprawling novel direction. Love was of course Richardson's great subject, and he had been attentive to its various guises in his earlier works. In their simplest sense, both *Pamela* and *Clarissa* are about the differences between pure and base desire, wise and foolish love. But *Grandison* is Richardson's most crystalline and categorical expression of such differences, a novel in which making distinctions is itself a primary theme. And if Richardson's letter reveals the direction of his thought at this time, it also hints at the dialectic which

Tendre" from the "pays d'Amour" and characterizes "tendresse," which depends on sympathetic identification with another—or sensibility—as "the overriding aim of love as well as friendship." *Mademoiselle de Scudéry and the Carte de Tendre* (Durham: Durham University Press, 1986), pp. 86–87.

18 *Selected Letters of Samuel Richardson,* ed. John Carroll (Oxford: Clarendon Press, 1964), letter dated 30 September 1751, p. 192. References are to this edition. Harris notes that Lady Bradshaigh seems to have been the first to learn towards the end of 1749 of Richardson's plan to write about a good man, and that Colley Cibber had seen the portion of the manuscript which describes Harriet's abduction as of May 1750 ("Introduction," p. viii).

emerges from *Grandison*'s narrative. He writes, citing Miss Mulso, "'Cannot all the natural and right affections of the heart, ask you, subsist together?' They can. 'Must one absorb and swallow up the rest?' It often does in the greenwood-love I have been mentioning [i.e. passion]" (p. 193). In *Grandison*'s exploration of "different sorts of Love," one does indeed absorb and swallow the rest.

Echoing sentiments similar to those in the letter, *Grandison*'s criticism of romantic love and the romances which enshrine it finds direct and polemical expression in the views of Mrs Shirley, Harriet's grandmother and *Grandison*'s female sage. She regrets that, in her youth, she was "over-run with the absurdities of that unnatural kind of writing" (romance), from which she derived "very high ideas of first impressions; of eternal constancy; of Love raised to a pitch of idolatry" (3:398). Because of these "romantic notions," she almost rejected her suitor Mr Shirley's offer of marriage, despite the fact that he was "a good sort of man; a sensible man" whose "character was faultless." "But what was a good sort of man to an Oroondates?" she asked, referring to the hero of La Calprenède's *Cassandra* (3:398). Moreover, she feared that if she married Mr Shirley, she might later fall in love with someone else, "the kindred soul, who must irresistably claim my whole heart" (3:399), as does the main character in Mme de La Fayette's *La Princesse de Clèves*, a book she owns and admires (3:400). Mrs Shirley's youthful misconceptions give a comprehensive list of the conventions of romantic love: it is involuntary and always strikes the lover at first sight; it is passionate (that is, sexual) and fixated on one object, since a second love is impossible; and it inspires the male lover with courage and daring. It is important to keep these conventions in mind when looking at the ways in which *Grandison* and other novels revise romantic love.

If passion is unacceptable because it encourages vice and folly, it is also dangerous because it cannot guarantee socially or economically desirable marriages. If legitimated as grounds for marriage, lust and romantic love—both based ostensibly on pure and spontaneous feeling—threaten to destabilize society through a plethora of socially unacceptable marriages. As Sir Charles's sister Charlotte says, "If Love be not a voluntary passion, why not [fix her affections] upon a hostler, a groom, a coachman, a footman—A grenadier, a trooper, a foot-soldier?" (3:405). Companionate love provides an alternative.

Mrs Shirley's account of her mistaken notions gives her the opportunity to define companionate love, which the novel overtly endorses. An excellent pedagogue, she makes her point with an anecdote, telling how, when she was the girlish Henrietta rather than the venerable Mrs Shirley, her good friend Mrs Eggleton cured her of her romantic notions by urging her to accept Mr Shirley's proposal even though she was not passionately in love: "Esteem, heightened by Gratitude, and enforced by Duty ... will soon ripen into Love: The only sort of Love that suits this imperfect state; a *tender*, a *faithful*, affection" (3:398). She denies the legitimacy of her young friend's romantic notions, arguing that "The passions are intended for our servants, not our masters" (3:399).[19] In her view, practical motives are not to be ignored when choosing a husband—Henrietta is "one of many Sisters" (3:398)—although, of course, the primary consideration should not be economic. That Henrietta does not dislike Mr Shirley, together with the fact that he is a "worthy man," is enough to constitute a preference. Mrs Eggleton concludes, "I would not by any means ... have you marry a man for whom you have not a preferable inclination; but why may you not find, on admitting Mr. Shirley's addresses, young, agreeable, worthy, and every way suitable to you, as *he* is, that he is that man whom your inclination can approve?" (3:399).

Although a "preference" is necessary in "the most important article of life," this preference can be generated at will, as Mrs Eggleton's locution "whom your inclination can approve" suggests. The unusual use of the word "inclination" as the active agent of the clause enacts Mrs Eggleton's revision of romantic love: inclination should be an act of will rather than a passive predilection. Futhermore, the foundation of companionate love is not passion but *esteem*, which is inspired by "merit," a combination of intellectual and moral qualities, the most important of which is virtue. Although "understanding" (intelligence) is a desirable characteristic, a good man who is not particularly intelligent (such as Charlotte's husband, Lord

19 Harris also cites this passage as an instance of *Grandison*'s critique of romantic love, while also noting (in accord with the dialectic) that Harriet's love for Sir Charles "gains as much from romance as it loses" (*Samuel Richardson*, p. 147).

G.) is still a suitable lover.[20] Assessing the character of a prospect-
ive spouse is thus the most important part of determining his or
her eligibility. As Sir Charles observes, "Love at first sight" (that is,
romantic love) precludes this necessary evaluation, for it "must indicate a mind *prepared* for impression, and a sudden gust of passion,
and that of the least noble kind; since there could be no opportunity of knowing the *merit* of the object" (2:357). And contrary to the
romantic belief that true lovers are made for each other, companionate love implies that any two worthy people are capable of being
happy together. As Charlotte says, "The man who loves virtue for virtue's sake loves it where-ever he finds it ... there will be tenderness
in his distinction to everyone, varying only according to the difference of her circumstances" (2:352). Companionate love is indeed a
"voluntary passion."

Because it originates in the virtue of the lovers themselves, companionate love is an ethically suitable motive for marriage, unlike
lust and romantic love. Moreover, companionate love precludes undesirable alliances. The fact that it is voluntary means that the lover
can avoid directing his or her affections inappropriately. One can
make the decision to cross class boundaries in quest of superior
merit—such is the basis on which the Count of D. seeks Harriet's
hand in marriage—but one does not do so indiscriminately. And
since a person who loves virtue must be a virtuous person, one would
not wish for a marriage likely to injure one's family or the object of
one's affections. As Sir Charles says, a man whose love is a "pure
flame" would never "seek to gratify his own passion, at the expence
of the happiness or duty of the object pretended to be beloved"
(1:332–33). Thus, since titles and estates were inherited through the
male line and a woman adopted her husband's rank, a man who es-
teemed a woman of superior social rank would control his feelings,

20 *Grandison* tries to deflect attention from the fact that intelligence and virtue are distinct
   qualities by using the concept of merit to include both. This equation was attractive to
   middle-class ideology, which advocates meritocracy while insisting that virtue will lead to
   material success. In accord with *Grandison*, Adam Smith observes that "in the middling and
   inferior stations of life, the road to virtue and that to fortune ... are, happily in most cases,
   very nearly the same." *The Theory of Moral Sentiments* (Oxford: Clarendon Press, 1976), p.
   63. Doody observes that "the first edition of Smith's *Moral Sentiments* appeared five years
   after the last volume of *Grandison*, and might almost have been based upon it" ("Identity,"
   p. 121).

as their marriage would be detrimental to her economic and social standing.

Sir Charles experiences companionate love for his Italian pupil Clementina. He *chooses* to love her only after she falls in love with him first. Before this, he appreciates her attractions without personally desiring her. He confides to his mentor Dr Bartlett:

I had never seen the woman ... that I *could* have loved so well, had I not restrained myself, at first, from the high notion I knew they [her family] had of their quality and rank; from considerations of the difference in religion; of the trust and confidence the family placed in me; and by the resolution I had made, as a guard to myself from the time of my entering upon my travels, of never aiming to marry a foreigner. (2:176)

Sir Charles's statement shows that he does not restrain strong and unbidden emotions, as he does in the case of his English friend Harriet, as we shall see. On the contrary, he rationally acknowledges that Clementina possesses qualities that are capable of inspiring love. The emphatic "could" of his statement, which signals an act of will, reveals that his love for Clementina will require deliberation.

Sir Charles's response to Clementina always involves thought rather than feeling. For instance, when he imagines marriage to Clementina before it has been suggested by her family, his daydreams are motivated by rational considerations of the advantages of such a match:

For my own part, it was impossible (distinguished as I was by every individual of this noble family, and lovely as is this daughter of it, mistress of a thousand good qualities, and myself absolutely disengaged in my affections) that my vanity should not sometimes be awakened, and a wish arise, that there might be a possibility of obtaining such a prize: But I checked the vanity, the moment I could find it begin to play about and warm my heart. (2:123–24)

Sir Charles is thus momentarily tempted by Clementina's family's position and her own merits, both of which he coolly assesses. His metaphor, which figures vanity as a flame (it plays about and warms his heart), emphasizes that passion is *not* the basis of Clementina's attraction. Sir Charles's alteration of a conventional metaphor (flame as love) illustrates his true motives for desiring Clementina: vanity literally inhabits the place of love in the metaphor, as it does in Sir Charles's emotions.

The Erotics of Virtue

Although companionate love precluded the threat of unregulated social mobility, it nevertheless created problems within the very terms of the ideological riddles it ostensibly solved. As we have seen, the marriage for love ideally deflected random social mobility by providing seemingly isolated exceptional cases of marriage across class lines. But it did not completely obviate the threat to the hierarchical structure of English élite society, since the "exception" could in theory *become* rather than prove the rule. Companionate love solved this problem by encoding the social control of desire so that it focused only on appropriate objects. But this solution paradoxically recreated the original problem: companionate love had the potential to re-establish class lines on nearly as rigid a basis as those of the marriage of interest. Love must be involuntary if it is to enable marriages that transgress established norms. Companionate love might justify the Count of D.'s suit to to Harriet, who is a member of the gentry, but it could not authorize the marriage between Mr B. and Pamela (who represents the working middle class, despite her ostensible status as a servant). A completely "voluntary passion" could never alter the social order, not even in order to justify the limited number of inter-class marriages that were deemed suitable and necessary to the economic health of the nation.

Furthermore, the companionate ideal continually undermines its own ethical basis, threatening to collapse into the very motives of interest that it presumably opposes. Although interest is supposedly subordinated to inclination in the companionate marriage, since one should not marry unless a "preference" exists, this preference, based as it is on balanced and deliberate judgment, is in danger of overvaluing the material or social advantages of marriage. This situation is illustrated by the marriage between Sir Charles's ailing uncle Lord W. and the impoverished Miss Mansfield. Miss Mansfield's family has fallen on hard times; Lord W. is aging, suffering from gout, and in need of a nurse. Although Harriet claims that the marriage is appropriate since "discretion and gratitude are the corner-stones of the matrimonial fabric" (3:281), the sort of gratitude that Miss Mansfield owes to Lord W. is very different from that which Harriet herself feels for Sir Charles. Harriet is initially grateful when Sir Charles rescues her from a kidnapper and later for his love, while Miss Mansfield is grateful for the material advantages Lord W.'s interest brings to her and her family. Although Harriet praises the match by citing the conventional arguments advocating companionate marriage— "Lady W. had no prepossessions in any other man's favour. My Lord loves her" (3:281)—the plot reveals the fact that the marriage is one of convenience, since the "lovers" agree to marry before either can have gained sufficient knowledge of the other's worth or character. Lord W.'s marriage shows that *Grandison* wants to advocate a certain kind of marriage of convenience because it is serviceable, while revising its true motives because marriages of interest are morally unacceptable. That the discourse of companionate love can be applied in this process of revision reveals the permeability of the boundary between prudence and interest.

These ideological dilemmas are solved by the last and best of the novel's "different sorts of Love"—sentimental love—as exemplified by Harriet's feelings for Sir Charles. On the surface, Harriet's love resembles romantic love. She adores Sir Charles at first sight and persistently denies her ability to care for another man. Even when it appears that he is almost certain to marry Clementina, Harriet refuses to consider the Countess of D.'s proposals for her son, claiming that her heart is "*already* a wedded heart: It is wedded to his [Sir Charles's] merits ... I can never think of any *other,* as I *ought* to think of the man to whom I give my hand" (2:289). As Harriet falls more and more deeply and (ostensibly) hopelessly in love, she suffers all the conventional symptoms of the romantic lover. She grows pale, sickly and thin, blushes and sighs, and prefers solitude to company. Sentimental love, like romantic love, includes sexual desire: Sir Charles is dashing and handsome, and as Harriet herself confesses, her love is "perhaps a little too personal" (2:13). In fact, unlike companionate love, its effects are always registered on the body through such responses as sighs and blushes.

Harriet's love is not romantic, however, because it is inspired by Sir Charles's merit. If Harriet adores Sir Charles at first sight, it is because her very first sight of him provides proof of his moral worth: in an action befitting the most impassioned romantic hero, Sir Charles risks his life in a disinterested act of goodness and mercy to save Harriet's honour. It is because Sir Charles is so much more virtuous than the merely good men Harriet esteems that her response to him is so much more intense. The reasonable criteria of companionate love thus inspire the passionate affect of romantic or physical love. The flamboyant plot and exalted passion of the romantic ethos remain intact, yet their driving force is virtue; merit has been eroticized in a dialectical resolution of reason and passion.

Sir Charles reveals his "sentimental love" for Harriet when he confesses his involvement with Clementina:

And now, madam, said he [and he was going to take my hand, but with an air, as if he thought the freedom would be too great—A tenderness *so* speaking in his eyes; a respectfulness *so* solemn in his countenance; he just touched it, and withdrew his hand] What shall I say? ... Honour forbids me!—Yet honour bids me—Yet I cannot be unjust, ungenerous—selfish! ... And, bowing low, he withdrew with precipitation, as if he would not let me see his emotion. He left me looking here, looking there, as if for my heart. (2:132)

Sir Charles struggles to control himself. He cannot resist touching Harriet. Moreover, his feelings are betrayed by his body language, the infallible sign of sentimental love. He obviously has tears in his eyes ("he would not let me see his emotion"), as the muted pun on "precipitation" (hurry and moisture) emphasizes. The dashes in his speech indicate his overwrought condition. He is so overcome with emotion that he departs from the usual procedures of etiquette, quite a statement from this "complete gentleman"; he fails to conduct Harriet out of the room and abruptly leaves her in great agitation, casting "looks that seemed to carry more meaning than his words" (2:134). Although Sir Charles does not (cannot) completely voice his thoughts about the conflict he is suffering ("Honour bids me—Yet Honour forbids me"), the context of the conversation makes it clear that honour bids him to be faithful to Clementina and forbids him to make his addresses to Harriet. Even Harriet herself, who misconstrues this conversation in Clementina's favour on several occasions, finally understands that Sir Charles's confusion and distress indicate his love (2:387).

Sir Charles's love for Harriet, unlike his feeling for Clementina, is involuntary. Although he claims that he had restrained himself from loving Clementina because circumstances were not conducive to their union, how much truer ought this to have been where Harriet is concerned, when he had already pledged himself to another woman. And yet he cannot control his love for Harriet any more than she can control her love for him. Although both are capable of restraining their passion in the interest of virtue and justice, the initial impulse to love is unsought and immediate. Thus Sir Charles, like Harriet, loves at first sight; as he later confesses, "the moment I saw you first ... I loved you" (3:284). And Sir Charles's passion registers the courtly, bodily language of love throughout the novel. He blushes several times at the mention of Harriet's name in connection with his own (2:81; 2:339, 658). When he speaks of Harriet, "His voice then is the voice of Love" (2:352). The most devoted reader of romance could wish for no more.

What writers identify as "sentimental love" has much in common with the mid-century conception of sentiment itself, for sentimental responsiveness provides the implicit model for a kind of love that corrects the ethical and disciplinary deficiencies of other modes of feeling. Richardson and his contemporaries thought of sentiment as a combination of reason and spontaneous feeling, a double valence which safeguards the sentimental subject from the opposing dangers of irrationality and calculation, as does sentimental love.[21] Moreover, as John Mullan notes, sentiment takes the body as an absolute ground and guarantor of sincerity: "The vocabulary [of sentiment] is that of gestures and palpitations, sighs and tears ... powerful because it is not spoken," whereas speech "can be a terrain of blandishment and deceit."[22] The sentimental ethics of "embodiment" enables an ingenious co-optation of romantic feeling on the part of

21 On sentiment as a blend of reason and passion see especially R.F. Brissenden, *Virtue in Distress* (New York: Harper and Row, 1974), chap. 2; Hagstrum, chap. 5; and John Mullan, *Sentiment and Sociability: The Language of Feeling in the Eighteenth Century* (Oxford: Clarendon Press, 1988), pp. 57–58.

22 Mullan, p. 61. On the physical basis of sentiment see also G.J. Barker-Benfield, *The Culture of Sensibility* (Chicago: University of Chicago Press, 1993), chap. 1; Brissenden, pp. 39–48; R.S. Crane, "Suggestions toward a Geneology of 'The Man of Feeling,'" *ELH* 1 (Decem-

sentimental love: its imprint on the body becomes not only the sign of its involuntariness and eroticism, but also of its ethical character. The very physicality which was formerly a source of danger (lust) is transformed into a virtue. And sentiment is also a tool of reciprocal hegemony because, as Robert Markley observes, it "negotiates the class struggle between aristocratic and mercantile classes" by reformulating "the problematic between birth and worth as a celebration of qualities that both can celebrate."[23] Similarly, sentimental love legitimates both aristocratic and middle-class ideals through its appropriation of the elements of romantic love in the interest of virtue.

Sentimental love retains the encoded social controls of companionate love, but they operate subconsciously. This is made clear when Harriet reassures her friend Lucy that falling in love is nothing to be ashamed of. "What better assurance can I give to my Uncle, and to all my friends, that if I were caught, I would own it, than by advising *you* not to be ashamed to confess a sensibility which is no disgrace, when duty and prudence are our guides, and the object worthy?" (1:66). In Harriet's locution (an unwitting description of sentimental love), the lover must be "caught," surprised by love, yet at the same time guided by motives that would seem to preclude such a passive and unconsidered entanglement. This is possible only if duty and prudence are internalized. While the companionate lover deliberately obeys the dictates of his or her social world, the sentimental lover is a thoroughly disciplined subject.

ber, 1934), 228–29; Todd, pp. 7–8; and Ann Jessie Van Sant, *Eighteenth-Century Sensibility and the Novel* (Cambridge: Cambridge University Press, 1993, chaps 5 and 6. The relationship between bodily and moral sensibility was widely accepted by scientists, including George Cheyne, Richardson's friend and doctor. It was believed that sentiment had a physical basis, originating in the nervous system: "'sensibility', 'sentiment', and 'sympathy' were terms with precise meanings in the newly developing sciences of physiology and neurology" (Brissenden, p. 39). On the significance of the body in *Grandison* see Juliet McMaster, "*Sir Charles Grandison*: Richardson on Body and Character," *Eighteenth-Century Fiction* 1 (January 1989), 83–102, and pp. 246–67 above. McMaster justly claims that "the drama and sensational interest that balance overt moralizing of the novel is the felt presence of the body" (p. 85).

23 Robert Markley, "Sentimentality as Performance: Shaftesbury, Sterne, and the Theatrics of Virtue," *The New Eighteenth Century*, ed. Felicity Nussbaum and Laura Brown (New York: Methuen, 1987), p. 218.

Sentimental love thus allows for the limited social mobility companionate marriage paradoxically threatens to prohibit. Since it is passionate and involuntary, it can inspire the interclass marriages that companionate love necessarily precludes. At the same time, however, because the foundation of sentimental love is virtue, it cannot lead to a truly subversive passion. Sentimental love is therefore superior to companionate love, since it synthesizes the best aspects of all other "sorts of love": it retains the proper motives of companionate love, yet it is purified of the taint of interest through its spontaneity. Its superiority is obvious in *Grandison*, since it is the sort of love experienced by its morally superior hero and heroine; as ideal characters, they achieve an ideal sort of love.

Yet, despite the superiority of sentimental love, it cannot be openly advocated. Because it manifests itself as pure feeling, there is no way for the text to endorse it overtly without legitimating other dangerous and potentially subversive forms of love that also exalt passion over reason. Thus, *Grandison* explicitly advocates the companionate ideal while enacting a more forceful vindication of the sentimental ideal. Even the faultless Sir Charles urges companionate love to his followers, while his own story glorifies sentimental love. This double message necessitates his double love.

Grandison's need to endorse two different forms of love involves a fundamental contradiction within the novel's code of virtue, as I hinted at the beginning of this essay. However excusable Sir Charles's involvement with two women might be, and however rarefied his love for each, a double love conjures the Lovelacian demons of libertinism and polygamy.[24] This creates the paradox of a less-than-perfect paragon, a problem which generates a certain amount of defensiveness within the text. Characters repeatedly comment on the extraordinary nature of the characters and circumstances involved. For instance, Charlotte observes, "There might be a law made, that the case should not be brought into precedent till two such women

24 Flynn notes that Sir Charles approaches polygamy in his triangular relationship with Harriet and Clementina, and discusses Sir Charles as a successful Lovelace (pp. 231–34), a comparison first observed by Morris Golden, *Richardson's Characters* (Ann Arbor: University of Michigan Press, 1963), p. 97. For an analysis of polygamy in *Grandison*, see Doody, "Identity," pp. 128–30.

should be found, and such a man; and all three in the like situation" (3:195). Sir Charles's ineluctable entanglement in this triangle is also stressed by both himself and others; although he and Harriet are in love, he has not "sought to engage her affections" (2:383). Far from encouraging the love of two women, Sir Charles cannot help inspiring unsought passion in the female breast: "A woman of virtue and honour cannot *but* love him" (2:381). The type of love triangle that would ordinarily be the consequence of morally questionable behaviour on the part of a gentleman is here generated by Sir Charles's very excellence—by his sense of honour and his love of virtue; he cannot help but respond to both the vulnerable Clementina and the morally excellent Harriet.

The most brilliant of Richardson's solutions to the paradox of a virtuous double love is also is also the novel's notable formal quirk: the curious absence of Sir Charles in his eponymous novel.[25] *Grandison* must reveal Sir Charles's thoughts and feelings in order to establish both his virtue and the nature of his feelings for Clementina and Harriet. But it does so in indirect ways so that Sir Charles's interiority is always mediated, but his feelings are nevertheless always legible. He writes relatively few letters, and they are rarely of the self-probing kind that constitutes so much of Harriet's correspondence. His most revealing moments are almost always reported by other characters, thereby blunting their confessional character—and yet such moments of revelation occur with regularity. This strategy ensures that we know the truth about Sir Charles's divided love, yet we do not experience it through his eyes. We are therefore distanced from his internal struggle and spared the concomitant moral queasiness of a divided affection. Through Richardson's persistent sleight of hand, different sorts of love and different sorts of lovers—the very material of aristocratic excess—accord with Christian virtue.

In his last novel Richardson finalized the views on love that had been so important throughout his work. He was here able to portray a perfect kind of love which was unrepresentable in *Pamela* and

---

25 Sir Charles's absence is noted by Doody, *Natural Passion,* p. 274; T.C. Duncan Eaves and Ben D. Kimpel, *Samuel Richardson* (Oxford: Oxford University Press, 1971), p. 337; and Laura Brown, *English Dramatic Form, 1660–1760* (New Haven: Yale University Press, 1981), p. 198.

Clarissa because of the nature of Mr. B. and Lovelace. While libertinism and romance form much of the subject of the earlier novels, sentimental love is only sketchily indicated. Mr B. indeed falls in love with Pamela's virtue, and she responds to the best in him. But Richardson's pessimism about reformed rakes led ultimately to Mr B.'s moral teeter-tottering in *Pamela* 2, where he becomes involved with a Countess. Marred by Mr B.'s imperfections, the love between Mr B. and Pamela falls short of the pinnacle of emotional and moral perfection enjoyed by Harriet and Sir Charles, although of course Pamela (like Sir Charles's mother, Lady Grandison) remains constant in her loyalty and affection. For Clarissa, the relationship between love and merit is represented in a primarily negative way. Clarissa progressively loses her regard for Lovelace as she gradually realizes his true nature. Lovelace's feelings are murkier and more complicated than anything we find in *Grandison* or *Pamela*. Power, lust, and genuine regard all fuel his desire, and in the end, it is Lovelace who ironically falls in love with Clarissa's goodness, as she has been repulsed by his evil. But by creating the faultless Sir Charles, Richardson could represent sentimental love as a fully mutual, erotic response to moral excellence. And it could then be distinguished clearly from companionship, romance, and lust.

Given *Grandison*'s considerable influence, it is not surprising that, in subsequent novels, the *dialectic* of love, which is mapped so clearly in *Grandison*, functions as a *typology* of love. If the courtship novel typically represents and evaluates a spectrum of sorts of love (and such didacticism is especially important for female readers who might otherwise be ensnared by the values of romance), *Grandison* demonstrates the lexicon of available modes of feeling. A brief example must suffice in Austen, Richardson's admirer and, to a great extent, his literary heir.[26] Her novels repeatedly evince the categories of love that we find in *Grandison*. In *Pride and Prejudice*, Darcy's sentimental love for Elizabeth Bennet contrasts with the companionate

26 On *Grandison*'s influence on Austen see Jocelyn Harris, *Jane Austen's Art of Memory* (Cambridge: Cambridge University Press, 1989), chap. 4; Kenneth Moler, *Jane Austen's Art of Allusion* (Lincoln: University of Nebraska Press, 1968), pp. 77–81, 105–7, 193–94; and Park Honan, "Richardson's Influence on Jane Austen," *Samuel Richardson: Passion and Prudence*, ed. Valerie Grosvenor Myer (Totowa, NJ: Barnes and Noble, 1986), pp. 165–77.

feelings she is eventually able to return, and both are sharply distinct from Charlotte Lucas's prudent interest in Mr Collins and Lydia's romantic passion for Wickham. Sentimental love and companionship are equally attractive alternatives to apathy and folly. Marianne Dashwood's romantic tendencies are suitably thwarted in *Sense and Sensibility*; she must settle for companionship, while Elinor's "sense" is rewarded with a far more romantic ending. In *Persuasion*, Austen represents sentimental love as the greatest good; Anne Elliot's passion for Wentworth is virtuous and proper because of the integrity of each. Representations of these categories of love—of lust, romantic love, companionship, and "rational passion"—characterize countless other novels. As we might expect, however, these distinctions are not always made with *Grandison*'s rigour (not even by Richardson himself, as we have seen). Indeed, *Grandison* is all about making fixed distinctions among modes of feeling, of pinning down what is really quite slippery. Moreover, *Grandison*'s categories, even in tendentious form, do not have the same ideological valence throughout the eighteenth and nineteenth centuries. Yet, if distinct modes of feeling are born of a specific historical moment, they outlive that moment to be articulated in other concerns and ideals. *Grandison*'s dialectic of love provides the material for such revision.

Sir Charles Grandison and the "Language of Nature"

George E. Haggerty

At one point early in her involvement with the Grandison family circle, Harriet Byron asks a series of rhetorical questions which expose the central obsessions of Richardson's final novel:

And why is the Grecian Homer, to this day, so much admired, as he is in all these nations, and in every other nation where he has been read, and will be, to the world's end, but because he writes to nature? And is not the language of nature one language throughout the world, tho' there are different modes of speech to express it by?[1]

Harriet gives vent to this seemingly self-evident expostulation as a way of matching her own circumscribed experience against the worldly wisdom of Sir Charles. (She is writing from London to her cousin Lucy, with whom she is in constant correspondence and who reads her letters to a close-knit family circle.) Harriet's point is that a lively sensibility will make even radically limited experience harrowing and eventful. Indeed, as critics have noted, it is the nature of this novel to find more richness, variety, and depth in the largely female

---

1 Samuel Richardson, *The History of Sir Charles Grandison* (1753–54), ed. Jocelyn Harris, 3 vols. (London: Oxford University Press, 1972), 1:185. References are to this edition. "*Sir Charles Grandison* and the 'Language of Nature'" was first published in *Eighteenth-Century Fiction* 2:2 (1990), 127–40.

world of private experience and epistolary correspondence than in the public world of heroic action and restraint.[2]

The real world of the novel is a world which expends its energy in the inscription of feelings in language, searching for what Harriet elusively calls the "language of nature." Margaret Anne Doody argues that the private circle of which Sir Charles is an intimate member is a comic version of those imprisoning households in Clarissa.[3] In the English group, parents have in one way or another been disposed of, and a circle of young adults live together as brothers and sisters in what seems at times like an orgy of mutual admiration. Yet this circle is also a hornet's nest of private intrigue. With no parents to regulate behaviour, freedom is nearly absolute—Harriet's relatives are extraordinarily careless about her well-being—and the characters have only their own moral sense and their mutual example to guide them in a world fraught with danger from both without and within. The challenge for these characters is to balance private strength with public necessity and to establish a context in which they can be themselves. They meet this challenge in and through language.

Harriet herself and Charlotte Grandison are the most fascinating members of this circle, because they are the most fully developed and the most actively engaged in discovering who they are. Harriet at one stage calls Charlotte "A very Miss Howe" (1:229); this not only reminds us of some of the less excruciating concerns of the earlier novel but also suggests a reworking of constant themes.[4] Charlotte is a "new" Anna Howe, though, only in the sense that she is a richer, more fully characterized, and a more boldly experimental

---

2 See Margaret Anne Doody, *A Natural Passion: A Study of the Novels of Samuel Richardson* (London: Oxford University Press, 1974), pp. 277–81; and John Sitter, *Literary Loneliness in Mid Eighteenth-Century England* (Ithaca: Cornell University Press, 1982), pp. 208–10. Other studies which have dealt interestingly with *Sir Charles Grandison* are Terry Castle, *Masquerade and Civilization: The Carnivalesque in Eighteenth-Century English Culture and Fiction* (Stanford: Stanford University Press, 1986); Carol Houlihan Flynn, *Samuel Richardson: A Man of Letters* (Princeton: Princeton University Press, 1982); James Allen Stevenson, "'A Geometry of His Own': Richardson and the Marriage Ending," *SEL* 26 (1986), 469–83.

3 Doody, pp. 278–79.

4 Sitter emphasizes this connection (pp. 202–4); see also Mary V. Yates, "The Christian Rake in *Sir Charles Grandison*," *SEL* 24 (1984), 545–61.

statement of what has been called *ur*-feminism.[5] Harriet, however, is by no means a second Clarissa. Excitement rather than misery keeps her up late writing: her minutely described responses to every detail of the history of Sir Charles and his family constitute by far the bulk of the novel. She is often accused by her friends of spending too much time at her pen. In a world of such intense socializing, this closeted scribbling becomes vaguely suspect; but it is absolutely essential to Harriet's well-being. *Grandison* insists on a fully developed private life as well as a constant and aggressive self-questioning in response to experience in the world. But private experience is not sacrosanct. Harriet's letters become the public property of her family once they are written, and her private thoughts are publicized before she has had a chance to censor them. Once thoughts or feelings have been articulated, then, they are in danger of becoming public property. Harriet discovers this abruptly:

My dear Charlotte, whispered I—Pray, say something encouraging to Lord G. [her suitor]. He is pleased with every-body; but no-body says anything to him. ...

My Lord, What do you think Miss Byron says?

For Heaven's sake, dear Miss Grandison!

Nay, I will speak it.

Pray, Madam, let me know, said my Lord.

You will know Miss Grandison in time, said Sir Charles. I trust her not with any of *my* secrets, Miss Byron.

The more ungenerous you, Sir Charles; for you get out of me all mine. (1:236–37)

The intimacy of the extended family repeatedly demands this kind of self-exposure. A whispered aside is made public because in a world of mutual admiration, secrecy is suspect. To be private suggests the unhealthy, as indeed Clementina's fate dramatizes in vivid and nearly scientific detail later on. There is of course an uneasy tension between the profession of absolute openness and such central

---

5 Stevenson sees a "feminist unity in Richardson's canon," but his true concerns lie elsewhere (p. 477). The most salient assertions of feminism in *Clarissa* are Terry Castle, *Clarissa's Ciphers: Meaning and Disruption in Richardson's "Clarissa"* (Ithaca: Cornell University Press, 1982), pp. 25–31, 184–87; and Terry Eagleton, *The Rape of Clarissa: Writing, Sexuality, and Class Struggle in Samuel Richardson* (Minneapolis: University of Minnesota Press, 1982), pp. 88–91.

concerns as Harriet's unspoken love for Sir Charles, but this tension is precisely what the novel attempts to dramatize. The novel teaches that there is no place for deception in this world of effusive directness, that nothing need be hidden, and that no one need protect a private self from public exposure. As a result, it becomes paramount that every letter sooner or later gets read by everyone else—to the infinite edification of all. Private embarrassment gives way to a kind of domestic public spirit, with the vague promise that the self can always find ideal reflection in the supportive and encouraging "other" of family life.

The heart as the well-spring of affection is as much at issue here as it is in Richardson's earlier novels. And it is understood as equally the centre of a range of beliefs about human experience and individual response to the world. Just as it existed in scientific discussions of the period as the source of sensation or feeling, in this novel it becomes the physical as well as the spiritual source of love, honesty, and sympathetic response.

As R.F. Brissenden suggests in *Virtue in Distress,* the "redefinition of man as a social and moral being took place in the context of a redefinition of man as a physical being. ... 'Sensibility,' 'sentiment,' and 'sympathy' were terms with precise meanings in the newly developing sciences of physiology and neurology."[6] If scientists were tearing open the rib cages of animals during this period to see just how much the creatures' hearts could feel, writers like Richardson were anatomizing their characters in an attempt to find a language for human feeling and the sources of physical response, a language of nature. The dissection essential to this search was an horrific and excruciating process, but it produced seemingly objective, scientific results.[7]

"My pen shall be honest to [my] heart" (1:179), Harriet tells Lucy as she attempts to describe the bounty of the Grandisons; and later:

6 R.F. Brissenden, *Virtue in Distress: Studies in the Novel of Sentiment from Richardson to Sade* (London: Macmillan, 1974), p. 39.

7 For a discussion of the scientific background to Sensibility, see Brissenden (pp. 40–41); John A. Dussinger, "The Sensorium in the World of *A Sentimental Journey,*" *Ariel* 13 (1982), 6–7; John Mullen, "Hypochondria and Hysteria: Sensibility and the Physicians," *The Eighteenth Century: Theory and Interpretation* 25 (1984), 141–74; and G.S. Rousseau, "Nerves, Spirits, and Fibres: Toward Defining the Origins of Sensibility," *Studies in the Eighteenth Century* 3, ed. R.F. Brissenden (Toronto: University of Toronto Press, 1976), pp. 137–57.

"And what have I in my heart, were it to be laid open to all the world, that I should be—afraid—I was going to write, that I should be *ashamed* of?" (1:279). Harriet and Charlotte go through a painstaking ritual of "opening their hearts" to one another, and Harriet's aunt even counsels her to give in to her "natural openness of heart" (1:301). Because Harriet is expected to pour out her heart so "naturally" to her relatives and her new-found friends, she learns to control her responses (for the most part) and weather the storms of her growing affection for Sir Charles. Her reserve on the subject of Sir Charles is a signal to the others, however, to probe and analyse, if ever so delicately, in order to expose her secrets. If the results are painful, at least the analysts could claim that in removing from her heart such obstructions as hidden love, they were encouraging the free flow of spirits and their proper circulation that was in the eighteenth century the guarantee of physical and mental health.[8]

Supposedly for her own good, then, Harriet is forced to admit her love for the man who seems least accessible, Sir Charles Grandison. She must question every one of her responses, however, and check and recheck her relation to language before she can trust herself with her feelings. Harriet comes to dissect her own responses with a single-minded determination that echoes that of Haller and van Whyt in probing the organs of their experimental subjects for some sign of a response:[9]

But, my Lucy, one silly question to *you*, who have been a little *entangled*, and more happily *disentangled*—I catch myself of late in saying *him* and *he*, and writing to you *somebody*, and such-like words, instead of saying and writing boldly, as I used to do, Sir Charles, and Sir Charles Grandison; which would sound more respectfully, and yet am sure I want not respect. What is the meaning of this?—Is it a sign—Ah! my Lucy! you said you would keep a sharp look-out; and did I not say I would upon myself? (1:278–79)

Harriet seems to view her growing emotional attachment to Sir Charles as a dangerous "entanglement" and to suspect that language

8 Brissenden, pp. 33–41; see also Michel Foucault, *Madness and Civilization: A History of Insanity in the Age of Reason*, trans. Richard Howard (New York: Vintage-Random House, 1965), pp. 146–50.

9 Brissenden, pp. 40–41; see also John A. Dussinger, *The Discourse of the Mind in Eighteenth-Century Fiction* (The Hague: Mouton, 1974), pp. 28–29.

has become a "sign" of her vulnerability. Here she tries to call in Lucy as a censor to check her freedoms of speech. But she understands that her language has already betrayed her feelings. Instead of worrying about the inability of language to create an authentic reflection of her emotions, that is, she is concerned lest language reveal feelings that she would prefer to conceal.

Later she tries valiantly to find a label for her feelings that can exonerate her from the charge of self-interest. She has been reading to the Grandison circle her own letters describing the various proposals of marriage that she has received. The ladies, her companions, have made it clear that they support the idea of her marriage and that one of the suitors, Lord D., seems to them a fully appropriate match for such a promising young girl as Harriet. Harriet rejects the proposal, but finds it difficult to explain herself. When she is alone, she disburdens herself to her supporters at home:

It is now, my dear friends, some-how or other, become necessary, I think, to let you minutely into my situation, that you may advise, caution, instruct me—For, I protest, I am in a sort of wilderness.—Pray, my Lucy, tell me—But it cannot be from *Love*. So I don't care—Yet to lie under such a weight of obligation; and to find myself so much surpassed by these ladies—Yet it is not from *Envy*, surely: That is a very bad passion. I hope my bosom has not a place in it for such a mean self-tormentor. Can it be from *Pride*? Pride is a vice that always produces mortification: And proud you all made me of your favour—Yet I thought it was grateful to be proud of it. (1:284)

The uneasiness that Harriet had just expressed about the potential of language to expose her has become intensified to the point of crisis. Harriet surely is in a "wilderness" here, a wilderness of language and syntax that confounds her attempts to distinguish her real feelings from the public forms of interpretation that could humiliate her. She wants to be honest with herself and her interlocutors at the same time that she wants to retain a private self. Language seems inadequate to her needs and quite likely to betray her. The labels she proposes are rejected in a near-hysteria of disjunction. Inner conflict is represented as a series of contradictions which leave her seeming almost childish. Emotion renders her speechless.

Her experience of love, however, when she finally understands it as such, leads her to the extreme position of rejecting "self" in favour of a vaguely defined "truth":

SELF, my dear Lucy, is a very wicked thing; a sanctifier, if one would give way to its partialities, of actions, which, in others, we should have no doubt to condemn. DELICACY, too, is often a misleader; an idol, at whose shrine we sometimes offer up our Sincerity; but, in that case, it should be called *Indelicacy*.

Nothing, surely, can be delicate, that is not true, or that gives birth to equivocation. (2:1)

This is not a case of simple self-betrayal. Harriet senses her own vulnerability and begins to understand that she must use language defensively. In establishing an unequivocal relation to the truth of her own emotions, which she calls sincerity, Harriet is establishing the only relation to language capable of sustaining her in the crisis ahead. Just as Clarissa's personal honesty is her final refuge, Harriet finds strength in the kind of self-questioning that will enable her to survive the tide of her passion. "Why was I born with an heart so open and sincere?" she asks rhetorically (2:1), for she already knows the answer.[10] In a world of male supremacy and the impossibility of action for women, sincerity becomes a kind of power. It is the only means of maintaining a coherent self in the midst of the conflict between language and feeling. If truth can become the basis of goodness, Harriet comes to understand, her own weakness will become her strength; if emotions can be expressed in language they lose their power to pervert identity. Once she has learned this, Harriet can face the letters from Italy that spell out her crisis. If language can give vent to her feelings, in other words, she knows she will survive.

In this knowledge she is unlike her great and respected rival for the love of Sir Charles, Clementina della Poretta. Unlike Harriet's, Clementina's love is inarticulate and self-destructive. Significantly, Sir Charles is Clementina's tutor in English, and it is in teaching her his language that he works his way into her heart. Their cultural difference is offered as the stumbling block to a profession of love, both because the family will not consent to lose their daughter to an English Protestant and because Clementina fears both the safety of her own soul and the damnation of Sir Charles's.

10 Doody discusses early reactions to Harriet's "frankness" (pp. 312–13).

Clementina, then, represses her love and is forced by the family to give over even thinking about her "Chevalier." The brutal regime she is forced by jealous cousins to follow is an attempt to drive her out of her mind. She is susceptible to such attempts, as Jocelyn Harris notes, because her unspoken love and seemingly hopeless passion have led her to sacrifice reason to emotion and to succumb to an extreme example of that version of melancholy that Richardson's own physician, George Cheyne, dubbed the "English Malady." As Harris reminds us, Richardson had himself printed Robert James's *Medicinal Dictionary* (1743), in which the entry for "mania" reads: "Among the causes which dispose to the most violent delirium, and ... destroy the Force of the Mind and Body, none is more powerful than an Excess of Love."[11] Clementina's physical degeneration is patterned after Cheyne's three stages of vapours, Harris says, "proceeding from fits, fainting, lethargy or restlessness to hallucination, loss of memory, and despondency (bleeding and blistering are here recommended), with a final decline toward consumption."[12] For Michel Foucault, Clementina's madness could be ascribed simply to "an excess of sensibility."[13] Clementina is lost in the private horror of her own unexpressed emotions.[14]

Clementina's crisis seems largely to result from her inability to articulate her distress. Without language to give public meaning to her private pain, she comes close to total self-destruction: "When her mamma went to her, she found her spiritless, her eyes fixed, and

11 See Robert James, *Medicinal Dictionary* (London: T. Osborne, 1743), s.v. "mania."

12 Harris, notes to *Sir Charles Grandison* (2:673–74).

13 "As long as vapours were convulsions or strange sympathetic communications through the body, even when they led to fainting and loss of consciousness, they were not madness. But once the mind becomes blind through the very excess of sensibility—then madness appears" (Foucault, p. 158); see also Tony Tanner, *Jane Austen* (Cambridge: Harvard University Press, 1986), pp. 81–85; and George E. Haggerty, "The Sacrifice of Privacy in *Sense and Sensibility*," *Tulsa Studies in Women's Literature* 7 (1988), 221–37.

14 On the dangers of female emotion, see Mary Poovey, *The Proper Lady and the Woman Writer: Ideology as Style in the Works of Mary Wollstonecraft, Mary Shelley, and Jane Austen* (Chicago and London: University of Chicago Press, 1984); Poovey argues that "feeling was one significant theater of experience that could not be completely denied to women" and that "although women found in the sentimental novel a subject and even a genre, these works ... helped to drive further underground the aggressive, perhaps sexual, energies that men feared in women" (p. 38).

as gloomy as ever. She was silent to two or three of her mother's questions; and when she *did* speak, it was with wildness" (2:185). Only Sir Charles can save her from herself. Once her family has retrieved her from the clutches of her vindictive relatives, who had only exacerbated Clementina's hysteria by practising a kind of primitive aversion technique to stop her from continuing to babble the name of her beloved Chevalier, they decide to overcome their resistance to Sir Charles. For they suspect that only he can break down the wall she has established between herself and the world. Her emotions are stopped up, as it were, and only Sir Charles can cause the spirits to flow and induce expression therefore to relieve the pent-up feelings. The sexual implications of this homeopathic cure are clear, but Richardson substitutes for private sexuality a public rehabilitation scene fraught with emotional tension. The nearly catatonic girl is introduced carefully to Sir Charles:

Know you not the grateful Grandison, whom all your family have honoured with their regard?

O yes!—Yes,—I think I do.—They rejoiced to hear her speak.—But where have you been all this time?

In England, madam—But returned, *lately* returned, to visit you and your Jeronymo [her wounded brother whose life Grandison has saved].

Jeronymo! one hand held up; the other not withdrawn. Poor Jeronymo!

God be praised! said the General: Some faint hopes. The two Marchionesses wept for joy. (2:474)

In this novel, it is success to become social again, to leave the world of private woe and terror and communicate once more through the medium of language. Soon Clementina is even attempting a few phrases in English (the above passage is "translated") and the fullest expression of her recovery is her ability to compose a long letter in which she articulates her desire to live a life of her own, separate from her Chevalier. Language then becomes the sole mode of self-determination. Clementina has the freedom of choice, and she decides: "Were I to be thine, my duty to thee would mislead me from that I owe to my God, and make me more than temporarily unhappy" (2:565). The care with which she uses language here, the discriminating vocabulary of future possibility, suggests that Clementina has regained control of her fate. Clementina's fear

326 GEORGE E. HAGGERTY

of Grandison is a fear of the world beyond the capability of her own syntactical power. For God is the final source of meaning in Clementina's circumscribed world, and even Grandison cannot provide a substitute version of reality. In any case, the experience of the novel is to believe in Clementina's simplicity of heart and to rejoice that this endearing character has been so able to articulate an independent stance.[15] When later tempted to renege even by Sir Charles, she returns to "this paper, which has cost me so many tears" (2:565).[16] The words expressed on that paper become her only support.

Charlotte Grandison is no less sensitive than Harriet or Clementina, but she offers yet another version of linguistic confusion. As Sir Charles rescued Harriet from abduction at a masquerade, he rescues Charlotte from an equally harrowing adventure, that of a careless promise. Charlotte's verbal commitment to Captain Anderson seems as dangerous as Harriet's portrayal of an Arcadian princess, in which costume she was abducted by Sir Hargrave Pollexfen:[17]

Women should never be drawn-in to fetter themselves by promises [Sir Charles advises]. On the contrary, they ought always to despise, and directly to break with the man, who offers to exact a promise from them. To what end is a promise of this kind endeavour'd to be obtained, if the urger suspects not the fitness of his addresses in the eyes of those who have a right to be consulted; and if he did not doubt either his own merit, or the lady's honour and discretion? (1:408)

In other words, Sir Charles implies, a promise is a perversion of the public role of language. An extracted promise is a form of deception, and like the converse of a vow it contracts its adherents to a course of action almost certainly dishonourable. In using language to pervert meaning, an extracted promise violates the very premises of the self-reliance of the female characters, and nothing could threaten their emerging power more. Sir Charles suggests that Charlotte's

---

15 See Cynthia Griffin Wolff, *Samuel Richardson and the Eighteenth-Century Puritan Character* (Hamden, Conn.: Shoe String Press, 1972), pp. 217–18, for a discussion of the heritage of this conflict.

16 Also see 2:573–75, where Clementina gives the motives of her "*self-denial*"; and 584–86, where she articulates her religious reservation more fully.

17 For a provocative discussion of the implications of the masquerade in *Sir Charles Grandison*, see Castle, *Masquerade*, p. 123.

father could have absolved her from her promise on nothing less than biblical authority (Num. 3:3–5), and laments that "You have not now ... any-body to controul you: You are absolutely your own mistress" (1:408). Charlotte's careless use of language, in other words, emphasizes her lack of paternal "authority" and the dangers of conversation. Like Harriet, she needs to learn how to claim authority for herself. After this initial misalliance, Charlotte is loath to commit herself to any of her suitors. Much of the central section of the novel is given over to her resistance and final capitulation to the suit of Lord G. Richardson has provided Charlotte with a ridiculous suitor to highlight the potentially confining and restrictive implications of personal relations. When the adoring Lord G. has finally won her hand in marriage, Charlotte's seemingly destructive independence of spirit becomes expressed publicly in the linguistic pertness with which she treats him. Again and again she short-circuits communication with verbal sharpness, until the happiness of the marriage seems in danger:

> I beg pardon for intruding, madam—But I thought—
> That you had a privilege, Sir—But marriage itself, Sir, shall not give you a privilege to break into my retirements. You *thought*, Sir—You could *not think*—So much the worse if you did— (2:329)

If Charlotte seems like a latter day Millamant in her concern for privacy, her tone is much more frantic and the urgency of her demand as a result more deeply felt.[18] Her expostulations cause discomfort, but it is the circumstance of the woman herself that is uncomfortable. Charlotte's syntactical violence and her ironic emphases suggest that Lord G.'s gracious self-insinuation is exactly what she fears. Only by shouting him down, it seems, can she maintain her integrity. When Charlotte does consent to enter into intercourse with her husband, however, she seems threatened to become the literal victim of his insatiable appetite for her person. The following playful interchange probes the sexual implications of "conversation," and it explains the anxieties behind Charlotte's intransigence. She is certainly in danger of losing more than her independence here, but

18 See Doody, pp. 288–91.

rather than allowing her husband to "devour" her in a burst of in-articulate passion, she trains him to converse with her. She wants to talk him out of a solitary visit to friends and have him accompany her instead on her own journey. She also wants to establish a new re-lation of language and meaning in which she retains authority yet still admits the fact of her desire:

> Only answer me, my Lord; Are you willing I should go to Northampton-shire?
> If you choose to go, I have no objection. Miss Byron is an angel.
> Now, don't be perverse, Lord G. Don't praise Miss Byron at the expence of somebody else.
> Would to heaven, madam—
> I wish so too—And I put my hand before his mouth—*So* kindly!
> He held it there with both his, and kissed it. I was not offended. But do you actually set out for Windsor and Oxford to-morrow, my Lord?
> Not, madam, if you have any commands for me.
> Why, now, that's well said. Has your Lordship any-thing to propose to me?
> I could not be so welcome as your *escorte*, as I am sure I should be to Miss Byron and her friends, as her *guest*.
> You *could* not! How can you say so, my Lord? You would do me both honour and pleasure.
> What would I give, that you mean what you say!
> I *do* mean it, my Lord—My hand upon it—I held out my hand for his. He snatched it; and I thought would have devoured it.
> We will take the coach, my Lord, that I may have your company all the way.
> You equally astonish and delight me, madam! Is it possible that you are—
> Yes, yes, don't, in policy, make it such a wonder, that I am disposed to be what I *ought* to be.
> I shall be too, too, too happy! sobbed the man. (2:508)

Beneath the obvious concerns of marital duty and the problems Charlotte has had conforming to that ideal, Richardson has intro-duced a discussion of language that is both penetrating and amus-ing. After weeks of teasing, Charlotte has finally condescended to speak to her admittedly silly husband without mocking his love. In doing so, she teaches him both what he can expect as her husband and how he is to express those expectations. She may feel the danger of losing her independence, if not her very being, to her husband, but at the same time she seems to realize that without the bond of language their relationship will become meaningless. Charlotte begins to understand the domesticating power of language: Lord G.'s inarticulate passion threatens her freedom, but if she can teach him to speak, she will be able to reason with him, convince him of her willingness to communicate at the same time that she establishes her otherness. Hence she experiments with saying what she means, really for the first time with Lord G., and finds that he can hardly believe her sincere. This is the dilemma to which her ironic use of language has led her, and her only escape is to admit her sense of obligation and to articulate it publicly. After this, their relationship can flourish in direct speech rather than flounder in irony.

That Charlotte has had to insist that she means what she says is a measure of how far she has slipped below the ideal of social intercourse that the novel has set. If she is more entertaining as a result, she also has more to repent when she realizes the depth of her attachment to this silly, but good, man:

Lord bless me, my dear Lady L.! [she exclaims to her sister] I have been frightened out of my wits. This Lord G.—What do we do by marriage, but double our cares?—He was taken very ill two hours ago; a kind of fit. The first reflexion that crossed me, when he was at worst, was this—What a wretch was I, to vex this poor man as I have done!—Happy, happy is the wife, in the depth of her affliction, on the loss of a worthy husband; happy the husband, if he *must* be separated from a good wife; who has no material cause for self-reproach to imbitter reflexion, as to his or her conduct to the departed. Ah, Caroline, how little do we know of ourselves, till the hour of trial comes! I find, I find, I have more Love for Lord G. than I thought I had, or could have, for any man! (2:545)

By putting her love into words for the first time, Charlotte seems to accept the public implications of her married state. When Lord G. recovers, she fears she has "*exposed*" herself. That is precisely the point. She has attempted to disguise her emotions in a kind of self-defence but finds that there is a different kind of safety available in open and honest exposure. Her distortion of her true feelings, like the masquerade and the promise, threaten, as here, to alienate her from herself. She has come to know herself, and with that knowledge she can become a healthy member of society.

In this novel, then, the language of nature is a liberating language. It encourages self-knowledge and teaches the means of self-expression in the public world. Private isolation is overcome; indeed, public and private are joined in a language which establishes communities rather than destroys them. Deception and dishonesty of any kind are deplored in the novel. Language that comes from the heart can only release emotional tension if it is honest and direct. Any other use of language is obstructive and debilitating. Literary flourishes are clearly relegated to the unserious or even the dangerous. In discussing Charlotte's love life, for instance, Sir Charles insists that "The matter is too serious to be spoken of in metaphor" (1:397), and later, in addressing the same topic, he puts down his sister's archness by observing that "Wit ... is a dangerous weapon: But that species of it which cannot shine without a foil, is not a wit to be proud of" (2:86). Harriet even goes so far as to exclaim to Charlotte: "Wicked wit! What a foe art thou to decent chearfulness!" (3:117). When the elder Grandison rejects his daughter Caroline's suitor Lord L. and calls L.'s letter proposing marriage an "artful letter," for instance, Harriet gives way to the following reverie:

Thus spoke the *rakish*, the *keeping* father, Lucy, endeavouring to justify his private vices by general reflexions on the sex. And thus are wickedness and libertinism called a knowlege of the world, a knowlege of human nature. Swift, for often painting a dunghil, and for his abominable Yahoe story, was complimented with this knowledge: But I hope, that the character of human nature, the character of creatures made in the image of the Deity, is not to be taken from the overflowings of such dirty imaginations. (1:348)

In this account, imagination is intrinsically at odds with nature. In coining the notion of a dirty imagination, Richardson was giving notoriety to what he saw as a force of corruption in language. For imagination not only colours truth and makes "additions to nature," it perverts language itself in the pursuit of private desire.[19] Like all else which sacrifices public to private experience in *Sir Charles Grandison*, imagination is held in deepest contempt. Richardson would agree surely with Johnson, when in *Rasselas* he says that "All power of fancy over reason is a degree of insanity."[20]

19 The quotation is from Addison, a favourite of Richardson's. See *Spectator* 421.

20 Samuel Johnson, *The History of Rasselas, Prince of Abyssina*, ed. Geoffrey Tillotson and Brian Jenkins (London: Oxford University Press, 1971), chap. 44, p. 114.

Johnson's terminology suggests a distrust of the imagination that remains central to literature of Sensibility. Writers beyond Richardson address the issue of madness with alarming regularity, often blaming it on unbridled imagination. "When the imagination," says Hume, "from any extraordinary ferment of the blood and spirits, acquires such a vivacity as disorders all its powers and faculties, there is no means of distinguishing betwixt truth and falsehood; but every loose fiction or idea, having the same influence as the impressions of the memory, or the conclusions of the judgment, is receiv'd on the same footing, and operates with equal force on the passions."[21] Richardson's commitment to the exploration of response seems inspired at least in part by a fear that imagination is a threat to social stability. Imagination isolates individuals from the natural world and restricts them to a world of their own creation; they therefore sacrifice public responsibility to the privacy of emotion. Problems arise when this emotion cannot be redirected outward. The language of nature offers the basis of this redirection.

Emotionality, as noted by Foucault and others, becomes increasingly problematic in the later eighteenth century. "From now on," Foucault says, "one fell ill from too much feeling."[22] In *Sir Charles Grandison* recovery becomes possible by means of openness and direct expression. If the dangers of the public world are legion, they are less detrimental than the kinds of debility that imaginative isolation suggests. If there is a kind of self-betrayal inherent in laying open the heart, it must be measured against the self-oppression implied in the silent world of emotion.[23] For Harriet Byron, the language of nature is a means of self-realization. The self she realizes, married and publicly established, has escaped the harrowing confines of private sensibility, for better or worse.

---

21 David Hume, *A Treatise of Human Nature*, ed. L. Selby-Bigge (1888); 2nd ed., revised P.H. Nidditch (Oxford: Oxford University Press, 1978), p. 123 (book 1, part 3, section 10).

22 Foucault, p. 157.

23 See Nina Auerbach, *Romantic Imprisonment: Women and Other Glorified Outcasts* (New York: Columbia University Press, 1985), p. 15.

Index

Halsband, Robert, 29n2
Hanson, Laurence, 41n28
Hardwicke, Lord, 300
Harevit, Lars, 13n10
Harris, Jocelyn, 92–113; "As If They
  Had Been Living Friends,"
  284n39; Notes to *Sir Charles
  Grandison*, 324; "The Reviser
  Observed," 290–3, 297n6; *Samuel
  Richardson*, 35, 142n10, 269n2,
  274nn13–14, 285, 295n1,
  300n12, 302n16, 303n18, 305n19
Harris, Michael, 33n13, 36n19,
  41n28
Harth, Erica, 295n3, 296n5, 297n7,
  300, 300n14
Hartley, David, 120n19
Harvey, William, 171
Hayman, Francis, 11
Haywood, Eliza, 125
Hegel, Georg Wilhelm Friedrich,
  225, 230
Heidegger, Martin, 225
Hermeticism, 228
Hervey, Lord, 29, 45–6, 48
Hieroglyphics of Horapollo, The,
  240
Highmore, Joseph, 151
Hill, Aaron, 26n28, 73n4, 90, 147
Hill, Christopher, 136, 137n2,
  138–9, 189n29, 298n8
Hobbes, Thomas, 93–8, 108–9,
  113, 118; *Elements of Law*, 94n8;
  Human Nature, 94n7; *Leviathan*,
  94n6, 97; philosophy, 93–5
Hobhouse, Stephen, 229
Hogarth, William, 97n10, 177
Hornbeak, Katherine, 19n20
Hume, David, 118, 120n19, 125–6,
  331n21; "Of Passive Obedi-
  ence," 126
Hunter, J. Paul, 14, 178n14, 294n64

"Hymn of the Pearl, The," 213–14,
  222, 233
Hypostasis of the Archons, The, 219

Ibsen, Henrik, 170
Irenaeus of Lyons, St, 211, 214
Isle, Duncan, 131n39

Jacobitism, 40, 120, 122, 123
James, Henry, 248
James, Robert: *Medical Dictionary*,
  324
James I, king of England, 119
Jameson, Fredric, 144n13, 145–6,
  149
Johnson, Samuel, 32, 43, 170n1,
  225; Boswell's life of, 31n8; *Dic-
  tionary*, 173n7; life of Rochester,
  98; *Rasselas*, 290, 330–1
Jones, Wendy, 295–316
Jordan, Constance, 120n17
Journal of the House of Commons,
  36
*Judgement of Whole Kingdoms and
  Nations* (1710, anon.), 122
Jupiter, 93
Juvenal, 45

Kabbala, 228
Kauffman, Linda S., 175n10
Kay, Carol, 73, 78, 116n5, 118
Kearney, A.M., 25–6
Kermode, Frank, 72, 85
Kettle, Arnold, 139n8
Keymer, Thomas, 28n1, 36n19,
  37n21, 142n10, 150n25, 153n1,
  196n36, 284n37
Kilfeather, Siobhan, 136n1
Kimpel, Ben D. *See* Eaves, T.C.
  Duncan
King, Karen L., 219
Kinkead-Weekes, Mark, 54, 56,

Smith, Adam: *The Theory of Moral Sentiments*, 305n20
Smith, Virginia, 228n27
Smollett, Tobias George, 266
social contract theory, 95, 97, 118n12, 120, 122, 123–4, 125
Socrates, 197, 254
South, Robert, 155, 173, 200, 202, 277
Spacks, Patricia Meyer, 8n3, 12, 55n8, 79, 81n15
Spanish Inquisition, 40
Sparrow, John, 225, 231
Speck, W.A., 143n12
Spectator, 299
Spenser, Edmund, 183; *The Faerie Queene*, 111–12, 255; *Mutability Cantos*, 92
Spinoza, Benedict de, 287
Starr, G.A., 178n14
Staves, Susan, 153n2
Steele, Richard, 179; *The Christian Hero*, 299
Stephen, Leslie, 256
Stepney, George, 45
Sternberg, Meir, 176n10
Sterne, Laurence, 12, 252; *Tristram Shandy*, 290
Stevenson, James Allen, 318n2, 319n5
Stinstra, Johannes, 121, 127n34, 178
Stone, Lawrence, 117n10, 189n29, 294n64, 295n3, 296n5, 297n7, 299n11
Stuber, Florian, 57n11, 123, 128n38, 163, 180n21, 227n25
Sussman, Charlotte, 55n8
Swift, Jonathan, 153n2, 176, 204, 207n51

Talbot, Catherine, 31n8

Tanner, Tony, 117n10, 324n13
Tatler, 299
Thackeray, William Makepeace, 248, 250, 263
Theresa, St, 261
Thickstun, Margaret Olofson, 176n10
Thomas, John, 160
Thomas à Kempis: *Imitation of Christ*, 110, 201, 211n2
Thompson, E.P., 143–5, 296n4
Thompson, Martyn P., 120n18
Thompson, Peggy, 152–69
Thomson, James: *Edward and Elenora*, 39n24
Tillotson, John, 155, 173, 179, 276, 278
Todd, Janet, 55n8
Todd, Margo, 298n8
Tottie, John, 159
Traherne, Thomas, 229
Trapp, Joseph, 160, 212n3, 226–7
Traugot, John, 153n1
Treaty of Utrecht, 117
Trollope, Anthony, 263
True Briton, 121
Trumbach, Randolph, 189n29
Turner, James Grantham, 28n1, 98, 269n2, 302n16
Tyrrell, James, 119, 122; *Bibliotheca Politica*, 126
Tytler, Graeme, 254n12

Valentinus and Valentinians, 211n1, 214
Van Ghent, Dorothy, 136, 138, 138n5
Van Sant, Ann Jessie, 152–3n1, 312n22
Varey, Simon, 33n13
Virgil, 191n31
Vives, Juan Luis, 92

Waller, Edmund, 102
Walpole, Robert, and Walpole
administration, 27, 29, 36,
39–40, 39n24; Licensing Act
(1737), 34, 37, 39, 42
Walsingham, Francis (William
Arnall), 34, 41n27
Warner, William Beatty, 57n11,
118n10, 139, 157–8, 175n10,
200n40, 201, 283, 284, 291,
292n58
Watkins, Owen C., 178n14
Watson, Thomas, 173, 178, 179,
199–200, 204, 205
Watt, Ian, 46n39, 72n1, 121n20,
136, 137n2, 138, 153n1
Weekly Miscellany, 36n19
Weinbrot, Howard, 238
Wendt, Allan, 147n18, 154n7
Wesley, John, 228n27
Westcomb, Sophia, 170n1
Wheeler, Roxann, 112n30

Whitefield, George, 160–2, 165,
167; portrait of, 161
Wiles, Maurice, 276, 278
Willey, Basil, 94n7
Williams, Raymond, 149
Wilson, Stuart, 13n12
Wither, George, 240
Wolff, Cynthia Griffin, 79, 117n10,
121n20, 157, 175n10, 202n45,
268n2, 271, 326n15
Wood, Anthony à, 93n4
Wood, James, 165
Wright, Robert, 155, 159–60
Wycherley, William, 97

Yates, Mary V., 279n30, 318n4
Yeats, William Butler, 170, 261
Young, Edward, 34, 42, 117, 173

Zomchick, John B., 272n12
Zopyrus, 254